DIMENSIONS OF DIGNITY

In an age of constitutional revolutions and reforms, theory and practice are moving in opposite directions. As a matter of constitutional practice, human dignity has emerged in jurisdictions around the world as the organizing idea of a groundbreaking paradigm. By reconfiguring constitutional norms, institutional structures, and legal doctrines, this paradigm transforms human dignity from a mere moral claim into a legal norm that persons have standing to vindicate. As a matter of constitutional theory, however, human dignity remains an enigmatic idea. Some explicate its meaning in abstraction from constitutional practice, while others confine themselves to less exalted ideas. The result is a chasm that separates constitutional practice from a theory capable of justifying its innovations and guiding its operation. By expounding the connection between human dignity and the constitutional practices that justify themselves in its light, Jacob Weinrib brings the theory and practice of constitutional law back together.

JACOB WEINRIB is an assistant professor at the Faculty of Law at Queen's University, Kingston, Ontario. His research interests include legal theory and comparative public law.

CAMBRIDGE STUDIES IN CONSTITUTIONAL LAW

The aim of this series is to produce leading monographs in constitutional law. All areas of constitutional law and public law fall within the ambit of the series, including human rights and civil liberties law, administrative law, as well as constitutional theory and the history of constitutional law. A wide variety of scholarly approaches is encouraged, with the governing criterion being simply that the work is of interest to an international audience. Thus, works concerned with only one jurisdiction will be included in the series as appropriate, while, at the same time, the series will include works which are explicitly comparative or theoretical - or both. The series editors likewise welcome proposals that work at the intersection of constitutional and international law, or that seek to bridge the gaps between civil law systems, the US, and the common law jurisdictions of the Commonwealth.

Books in the series

Dimensions of Dignity: The Theory and Practice of Modern Constitutional Law
Jacob Weinrib

Reason of State: Law, Prerogative, Empire
Thomas Poole

Bills of Rights in the Common Law
Robert Leckey

The Guardian of the Constitution: Hans Kelsen and Carl Schmitt on the Limits of Constitutional Law
Translated by Lars Vinx, with an introduction and notes by Lars Vinx

Parliamentary Bills of Rights: The Experiences of New Zealand and the United Kingdom
Janet L. Hiebert and James B. Kelly

Lawyering for the Rule of Law: Government Lawyers and the Rise of Judicial Power in Israel
Yoav Dotan

Balancing Constitutional Rights: The Origins and Meanings of Postwar Legal Discourse
Jacco Bomhoff

Judges on Trial: The Independence and Accountability of the English Judiciary
Shimon Shetreet and Sophie Turenne

Proportionality and Constitutional Culture
Moshe Cohen-Eliya and Iddo Porat

The Politics of Principle: The First South African Constitutional Court, 1995–2005
Theunis Roux

The New Commonwealth Model of Constitutionalism: Theory and Practice
Stephen Gardbaum

Searching for the State in British Legal Thought: Competing Conceptions of the Public Sphere
Janet McLean

Judging Social Rights
Jeff King

Proportionality: Constitutional Rights and Their Limitations
Aharon Barak

Parliamentary Sovereignty: Contemporary Debates
Jeffrey Goldsworthy

DIMENSIONS OF DIGNITY

The Theory and Practice of Modern Constitutional Law

JACOB WEINRIB
Queen's University, Faculty of Law

CAMBRIDGE
UNIVERSITY PRESS

CAMBRIDGE
UNIVERSITY PRESS

University Printing House, Cambridge CB2 8BS, United Kingdom

Cambridge University Press is part of the University of Cambridge.

It furthers the University's mission by disseminating knowledge in the pursuit of education, learning and research at the highest international levels of excellence.

www.cambridge.org
Information on this title: www.cambridge.org/9781107084285

First published 2016

A catalogue record for this publication is available from the British Library

Library of Congress Cataloging in Publication data
Weinrib, Jacob, 1982– author.
Dimensions of dignity : the theory and practice of modern constitutional law / Jacob Weinrib.
pages cm. – (Cambridge studies in constitutional law ; 15)
Includes bibliographical references and index.
ISBN 978-1-107-08428-5 (hardback)
1. Respect for persons – Law and legislation. I. Title.
K3249.W45 2016
342.08′5–dc23
2015022588

ISBN 978-1-107-08428-5 Hardback

To my teachers

Peddlers of verbiage – and there are some – endlessly make vacuous pronouncements about what they call the importance of practice and the uselessness and danger of theory. There is only one thing to say on this. Imagine any sequence of the most useful, excellent, and considered facts that you possibly can. Can you imagine that the theoretical order does not contain a sequence of ideas and truths that corresponds exactly to your practical chain? Unless you have entirely lost your reason, you will see that the one follows from the other or, better, precedes it. What, pray, is theory unless it is that connected sequence of truths that you might not be able to see until it has been made *real* but which someone has to have seen, unless of course everyone proceeds on the basis of not knowing what they are doing?

Emmanuel Joseph Sieyès, "What is the Third Estate?" in *Political Writings*, trans. Michael Sonenscher (Indianapolis: Hackett, 2003), 161.

CONTENTS

ACKNOWLEDGMENTS

I am grateful to everyone who contributed to this project.

For conversations and comments on chapters, I would like to thank T. R. S. Allan, Alan Brudner, Bruce Chapman, Sujit Choudhry, Chris Essert, Harry Fox, Evan Fox-Decent, Stephan Hann, Louis-Philippe Hodgson, James Hunter, Tsvi Kahana, Lisa Kerr, Roy Kreitner, Mattias Kumm, Joanna Langille, Shai Lavi, Jed Lewinsohn, Ryan Liss, Andrew Max, Christopher McCrudden, Tamar Megiddo, Mariano C. Melero, Sophia Moreau, Liam Murphy, Hillary Nye, Sagi Peari, Sareh Pouryousefi, Diana Raffman, Gurpreet Rattan, Kristen Rundle, Wojiech Sadurski, Lena Salaymeh, Samuel Scheffler, Richard Stacey, Hamish Stewart, Azin Tadjdini, Jean Thomas, Malcolm Thorburn, Jeremy Waldron, Kathryn Walker, Mark Walters, Emily Kidd White, and Manuel Wörsdörfer. I am incredibly grateful to Judita Pamfil, who launched me on my philosophic odyssey and suggested the cover image. Thanks are also due to Finola O'Sullivan and Richard Woodham and their team at Cambridge University Press, and to Jeevitha Baskaran.

I am deeply indebted to Peter Benson, Joseph Heath, Jason Neyers, Scott Shapiro, Grégoire Webber, and Ariel Zylberman for reading the entire manuscript and offering many thoughtful suggestions. Dieter Grimm provided guidance on the constitutional and doctrinal dimensions of the project. Aharon Barak generously shared his vast "Dignity Library" with me and took the time to discuss the project's doctrinal dimension. Martin Stone helped me clarify the argument in the opening chapters. David Dyzenhaus provided incredibly valuable comments at every stage. Arthur Ripstein supervised the initial version of this project. I simply cannot imagine supervision of a higher calibre.

I gratefully acknowledge the support of the Social Science and Humanities Resource Council of Canada for a Vanier Canada Graduate Scholarship and a Postdoctoral Fellowship. I also thank the New York University School of Law, where I worked on this book as a Hauser Global Research Fellow at the Center for Constitutional Transitions and, subsequently, as a Dworkin-Balzan Fellow at the Center for Law and Philosophy.

Finally, I am endlessly grateful to my family: to my parents who in so many ways made this project possible, to Debra for all of her love, and to Max, who, in his first months, stayed up into the night to keep me company while I worked.

Chapter 2 is based on "Authority, Justice, and Public Law: A Unified Theory," *University of Toronto Law Journal* 64 (2014): 703–35. It is reprinted with permission of the University of Toronto Press. Chapter 5 originally appeared as "The Modern Constitutional State: A Defense," *Queen's Law Journal* 40 (2014): 165–211. It is reprinted with permission of the Queen's University Press.

TABLE OF CONSTITUTIONS

TABLE OF CASES

1

Human dignity and public law

We live in a legal world in which the idea of human dignity is everywhere invoked and everywhere contested.

As a matter of *constitutional practice*, in the decades since the end of World War II, human dignity has emerged as the organizing idea of a groundbreaking paradigm in public law.[1] In jurisdictions around the world, human dignity is invoked as a right or value that imposes an overarching obligation on all public authority,[2] as the underlying basis of

[1] Arthur Chaskalson, "Human Dignity as a Foundational Value of Our Constitutional Order," *South African Journal on Human Rights* 16 (2000): 196: 'The affirmation of human dignity as a foundational value of the constitutional order places our legal order firmly in line with the development of constitutionalism in the aftermath of the second world war.' On the connection between human dignity and postwar constitutionalism, see Roger Berkowitz, "Dignity Jurisprudence: Building a New Law on Earth," in *The Dignity Jurisprudence of the Constitutional Court of South Africa*, ed. Drucilla Cornell et al. (New York: Fordham University Press, 2013), 65–72; Judge Christian Byk, "Is Human Dignity a Useless Concept? Legal Perspectives," in *The Cambridge Handbook of Human Dignity: Interdisciplinary Perspectives*, ed. Marcus Düwell (Cambridge: Cambridge University Press, 2014), 362–7; Paolo G. Carozza, "Human Dignity in Constitutional Adjudication," *Comparative Constitutional Law*, ed. Tom Ginsberg and Rosalind Dixon (Cheltenham: Edward Elgar, 2011), 459; C.J. Friedrich, "The Political Theory of the New Democratic Constitutions," *Review of Politics* 12 (1950): 217; Catherine Dupré, "Human Dignity in Europe: A Foundational Constitutional Principle," *European Public Law* 19 (2013): 319–40; Matthias Mahlmann, "Human Dignity and Autonomy in Modern Constitutional Orders," in *The Oxford Handbook of Comparative Constitutional Law*, ed. Michel Rosenfeld and András Sajó (Oxford: Oxford University Press, 2012), 371–5; Lorraine Weinrib, "Human Dignity as a Rights-Protecting Principle," *National Journal of Constitutional Law* 17 (2004): 325–45.

[2] Basic Law of the Federal Republic of Germany, 1949, article 1(1) [hereinafter Grundgesetz]. See also Armenia, 1995, article 14; Bulgaria, 1991, article 4(2); Dominican Republic, 2010, article 38; Greece, 1975, article 2(1); Peru, 1993, article 1; Poland, 1997, article 30; and Sweden, 1974, article 2. See also Paolo G. Carozza, "Human Rights, Human Dignity, and Human Experience," in *Understanding Human Dignity*, ed. Christopher McCrudden (Oxford: Oxford University Press, 2013), 620; Aharon Barak, "Human Dignity: The Constitutional Value and the Constitutional Right," in *Understanding Human Dignity*, 361–80.

constitutional rights,[3] as an interpretive principle for determining the protections that particular constitutional rights afford,[4] as a constraint on the kinds of constitutional amendments that may be lawfully enacted,[5] and as a standard against which limitations of constitutional rights must be justified.[6] From the standpoint of constitutional practice, the significance of human dignity cannot be overstated.[7]

As a matter of *constitutional theory*, however, the idea of human dignity remains enigmatic. When human dignity is the subject of theoretical exploration, it typically arises within the context of religious or philosophic worldviews formulated in abstraction from constitutional concerns. This leaves the idea open to the charges that it is empty or dangerous: either it lacks resources for resolving constitutional disputes or the resources that it brings are hostile to the very rights and freedoms that a just constitutional order seeks to secure. Consequently, a chasm separates the practice of modern constitutionalism from the prevailing theoretical approaches. In this context, this new paradigm in constitutional governance has had to develop not merely without a guiding theory but also in opposition to established theoretical frameworks.

The purpose of this book is to formulate a general theory of public law that not only captures the distinctiveness of modern constitutional practice, but also delineates the obligation of all states to bring themselves

3 Armenia, 1995, article 14; Grundgesetz, article 1; Kenya, 2010, article 19(2); Kosovo, 2008, article 23; Poland, 1997, article 30; *S.* v. *Makwanyane and Another* (1995) 3 SA 391 (CC), para. 328. In the Canadian context, see, for example, *Hill* v. *Church of Scientology of Toronto*, [1995] 2 SCR 1130, para. 120; *Blencoe* v. *British Columbia (Human Rights Commission)*, [2000] 2 SCR 307, para. 76.

4 Dieter Grimm, "Dignity in a Legal Context: Dignity as an Absolute Right," in *Understanding Human Dignity*, 385. See also Stu Woolman, "The Architecture of Dignity," in *The Dignity Jurisprudence of the Constitutional Court of South Africa*, 87.

5 Grundgesetz, article 79(3); Angola, 2010, article 236; Greece, article 110(1). See also Yaniv Roznai, "Unconstitutional Constitutional Amendments – The Migration and Success of a Constitutional Idea," *American Journal of Comparative Law* 61 (2013): 684–5 and 692 (describing human dignity as a judicially recognized constraint on constitutional amendments in Peru and India).

6 Drucilla Cornell and Sam Fuller, "Introduction," in *The Dignity Jurisprudence of the Constitutional Court of South Africa*, 19; *R.* v. *Oakes*, [1986] 1 SCR 103, para. 64.

7 *S.* v. *Makwanyane and Another*, para. 328: 'The importance of dignity as a founding value of the new Constitution cannot be overemphasised.' On the centrality of dignity in German constitutional law, see *Lüth*, 7 BVerfGE 198, 205 (1958): '[T]his value system, which centers upon the dignity of human personality developing freely within the community, must be looked upon as fundamental constitutional decision affecting all spheres of law.' Translated in Donald P. Kommers and Russell A. Miller, *The Constitutional Jurisprudence of the Federal Republic of Germany* (Durham: Duke University Press, 2012), 444.

within its parameters. The animating idea of this theory is human dignity, conceived of in terms of the right of each person to equal freedom. By systematically unpacking the normative, institutional, and doctrinal ramifications of this simple idea for the public law relationship between rulers and ruled, a theory illuminating modern constitutional practice materializes.

By *modern constitutional practice*, I refer to the sum of conditions that legal systems in the postwar era have introduced to make the exercise of public authority accountable to the human dignity of all who are subject to it. These conditions include a constitution that establishes the terms for the lawful exercise of all public authority; a set of constitutional rights that bind all branches of government; an accessible judicial body authorized and obligated to respond to constitutional complaints by reviewing the conformity of government conduct to constitutional norms; substantive constraints on the amending power that preserve the essentials of the constitutional order; and doctrines that determine both the protections that constitutional rights afford and the limits to which rights are subject in reference to the overarching idea of human dignity. Together these conditions create, sustain, and refine a legal order in which the human dignity of each person forms a justiciable constraint on the exercise of all public authority.

At issue in this book is the idea that justifies and guides modern constitutional practice. As I argue below, this idea is captured neither by the meanings that have, as a historical matter, been associated with the word *dignity* nor by the meanings that various philosophic traditions attribute to this term. Just as the word can appear in the absence of the idea, so too the idea can appear in the absence of the word. It is therefore not surprising that some are eager to reject *human dignity* as a superfluous notion that can be expressed using more familiar and less exalted terminology. But even if one acknowledges that there are other ways of referring to the idea, the task of explaining the connection between the idea and the constitutional practices that invoke it remains. It is to the challenge of expounding this connection that I now turn.

1.1 Dignity's dilemma

A dilemma awaits any constitutional theory that appeals to the idea of human dignity. This dilemma stems from the fact that the idea can be formulated as either a concept or a conception.[8] Each possibility brings its own difficulty.[9]

In constitutional jurisprudence, the *concept* of human dignity usually refers to the constraint that the intrinsic worth of each free and equal person imposes on how individuals may be treated. If the virtue of the concept is that it is relatively uncontroversial, its vice is that it is uninformative: it offers no account of what exactly human dignity consists in or what kind of treatment human dignity requires, prohibits, or permits. Thus, human dignity has been called a 'vacuous concept' bereft of any boundaries,[10] a subjective idea that varies 'radically with the time, place, and beholder,'[11] an indistinct idea that 'masks a great deal of disagreement and sheer confusion,'[12] a noble sentiment that 'can have no place in an attempt at rational persuasion,'[13] and an 'impossibly vague'[14] idea that fails to 'provide a universalistic, principled basis for judicial decision-making in the human rights context.'[15] In the eyes of its critics, the concept is too hollow to fill the constitutional jurisprudence that invokes it.[16]

To render the *concept* of human dignity determinate, other scholars have developed *conceptions* of human dignity. These conceptions invariably appeal to some religious or philosophic worldviews to make the case that human beings have intrinsic worth and to set out the beliefs that they should affirm and the conduct that they must undertake. Such

[8] On the distinction between a concept and a conception, see John Rawls, *A Theory of Justice* (Cambridge: Harvard University Press, 1971), 5–10.

[9] Here I follow Christopher McCrudden, "Human Dignity and Judicial Interpretation of Human Rights," *European Journal of International Law* 19 (2008): 679–80.

[10] Mirko Bagaric and James Allan, "The Vacuous Concept of Dignity," *Journal of Human Rights* 5 (2006): 269.

[11] Stephen Pinker, "The Stupidity of Dignity," *The New Republic* (May 28, 2008).

[12] Rosen, *Dignity: Its History and Meaning* (Cambridge: Harvard University Press, 2012), 67. For a similar view, see Dennis Davis, "Equality: The Majesty of Legoland Jurisprudence," *South African Law Journal* 116 (1999): 413 (criticizing the South African Constitutional Court for affording 'dignity both a content and a scope that make for a piece of a jurisprudential Legoland – to be used in whatever form and shape is required by the demands of the judicial designer').

[13] Friedrich A. Hayek, *The Constitution of Liberty* (Chicago: University of Chicago Press, 1960), 6. But see 79.

[14] McCrudden, "Human Dignity and Judicial Interpretation of Human Rights," 723.

[15] Ibid., 655.

[16] For an early formulation of this attack on dignity as a concept in ethical philosophy, see Arthur Schopenhauer, *The Basis of Morality*, trans. Arthur Brodrick Bullock (New York: MacMillan, 1915), 101 (denouncing the conception of human dignity that appears in Kantian ethics as 'hollow hyperbole' and the 'shibboleth of all perplexed and empty headed moralists').

conceptions can be found in the Jewish, Catholic, and Islamic religious traditions, as well as in various philosophic frameworks.[17] While such conceptions of human dignity are sometimes challenged for lacking the determinacy necessary to resolve constitutional disputes,[18] they would generate a serious problem even if they were perfectly determinate.

This problem is that these conceptions of human dignity inevitably clash with the very concept that they purport to explicate. These conceptions typically proceed by, first, identifying the kinds of beliefs and actions that make up a good or valuable life and, then, enlisting the coercive authority of the state to bring them about. The illiberalism of leading conceptions thereby comes into conflict with the liberal commitments of the concept to the freedom and equality of each individual.[19] These conceptions violate freedom by compelling individuals to conform to a particular conception of the good life. These conceptions violate equality by elevating what some persons understand to be the good life into a standard that others are forced to follow. Instead of specifying the liberal concept of human dignity, they subvert it.

Thus, whether defenders of the idea of human dignity appeal to a concept or a conception, a difficulty ensues. For some, the concept of human dignity is empty; it offers no resources for resolving concrete constitutional disputes. For others, conceptions of human dignity are dangerously illiberal; they violate the concept of human dignity by

[17] For an overview of various conceptions of human dignity, see Anne Hughes, *Human Dignity and Fundamental Rights in South Africa and Ireland* (Pretoria: Pretoria University Press, 2014), 36–49, and Aharon Barak, *Human Dignity: The Constitutional Value and the Constitutional Right* (Cambridge: Cambridge University Press, forthcoming), ch. 2.

[18] Rosen, *Dignity: Its History and Meaning*, 9.

[19] On the appropriation of the term *dignity* by proponents of illiberal ideologies, see Rosen, "Dignity: The Case Against," in *Understanding Human Dignity*, 152 (asking 'how could it be legitimate for democratic societies, in which the fact of moral pluralism appears to be fundamental, to plump for either one of these controversial comprehensive moral theories and impose it on their citizens?'); Pinker, "The Stupidity of Dignity" (responding to those who, in the biomedical context, conceive of dignity in terms of a religious comprehensive doctrine by emphasizing that a 'free society disempowers the state from enforcing a conception of dignity on its citizens'); and Horst Dreier, "Human Dignity in German Law," in *The Cambridge Handbook of Human Dignity: Interdisciplinary Perspectives*, 383 (warning against the dangers of paternalistic misconceptions of human dignity, which pit the concept 'against its actual foundations, namely, individual autonomy and self-determination over one's own life and the way it is lived. [Human dignity] then mutates from a promise of freedom and equality for all persons into a rule giving the state the power to intervene in people's lives. This would lead to the opposite of what was intended').

subjugating the freedom and equality of individuals to some higher cause. Each of these possibilities poses a fundamental challenge to modern constitutionalism. If human dignity is an empty notion, then constitutional jurisprudence that relies on it must be a sham.[20] If human dignity subordinates freedom and equality to a particular conception of the good life, then the idea stands in opposition to the very rights that modern constitutionalism seeks to secure.[21]

Accordingly, the question that any theory of modern constitutional practice must answer is clear: Can an account be formulated that refrains from violating the freedom of persons to determine their own commitments, whether religious, philosophic, or otherwise, and that nevertheless possesses the resources to explain how the idea of human dignity directs the resolution of constitutional disputes? The same question can be put in terms of the dilemma to which it responds: What would a conception of human dignity look like that adhered to the liberalism of the concept? This book offers an answer to this question.

On the one hand, I develop an account that sidesteps the illiberalism of prominent *conceptions* of human dignity. Proceeding from a concept of human dignity evident in modern constitutional practice,[22] I reject the view that human dignity concerns the relationship between an individual and some particular end – whether religious or philosophic – to which his or her thoughts and actions must conform and that the state would be

20 Ibid.

21 On this point, see Barak, *Human Dignity: The Constitutional Value and the Constitutional Right*, ch. 7; *R.* v. *Morgentaler*, [1988] 1 SCR 30, 166, Wilson J.: 'The idea of human dignity finds expression in almost every right and freedom guaranteed in the [*Canadian Charter of Rights and Freedoms*]. Individuals are afforded the right to choose their own religion and their own philosophy of life, the right to choose with whom they will associate and how they will express themselves, the right to choose where they will live and what occupation they will pursue. These are all examples of the basic theory underlying the *Charter*, namely that the state will respect choices made by individuals and, to the greatest extent possible, will avoid subordinating these choices to any one conception of the good life.'

22 See, for example, Drucilla Cornell and Sam Fuller, "Introduction," in *The Dignity Jurisprudence of the Constitutional Court of South Africa*, 14 (attributing to Justice Ackermann the view that freedom is the 'originary right of all human beings, and therefore the basis of their dignity'). On the general right to freedom, see Edward J. Eberle, "Human Dignity, Privacy, and Personality in German and American Constitutional Law," *Utah Law Review* (1997): 965 (arguing that 'each person should be free to develop his own personality to the fullest, subject only to restrictions arising from others' pursuit of the same'). See also Christoph Enders, "A Right to Have Rights – The German Constitutional Concept of Human Dignity in German Basic Law," *Revista de Estudos Constitucionais, Hermenêutica e Teoria do Direito* 2 (2010): 4.

justified in coercively enforcing. Instead, the concept concerns the equal right of each person to freedom. As free, each person has the right to determine the purposes that he or she will pursue. As equal, each person has a duty to pursue his or her purposes in a manner that respects the right of others to freedom. Taking these aspects together, human dignity means that no one may rightfully compel you to direct your freedom to a purpose that is not your own. If this concept of human dignity forms the organizing idea of public law, then the basis and boundaries of public coercion must be reconsidered. Any exercise of public authority – indeed, public authority itself – would have to be justified in terms of its fidelity to the equal right of each person to freedom. A legal system that operated in accordance with this idea would 'be in keeping with the purest liberalism' insofar as the persons within it would not be 'coercible by any ancestral tradition, being vassals neither of their race, nor to their religion, nor to their condition of birth, nor to their collective history.'[23]

On the other hand, I offer an account that explains how the *concept* of human dignity gains the specificity to guide the development of constitutional jurisprudence in jurisdictions around the world. Critics of human dignity attack the concept for failing to provide a 'clear test or set of criteria that leads from fundamental value to appropriate action – something to compete with the simple maximizing principle of utilitarians.'[24] The utilitarian theory of the good represents one way of proceeding from an abstract principle to a determinate moral conclusion. That theory begins by positing a principle – bring about the greatest happiness of the greatest number – and then explores how this principle can be most fully realized in the circumstances in which we find ourselves. The more knowledge one has about these circumstances, the more determinate guidance the theory provides.

The conception of human dignity that I elaborate introduces determinacy in a different way. I begin with the abstract concept of human dignity as independence, that is, the right to interact with others on terms of equal freedom. Instead of following the utilitarian approach by applying this concept directly to the contingent circumstances that experience presents, the theory develops the concept into an increasingly determinate conception as the argument progresses through a series of sequenced stages. I will refer to these stages as *dimensions*. Each

[23] Pierre Elliot Trudeau, *The Essential Trudeau*, ed. Ron Graham (Toronto: McClelland and Stewart, 1998), 80. Trudeau was the Canadian prime minister who was responsible for the constitutional reforms that brought Canada into the modern constitutional paradigm.

[24] Rosen, *Dignity: Its History and Meaning*, 155.

dimension distills what human dignity means for some aspect of the public law relationship between rulers and ruled. Within this sequenced argument, each dimension both presupposes and is more specific than the one that preceded it. Together, the dimensions of dignity constitute a conception that traverses public law, beginning with the most general features of the relationship between rulers and ruled and proceeding to fine-grained problems involving the institutional structure and doctrinal commitments of a modern constitutional state.

Unlike the principle of utility, human dignity is not a monolithic principle that makes the same demands of all agents in all circumstances.[25] The implications of the right of each person to equal freedom both justify and direct the authority of the public institutions that together comprise a legal system. These public institutions have rights that no private person possesses and duties that no private person owes. Thus within the public law relationship, what one must do reflects the position that one occupies. To understand what human dignity demands, we must attend to its dimensions.

By conceiving of the dimensions of the public law relationship between rulers and ruled as comprising a conception of human dignity, I depart from a range of conceptions in which human dignity is presented as a concept that can be fully specified without referring to the relationship between the individual and the state. Consider Christoper McCrudden's approach. On his view, the concept of human dignity emerges as an ontological claim about 'what the intrinsic worth of the individual human being consists in.'[26] This concept, McCrudden explains, is then specified through a further claim concerning the 'forms of treatment' that 'are inconsistent with this worth.'[27] Once the idea of human dignity is rendered determinate, it can then be applied to a range of subjects. Thus, he suggests that when human rights jurisprudence arose, it applied these earlier understandings of what human dignity requires to 'the relationship between the state and the individual.'[28] The assumption that underlies McCrudden's approach is that the concept of human dignity can be fully specified by a conception that does not refer to the public law relationship.

[25] Jeremy Bentham, *An Introduction to the Principles of Morals and Legislation* (Oxford: Clarendon Press, 1879), 3 (c. I, 7th para.) (holding that a 'measure of government (which is but a particular kind of action, performed by a particular person or persons) may be said to be conformable to or dictated by the principle of utility, when in like manner the tendency which it has to augment the happiness of the community is greater than any which it has to diminish it').

[26] McCrudden, "Human Dignity and Judicial Interpretation of Human Rights," 680.

[27] Ibid. [28] Ibid.

On this view, human dignity makes no essential reference to the authority of public institutions, the fundamental norms or institutional arrangements promulgated by a constitution, or the legal doctrines through which those normative commitments are brought to bear on disputes that arise contingently in experience. Of course, this is not to say that the idea of human dignity, once specified through a conception, cannot be applied to aspects of the public law relationship. Rather, it is to say that what human dignity means for public law is derivative of what human dignity would mean even if there was no such thing as public law. An exhaustive conception of human dignity need not mention public law.[29]

This book contrasts with this approach in two respects. First, because the concept of human dignity has implications for the normative, constitutional, and doctrinal dimensions of the public law relationship, the subject matter of the conception that I offer is public law. Of course, this is not to deny that human dignity may have a central role to play in our understanding of private or international law, but to insist on its centrality to our understanding of public law. While the claim that the concept of human dignity cannot be fully explicated without engaging with public law might seem trite, it orients us away from a range of conceptions that focus on the relation of persons to something other than the state[30] – whether the values that a successful life instantiates,[31] the duties that a rational will gives to itself,[32] the natural world,[33] or the supernatural.[34]

29 For a parallel discussion of how utilitarians think about the relationship between law and morality, see Martin Stone, "Legal Positivism as an Idea about Morality," *University of Toronto Law Journal* 61 (2011): 319.

30 On the gulf between the constitutional meaning of human dignity and philosophic conceptions, see Barak, *Human Dignity: The Constitutional Value and the Constitutional Right*, ch. 7 (asking '[h]ow is it possible to base a constitutional understanding of the value of human dignity upon a philosophic view that has nothing to do with the constitutional character of that value?').

31 Ronald Dworkin, *Justice for Hedgehogs* (Cambridge: Harvard University Press, 2011), 191–218.

32 Immanuel Kant, *Groundwork of the Metaphysics of Morals*, in *Practical Philosophy*, ed. Mary Gregor (Cambridge: Cambridge University Press, 1996).

33 See, for example, George Kateb, *Human Dignity* (Cambridge: Harvard University Press, 2011); Hubert Cancik, "'Dignity of Man' and '*Persona*' in Stoic Anthropology: Some Remarks on Cicero, *De Officiis* I 105–107," in *The Concept of Human Dignity in Human Rights Discourse*, 19–39. As one of the fathers of Germany's postwar constitution remarked about the stoic conception: 'Epictetus once expressed that even the slave chained to his oar was free if he had the right attitude. But, comrades, we do not want to be satisfied with this freedom of the galley slave. We do not only want the opportunity to have this inner freedom.' Christoph Goos, "*Würde des Menschen*: Restoring Human Dignity in Post-Nazi Germany," in *Understanding Human Dignity*, 89.

34 *Genesis* 1:27; *Psalm* 8:5–6; *Ephesians* 4:24.

Second, instead of formulating a theory to justify the concept of human dignity, my argument moves in a different direction. I begin with the idea that human dignity is a *juridical* concept, that is, a concept that concerns not the public laws that happen to have been posited in a particular time and place, but the moral possibility and purpose of public law conceived of as a relationship between rulers and ruled. The remaining chapters develop a corresponding juridical conception by working out the implications of the concept for the public law relationship between rulers and ruled. This conception explains why human beings must interact under the public authority of a legal system, why a legal system has an overarching obligation to respect and protect the dignity of each person subject to its authority, and why this obligation cannot be fully satisfied in the absence of the constitutional structure and doctrinal commitments that characterize modern constitutional governance. The task, then, is not to offer a justification of the concept of human dignity, but rather to show how the concept justifies modern constitutional practice and generates the duty of all legal systems to bring themselves within its parameters.[35] By delineating the conditions under which each person can be free from the choice of another rather than the good that each person should pursue, a conception emerges that is true to the liberalism of the concept.

1.2 The antinomy of public law

The claim that the dilemma of dignity can be unraveled by formulating a theory of public law may seem to simply relocate the problem it aims to address. The dilemma consists in the opposition between two unsatisfactory accounts of human dignity: those that present a concept devoid

[35] Conceptions of human dignity often proceed by identifying a particular capacity for exercising intellectual or moral virtue and then arguing that this capacity forms the basis for acknowledging human dignity and fundamental rights. These conceptions have been criticized for being underinclusive. Since there are human beings who do not have the capacity to exercise the relevant virtues, these conceptions withdraw legal protection from the most vulnerable among us. On this point, see Sigrid Graumann, "Human Dignity and People with Disabilities," in *The Cambridge Handbook of Human Dignity: Interdisciplinary Perspectives*, 486 and Christoph Goos, "*Würde des Menschen*: Restoring Human Dignity in Post-Nazi Germany," in *Understanding Human Dignity*, 81–2. This book offers a more inclusive approach, in which human dignity enters not as a consequence of a capacity that some possess but others lack, but as a normative assumption about human persons *as such* that renders the normative, constitutional, and doctrinal dimensions of public law intelligible.

of content and those that are filled with content that does not cohere to the relevant concept. However, when one's attention shifts from human dignity to public law, a parallel dilemma surfaces.

Theories of public law usually take one of two forms.[36]

For some, the fundamental insight that a theory must capture is that public law is simply the sum of rules that have been validated in a particular jurisdiction by the contingent exercise of public authority. Accordingly, what a theory of public law must explain is how rules that are valid can be differentiated from ones that are invalid. This is a factual inquiry about how public authority has actually been exercised rather than a moral inquiry about how it should have been exercised. After all, that a rule is moral does not mean that it has been validated through the exercise of public authority, just as the fact that a rule has been validated does not mean that it is moral.[37] Since public law is merely the contingent product of the exercise of public authority within a particular jurisdiction, an exhaustive account of public law need not refer to moral ideas of human dignity and fundamental rights. On this view, public law can be filled with an endless variety of rules because it is empty. Public law has no necessary content.

Others explicate the converse view that public law is not a factual phenomenon but a moral one. The purpose of a theory of public law is to explain the nature of morality or justice to which all conduct must conform. Because the question of how one should act is wholly moral, it can be answered without referring to the way in which public authority happens to have been exercised within a particular jurisdiction at a particular time. As for the rules that have been validated through the exercise of public authority, they are either redundant or pernicious. If positive laws conform to what morality demands, then they are redundant and can be disregarded. Alternately, if positive laws violate what morality demands, then they are pernicious and must be disobeyed. In either case, morality alone provides the relevant standard for human conduct in all times and places. On this view, the actual practice of public law is extraneous to what public law actually demands.

When Lon L. Fuller surveyed these disparate ways of thinking about public law, he saw that the leading theories were caught up in an

[36] See, for example, Lon L. Fuller, "Reason and Fiat in Case Law," *Harvard Law Review* 59 (1946): 376–95.

[37] Hart, "Positivism and the Separation of Law and Morals," *Harvard Law Review* 71 (1958): 599.

'antinomy.'[38] The antinomy consisted in the conflict between competing attempts 'to treat a partial view of the law as if it were the whole view.'[39] By this, Fuller meant that when we leave the stipulations of legal philosophers behind, 'we inevitably see that [law] is compounded of reason and fiat, of order discovered and order imposed, and that to attempt to eliminate either of these aspects of the law is to denature and falsify it.'[40] But that is exactly what the leading theories do, whether by attempting to 'cut the fiat branch loose from the ethical considerations that have shaped it'[41] or by attempting to 'eliminate the branch of fiat by maintaining that the whole of law is, or at least can be, the expression of reason.'[42] Thus, Fuller remarked, 'In dealing with the antinomy of reason and fiat, the main effort of the various schools of legal philosophy has been to obliterate one of its branches.'[43]

The standard way to overcome an antinomy is to identify the problematic presupposition that generates its conflicting branches. The fundamental challenge that any theory must confront is that public law seems to involve two discrete kinds of claims, which appear to be antagonistic rather than complementary.[44] On one hand, legal practice involves contingent claims that issue from the exercise of public authority – or what Fuller called *fiat* – within a particular legal system at a particular time. On the other, legal practice involves moral claims of justice – or what Fuller called *reason* – often appearing in the language of human dignity and fundamental rights. The challenge for theories of public law is that these claims might pull in different directions. Justice denies the adequacy of what authority establishes. Authority denies the actuality of what justice demands. Since the norms that are authoritative within a given legal system are often unjust, while just norms too often fail to be legally

[38] Fuller, "Reason and Fiat in Case Law," 377. [39] Ibid., 382. [40] Ibid. [41] Ibid., 384.
[42] Ibid., 381. [43] Ibid.
[44] See, for example, Carl Schmitt, *Constitutional Theory*, trans. Jeffrey Seitzer (Durham: Duke University Press, 2008), 65 (suggesting that it is arbitrary 'to speak of legal order without further clarification. The concept of legal order contains two entirely different elements: the normative element of justice and the actually existing element of concrete order'). See also Harold J. Berman, *Law and Revolution: The Formation of the Western Legal Tradition* (Cambridge: Harvard University Press, 1983), 21–2 (noting the inherent contradiction in Western legal systems between conceiving of law as order and conceiving of law as justice); Stefano Bertea, "How Non-Positivism Can Accommodate Legal Certainty," in *Law, Rights, and Discourse: The Legal Philosophy of Robert Alexy*, ed. George Pavlakos (Oxford: Hart Publishing, 2007), 70 (emphasizing that the 'essential dichotomy' in law between 'certainty and justice – both of them being fundamental values in law, and yet each colliding with the other – has been a source of serious theoretical problems').

authoritative, a legal theory cannot hold that persons are simultaneously bound both by the sum of validly enacted norms and by the eternal precepts of justice. Rather, the line of thought goes, a theory must focus on either authority in abstraction from justice or justice in abstraction from authority. The antinomy of public law consists in the conflict between these one-sided approaches.

By developing a conception of human dignity, this book offers a theory of public law that integrates the components that the leading theories sever. My guiding idea is that the dimensions of human dignity form a theory of the public law relationship between rulers and ruled. Within this relationship, each party has distinctive rights and duties. Rulers have the right to exercise public authority by imposing coercible legal obligations on the ruled. In turn, the ruled have the right to just governance, which imposes a corresponding obligation on rulers to bring the existing legal order into the deepest possible conformity with the dignity of all who are subject to it. Since notions of authority and justice bind different parties to the public law relationship, no contradiction arises from uniting them in a common framework. Because this framework rejects the fragmentation of competing theories that attempt to render the practice of public law intelligible by reducing the whole to one of its aspects, I call it the *unified theory of public law*. In articulating a juridical standpoint from which the distinctive claims of authority and justice may each be given their due, the unified theory of public law succeeds where its fragmented counterparts fail. The unified theory illuminates the general practice of public law and, in particular, the inner workings of the modern constitutional state.

The branches of the antinomy of public law are generated by overlooking the significance of human dignity as a moral idea that concerns the public law relationship. Once one excludes the possibility that there is a branch of morality that focuses on public law in this manner, two ways of thinking about public law remain. Each approach grabs on to one side of the distinction between *is* and *ought*. One could conceive of the nature of public law in terms of what is the case, that is, in terms of facts about how public authority in a particular jurisdiction has been exercised. Such an approach need not refer to morality. Or one could conceive of the nature of public law in terms of what ought to be the case, that is, in terms of moral considerations that make no essential reference to the rules that the public authority happens to validate. Whichever path one takes, one retains the conviction that the juridical conception of human dignity denies – that it is possible to provide an exhaustive account of morality without referring to public law.

Within the unified theory, human dignity and public law are concepts that cannot be understood in abstraction from one another. As a juridical concept, human dignity justifies public authority and regulates its ongoing operation. As a practice in which notions of authority and justice are ineliminable, public law presupposes human dignity as its unifying basis. So long as human dignity and public law are not explored together, each remains an isolated mystery.

Someone might object that the unified theory is circular because human dignity is explicated in terms of public law, which is, in turn, explicated in terms of human dignity. The sin of a circular argument is that the conclusion simply reiterates the premises. An argument in which the output merely restates the input proves nothing, even if the inputs are true. The unified theory of public law is not circular in this sense because its conclusions do not simply restate the bare concept of human dignity. Rather, the concept is developed into a conception by exploring its normative, constitutional, and doctrinal dimensions. As each dimension unfolds, our understanding of both human dignity and public law simultaneously deepens. It is to these dimensions that I now turn.

1.3 Dignity's dimensions

Modern constitutional practice raises a series of theoretical questions about the nature of public law. Consider the first article of Germany's Basic Law, which offers one of the earliest pronouncements of the modern constitutional paradigm by encapsulating the relationship that is to obtain between the free and equal individual and the coercive state: 'Human dignity shall be inviolable. To respect and protect it shall be the duty of all state authority.'[45] A set of normative, constitutional, and doctrinal questions ensue from this article. These questions delineate the dimensions of public law:

1. As a matter of the *normative dimension* of public law, if persons are free and equal in their dignity, what right has the state to exercise authority over them by imposing and enforcing legal obligations? And why must state authority respect and protect human dignity over other preferred objectives?

[45] Grundgesetz, article 1(1).

2. As a matter of the *constitutional dimension* of public law, can a state respect and protect the dignity of its inhabitants in the absence of the constitutional norms and institutional arrangements that characterize modern constitutionalism?
3. As a matter of the *doctrinal dimension* of public law, can a state respect and protect the dignity of its inhabitants in the absence of the doctrines that characterize modern constitutionalism?

In providing an integrated response to these questions, the unified theory develops the concept of human dignity into an increasingly determinate conception of the public law relationship between rulers and ruled. I will now outline how subsequent chapters of this book explicate these dimensions.

1.3.1 The normative dimension

In Chapter 2, I flesh out the normative dimension of public law by showing that human dignity is both the legitimating basis of public authority and the purpose to which all public authority must be directed. Human dignity is the legitimating basis of public authority because the concept of human dignity holds that each person has both a right and a duty to interact with every other on terms of equal freedom. However, in the absence of publicly authoritative institutions that establish, interpret, and implement law, it is impossible for private persons to interact with one another on such terms. Thus, human dignity generates a duty incumbent on private persons to interact within a legal system. Such a justification of public authority constrains the way in which it must be exercised. If the right of government to exercise public authority rests on the dignity of all who are subject to it, then public authority contains its own internal standard of moral adequacy. The exercise of public authority conforms to the terms of its justification to the extent that it is directed toward bringing the existing legal order into the deepest possible conformity with its internal moral standard – human dignity under law. This standard requires the adoption of a democratic mode of lawgiving and a system of positive law that is adequate to the human dignity of the free and equal persons subject to it.

The unified theory makes a fundamental departure from theories of public law that focus on either the contingent exercise of public authority or the necessary demands of justice. For the unified theory holds that claims of authority and justice are not antithetical virtues of opposing theoretical frameworks but mutually implicating norms. The right of government to exercise public authority over private persons does not exist in the absence of a duty to govern justly. The right of private persons to justice cannot be fulfilled in the absence of publicly authoritative institutions.

When public law is conceived of in these terms, a regime might violate human dignity in one of two ways. A regime might fail to establish public institutions that render private persons accountable to one another in their conduct. This pathology, which involves the violation of the *horizontal* demands of dignity, forms the focus of Chapter 3. Alternately, a regime might exercise public authority in a manner that imposes arbitrary constraints on the freedom of one or more persons subject to its lawgiving. This pathology, which concerns the *vertical* demands of dignity, is explored in Chapter 4.

Within the unified theory, a legal order is a condition in which public institutions establish, interpret, and enforce norms of conduct and thereby secure each private person from the arbitrary power of every other. It follows that when force is exercised in a manner that is incompatible with one or more persons enjoying freedom in relation to others, that force cannot be authoritative. Thus, the concept of a legal order involves coercive power, but is not reducible to it. In Chapter 3, I develop this distinction between public authority and private violence and argue that it resolves difficulties that various legal theorists, including Gustav Radbruch, Lon Fuller, and Robert Alexy, encountered in differentiating the public authority of a legal system from the organized violence of the Nazi years. I then apply this framework to the concrete circumstances of Nazi power and argue that, from the standpoint of public law, the problem with Nazism was not that it was an unjust legal order, but rather that it was not a legal order at all. Nazism cast off every legal norm and procedure that secured the dignity of private persons in relation to one another until violence was the only aspect of law that remained, which is to say that there was no law at all.

While Chapter 3 concerns the distinction between public authority and private violence, Chapter 4 concerns the distinction between just and unjust exercises of public authority. A distinguishing feature of contemporary political and legal theory is its rejection of earlier approaches that sought *either* to justify existing societies, which are to varying extents mired in injustice, *or* to explicate the nature of a perfectly just society. By contrast, the aspiration of contemporary theories is to articulate a framework for thinking about the progressive transformation of the actual societies in which we live into the increasingly just societies we seek to realize. I argue that to satisfy this aspiration, a theory must have a structure that integrates three elements: (1) an underlying subject, for example, legal systems; (2) a moral standard against which instances of the underlying subject can be assessed; and (3) a framework for discerning what must be done when instances of the underlying subject are defective in relation to the relevant moral standard. This is exactly what the unified theory provides. By attending to the implications of human dignity, the unified theory formulates what a legal system is, why human dignity forms the moral standard for assessing a legal system's adequacy, and why all public authority must be directed toward bringing the legal order into the closest possible conformity with the dignity of all who are subject to it. I also argue that the leading theories in political and legal philosophy – whether John Rawls's theory of justice as fairness or H.L.A. Hart's legal positivism – do not possess the requisite structure. I close by explaining why legal systems that share a common ideal of public justice need not enact identical laws and create identical institutional arrangements.

1.3.2 The constitutional dimension

The constitutional dimension of the unified theory addresses the question: Can a state respect and protect the dignity of its inhabitants in the absence of the constitutional norms and institutional arrangements that characterize modern constitutionalism? These structures include (1) a constitution that exhaustively establishes the conditions for the valid exercise of all public authority, (2) a constitutionally entrenched bill of rights that delineates the right of persons, by virtue of their dignity, to just governance, and (3) a politically independent judicial body to which any individual can bring a constitutional complaint challenging the validity of any exercise of public authority that violates a constitutional right.

The standard way to defend these arrangements is to identify a morally beneficial outcome and then maintain that this structure contributes to its realization. Ronald Dworkin is representative of this approach. He defends the use of judicial review to protect constitutional rights on the grounds that it raises the level of public debate and culminates in just decisions.[46] This instrumental justification is vulnerable to a devastating objection. As Jeremy Waldron has argued, these and other benefits that constitutionalism purports to bring may be realized in its absence, while

[46] Dworkin, *Freedom's Law: The Moral Reading of the American Constitution* (Oxford: Oxford University Press, 1996), 34 and 345.

the presence of constitutional arrangements provides no guarantee that the benefits will accrue.[47]

Instead of justifying modern constitutionalism by appealing to benefits that could, in principle, be achieved in its absence, I argue in Chapter 5 that modern constitutionalism is a systematic response to a moral problem that every legal system must address, but that cannot be addressed apart from the legal and institutional structure of a modern constitutional state. The problem – common to all precursors of modern constitutionalism – is not that rulers *necessarily* exercise public authority in a manner that violates the inherent dignity of the ruled, but that in the event of a violation there is no legal recourse for those affected. In legal systems in which public authority is exercised by the few, as in autocratic or oligarchic forms of government, it is the many who are left susceptible to injustice. Conversely, in legal systems in which public authority is exercised by the many, as in majoritarian democracies, it is the few who remain vulnerable. By contrast, modern constitutionalism stands as a fundamental innovation in public law designed to make the exercise of public authority accountable neither to the many nor to the few, but to the human dignity of each and every person subject to law's authority. This accountability is established by the legal and institutional structure of a modern constitutional state, which creates the conditions under which any person who believes that his or her dignity has been violated (and, in some circumstances, representative or surrogate actors) may bring a constitutional complaint to an impartial judicial body that is empowered and obligated to constrain the exercise of public authority to the terms of its justification. Because such a form of accountability is not possible apart from the legal and institutional structure of a modern constitutional state, this justification is not vulnerable to the skeptical challenge that Waldron raised against Dworkin.

1.3.3 The doctrinal dimension

The doctrinal dimension of the unified theory responds to the question: Can a state respect and protect the dignity of its inhabitants in the absence of the doctrines that characterize modern constitutionalism? While a variety of doctrines could be considered, I focus on the doctrines

47 See, for example, Jeremy Waldron, "Judicial Review and the Conditions of Democracy," *Journal of Political Philosophy* 6 (1998): 339–40; and "The Core of the Case Against Judicial Review," *Yale Law Journal* 115 (2006): 1349–50.

that modern constitutional states have developed to impose substantive constraints on constitutional amendments and to structure the adjudication of constitutional rights. My claim is that these doctrinal commitments play an integral role in fulfilling modern constitutionalism's overarching purpose: the realization of a legal order in which the exercise of power is accountable to the inherent dignity and fundamental rights of each person subject to its authority. The doctrinal commitments of a modern constitutional state reflect the reason why modern constitutionalism is itself required.

When it comes to constitutional amendments, constitutional theory and practice could not be more out of step. In the constitutional practice of legal systems around the world, more and more states are not only adopting a modern constitutional form of governance, but insulating its essential features from hostile amendments. Some states have followed Germany in enacting a constitutional provision identifying a set of sacrosanct constitutional commitments that may neither be diminished nor dissolved through a constitutional amendment, however popular. In Germany, these commitments include dignity, democracy, and the rule of law. Other jurisdictions have followed India in formulating interpretive doctrines that implicitly acknowledge similar commitments. Within such legal systems, the legal and institutional structure through which dignity and fundamental rights are protected may be refined through a constitutional amendment, but not dismantled.

From the standpoint of constitutional theory, however, these developments are perplexing. The traditional view conceives of the amending power as an instrument that may be directed toward the pursuit of any preference that garners sufficient popularity.[48] On such a view, the amending power should be subject only to procedural constraints that specify the threshold of support that a successful amendment must attract. An alternative view suggests that the amending power is subject to substantive constraints that stem from the fundamental commitments of the relevant constitutional order.[49] The difficulty with this doctrine is that it is only as adequate as the context in which it happens to be raised. The doctrine insulates the fundamental features of the constitutional

[48] Martin Loughlin, "The Concept of Constituent Power," *European Journal of Political Theory* 13 (2014): 218–37; Bruce Ackerman, *We the People: Foundations* (Cambridge: Harvard University Press, 1991), 14–16.

[49] John Rawls, *Political Liberalism* (New York: Columbia University Press, 1996), 238–9; Carl Schmitt, *Constitutional Theory*, trans. Jeffrey Seitzer (Durham: Duke University Press, 2008), 150.

order from amendment, but is indifferent to the relation of these features to human dignity. Thus, the doctrine was invoked in the Indian context to safeguard the rule of law, democracy, and judicial review, but it was also invoked in the antebellum South by those seeking to perpetuate racial slavery.

In Chapter 6, I draw on the unified theory to justify the substantive constraints that bind the amending power of a modern constitutional state. Modern constitutionalism is a form of governance in which the duty of government to respect, protect, and fulfill the dignity of all who are subject to it forms a justiciable condition of the valid exercise of public authority. The transition to such a form of governance has significant ramifications for the future employment of the amending power. Since a constitutional amendment is an exercise of public authority, it follows that amendments that violate the duty of just governance are not merely unjust but invalid. And since this duty is violated by exercises of the amending power that undermine the state's commitment to human dignity or the legal and institutional structure entailed by this commitment, such amendments cannot be valid. Thus, the unified theory explains why a modern constitutional state may use its amending power to refine its form of governance, but may not direct that power toward its diminishment or destruction.

Chapter 7 explores two doctrines that modern constitutional states invoke to adjudicate constitutional rights: purposive interpretation and proportionality. Through purposive interpretation, courts determine the protections that constitutional rights afford to their bearers. In turn, proportionality sets out the conditions that government must satisfy to justify the limitation of a constitutional right. This approach has been criticized for extending constitutional protections with one hand that are then taken away with the other. In the eyes of its critics, this approach does 'violence to the idea of a constitution.'[50] After all, the reason why constitutional rights are entrenched is to establish that certain kinds of state conduct are impermissible. Doctrines through which impermissible conduct is rendered permissible must be repudiated.

[50] Grégoire C.N. Webber, "Proportionality, Balancing, and the Cult of Constitutional Rights Scholarship," *Canadian Journal of Law and Jurisprudence* 23 (2010): 198. See also George Kateb, *Human Dignity*, 30–1; Jürgen Habermas, *Between Facts and Norms: Contributions to a Discourse Theory of Law and Democracy* (Cambridge: MIT Press, 1998), 258–9; Neomi Rao, "On the Use and Abuse of Dignity in Constitutional Law," *Columbia Journal of European Law* 14 (2008): 232–38; Stavros Tsakyrakis, "Proportionality: An Assault on Human Rights," *International Journal of Constitutional Law* 7 (2009): 489.

I respond by establishing the moral continuity between the commitment of a modern constitutional state to respect, protect, and fulfill the human dignity of all who are subject to its authority and the doctrines through which it adjudicates constitutional disputes. The doctrine of proportionality, I argue, is the solution to a moral problem raised by the purposive interpretation of constitutional rights. If human dignity is to form a justiciable legal constraint on all public authority, it must be rendered sufficiently determinate for public officials to relate it to the particulars of governance. Thus, modern constitutional states delineate human dignity into a set of constitutional rights. While constitutional rights are more determinate than human dignity, they are more general than the instances to which they apply. Accordingly, they must be brought to bear on their instances through interpretation. Given the basis of constitutional rights, the protections must be interpreted purposively in reference to the overarching idea of human dignity. Such an approach will often afford a broad range of protections to constitutional rights. But the more broadly particular constitutional rights are interpreted, the more likely it is that conflicts will arise between a particular constitutional right and a competing specification of human dignity. Since a modern constitutional state is committed to interpreting constitutional rights purposively, and purposive interpretation culminates in conflicts between specifications of the constitutional order's most basic norm, a doctrine is required to identify cases of conflict and determine when government is *morally justified* in responding by limiting a constitutional right through law. I argue that this is exactly what the branches that make up the doctrine of proportionality provide. Far from introducing exceptions to the duty that human dignity imposes on all public authority, purposive interpretation and proportionality formulate what this duty requires in cases in which its various specifications cannot be fully realized.

The doctrinal dimension of the unified theory provides a rebuttal to those who allege that the idea of human dignity is too impoverished to guide or constrain constitutional adjudication.[51] My answer is not that constitutional adjudication should proceed by applying the concept of human dignity directly to constitutional disputes. Nor is my claim that lawyers and judges have superior judgment about the concrete meaning of constitutional rights. Instead, I explain how the concept of human dignity

[51] See, for example, McCrudden, "Human Dignity and Judicial Interpretation of Human Rights," 655; Rosen, "Dignity: The Case Against," in *Understanding Human Dignity*, 152.

can be brought to bear on contingent constitutional disputes in a series of stages that proceed from the normative structure of the public law relationship, to the constitutional structure that this relationship demands, and finally to the legal doctrines, such as purposive interpretation and proportionality, that bring the normative and constitutional dimensions of human dignity into contact with their instances. As a theory of modern constitutional practice, the unified theory explicates and justifies the inner logic of these doctrines.[52] Determining what human dignity and constitutional rights require with respect to a contingent dispute involves not an all-things-considered judgment, but rather a judgment sensitive to the considerations that these doctrines identify.

In the Conclusion, I bring the theoretical and practical dimensions of this project together by asking a critical but neglected question: Why did the foremost Anglo-American legal theorists in the postwar era fail to recognize the innovation of the modern constitutional state? I begin by setting out how Hart, Fuller, and Dworkin thought about the core components of modern constitutionalism, such as constitutional supremacy, the protection of dignity and rights, and judicial review. I then suggest that they overlooked modern constitutionalism for systematic, not incidental, reasons. As I note in Chapter 5, a legal system is defective when it is organized in such a way that persons susceptible to public wrongs are left without legal recourse. Because the leading Anglo-American legal theories lack the resources to recognize this defect, they fail to illuminate the constitutional and doctrinal innovations designed to alleviate it. In elaborating my argument, I distinguish the conception of human dignity that I defend from those advanced by Fuller and Dworkin.

Three clarifications about the nature of this project are in order from the outset.

First, the overarching purpose of this book is to formulate a theoretical justification of modern constitutional practice. The bridge between

[52] For a deflationary view of the doctrinal dimension of public law, see Martin Loughlin, *The Idea of Public Law* (Oxford: Oxford University Press, 2003), 163: 'Although public law discourse revolves around a common core of general principles – such as necessity, rationality, propriety, reasonableness, and proportionality – the application of these principles to specific cases remains indeterminate. This is because public law is not an exercise in moral reasoning built on philosophical premises, but a form of political reasoning driven by prudential considerations . . . Although such decisions may subsequently be justified in the generalized forms of constitutional adjudication, these rational forms do not yield the substance of public law decision.'

theory and practice can be built in either direction.[53] One can begin by looking to a practice and reflecting on its theoretical presuppositions. The present chapter adopts this approach. Alternately, one can elaborate a general theory of public law and then work out its practical ramifications. The subsequent chapters adopt this approach. The difference between these approaches lies in the direction that the argument moves rather than the ground that it covers.

Second, in expounding the unified theory, I focus on constitutional law. This is not to imply that public law and constitutional law are synonymous, but to stipulate that constitutional law sets out the conditions for the valid exercise of all public authority. Constitutional law constructs the parameters for the operation of other domains of public law, including administrative and criminal law. All branches of public law, insofar as they involve the constitutional exercise of public authority, must adhere to constitutional constraints.

Third, the justification of modern constitutionalism that I present does not offer a complete catalog of the constitutional norms and institutional arrangements appropriate for legal systems in general. Instead, the argument aims to articulate the moral problem inherent in the public law relationship between rulers and ruled – the problem of accountability – and then to explain how a modern constitutional state addresses this problem by integrating the following components: constitutional supremacy, constitutional rights, and judicial review. In Chapters 5, 6, and 7, my discussion of modern constitutionalism in a range of jurisdictions – including Canada, Germany, South Africa, and India – illustrates that a variety of approaches for addressing the problem of accountability are available, although all involve the integration of these components. The purpose of the constitutional theory that I elaborate is to set out a general normative standard against which legitimate variation can be distinguished from injustice. My hope is that by formulating an integrated answer to a set of normative, institutional, and doctrinal problems in public law, a standpoint materializes for profitably exploring a range of further issues.

1.4 Dignity: the concept and the word

Human dignity is the term that modern constitutional states employ to refer to the most abstract concept that justifies their practices. Of course, other

[53] Ronald Dworkin, *Life's Dominion: An Argument about Abortion, Euthanasia, and Individual Freedom* (New York: Alfred A. Knopf, 1993), 29.

terms could be used to refer to this concept, just as this term could refer to other concepts.[54] In exploring the relationship between modern constitutional practice and the concept of human dignity, scholars often explicate the concept by appealing to historical meanings of the word *dignity* or its counterparts in Latin (*dignitas*), German (*Würde*), and other languages. The attempt to explicate the practice of modern constitutional law in terms of the historical meanings of the word *dignity* characterizes the influential, but unsatisfactory, accounts of Michael Rosen and Jeremy Waldron.

Rosen's approach purports to explicate the meaning of dignity both within and beyond contemporary constitutional law by investigating the intellectual history of the term:

> To untangle the idea of dignity, the best way, I think, is to reach back to its roots, and these – like all concepts of significant interest in political life – are historical . . . History shows the existence of significant distinct strands in the meaning of dignity, strands that come together and move apart at different times.[55]

Canvassing historical discussions of dignity from religion, moral philosophy, aesthetics, and literature, Rosen delineates four strands of meaning: (1) dignity as a conferred 'rank or status,' (2) dignity as the 'intrinsic value' of a human being, (3) dignity as 'self-possessed behavior,' and (4) dignity as a particular right to respectful treatment.[56] Rosen argues that these strands fail to make sense of central features of the contemporary legal meaning of human dignity. When dignity is conceived as a rank or status that is established through a kind of legal or social convention, it fails to offer a moral standpoint for the critical assessment of that convention.[57] Turning to the view each person has intrinsic value, Rosen explores the Kantian and Catholic roots of this idea and rejects them for two reasons: first, because a liberal democratic state may not adopt and enforce metaphysical or theological doctrines[58] and, second,

[54] Matthias Mahlmann, "The Good Sense of Dignity: Six Antidotes to Dignity Fatigue in Ethics and Law," in *Understanding Human Dignity*, 595: '[O]ne should not look only for the *term* dignity . . . but for historical manifestations of the *idea* designated by these terms. In these manifestations, the idea may not be called dignity at all. This may be the case because the same or a similar idea can be expressed by many different linguistic means and, of course, not necessarily according to the linguistic expectations of posterity.' For an instance of the mistaken inference that the absence of the word *dignity* indicates the absence of the concept, see Samuel Moyn, "The Secret History of Constitutional Dignity," in *Understanding Human Dignity*, 96.

[55] Rosen, *Dignity: Its History and Meaning*, 7–8. [56] Ibid., 114.

[57] Rosen, "Dignity: The Case Against," in *Understanding Human Dignity*, 145.

[58] Ibid., 152.

because Kantian and Catholic conceptions of dignity fail to establish a 'cogent route from principle to application.'[59] Nor can human dignity refer to self-possessed behavior, or as Friedrich Schiller characterized it 'tranquility in suffering.'[60] Such a quality might be exhibited by certain persons at certain times, but it is 'not a universal and inalienable property of human beings, something that gives a foundational reason for their having equal basic entitlements in relation to the actions of the state and fellow members of the human race.'[61] Finally, the legal practice is not elucidated by conceiving of dignity as a right to treatment that is neither degrading nor contemptuous. In constitutional jurisprudence, human dignity is often conceptualized not as a particular right to a certain kind of treatment, but as the 'foundation for rights in general.'[62]

Having established that the intellectual history of the word *dignity* fails to elucidate its constitutional meaning, Rosen issues a skeptical conclusion. When courts appeal to human dignity to resolve questions about rights, 'it would appear that courts are operating freelance, and that their decisions – rhetorically framed in the grandiloquent language about dignity as they may be – lack basic moral legitimacy.'[63] Rosen's conclusion is broader than the argument that supports it. Even if the historical meanings of the word *dignity* fail to illuminate contemporary constitutional practice, this does not render that practice deficient or fraudulent. It simply means that earlier meanings of the word *dignity*, which were not formed in reference to public law, fail to shed light on its current practice. And this should not be surprising. For constitutional lawyers agree that in the aftermath of the horrors of World War II, dignity took on a new meaning that fundamentally reoriented public law.[64] Nothing that Rosen

[59] Rosen, *Dignity: Its History and Meaning*, 9. [60] Ibid., 31–2. [61] Ibid., 6.

[62] Ibid., 62.

[63] Rosen, "Dignity: The Case Against," in *Understanding Human Dignity*, 152.

[64] Stephen J. Wermiel, "Law and Human Dignity: The Judicial Soul of Justice Brennan," *William & Mary Bill of Rights Journal* 7 (1998): 224–8. Wermiel explains that in American jurisprudence of the nineteenth and early twentieth century, dignity referred to an elevated status. Thus, courts referred to the 'dignity of an argument,' the 'dignity of an invention' underlying a patent, the 'dignity of the State of Oregon,' and the 'dignity of citizenship.' In the aftermath of World War II, courts began to refer to the 'dignity of man,' the dignity of the 'human personality,' and 'human dignity.' On this point, see also Brenda Hale, "Preface," in *Understanding Human Dignity*, xv; Stu Woolman in *The Dignity Jurisprudence of the Constitutional Court of South Africa*, 74 (noting that the South African Constitutional Court 'recognizes that the history of dignity is a history of the world after World War II').

On the discrepancies that distinguish the meaning of the word *dignity* in postwar human rights law from the philosophic tradition extending from Cicero to Kant,

says about the meanings that were previously associated with the word *dignity* excludes the possibility of formulating a theory that captures the significance of the concept for contemporary constitutional law.

Like Rosen, Waldron seeks to explicate the meaning of dignity in both ancient and contemporary legal systems.[65] But where Rosen discovers conflicting meanings, Waldron finds continuity between ancient and contemporary understandings.[66] On the ancient understanding, dignity (*dignitas*) refers to the honor that one bears by virtue of the rank or office that one occupies.[67] One can therefore speak of the dignity of a monarch, or the lesser levels of dignity afforded to dukes, barons, or clergy.[68] Further, one can identify the particular rights and privileges that persons possess by locating their rank or office within the social hierarchy. By contrast, the contemporary understanding reflects a 'sea change in the way that "dignity" is used, enabling it to become a leading concept of *universal* rights (as opposed to special privileges).'[69]

Waldron acknowledges the tension between the ancient understanding of dignity as rank and the modern understanding of dignity as equal rights, but insists that these understandings can be reconciled.[70] His approach centers on the claim that dignity is a kind of convention regarding rank, or as he puts it, a 'term used to indicate a high-ranking legal, political, and social status.'[71] Over time, the content of the convention has changed. The ancient conception that stratified persons into higher and lower ranks has been supplanted by a 'single-status system . . . that entitles everyone to something like the treatment that was previously confined to high-status individuals.'[72] Thus, the dignity previously afforded to the superior alone is now extended to all of humanity. The notion of dignity as a convention about legal, political, or social rank is sufficiently capacious to envelop, on the one hand, stratified societies in

see Oliver Sensen, "Human Dignity in Historical Perspective: The Contemporary and Traditional Paradigms," *European Journal of Political Theory* 10 (2011): 71–91. For an account that explains how the *idea* of legal personality developed into contemporary dignitarian jurisprudence, see Joern Eckert, "Legal Roots of Human Dignity in German Law," in *The Concept of Human Dignity in Human Rights Discourse*, ed. Eckart Klein and David Kretzmer (Dordrecht: Kluwer Law International, 2002), 41–53.

65 Jeremy Waldron, "Dignity and Rank," in *Dignity, Rank, and Rights*, ed. Meir Dan-Cohen (Oxford: Oxford University Press, 2012), 14.

66 Ibid., 30. 67 Ibid. 68 Ibid., 30–1. 69 Ibid., 33. 70 Ibid., 31 and 33.

71 Jeremy Waldron, "Law, Dignity, and Self-Control," in *Dignity, Rank, and Rights*, 47. On the conventional character of Waldron's conception of dignity, see Meir Dan-Cohen, "Introduction: Dignity and Its (Dis)content," in *Dignity, Rank, and Rights*, 5–6; and Michael Rosen, "Dignity Past and Present," in *Dignity, Rank, and Rights*, 81.

72 Waldron, "Law, Dignity, and Self-Control," 57.

which persons stand in relations of superior and inferior, and, on the other, the egalitarian societies of the present day, in which persons can 'look up to each other from a position of upright equality.'[73]

Waldron emphasizes that his account offers resources for the immanent criticism of legal systems.[74] Rather than evaluating and criticizing legal systems for their conformity to some extrinsic moral theory, legal systems can instead be critically evaluated by looking to their own conventions. A legal system that commits itself to human dignity, whether explicitly in the text of its constitution or implicitly in its institutional arrangements and traditions of governance, can be criticized to the extent that it betrays its own dignitarian commitments.[75] Thus, Waldron's account takes the form of a conditional: *if* a legal system commits itself to human dignity, *then* it may be criticized in relation to that standard. Of course, where the convention has not been established, the duty that issues from it does not obtain.[76]

Although Waldron formulates his theory to expound the idea of human dignity in the legal practice of modern constitutional states like Germany and South Africa,[77] an antagonism obtains between the jurisprudence of these legal systems and the conventionalism of his account. This antagonism is evident in the way that these regimes understand both their own constitutional arrangements and the barbarism of the regimes that they supplanted. For Waldron, *human* dignity results from the 'assignment'[78] or 'attribution of high legal rank or status to every human being.'[79] By contrast, in German and South African jurisprudence, the duty that human dignity imposes on public authority is understood not to be assigned or attributed, but *acknowledged*. Arthur Chaskalson, the former Chief Justice of the South African Constitutional Court, explains that in referring to human dignity as inherent, the constitution indicates 'that respect for human dignity, and all that flows from it' is 'not a privilege granted by the state.'[80] His colleague Justice Ackermann shares this view: 'all humans have inherent dignity as an

[73] Ibid., 60. [74] Ibid., 67. [75] Ibid., 65–6.

[76] Ibid., 59. When Waldron considers legal systems in which the convention establishing *human* dignity was not present, he concludes not that these societies were defective because they violated human dignity by dividing persons into ranks of superior and inferior, but that our contemporary understanding of dignity is fundamentally different than it was in prior ages.

[77] Waldron, "Dignity and Rank," in *Dignity, Rank, and Rights*, 14.

[78] Waldron, "Law, Dignity, and Self-Control," in *Dignity, Rank, and Rights*, 47.

[79] Ibid., 66.

[80] "Human Dignity as a Foundational Value of Our Constitutional Order," 196.

attribute independent of and antecedent to any constitutional protection thereof.'[81] The same conviction is embedded in the German context. As Günter Dürig explains, the state's duty to respect and protect human dignity and fundamental rights is not created by the constitution. Rather, the constitution 'simply recognizes' this obligation.[82] From the standpoint of South African and German jurisprudence, human dignity binds the state even in the absence of a legal convention that acknowledges it. This obligation is also evident in the way that South Africa and Germany understand their brutal pasts. Human dignity is understood not as a norm that was established following Nazi and Apartheid violence, but as a norm that bound these regimes in their own day and that they systematically violated.[83]

A theory that seeks to explain the connection between human dignity and modern constitutional practice in these and other constitutional jurisdictions must confront a distinctive challenge. If the duty of a legal system to respect and protect human dignity binds regardless of that legal system's conventions, then a theory of human dignity would have to explain why this norm binds not only legal systems that have (explicitly or implicitly) committed themselves to it, but legal systems generally. To put the problem in Waldron's terms, why does human dignity form the immanent standard for the criticism of legal systems as such? Waldron's theory is unable to answer this question because it gets things backwards. Instead of explaining why human dignity forms the relevant standard for critically assessing legal conventions, he argues that human dignity is itself the product of legal conventions. By explicating human dignity in

[81] Lourens W.H. Ackermann, "The Legal Nature of the South African Constitutional Revolution," *New Zealand Law Review* (2004): 647.

[82] Günter Dürig, "An Introduction to the Basic Law of the Federal Republic of Germany," in *The Constitution of the Federal Republic of Germany*, ed. Ulrich Karpen (Baden-Baden: Nomos Verlagsgesellschaft, 1988), 13. See also Donald P. Kommers and Russell A. Miller, *The Constitutional Jurisprudence of the Federal Republic of Germany* (Durham: Duke University Press, 2012), 56 ('[The Basic Law] does not regard the state as the source of fundamental rights. The core of individual freedom, like human dignity itself, is regarded as anterior to the state').

[83] See, for example, Dieter Grimm, "The German and American Constitutionalism: A Comparison," *The Berlin Journal* 7 (2003): 11: 'What had separated the Nazi regime from Western civilization was its total neglect of human dignity.' In the South African context, see *Prinsloo* v. *van der Linde*, [1997] 6 B.C.L.R. 759 (S. Afr. Const. Ct.), para. 31 (lamenting that in Apartheid South Africa, the majority of the inhabitants of the country 'were treated as not having inherent worth; as objects whose identities could be arbitrarily defined by those in power rather than as persons of infinite worth. In short, they were denied recognition of their inherent dignity').

terms of the ancient notion of *dignitas*, Waldron's theory clashes with the constitutional practice that it claims to illuminate.

Others seek to explain the significance of dignity in constitutional law by looking to the philosophic theories that invoke the term, such as Immanuel Kant's ethics. Kant is well-known in constitutional circles for insisting that each person is an 'end in itself' and has an 'inner worth, that is, *dignity*.'[84] His ethical theory asserts that dignity (*Würde*) is the capacity to act from and in accordance with ethical duties that spring from the rationality of one's own free will. Germany's Basic Law, as we have seen, opens with the proclamation that human dignity (*Die Würde des Menschen*) is inviolable and that it is the duty of all state authority to respect and protect it.[85] Given the terminological overlap, jurists and moral philosophers appeal to Kant's ethical thought to explain the meaning of this article[86] and its counterparts in other legal systems.[87] But whatever its merits as a theory of virtue, Kant's *ethical* thought is unsuited for explicating the *legal* significance of human dignity.

On the one hand, Kantian ethics offer no account of how state authority is possible, that is, of how the state could have the right to

[84] Kant, *Groundwork of the Metaphysics of Morals*, 4:435. Page reference to Kant's corpus refer to the pagination of the Prussian Academy.

[85] Grundgesetz, article 1.

[86] See, for example, Dieter Grimm, "Dignity in a Legal Context: Dignity as an Absolute Right," in *Understanding Human Dignity*, 384; Edward J. Eberle, "The German Idea of Freedom," *Oregon Review of International Law* 10 (2008): 11 ('Kantian dignitarian ethics form a guiding principle of the [Germany's Basic Law], an ideal around which the whole legal order has been reconceived'); Thomas Hill, "In Defence of Human Dignity: Comments on Kant and Rosen," in *Understanding Human Dignity*, 313–25; G.P. Fletcher, "Human Dignity as a Constitutional Value," *University of Western Ontario Law Review* 22 (1984): 171–82.

[87] Allen Wood, "Human Dignity, Right and the Realm of Ends," *Acta Juridica* (2008): 48 (arguing that Kantian ethics provides 'the fullest philosophical articulation' of human dignity, as protected by the South African Constitution); L.W.H. Ackermann, "The Legal Nature of the South African Constitutional Revolution," 645–50; Stu Woolman, "The Architecture of Dignity," 73–123. Woolman's aim is to articulate the unity that underlies the various ways in which dignity is invoked in South African jurisprudence. His central claim is that the unifying basis of dignitarian jurisprudence is the injunction articulated in Kantian ethics to treat persons as ends and never merely as a means (76 and 116). While Woolman claims to offer an account of human dignity rooted in the idea of autonomy, as he develops his account, conflicting philosophic commitments begin to appear. Thus Woolman assimilates some dimensions of dignitarian jurisprudence to autonomy, but in explaining others he appeals alternately to utilitarianism (77) and the importance of diminishing suffering (81), Ronald Dworkin's ideal of equal concern and respect (116), and Amartya Sen's capabilities approach (81 and 119). Since this explication of human dignity relies on incompatible philosophic commitments, its components do not cohere into a larger whole.

impose coercible obligations on rational agents. The focus of Kantian ethics is those duties that the individual rational will gives to itself and that also form the incentive for action. Consequently, each rational agent must act from and in accordance with a common set of imperatives generated by practical reason. By contrast, public law involves duties that state authority imposes on private persons through the contingent enactment of positive law. Because these duties bind only those who find themselves within a given jurisdiction, individuals who occupy different legal systems may find themselves bound by different duties. Further, while legal authority requires that one acts in accordance with the relevant duties, the duty need not form the incentive for one's action. So far as law is concerned, persons must act in accordance with it regardless of whether they feel duty-bound to do so. Kantian ethics, accordingly, captures neither the right of government to exercise state authority nor the obligation of private persons to obey its lawgiving.

On the other, Kantian ethics do not capture the way in which human dignity and fundamental rights bind state authority. The disjunction emerges from the form and content of the duties that comprise Kantian ethics. As a matter of form, these duties are not correlative to the rights of others. At issue is the internal coherence of a single rational will, not the conduct of the state toward individuals subject to its authority. As a matter of the content of Kantian ethics, each agent must develop his or her talents and contribute to the happiness of others.[88] A fundamental discrepancy thus separates the conception of dignity that appears in Kant's ethics from the account that arises in modern constitutional law. Within Kantian ethics, dignity demands that individuals direct their freedom toward the pursuit of certain mandatory ends. By contrast, within modern constitutional jurisprudence, human dignity involves the recognition that each person is free to determine his or her own ends.[89]

In pointing to the inaptness of Kantian ethics to public law, I am not criticizing Kant but reiterating a fundamental tenet of his philosophy. Kant himself emphasized the sharp distinction between the ethical and

[88] *Doctrine of Virtue*, in *Practical Philosophy*, trans. Mary J. Gregor (Cambridge: Cambridge University Press, 1996), 6:385–6.

[89] For an account of the danger that attends conceiving of human dignity as the duty of individuals to live virtuously that the state may enforce, instead of as a right of individuals to freedom that imposes a duty on all state authority, see Denise Meyerson, "Does the Constitutional Court of South Africa Take Rights Seriously? The Case of S v. Jordan," *Acta Juridica* (2004): 138–54.

the juridical.[90] Indeed, the inspiration for the unified theory of public law stems not from Kant's ethical philosophy, but from the account of public right that appears in his mature juridical thought.[91] While the *word* dignity plays a peripheral role in Kant's legal and political thought,[92] the *concept* of human dignity takes center stage in his argument. Adopting the language of innate right (*angeboren Recht*), Kant argues that the right of each person to freedom – independence from the constraint of another's choice – must answer to nothing other than its own systematic requirements. In elaborating this idea, Kant creates a theory of public law that may follow from features of his philosophic project, but that can stand independently of it.[93] In this book, I reformulate Kant's striking insights into public law in abstraction from his broader framework, as well as his challenging texts and terminology.

For many, Kant's legal and political thought will seem an unsuitable inspiration for a theory of public law that seeks to give notions both of public authority and of public justice their due. After all, Kant is typically interpreted as either a conservative defender of the status quo who dismisses the demands of justice when they fail to conform to the positive law[94] or a utopian liberal who dismisses positive law when it fails to conform to the demands of justice.[95] Neither interpretation considers the integrative possibility that Kant's theory of public right offers a theoretical framework that justifies the authority of existing states over their members, elucidates the nature of a just state, and expounds the ongoing duty of all public authority to bring itself into the deepest possible conformity with public justice. I flesh out this possibility in the second, third, and fourth chapters.

In the fifth, sixth, and seventh chapters, I extend Kant's thought by explaining how it serves as the justificatory basis for the legal,

[90] Kant, *Doctrine of Right* in *Practical Philosophy*, 6:218–21.

[91] For a systematic exposition of the distinction between these branches of Kant's moral philosophy, see Ripstein, *Force and Freedom*, 355–88.

[92] See, for example, *Doctrine of Right*, in *Practical Philosophy*, 6:295, 6:316, 6:318, 6:327–9, and 6:364.

[93] On the freestanding nature of the legal and political component of Kant's framework, see Thomas Pogge, "Is Kant's *Rechtslehre* a 'Comprehensive Liberalism'?" in *Kant's Metaphysics of Morals*, ed. Mark Timmons (Oxford: Oxford University Press, 2002), 133–58; and Ripstein, *Force and Freedom: Kant's Legal and Political Philosophy*, 357–8.

[94] Robert Alexy, *The Argument From Injustice: A Reply to Legal Positivism*, trans. Bonnie Litschewski Paulson and Stanley L. Paulson (Oxford: Clarendon Press, 2002), 116–21; Alexy, "On the Concept and Nature of Law," *Ratio Juris* 21 (2008): 288–90.

[95] Jürgen Habermas, *Between Facts and Norms: Contributions of a Discourse Theory of Law and Democracy*, 120–1.

institutional, and doctrinal features of the modern constitutional state. While Kant did not discover modern constitutionalism, I believe that his thought elucidates the relationship between authority and justice that the modern constitutional state strives to realize. Perhaps Kant would be receptive to this suggestion. In the Preface to the *Doctrine of Right*, he emphasizes the somewhat provisional character of his theory of public right:

> Toward the end of the book I have worked less thoroughly over certain sections than might be expected in comparison with the earlier ones, partly because it seems to me that they can be easily inferred from the earlier ones and partly, too, because the later sections (dealing with public right) are currently subject to so much discussion, and still so important, that they can well justify postponing a decisive judgment for some time.[96]

One of the reasons that Kant presents for failing to fully develop his theory of public right is that the discussions in his day had not reached a decisive conclusion. The meaning of such a comment might be evident if uttered by another philosopher, but coming from Kant it is puzzling. The *Doctrine of Right* appears in a work entitled *The Metaphysics of Morals* and concerns the a priori norms governing the external interaction of free and equal persons. How could the elaboration of a system of a priori norms be hindered by the discussions that were occurring in Kant's day (or any other)?

I suspect that the answer lies in the distinction between the normative domain of right and the empirical domain of political knowledge. Kant takes himself to have provided an exhaustive account of the normative structure of public right, but seems aware of his own inability to present the institutional and doctrinal conditions in which these norms would be most adequately realized. As I argue in Chapter 5, the norms of public right are most deeply fulfilled in the modern constitutional state. In this setting, the right of all persons, by virtue of their human dignity, to public justice is transformed from a mere moral ideal into a legal reality. Each person subject to law's authority has by virtue of his or her dignity a justiciable right to insist that all governance conforms to the terms of its own justification. In Kant's day, ideas of human rights had just begun to percolate into public consciousness, but the modern constitutional paradigm was not yet evident. It emerged following the moral horrors of World War II when peoples around the world finally began to confront the challenge of designing legal systems in

[96] *Doctrine of Right* in *Practical Philosophy*, 6:209.

which the demands of human dignity formed a justiciable constraint on the coercive exercise of public authority. While Kant had no knowledge of these future developments, his general theory of public right provides a powerful framework for illuminating their groundbreaking significance.

PART I

The normative dimension

2

Authority, justice, and public law

In "Positivism and the Separation of Law and Morals," H.L.A. Hart advanced three enduring theses about the relationship between law and morality.[1]

The first is that an adequate theory of law steers a middle course between anarchism and quietism.[2] Anarchism is the view that what is unjust cannot impose legal obligations. Quietism is the view that what imposes legal obligations cannot be unjust. Neither the anarchist nor the quietist can endorse Bentham's 'motto of a good citizen' under 'a government of laws': '*To obey punctually; to censure freely.*'[3] For the anarchist, the criticism of a legal system's adequacy leaves nothing to obey. For the quietist, the duty to obey a legal system excludes the possibility of criticizing its adequacy. Thus, from their diverging outlooks, anarchists and quietists both deny the truism that a legal system might be unjust. The disagreement between anarchists and quietists is confined to the issue of whether the absence of justice indicates the absence of legality or whether the presence of legality indicates the presence of justice.

The second thesis is that legal positivism avoids the twin pitfalls of anarchism and quietism by separating the question of whether something is legally valid from the question of whether it is just:

> What both Bentham and Austin were anxious to assert were the following two simple things: first, in the absence of an expressed constitutional or legal provision, it could not follow from the mere fact that a rule violated standards of morality that it was not a rule of law; and, conversely, it could not follow from the mere fact that a rule was morally desirable that it was a rule of law.[4]

1 Hart, "Positivism and the Separation of Law and Morals," *Harvard Law Review* 71 (1958): 593–629.
2 Ibid., 597–8.
3 Bentham, *A Fragment on Government* (Cambridge: Cambridge University Press, 2001), 10.
4 Hart, "Positivism and the Separation of Law and Morals," 599.

By distinguishing the question of whether something is a law from the question of whether it is just, legal positivism jointly rejects anarchism and quietism. Anarchism is rejected because justice is not the standard of legal validity. Quietism is rejected because legal validity is not the standard of justice.[5] The separation thesis is the key to the progressive orientation to which legal positivism aspires. The distinction between law and morals enables positivist reformers to recognize the injustice of existing laws and to seek the enactment of better ones.

The third thesis is that nonpositivist theories of law inevitably collapse into anarchism or quietism.[6] Since positivism is premised on the separation of law and morals, its proponents invariably suppose that nonpositivism must be premised on their unity. On this view, whether one is an anarchist or a quietist depends on whether one assimilates law to morality or morality to law. The anarchist bends the concept of law to fit the concept of justice, while the quietist bends the concept of justice to fit the concept of law. The claim that nonpositivist theories are either anarchist or quietist extends through the positivist corpus from the works of Bentham to the present day. As Hart notes, Bentham attributed to Blackstone the anarchic view that human laws were invalid if they conflicted with divine laws and an 'obsequious quietism' that fails to admit a distinction between what the law is and what it ought to be.[7] Similarly, Kelsen argued that nonpositivist theories were either revolutionary or conservative. In its revolutionary guise, which Kelsen attributed to Locke, nonpositivism calls 'into question the validity of the positive law by claiming that the positive law contradicts some presupposed absolute order.'[8] In its conservative guise, which Kelsen ascribed to Kant, nonpositivism shows 'that the positive law is simply the emanation of a natural or divine order or of a system of reason – the emanation of an absolutely "right," just order.'[9] With these one-sided accounts of nonpositivism in hand, positivists dismiss nonpositivist theories as blind to a fundamental aspect of law's nature. Since nonpositivist theories are either anarchist or quietist, and each of these frameworks denies the truism that

[5] Ibid., 598. [6] Ibid., 597–8. [7] Ibid., 598.

[8] Kelsen, *An Introduction to the Problems of Legal Theory*, trans. Bonnie Litschewski Paulson and Stanley L. Paulson (Oxford: Oxford University Press, 1997), 18. See also Kelsen, "The Natural-Law Doctrine before the Tribunal of Science," *Western Political Science Quarterly* 2 (1949): 493.

[9] Kelsen, *An Introduction to the Problems of Legal Theory*, 18; and "The Natural-Law Doctrine before the Tribunal of Science," 493.

a valid system of law may be unjust, positivists conclude that nonpositivist theories cannot account for a fundamental aspect of law's nature.

The objection continues to be raised today. Scott Shapiro has recently argued that nonpositivist theories – or as he terms them, natural law theories – are inherently incapable of accounting for the possibility of evil legal systems:

> By insisting on grounding legal authority in moral authority or moral norms, natural law theory rules out the possibility of evil legal systems . . . Just as theologians have struggled to explain how evil is possible given the necessary goodness of God, the natural lawyer must account for the possibility of evil legal systems given that the law is necessarily grounded in moral facts.[10]

Shapiro sugggests that a nonpositivist might respond to this objection in two ways.[11] The first involves rejecting the legal truism that a valid law might be unjust. The second involves admitting the inability to illuminate the truism but countering that the problems that legal positivism face are nevertheless worse. Neither of these possibilities confronts the objection.

In this chapter, I accept Hart's first thesis denying the adequacy of both anarchism and quietism, but reject both his second and third. I start with the second thesis by considering whether Hart's version of legal positivism succeeds in steering a middle path between the twin pitfalls of anarchism and quietism. I argue that Hart's positivism offers an explanation of how certain persons in a legal system could perceive themselves to be under obligations with respect to enacted laws, but does not explain how a legal system could actually have the authority to impose obligations on them. In the absence of such an account, Hart's theory collapses into the very anarchism that led him to reject the theories of his predecessors in both the positivist and nonpositivist camps. I then turn to consider Hart's third thesis that nonpositivist theories of law inevitably collapse into anarchism or quietism. The central purpose of this chapter is to provide a sketch of a nonpositivist legal theory, the *unified theory of public law*, which provides an alternative to anarchist and quietist paradigms by formulating an integrated justification of two distinctive aspects

[10] Scott Shapiro, *Legality* (Cambridge: Harvard University Press, 2011), 49. For an additional exposition of the positivist objection, see Jules L. Coleman and Brian Leiter, "Legal Positivism," in *A Companion to Philosophy of Law and Legal Theory*, ed. Dennis Patterson (Oxford: Blackwell Publishing, 1999), 230–1.

[11] Ibid., 50.

of legal systems generally: public authority and public justice. My claim is that by reconceptualizing the relationship between public authority and public justice, the unified theory is able to reject the positivist separation of law and morals while avoiding the collapse into anarchism or quietism. If my argument is correct, then Hart gets things backwards. Hart's positivism collapses into the very anarchy that he derides, while the nonpositivism of the unified theory offers the middle path that he sought.

I present my argument in four sections. In the first section, I explain why Hart fails to steer a middle course between anarchism and quietism. The remaining sections unpack the unified theory of public law by elaborating a conceptually sequenced account of the right of persons to interact with others on terms of equal freedom. In the second section, I sketch a justification of the *principle of authority*, which relates the right of government to impose, interpret, and enforce valid legal obligations to the corresponding duty of private persons to obey public lawgiving. I then argue, in the third section, that the justification of the right of government to exercise public authority implicates a distinctive moral standard for assessing the adequacy of existing legal systems and directing their reform. The *principle of justice* relates the right of persons to just governance to the corresponding duty incumbent on government in the exercise of its authority. The distinguishing feature of the unified theory is its claim that when authority and justice are appropriately conceived and justified, they are neither antithetical virtues of opposing theoretical frameworks nor isolated notions. Instead, authority and justice are the *mutually implicating* constitutive and regulative aspects of the public law relationship between rulers and ruled. The right of rulers to exercise public authority is always accompanied by a duty to govern justly, while the right of the ruled to just governance presupposes the presence of publicly authoritative institutions. In the fourth section, I defend the unified theory from the leading positivist objection, which claims that any theory that appeals to moral concepts to elucidate the concept of law must inevitably fail to recognize a legal truism: a particular law or a legal system might be valid even though it is unjust. I argue that the unified theory is not vulnerable to this objection because in articulating what a legal system is, it provides resources for thinking about what makes a particular law or a legal system as a whole just. The justification of the right to exercise public authority implicates the relevant moral standard for assessing the adequacy of its instances.

Although I present the unified theory as a nonpositivist view, I do not deny positivism's core theses that positive law must be enacted by an appropriate public institution in order to be valid or that positive law is neither validated by its justice nor invalidated by its injustice.[12] As I argue below, such a platitude is compatible with both positivist and nonpositivist theories. The central dispute between positivists and nonpositivists lies elsewhere.

2.1 Hart's middle path

The problem of legal obligation traverses Hart's thought from the criticism of his positivist and nonpositivist predecessors to his own innovative contributions. On the one hand, Hart seeks to distinguish his own view from Austin's command theory by introducing legal obligation into the positivist framework. On the other, Hart seeks to provide an alternative to nonpositivist theories by differentiating notions of legal and moral obligation. In this section, I consider Hart's conception of legal obligation in the context of his criticism of competing theories. I argue that the conception of legal obligation that Hart formulates is too thin to satisfy the aim that animates his project: the formulation of a middle path between anarchism and quietism.

Hart dismissed Austin's legal positivism because it lacked the resources to distinguish between the coercive power of a legal system and the violence of an outlaw. For Austin, law is the command of a legally unconstrained sovereign. A *command* is an expression of a desire that another commit or forego a certain action, coupled with a threat to be imposed in the event of noncompliance.[13] The violation of a threat is likely to result in a *sanction*.[14] A command is issued by a *sovereign*, that is, an agent that is habitually obeyed by others but that does not habitually obey others.[15] The issuance of a command is correlative to a duty or obligation, which consists in being liable to an evil for failing to comply with a command. Whenever a command is issued, an obligation is present; whenever an obligation is present, a command has been issued.[16] The affinity between Austin's account of a legal system and naked violence led Hart to remark:

[12] See, for example, John Gardner, "Legal Positivism: 5½ Myths," *The American Journal of Jurisprudence* 46 (2001): 200–1.
[13] John Austin, *Lectures on Jurisprudence* (New York: Henry Holt and Company, 1875), 13.
[14] Ibid., 12. [15] Ibid., 82.
[16] Austin, *The Province of Jurisprudence Determined* (London: John Murray, 1832), 7.

> The situation which the simple trilogy of command, sanction, and sovereign avails to describe, if you take these notions at all precisely, is like that of a gunman saying to his victim, "Give me your money or your life." The only difference is that in the case of a legal system the gunman says it to a large number of people who are accustomed to the racket and habitually surrender to it. Law surely is not the gunman situation writ large, and legal order is surely not to be thus simply identified with compulsion.[17]

When subjected to the whims of a gunman, a victim who is eager to secure his life may readily surrender his money. Prudence may even *oblige* the victim to comply with the gunman's wish, but, as Hart notes, the victim has no *obligation* to comply.[18] Austin fails to distinguish the lawgiving of the sovereign from the violence of the gunman because he lacks an account of how one person, the sovereign, could have the public authority to impose a legal obligation on another. In the absence of such an account, the coercive power of a legal order doubles as a description of mere violence.

Whereas Hart's positivist predecessors lacked an account of legal obligation, Hart's nonpositivist predecessors failed to draw a distinction between legal obligations and moral ones. The failure to distinguish between legal and moral obligation culminated in two kinds of intellectual confusion: quietism and anarchism.[19] Some nonpositivist theories collapsed into quietism by holding that any norm that was legally obligatory was also morally obligatory. These theories thereby precluded the possibility of subjecting valid law to moral criticism. Other nonpositivist theories collapsed into anarchism by holding that if a norm was not morally obligatory, it could not be legally obligatory. The problem with anarchism is not that principled anarchists always break the law, but that they always act in accordance with their own understanding of what morality requires. If positive law is not present, then they act in accordance with their moral obligations. If positive law is present, then it may conform to or deviate from the requirements of morality. Positive law that conforms to what morality requires is superfluous because one is already under a moral obligation to do what it enjoins. Alternately, positive law that deviates from what morality requires is reprehensible

[17] Hart, "Positivism and the Separation of Law and Morals," 603. Of course, Hart raised other criticisms against Austin's view, which I do not consider here.

[18] Hart, *The Concept of Law* (Oxford: Clarendon Press, 1961), 6–7 and 80–1. See also Hart, "Legal and Moral Obligation," in *Essays in Moral Philosophy*, ed. A.I. Melden (Seattle: University of Washington Press, 1958), 89–91 and 95–9.

[19] Hart, "Positivism and the Separation of Law and Morals," 597–8.

and should not be obeyed. Having rejected these approaches, Hart's aim was to formulate a theory of law that avoided the confusions of anarchism and quietism. But as Hobbes once observed, 'beset with those that contend, on one side for too great liberty, and on the other side for too much authority, 'tis hard to pass between the points of both unwounded.'[20] Hart believed that the key to passing between these points lay in maintaining what anarchists and quietists both denied, that a valid legal norm might depart from what morality requires. Thus, Hart set out to formulate an innovative account of legal obligation that was not reducible to the idea of moral obligation.

The basis of Hart's theory lies in a bifurcated account of rules and the perspectives that public officials and private persons adopt toward them. Law is the union of primary and secondary rules. Primary rules establish standards of behavior that impose legal obligations requiring human beings to commit or omit certain actions.[21] How does a primary rule acquire the authority to impose legal obligations? Hart's answer lies in his account of secondary rules, which, in addition to conferring the power to change primary rules and adjudicate disputes, establish the conditions of the validity of primary rules. The rule of recognition provides persons within a society, whether private citizens or public officials, with 'authoritative criteria for identifying primary rules of obligation.'[22] Primary rules are valid because the mode of their enactment conforms to the criteria specified by the rule of recognition. As the foundational rule of a legal system, the rule of recognition cannot be validated by a more fundamental rule. Rather, the rule of recognition exists as a social fact demonstrated in the convergent practice of 'courts, officials, and private persons in identifying the law by reference to a certain criteria.'[23] The criteria specified by the rule of recognition are binding simply because they are accepted as establishing a standard of behavior that is obligatory. Those who accept that a rule establishes an obligatory standard of behavior adopt, what Hart terms, the internal point of view toward a rule. From the perspective of those who take the internal point of view toward a rule, the violation of that rule is 'not merely a basis for the prediction that a hostile reaction will follow but a *reason* for hostility.'[24]

On Hart's account of legal obligation, officials deem the primary rules enacted in accordance with the rule of recognition to be obligatory because they adopt the internal perspective toward the rule of

[20] *Leviathan*, ed. Edwin Curley (Indianapolis: Hackett Publishing, 1994), 1.
[21] Hart, *On the Concept of Law*, 80–1. [22] Ibid., 97. [23] Ibid., 107. [24] Ibid., 88.

recognition. In a legal system, officials act as though legal enactments emerging from a convergent social practice are obligatory because they believe those enactments to be obligatory. In turn, private citizens too might adopt the internal perspective toward the same social practice and thus deem themselves to be under obligation with respect to the primary rules that issue from it.

When Hart discusses the rule of recognition, he sometimes suggests that both public officials and private citizens adopt the internal point of view toward it.[25] But Hart is clear that from a descriptive standpoint, the existence of a legal system entails only that officials accept the rule of recognition. Hart explains that there are

> two minimum conditions necessary and sufficient for the existence of a legal system. On the one hand those rules of behaviour which are valid according to the system's ultimate criteria of validity must be generally obeyed, and, on the other hand, its rules of recognition specifying the criteria of legal validity and its rules of change and adjudication must be effectively accepted as common public standards of official behaviour by its officials. The first condition is the only one which private citizens *need* satisfy: they may obey each "for his part only" and from any motive whatever ... The second condition must also be satisfied by the officials of the system. They must regard these as common standards of official behaviour and appraise critically their own and each other's deviations as lapses.[26]

The two minimum conditions of a legal system are that private citizens generally obey primary rules (even if motivated entirely by fear) and that officials adopt the internal perspective toward the rule of recognition and the primary rules that issue from it.[27] In a legal system, it is not the case that private citizens must accept that primary rules establish legally obligatory standards of behavior. However, a condition in which primary rules are not generally obeyed by private citizens is not a legal system.

The possibility that officials alone will perceive legal norms as imposing legal obligations prompts Hart to remark:

> In an extreme case the internal point of view with its characteristic normative use of language ('This is a valid rule') *might be confined to the official world*. In this more complex system, only officials might accept and

[25] Ibid., 97, 107, and 110. [26] Ibid., 113.

[27] On the function of the internal point of view in Hart's legal theory, see Coleman and Leiter, "Legal Positivism," 247; Scott J. Shapiro, "What is the Internal Point of View?" *Fordham Law Review* 75 (2006): 1165–7; and Benjamin C. Zipursky, "Legal Obligations and the Internal Aspect of Rules," *Fordham Law Review* 75 (2006): 1241.

> use the system's criteria of legal validity. The society in which this was so might be deplorably sheeplike; the sheep might end in the slaughter-house. But there is little reason for thinking that it could not exist or for denying it the title of a legal system.[28]

That the internal point of view may be confined to the official world indicates a fundamental feature of Hart's account. Hart does not seek to justify how it is possible for public officials to have public authority, that is, a right to change the normative situation of private citizens by, for example, imposing coercible obligations upon them. Rather, Hart seeks to describe the disposition of public officials toward their own activities. In a legal system, officials *believe* both that primary rules validated by the rule of recognition impose obligations on private persons and that the violation of a primary rule is a justification for a coercive response.

Hart's innovation consists in introducing a structured normativity into legal positivism. While Austin conceived of law in terms of specific commands issued by a superior power, Hart conceived of law in terms of general rules that officials regard to be obligatory and bring to bear on particulars. From the standpoint of the public officials of a legal system, Hart's account marks a fundamental departure from Austin's because it incorporates what Austin's excludes: an explication of the role that general and obligatory rules play in the thoughts and actions of officials. But from the standpoint of private citizens, Hart's normative innovation presents a trivial departure from Austin's. The objection that Hart raises against Austin is that a threat backed by force might compel performance, but it imposes no obligation on another. The question that Hart's own account raises is why a private citizen confronted by a public official who adopts the internal point of view toward a threat is any different. Surely the deficiency of Austin's framework is not that the gunman (or his entourage) fails to adopt the appropriate disposition toward his own threats, but that it is not clear how the unilateral imposition of threats can impose an obligation on another. Hart fails to address this problem. No matter how many officials believe a rule to be obligatory and to justify coercion – and no matter how fervent their beliefs – private persons are not thereby placed under an *obligation*, as opposed to being merely compelled or *obliged*. In the absence of an account of how one person can have the authority to impose and enforce legal obligations on others, Hart's account fails to escape from the coercive shadow cast by Austin's

[28] Hart, *On the Concept of Law*, 114 (my emphasis).

framework. A gunman who believes that he is acting in accordance with a general and obligatory rule is still a gunman.[29]

Hart's account culminates in a defect that prompted his rejection of nonpositivist theories. Since positivists maintain that considerations of legal validity are independent of considerations of justice, they are sometimes accused of quietism, that is, of holding that valid law is not subject to moral criticism. This accusation must be mistaken, although not for the reason that positivists claim.[30] The problem of quietism is that a law is presumed to be just simply because it is obligation-imposing. Hart, however, never explains how laws can impose obligations. In the absence of such an account, what is obligatory is not the primary rules to which officials adopt the internal perspective, but moral norms that are obligatory apart from the dispositions that persons have toward them. Thus, when Hart discusses wicked legal systems, in which supposed legal obligations come into conflict with moral obligations, he insists that public officials should consult morality to determine whether a valid law should be applied[31] and private citizens should consult morality to determine whether a valid law should be followed.[32] Whether one is a public official or a private citizen, the question of how one should act in relation to a valid law is a moral question. Similarly, when positive law is absent (perhaps because a legal system does not exist or because the existing legal system contains a gap), persons must act in conformity with the dictates of morality. Whether positive law is present or absent, just or unjust, everyone is under an obligation to do what morality requires in their own eyes. Surely this is not the concept of law but a vision of anarchy.[33]

Legal positivism stems from the insight that law often commands what morality forbids. Accordingly, Hart attempted to provide an account of

[29] On this point, see Kenneth Einar Himma, "Positivism and the Problem of Explaining Legal Obligation," *American Philosophical Association Newsletter* 5 (2006): 17.

[30] For a response to this criticism from within the positivist camp, see John Gardner, "Legal Positivism: 5½ Myths," 209–10.

[31] Hart, "Positivism and the Separation of Law and Morals," 617–8.

[32] Hart, *On the Concept of Law*, 206: 'What surely is most needed in order to make men clear-sighted in confronting the official abuse of power, is that they should preserve the sense that the certification of something as legally valid is not conclusive of the question of obedience, and that, however great the aura of majesty or authority which the official system may have, its demands must in the end be submitted to moral scrutiny.'

[33] On this point, see Hart, "Legal and Moral Obligation," 104: 'The recognition of an obligation to obey *the law* must as a minimum imply that there is at least some area of conduct regulated by law in which we are not free to judge the moral merits of particular laws and to make our obedience conditional on this judgment.'

legal obligation that was wholly independent of moral considerations. In place of an account of how legal systems could have the right to impose and enforce obligations on private persons, Hart instead offered an account in which officials perceived rules to impose legal obligations. The difference between an obligatory rule and a rule that some perceive to be obligatory is critical. In the absence of an account of how it is possible for a legal system to impose legal obligations on its members, Hart's framework resurrects the very difficulties that he discerned in his positivist and nonpositivist predecessors. If we wish to overcome this difficulty, we must explain not how law could be perceived to impose obligations, but how it could actually do so. To overcome the specter of anarchy, what is required is not a theory of de facto authority, but a theory of de jure authority.

2.2 The principle of authority

Public authority is a troubling idea. It is the idea that the ruler (or rulers) of a legal system has the right to change the normative situation of the ruled by conferring rights, powers, or immunities, or – more problematically still – by imposing coercible obligations.[34] The reason that public authority is a troubling idea is that it seems to unduly augment the freedom of the ruler and to correspondingly diminish the freedom of the ruled. The very notion of public authority, apart from how it is exercised in particular instances, seems to conflict with our considered conviction that each person has human dignity or what I will call

Since the positivist holds that the obligation to obey law does not follow from the validity of law, when Raz reflects on whether there is a general obligation to obey the law, he looks beyond law to various moral and prudential grounds that might generate such a duty. The grounds that Raz considers furnish conclusions that are too narrow to ground a general obligation to obey the law. For Raz, as for Hart, whether one should act in conformity with a particular law does not hinge on its legal validity, but on the moral and prudential reasons that persons have to commit or forego a certain action. See *The Authority of Law* (New York: Oxford University Press, 2009), 233–49. The same holds for Raz's account of social coordination problems. Social coordination problems are undesirable for moral or prudential reasons. The government's solution to a social coordination problem does not change the obligations that are incumbent on private persons but rather changes the context in which private persons act pursuant to the moral and prudential reasons that obtain independently of the legal system. Law is not obligatory, although it may facilitate (or frustrate) the pursuit of ends that are independently obligatory. See *Authority*, ed. Joseph Raz (New York: New York University Press, 1990), 1–19.

[34] Stephen Perry, "Political Authority and Political Obligation," in *Oxford Studies in Philosophy of Law*, vol. II, ed. Leslie Green and Brian Leiter (Oxford: Oxford University Press, 2013) [Perry, "Political Authority"].

independence, which consists in the right to determine and pursue one's purposes, and a duty to respect the right of all others to the same. If each person is free and equal in the sense that each is his or her own ruler, then any division of persons into those who rule and those who are ruled stands in urgent need of justification.

The reason why public authority is problematic indicates the basis on which it must be justified. An adequate justification must establish that public authority is consistent with the right and the duty of each person to interact with every other on terms of equal freedom. In this section, I will provide a sketch of the justification of the principle of authority by arguing that in the absence of publicly authoritative legislative, executive, and adjudicative institutions that establish, interpret, and implement law, private persons could not interact with one another on terms of equal freedom. Since persons must interact on such terms, they must interact in the presence of publicly authoritative institutions.[35]

Suppose that private persons interact in a condition devoid of public institutions that establish, enforce, and interpret legal norms.

In the absence of a legislative institution capable of enacting general laws that publicly establish what is permitted, prohibited, or required, private persons might offer their own proposals about the norms that are appropriate for ordering interaction on terms of equal freedom. The problem that such an arrangement raises is neither that persons are unlikely to make proposals in good faith nor that given certain human tendencies the proposals are likely to disappoint, but that any proposal is simply a unilateral assertion. Since each person is the equal of every other, no one has standing to unilaterally impose a common set of rights that each person possesses and duties that each person owes. And since each person is free, each person may bring the idea of equal freedom to bear on particulars in whatever way seems good and right in his or her own eyes. In a condition in which every juridical agent is a private person, the problem of unilateral lawgiving is irresolvable. For if the idea of equal freedom can be rendered determinate with respect to particulars through a variety of general norms, and if different persons are not subject to a common set of determinations, then persons do not interact on the basis of a common set of restrictions on freedom. The solution to the problem of unilateral lawgiving is institutional. Private persons must submit to a

[35] The ensuing account of the conceptual problems that pervade private interaction in the absence of public institutions relies on Arthur Ripstein, *Force and Freedom* (Cambridge: Harvard University Press, 2009), 145–81; and Ripstein, "Authority and Coercion," *Philosophy & Public Affairs* 32 (2004): 2–35.

publicly authoritative legislative institution that possesses a right that all private persons lack – the right to enact a common set of general norms that bind private persons in their conduct.

Now suppose that there is a public legislative institution that enacts general laws but no institution capable of interpreting those laws in cases in which their meaning is disputed. Disputes regarding the meaning of legal norms remain possible because if norms are to govern action, they must be more general than the particulars to which they apply. Thus, even when legal norms are publicly promulgated through a legislative institution, disputes may arise about their meaning with respect to a contingent occurrence. We may have a dispute about who owns a particular piece of property or about where your property ends and mine begins. Or we may have a dispute about whether we have entered into a contract or about how the terms of that contract are to be interpreted. In the absence of a public adjudicative institution, legal disputes cannot be resolved rightfully. The reason that disputes cannot be resolved rightfully is not that private persons are selfish or averse to cooperation, but that the parties to the dispute, being free, are each entitled to assert their own interpretation of the rights and duties apposite to their interaction, and being equal, are not required to yield to another's judgment about the rights that either possesses and the duties that either owes. In the event of a legal dispute, I am entitled to stand on my right and refuse to capitulate to your contrary claim. But the same is true for you. The result is a deadlock in which each of us may insist on our own unilateral judgment about what law requires and refuse to defer to the other. Just as each party has a right to reject the unilateral judgment of the opposing party to the dispute, so too each party to the dispute has a right to reject the unilateral judgment of any other private person. When persons interact in a condition populated exclusively by private persons, disputes cannot be resolved rightfully. The solution to the problem of unilateral judgment is to submit private disputes to the authority of a public judiciary. The judiciary resolves disputes not by enabling one private person to unilaterally determine the rights and duties of another, but by providing an impartial public forum for the interpretation of a disputed legal norm. Because the judiciary is not a private party, it enables disputes to be resolved without subjecting either party to the unilateral judgment of another private person or imposing a unilateral judgment through a violent act.

Finally, suppose that there are legislative and adjudicative institutions but no executive institution empowered to implement and enforce the law. I may limit myself to exercising my freedom in a manner that respects your own, as established by a legislature or determined by the verdict of a court. But by acting in a manner that respects your independence, I have no assurance that you will reciprocate by acting in a manner that respects mine. In the absence of an executive power that protects the independence of each person with respect to every other, the independence of each person remains subject to the choice of other private persons. Others need not violently interfere with my rights, but whether they do so depends not on my entitlements as a member of a system of equal freedom, but on the particular purposes that they happen to have. In the absence of a public executive institution, the independence of each person remains subject to the unilateral acts of all others. Like the problems of unilateral lawgiving and unilateral judgment, the solution to the problem of unilateral enforcement is institutional. By exercising public coercion to protect the independence of private persons in relation to one another, an executive institution distinguishes public authority from an empty recommendation: public legislation is to be implemented, verdicts handed down by courts are to be enforced, and violations of law are to be prevented, detected, and prosecuted. In a legal system, private rights are secured through public coercion.

A public authority is comprised of legislative, adjudicative, and executive powers, which together form the condition in which private persons can enjoy their independence in relation to one another. This condition is a regime of *public law*. Such a condition supplants unilateral lawgiving with public legislation, unilateral judgment with public adjudication, and unilateral enforcement with public implementation of legal norms. Together, these institutions create a condition in which private persons may interact on the basis of publicly established norms and modes of adjudication and enforcement rather than the force of one or the goodwill of another. Each of the institutional powers of a legal condition is necessary to secure the independence of private persons in relation to each other, and each is a power that no private person can possess. Through its legislative will, the government acts on behalf of all private persons by providing a public determination of what is lawful and by empowering officials to enforce the law and adjudicate disputes about its meaning. Laws imposing obligations and conferring rights and powers cannot be enacted in the absence of a legislative power, disputes cannot be resolved rightfully in the absence of a publicly authorized judicial power, and persons cannot have assurance that others will respect their independence in the absence of a publicly authorized executive power.

Because the government acts on behalf of all private persons as a whole, no private person is subordinated to another by obeying public legislation, accepting the verdict of a judge, or yielding to authorized exercises of executive power.

Regardless of whether a state of nature ever existed, private persons have a coercible obligation to interact with others in a legal condition. The public institutions of a legal system create the conditions in which each person can enjoy his or her right to independence in relation to every other. Because interacting with others in a condition of public law is compatible with the right of every person to independence and interacting in a lawless condition is incompatible with the independence of anyone, every person must interact with all others in a condition of public law. The person who seeks to engage in lawless interaction rejects the legal condition in which all can enjoy their independence in relation to one another for a lawless condition in which none can. Persons who interact with others but refuse to submit to the public authority of a legal system may be compelled to do so because their refusal is incompatible with the independence of everyone, while their inclusion within a legal system is compatible with the independence of everyone, including their own. Further, the legal system to which a private person must submit is the legal system that that person occupies. Since rightful interaction requires that private persons interact on the basis of common norms of conduct, and different legal systems might promulgate a variety of different norms, no private person can enjoy a right to disregard the public authority of the legal system that he or she inhabits. Such a right would make the possibility of rightful interaction with others on the basis of common norms depend on the particular features of the legal systems to which particular persons happened to claim allegiance.

Having justified the legislative, executive, and judicial institutions that jointly comprise a government, we can now characterize the relationship between government and the private persons who are bound by it.

The *principle of authority* relates the right of government to rule – that is, to exercise public authority over its members – to the corresponding duty of the ruled to obey. A *government* is the sum of publicly authoritative institutions that represent the people as a whole by subjecting each of its members to common lawgiving, adjudication, and enforcement. A *people* is the totality of private persons subject to common governance. The presence of publicly authoritative institutions distinguishes a lawless condition from a condition of public law. In a lawless condition, every juridical actor is a private person. In a condition of public law, all private persons are subject to the authority of public institutions. The people acts not through the unilateral actions of its particular members, which being unilateral are incapable of imposing obligations on all others, but through the powers of the publicly authoritative institutions that comprise its government.[36]

The *rule of law* consists in the lawful exercise of public authority. The rule of law is possible only in a condition of public law – that is, a condition in which there is an authoritative process for the promulgation of legal rules. Under the rule of law, all private persons are subject to publicly enacted standards of behavior. These standards demarcate a publicly knowable domain of permissible action in which persons may

[36] Stephen Perry has argued that political authority involves the Hohfeldian correlates of a power to impose duties on the part of government and 'not a duty' on the part of private persons 'but, rather, a liability, meaning in this context a liability to be subjected to duties.' Perry, "Political Authority," 33. Perry explains that the distinction is not merely of technical significance. It matters because if the correlate of a power to impose a duty was itself a duty, then in the absence of a duty incumbent on the ruled, one might conclude that there was no corresponding power of the rulers. But such a conclusion would be erroneous because it overlooks the possibility that public authority exists prior to its exercise, in which case private persons are not subject to duties but rather liable to be subject to duties. Perry's point, which he formulates as the *prospectivity condition*, is that the liability to be subject to a duty must exist at the time of that duty's enactment. Ibid., 5, 34–7. Thus, any theory in which the 'argument for the conclusion that a given state possesses legitimate moral authority which depends on facts that only come into being at a time subsequent to the enactment of laws must be treated as suspect.' Ibid., 35.

The unified theory retains the correlates of right and duty without violating Perry's prospectivity condition. Private persons who interact with others have a duty to interact in the presence of publicly authoritative institutions. This duty obtains both in a lawless condition and in a condition of public law. In a lawless condition, private persons have a duty to enter into a legal condition. The violation of this duty is a wrong because it is incompatible with the formation and maintenance of a legal condition in which persons can enjoy their independence in relation to one another. In a condition of public law, the same duty requires that private persons submit to the existing public authority. A public authority is not present whenever persons have a duty to submit to it. For such a duty obtains in a lawless condition, but also in a legal condition in which a plurality of persons is subject to common legislative, executive, and judicial institutions. According to the justification of public authority supplied by the unified theory, that persons are under a duty rather than a liability to be subjected to duties is evident because persons can act wrongfully prior to the public authority's enactment – for example, by doing what lies in their power to perpetuate a lawless condition. Whereas Perry notes that public authority can exist prior to the particular duties enacted through its exercise, the unified theory holds that the duty to submit to the governance of public institutions precedes the existence of public authority. Since both of these positions retain the possibility that public authority (whether conceptualized as a right or a power) is not dependent on facts that contingently materialize after its exercise, neither violates the prospectivity condition.

formulate, develop, and pursue their own purposes in relation to one another. Interaction between private persons occurs in accordance with the rights that each is publicly known to possess and the duties that each is publicly known to owe. If persons are to conduct their affairs in accordance with law, lawgiving must be, inter alia, general, publicly knowable, prospective, clear, consistent, possible to obey, and relatively stable. Thus, the formal principles that make up Fuller's internal morality of law enter the unified theory neither in terms of a duty that government owes to those that it binds by exercising public authority nor as the aspiration internal to exercises of public authority,[37] but rather in terms of conditions under which persons who occupy public offices exercise public authority rather than private power.

Such a conception of the rule of law has important implications for the separation of powers. The problems of unilateralism are addressed through the establishment of legislative, executive, and adjudicative powers. If the actions of public officials who occupy executive and adjudicative offices are to be regarded as exercises of public authority rather than as lawless impositions of private power, those officials must act pursuant to law. This means that the officials who occupy executive offices cannot choose what general laws they will implement and what judicial verdicts they will carry out. Such an arrangement would subject private persons to arbitrary power. It also means that officials who occupy judicial offices must resolve legal disputes between private parties by appealing to general laws. To resolve private disputes by formulating general laws would be to subject the parties to arbitrary power.[38] To exercise public authority that each must obey rather than arbitrary power that each may resist, public officials must act pursuant to law.

The rule of law can be realized through a broad array of legislative arrangements that subjects the people as a whole to common lawgiving. Although it is not the case that all legal systems have an institution called a *legislature*, all legal systems have the legislative capacity to enact law. In an autocratic society, legislative power is held by a single individual. In such a society, all private persons are passive subjects who are bound by law but unable to contribute to its enactment. In an aristocratic society, legislative power is held by the plurality of individuals who comprise the aristocracy. All private persons excluded from the ranks of the nobility

[37] Fuller, *The Morality of Law* (New Haven: Yale University Press, 1964), 42: 'The inner morality of law . . . embraces a morality of duty and a morality of aspiration.'
[38] Ripstein, *Force and Freedom*, 175.

are passive. Finally, in a democratic society, legislative power is held by the totality of its adult citizens, who are not passive subjects bound by laws of another's making, but active citizens who contribute to the creation of the laws by which they are bound.

The rule of law does not require that laws be promulgated democratically through representative institutions. Whether legislative power is held by a single person, a few persons, or the citizenry acting collectively through its representatives, private persons are subject to the governance of public institutions. A just democratic order cannot exist without the rule of law, but the rule of law does not entail the existence of a just democratic order. The distinction between the lawful exercise of public authority and the lawless imposition of private power does not indicate the mode through which laws should be promulgated.

Nor does this distinction determine the appropriate content of enacted laws. The justification of the principle of authority establishes that lawgiving cannot be publicly authoritative if it is incompatible with the interaction of private persons on terms of equal freedom or if its secrecy, vagueness, or ad hoc character prevents persons from acting in light of it. But the principle of authority does not impose a duty on government to give laws of a certain kind. Indeed, the principle of authority imposes no duty on government at all. The principle concerns the *right* of government to give law and the corresponding *duty* of private persons to obey, not the *right* of private persons and the corresponding *duty* of government.

Just as the principle of authority can be satisfied by a variety of legislative arrangements, so too it can be satisfied by different judicial arrangements. From the standpoint of the principle of authority, what is crucial is that there is a judicial forum authorized to resolve contingent legal disputes between private parties. The common law and the civil law traditions provide different ways of constituting such a forum. Common law jurisdictions authorize judges to resolve private disputes in accordance with legal principles developed and refined in case law. Civil law jurisdictions authorize judges to apply a comprehensive legal code to the facts of a particular dispute. Each arrangement satisfies the principle of authority by offering private parties a public forum for resolving private disputes.

Private persons must act in conformity with valid public laws enacted by a public authority. The refusal to do so is a public wrong – that is, a wrong against the condition in which a plurality of persons can interact with one another in a manner that is consistent with the independence of everyone. Whereas wrongs that private persons commit against each other may be remedied by public institutions, a condition of public law could neither be created nor sustained if private persons had a right to disobey valid lawgiving. This claim is conceptual, not empirical. It would be empirical if it suggested that a causal relationship obtains between disobedience and the dissolution of society. Thus David Hume argued that a 'small degree of experience and observation suffices to teach us, that society cannot possibly be maintained without the authority of magistrates, and that this authority must soon fall into contempt where exact obedience is not paid to it.'[39] Such an empirical claim is susceptible to the empirical rebuttal that, in fact, legal systems persist even when obedience is not ubiquitous.[40] The conceptual claim focuses on the contrast between a legal system and a lawless condition. A legal system – comprised of legislative, adjudicative, and executive institutions that together subject a plurality of private persons to common norms – is the condition in which private persons can enjoy their independence in relation to one another. Such a condition would not be possible if private persons possessed the right to disregard laws that they deemed unjust because such a right would regenerate the problems of lawless interaction by subjecting private persons to the unilateral lawgiving, judgment, and enforcement of other private persons. Private persons cannot interact with others on terms of equal freedom in the absence of the publicly authoritative institutions that comprise a legal system.

Perhaps Hart's anarchic natural lawyer would object as follows: the principle of authority is too rigorous insofar as it imposes a duty on private persons to obey a regime of public law regardless of whether it is just. But why should private persons respect the right of government to rule when the government fails to create a legal order in which authority secures not only the private rights of persons in relation to one another, but also the independence of each person as a citizen of a just democratic order? Perhaps, the anarchist concludes, the government's right to impose legal obligations is confined to those cases in which law is the instrument of justice. In this way, authority and justice would be jointly realized.

[39] Hume, "Of the Original Contract," in *Essays, Moral, Political, Literary*, ed. E.F. Miller (Indianapolis: Liberty Classics, 1985), 480.

[40] Leslie Green, "Law and Obligations," in *The Oxford Handbook of Jurisprudence and Philosophy of Law*, ed. Jules L. Coleman, Kenneth Einar Himma, and Scott J. Shapiro (Oxford: Clarendon Press, 2001), 537; and Green, *The Authority of the State* (Oxford: Clarendon Press, 1990), 537.

The anarchist's objection frustrates the achievement of its own end, the realization of a just legal order. If each private person had the right to determine what norms are obligatory, then private persons would not be subject to common lawgiving and the problem of lawlessness, in which the independence of each is subject to the arbitrary choice of every other, would resurface. The right of each private person to act in accordance with what is just and good in his or her own eyes is incompatible with public law, conceived of as a relationship between a government and a people. It is incompatible with the notion of a *government* because such a right cannot be reconciled with a public authority that has the capacity to impose legal obligations upon a multitude of persons. In turn, such a right is incompatible with the notion of a *people* because if private persons had such a right, then the multitude would not be unified by their shared subjection to common legal institutions. The claim that the right and duty imposed by the principle of authority do not engage until a fully just democratic order is present obliterates the anarchist's aim of realizing a just society. By rejecting the principle of authority, the anarchist repudiates the very condition in which the realization of public justice is possible. The objection thereby culminates not in the joint realization of public authority and public justice but in the ongoing subjection of human beings to the indignity of lawless interaction.

Legal and political philosophers usually claim that 'no respectable theory of political obligation ever claimed that a person is obligated no matter what to obey the laws of a legal system to which he or she is subject.'[41] This is exactly what the unified theory claims in its justification of public authority: all private persons must obey all valid laws. This does not mean, however, that anything that calls itself a legal system thereby is one or that any decree buttressed by violence is a valid law. After all, the justification of public authority at work in the unified theory provides its own ground for distinguishing between the public authority of a legal system, which all must obey, and private violence, which all may resist. Public authority is that which secures the independence of each person from the arbitrary power of every other. It follows that arrangements that are incompatible with securing the right of each person to independence in relation to every other cannot be publicly authoritative. In such cases, the principle of authority does not require persons to capitulate to the

[41] Stephen Perry, "Associative Obligations and the Obligation to Obey the Law," in *Exploring Law's Empire: The Jurisprudence of Ronald Dworkin*, ed. Scott Hershovitz (Oxford: Oxford University Press, 2006), 183.

powerful – for the mere exercise of power, however organized, imparts no corresponding obligation. Rather, persons must submit themselves to the public authority of a legal system, in which each private person can enjoy independence from the arbitrary power of every other. I return to this point below, in differentiating the legal pathology that results from the violation of the principle of authority (barbarism) from the legal pathology that results from the violation of the principle of justice (injustice).

2.3 The principle of justice

Legal and political philosophers often think about justice by taking the existence of publicly authoritative institutions for granted and then asking, all things considered, what purpose (or purposes) they should pursue. The diverse suggestions that ensue have a common structure. Each stakes a claim to how public authority should be exercised that is isolated from the terms on which public authority is justified. The unified theory of public law adopts a different approach in which the question of how public authority should be exercised is considered from the standpoint of its justification.

The justification of the principle of authority establishes that government has the right to enact, interpret, and enforce legal obligations that bind private persons. If the government has the right to exercise public authority over private persons, why may the government not exercise its power by using persons as instruments to further the purposes of those who occupy public offices? Perhaps societies of human beings are nothing more than 'so many herds of cattle, each with its ruler, who keeps guard over them for the purpose of devouring them.'[42]

Within the unified theory, the right of government to exercise public authority over persons does not exist in a justificatory vacuum. The justification of public authority rests on the recognition that every person possesses a right to freely determine and pursue his or her own purposes in a manner compatible with the right of others to the same. Government is not the owner of a thing, which has no rights, imposes no duties, and suffers no wrongs. Rather, it is the representative of a totality of independent persons, who must subject themselves to public lawgiving because rightful interaction is impossible without it. Since the right to

[42] Jean-Jacques Rousseau, *On the Social Contract* in *The Basic Political Writings*, trans. Donald A. Cress (Indianapolis: Hackett Publishing Company, 1987), 142.

exercise public authority presupposes the human dignity of each person subject to it, internal to the justification of public authority is an account of what it would mean for a system of publicly authoritative institutions to be morally adequate and what it would mean for public institutions to exercise their authority in a morally adequate manner. A legal system is adequate on its own internal moral standard to the extent that it reconciles the authority of law with the human dignity of every person bound by it. In turn, the exercise of public authority conforms to the terms of its justification to the extent that it is directed toward bringing the existing legal system into the deepest possible conformity with its own internal standard of adequacy – dignity under law. Because the right of government to exercise public authority presupposes the right of every private person to equal freedom, government cannot deny the right of persons to independence without thereby denying the justificatory basis of its own authority.

The principles of public law delineate the juridical situation of the parties to the public law relationship. The principle of authority relates the *right* of government to the corresponding *duty* of persons to obey all valid lawgiving. The principle of justice traverses the public law relationship from the opposite direction by relating the *right* of every person to just governance to the corresponding *duty* of the government. Since the duty to govern justly accompanies the mere exercise of public authority, all branches of government – legislative, adjudicative, and executive – must bring the existing legal order into the deepest possible conformity with the independence of every person subject to its lawgiving. Accordingly, the juridical situation of a private person differs from that of government. Every private person has a right to independence – that is, to formulate his or her own purposes and pursue them with his or her own means – subject to the systematic constraint that each person respects the same right of all others. Unlike a private person, a government lacks the right to determine its own end. Government enters the world with a single obligatory end, the realization of a system of law that conforms to the terms of its own justification.[43] While private persons may direct their means toward the fulfilment of their own self-determined ends, the publicly authoritative means of government do not exist apart from their obligatory end.[44]

[43] For an opposing view, see Shapiro, *Legality*, 173 (describing law as a 'universal means' and claiming that 'there are no substantive goals or values that laws are supposed to achieve or realize').

[44] For such a conception of public authority, see Václav Havel, *The Art of the Impossible: Politics as Morality in Practice* (Toronto: Alfred A. Knopf, 1997), 72 and 84. The Czech

The principles of public law address two distinctive problems that arise in a conceptually sequenced exploration of the implications of the right of persons to independence. The problem that the principle of authority addresses is that in the absence of public institutions, the right of each person to interact with every other on terms of equal freedom remains subject to the arbitrary power of others. The solution to this problem of *horizontal* independence between private persons is, as I argued in the prior section, solved by the submission of private persons to a system of publicly authoritative institutions that establish, interpret, and enforce private rights. The second problem of independence presupposes the solution to the first. While the principle of authority addresses a problem that is unavoidable in the absence of public institutions, the principle of justice addresses a problem that can arise only when the public institutions comprising a government are present. The very public institutions that address the problem of *horizontal* independence by securing the right of each person to equal freedom in relation to every other create a problem of *vertical* independence because public institutions might themselves impose arbitrary restrictions on the freedom of one or more persons – that is, restrictions that a legal system does not itself require. This problem of vertical independence is addressed by the principle of justice, which requires government to direct all public authority toward bringing the legal order as a whole into conformity with the independence of each person bound by it. This requirement has implications for the way in which laws are enacted and the content of enacted laws.

Recall that the principle of authority requires that private persons submit to public lawgiving, but it draws no distinctions concerning the adequacy of autocratic, aristocratic, or democratic forms of lawgiving. By contrast, the principle of justice calls for the lawful transition to (and ongoing refinement of) a democratic legal order. Democracy is required because government must reconcile its public authority with the independence of those who are bound by it. In an autocracy, all persons are passive with respect to the legislative power. Autocracy is a defective mode of lawgiving because an arrangement in which persons are bound by laws that they cannot themselves enact imposes a constraint on the freedom of the ruled that freedom does not itself require. It thus fails to reconcile the public authority of the legal condition with the independence of all who

dissident, playwright, and statesman contrasts those who exercise public authority to further their own advantage and moral politicians who govern on behalf of the governed. Havel remarks about the latter: 'I have no idea whether I am such a person. I only know that I ought to be, because I have accepted this office.'

are bound by it. Aristocracy also runs afoul of the principle of justice. In an aristocracy some are passive with respect to the legislative power, while others are active. This arrangement is defective because it establishes ranks that defy the equality of independent persons insofar as some possess the right to contribute to the enactment of laws, while others are merely bound by laws of another's making. Democracy is the only mode of lawgiving in which citizens are *both* rulers *and* ruled, sovereign and subject. Democracy alone is capable of reconciling the independence of persons with legislative authority because it does not impose an arbitrary constraint on freedom by denying persons the right to contribute to the laws by which they are bound. Nor does it violate equality by granting this right to some persons but withholding it from others.

The duty to govern justly extends from the mode through which public legislation is to be enacted to its content. Because the right to exercise public authority over independent persons is always accompanied by a duty to govern justly, the duty applies to cases in which public authority is exercised by autocrats or aristocrats, but also to democracy, in which citizens collectively exercise legislative power through their representatives. Each citizen who contributes to public lawgiving must give laws to which all others, conceived of as free and equal members of a legal system, could consent. In a fully just democratic order, the system of laws that citizens collectively enact is fully congruent with the undiminished independence of each person bound by it. The ideal of public law is a democratic legal order in which each person contributes to and, in turn, is bound by lawgiving that leaves the independence of each person bound by it undiminished.[45]

[45] The unified theory of public law is liberal, not libertarian. It is liberal because its integrating idea is the right of persons to equal freedom. Freedom, in this sense, is not guaranteed by libertarianism. Libertarianism's organizing idea of self-ownership is compatible with the possibility that some persons may acquire the whole world, with the result that one would not be 'permitted to do anything without their consent – since that would involve the use of their property ... The protection that self-ownership affords is a basic protection against others doing certain things to one, but not a guarantee of liberty.' Peter Vallentyne and Bas van der Vossen, "Libertarianism," in *The Stanford Encyclopedia of Philosophy*, ed. Edward N. Zalta, http://plato.stanford.edu/archives/fall2014/entries/libertarianism/. While I believe that a theory of public right that turns on the idea of human dignity as equal freedom has significant ramifications for the affirmative duty of the state, in general, and the state's duty to alleviate poverty and fulfill socioeconomic rights, in particular, I leave these important issues to a subsequent occasion. On the distinctive problem that poverty raises for Kant's theory of public right and the positive duty of the state to address it, see Ripstein, *Force and Freedom*, 272–86; Ernest Weinrib, *Corrective Justice* (Oxford: Oxford University Press, 2012), 263–96.

Perhaps one might object that the principle of justice is overly demanding because it requires government do the impossible by creating a democratic utopia in which the exercise of authority leaves the independence of each person bound by it undiminished. If the creation of such an order is impossible, then it cannot be obligatory. Thus, the objection concludes, the principle of justice must be rejected.

This objection overlooks a crucial distinction between the principles of public law. The principle of authority is the *constitutive principle* of a legal system: it articulates what a legal system is and thereby enables a legal system to be distinguished from other entities within and beyond the juridical world. A legal system consists in the publicly authoritative institutions under which private persons can interact with one another on terms of equal freedom. By contrast, the principle of justice is the *regulative principle* of a legal system: it articulates the relevant moral standard for assessing the extent of a legal system's adequacy, and it requires the government of a legal system to direct its public authority toward bringing the existing legal order into the closest possible approximation of that standard. Since the principle of justice is not a constitutive principle that calls for the creation of a perfectly just legal order, government is not under a duty to do the impossible by creating such an order, whether in a single moment or in a finite series of acts. Rather, the duty of government is to exercise public authority in accordance with the terms on which that right is justified by bringing the existing legal system into the closest possible conformity with its own internal ideal of equal freedom under law. Regardless of whether a perfectly just legal system can be realized, it is certainly possible for existing legal systems to approximate the ideal of equal freedom under law to a greater or lesser extent. Because the principle of justice is a regulative principle that calls for the ongoing approximation of a just legal system rather than a constitutive principle that calls for the realization of a perfectly just one, the duty to govern justly does not exceed the boundaries of possibility.

The bifurcated structure of public law enables a distinction to be drawn between two distinct kinds of legal pathologies that are often blurred: injustice and barbarism. *Injustice* consists in the violation of the regulative principle of public law. A legal condition is unjust to the extent that it fails to reconcile the authority of law with the vertical independence of each person bound by it. In an unjust legal condition, public institutions must realize a legal order that to the greatest possible extent reconciles the authority of law with independence. Such a duty may require democratizing the process of lawgiving or liberalizing the positive law. By contrast, *barbarism* consists in the violation of the constitutive principle of public law. Barbarism is the pathology of a condition that by subjecting the freedom of one or more persons to the arbitrary power of others fails to secure horizontal independence. In such a condition, private persons are under a duty to submit themselves to the authority of public institutions, which render rightful interaction possible.

Insofar as the pathologies of public law emerge from the violation of distinct relations of independence, the difference between injustice and barbarism is not a matter of degree, as those who conceptualize barbarism as extreme injustice claim.[46] Rather, the pathologies are different in kind as each stems from a different aspect of the public law relationship. The question of whether private persons occupy a lawful or a lawless order concerns the presence of public institutions that secure the horizontal independence of each person in relation to every other. The question of whether a legal order is just concerns the adequacy of the vertical relationship between publicly authoritative arrangements and the independence of each individual subject to them. In Chapter 3, I will argue that – from the standpoint of the normative structure of public law – the problem with Nazi power was not that it was unjust but that it was barbaric. Nazism was not a lawful but defective mode of legal ordering but rather a condition of arbitrary power. In Chapter 4, I explore the duty incumbent on existing legal systems to address their defects.

Earlier, in explicating the principle of authority, I argued that the exercise of public authority presupposes that the indicia of the rule of law – generality, publicity, prospectivity, clarity, consistency, and so forth – are, at least to some extent, satisfied. We can now situate these indicia in relation to the principle of justice. The undiminished satisfaction of the indicia of the rule of law is a necessary but not a sufficient condition of just governance. Their satisfaction is a *necessary* condition of just governance because public authority cannot be reconciled with the greatest possible freedom of each person bound by it if the laws are, for example, vague and so admit of interpretations that place arbitrary constraints on freedom. Similarly, laws that lack generality and culminate in ad hoc decisions are inimical to the realization of public justice because

[46] Gustav Radbruch, "Statutory Lawlessness and Supra-Statutory Law (1946)," *Oxford Journal of Legal Studies* 26 (2006): 7: 'The conflict between justice and legal certainty may well be resolved in this way: The positive law, secured by legislation and power, takes precedence even when its content is unjust and fails to benefit the people, unless the conflict between statute and justice reaches such an *intolerable degree* that the statute, as "flawed law," must yield to justice.'

the disparate application of norms violates the equality of legal subjects and deprives them of a stable and calculable legal order in which to formulate and pursue their purposes. The latter problem also arises with respect to laws that are, to some extent, contradictory, secret, or retrospective. While the ideal of just governance requires the full satisfaction of the indicia of the rule of law, the satisfaction of these indicia is not a sufficient condition of just governance. Even a law that limits freedom arbitrarily by constraining it for the sake of a purpose that freedom itself does not require – for example, a prohibition on smelling the violets[47] – might nonetheless be formulated, enacted, and applied in such a way that the indicia of the rule of law are fully satisfied.

The unified theory of public law articulates the principles that constitute and regulate the juridical relationship between a government and its members. These principles are contrasted in Table 2.1.

The principles of authority and justice form the normative architecture of a legal system as such. That these principles are apposite to legal systems in general distinguishes the unified theory from competing frameworks that attempt to ground the right of government to exercise public authority or the right of persons to membership in a just democratic order on particular facts or states of affairs that might be present in one legal system but absent in another. As I argued in the prior section, the principle of authority emerges from the systematic implications of the right of each person to equal freedom rather than, as other theorists propose, the justice of the rules,[48] the superior wisdom of the rulers,[49] or some voluntary act on the part of the ruled, whether consent[50] or the

[47] Ebbinghaus, "The Law of Humanity and the Limits of State Power," *Philosophical Quarterly* 3 (1953): 20.

[48] See, for example, John Rawls, *A Theory of Justice* (Cambridge: Harvard University Press, 1971), 115: 'From the standpoint of justice as fairness, a fundamental natural duty is the duty of justice. This duty requires us to support and to comply with just institutions that exist and apply to us. It also constrains us to further just arrangements not yet established…'

[49] Joseph Raz, "Authority and Justification," *Philosophy & Public Affairs* 14 (1985): 18–9 (emphasis in original): '*the normal and primary way to establish that a person should be acknowledged to have authority over another person involves showing that the alleged subject is likely better to comply with reasons which apply to him (other than the alleged authoritative directives) if he accepts the directives of the alleged authority as authoritatively binding and tries to follow them, rather than by trying to follow the reasons which apply to him directly.*'

[50] See, for example, Leslie Green, *The Authority of the State* (Oxford: Clarendon Press, 1990), 18.

Table 2.1 *The Principles of Public Law*

Principle of Authority	Distinguishing Feature	Principle of Justice
Constitutive of public law: establishes what a law or legal system is	**Nature of the principle**	Regulative of public law: establishes a law or legal system's internal standard of moral adequacy
The presence of private interaction (within and beyond a legal system)	**Condition of application**	The presence of public authority over persons (solely within a legal system)
Satisfied by the presence of public institutions that secure independence between private persons	**Condition of satisfaction**	Satisfied to the extent that authority is reconciled with the independence of the ruled
private persons in relation to one another (horizontal)	**Satisfaction secures the independence of...**	each person subject to law's authority (vertical)
on public institutions to exercise authority	**Confers a right...**	on private persons to just governance
on private persons to submit to public authority	**Confers a duty...**	on public institutions to govern justly
Barbarism is the character of a condition/norm that renders horizontal independence insecure	**The pathology that follows from the principle's violation**	*Injustice* is the character of a valid law or legal system that violates vertical independence

acceptance of a benefit.[51] Such justifications culminate in a patchwork in which the public authority of the state varies from law to law and from individual to individual.[52] The unified theory departs from these

51 Simmons, "The Principle of Fair Play," *Philosophy & Public Affairs* 8 (1979): 307.

52 See, for example, Raz, *The Morality of Freedom* (Oxford: Clarendon Press, 1986), 80 (arguing that the service conception of authority 'invites a piecemeal approach to the question of authority of governments, which yields the conclusion that the extent of governmental authority varies from individual to individual, and is more limited than the authority governments claim for themselves in the case of most people'). For a criticism of this aggregative approach, see Perry, "Political Authority," 8, 63–6.

frameworks by holding that in every legal system, all private persons must obey all valid laws. Like the right and duty encompassed by the principle of authority, the right and duty encompassed by the principle of justice follow from a feature common to legal systems as such: the mere presence of publicly authoritative institutions governing persons. The right of persons to just governance does not stem from a state of affairs that might obtain in one legal system but not in another, such as the presence of a democratic form of lawgiving, a rights-protecting constitution, or a public culture committed to ideas of free and equal citizenship.[53] Theories that generate a duty to govern justly from such features might succeed in explaining why a legal system characterized by liberal practices should govern in accordance with a liberal conception of justice. What they do not explain is why a legal system that lacks these practices must adopt them. Rather than treating these practices as conferring justification upon a conception of justice, the unified theory articulates a conception of justice that indicates why the adoption of practices of this kind is itself obligatory.

2.4 Between anarchism and quietism

The central fault line in legal philosophy separates positivist theories, which hold that law is grounded in social facts, from nonpositivist theories, which hold that law is grounded in moral norms. Positivists account for the legal truism that a valid law might be unjust by distinguishing the question of whether a particular norm is valid, which hinges on social facts concerning its pedigree, from moral questions concerning its merit. As I explained earlier, for centuries legal positivists have claimed that nonpositivist theories generate two dangerous kinds of confusion: anarchism and quietism. These views are dangerous because they collapse the distinction between what the existing law is and what law ought to be and so deprive their proponents of the capacity to recognize and respond to unjust laws. For Hart, the danger of anarchism is that 'law and its authority may be dissolved in man's conceptions of

[53] See, for example, Rawls, *Justice as Fairness: A Restatement* (Cambridge: Harvard University Press, 2001), 39: '[J]ustice as fairness is framed for a democratic society. Its principles are meant to answer the question once we view a democratic society as a fair system of social cooperation between citizens regarded as free and equal, what principles are most appropriate to it. Alternatively: which principles are most appropriate for a democratic society that not only professes but wants to take seriously the idea that citizens are free and equal, and tries to realize that idea in its main institutions.'

what law ought to be,' while the danger of quietism is 'that the existing law may supplant morality as a final test of conduct and so escape criticism.'[54] The unified theory is nonpositivist insofar as it generates its principles of public law by elaborating on the systematic implications of the right of persons to independence. In this section, I demonstrate that the unified theory is neither anarchist nor quietist. As such, it is not vulnerable to the line of objection that legal positivists raise against nonpositivist theories.

Anarchism and quietism rest on a common mistake: the failure to maintain a distinction between the constitutive and regulative dimensions of public law. The constitutive dimension concerns what it means for a norm or condition to be lawful. The regulative dimension concerns what it means for a law or legal system to be adequate or just. The mistake that underlies both anarchism and quietism lies in reducing the whole of public law to either its constitutive or its regulative aspect. The anarchist holds that the regulative principle of a legal system is also its constitutive principle. On this view, justice is not only the standard of a law's moral adequacy but the condition of its authority. That which is unjust cannot be publicly authoritative. The quietist commits the opposing error by asserting that the constitutive principle of a legal system is also its regulative principle. On this view, the features of a particular law or legal system form the standard for assessing its moral adequacy. The result is that whatever arrangements are authoritative must also be just. By collapsing the distinction between the constitutive and regulative dimensions of public law, both anarchism and quietism reject the truism that a legal system in general or a particular norm within one might be authoritative and yet unjust.

The same cannot be said about the unified theory. The unified theory appeals to the part of morality that bears on public law to formulate principles that constitute and regulate the juridical relationship between rulers and ruled. Because the unified theory distinguishes between the constitutive and regulative aspects of the public law relationship, it is neither an anarchist nor a quietist theory. Recall that anarchism is the view that what is unjust cannot be publicly authoritative. The unified theory cannot be anarchist because public justice is the standard for assessing the adequacy of a publicly authoritative arrangement. Thus, the claim that an arrangement is unjust presupposes that it is publicly authoritative. When individuals adopt the standpoint of the principle of

[54] Hart, "Positivism and the Separation of Law and Morals," 598.

justice and criticize the adequacy of the legal order or a publicly authoritative arrangement within it, neither the authority of the legal order nor the binding character of its laws is called into question. Further, the unified theory cannot be quietist. Quietism is the view that what imposes legal obligations cannot be unjust. The unified theory cannot be quietist because the justification of the right of government to exercise public authority over persons implicates a demanding standard for assessing the moral adequacy of all publicly authoritative arrangements. The right to exercise public authority is always accompanied by a duty to bring the existing legal order into the closest possible conformity with this standard. Thus, the unified theory of public law jointly rejects the uncritical resignation of the quietist and the lawless freedom of the anarchist.

The distinction between the principles of authority and justice gives rise to an exhaustive classification of legal conditions. A *just legal condition* satisfies the principles of authority and the internal ideal of public justice by uniting the authority of law with the independence of all who are bound by it. An *unjust legal condition* satisfies the principle of authority but fails to satisfy the ideal of public justice. Existing legal systems are instances of this category and satisfy the ideal of public justice to varying extents. The duty of the public authority of such legal systems is to bring the legal order as a whole into the closest possible conformity with the vertical independence of each person bound by the authority of law. Finally, a *lawless condition* fails to satisfy the principle of authority because the horizontal independence of private persons has not been secured. These possibilities are exhaustive: a legal condition can be valid and just, valid but unjust, or simply invalid. A legal system cannot be both invalid *and* just because public justice concerns the adequacy of the public law relationship between a people and its government. If the parties to this relationship are not present, then questions about the adequacy of this relationship cannot arise. The same classification obtains with respect to particular norms: a norm can be valid and just, valid but unjust, or simply invalid.[55]

[55] The unified theory departs from the Lockean theory of institutional evaluation developed in A. John Simmons, "Justification and Legitimacy," *Ethics* 109 (1999): 739–71. Simmons defines *legitimacy* as the exclusive moral right of the state 'to impose new duties on subjects by initiating legally binding directives, to have those directives obeyed, and to coerce noncompliers.' Ibid., 752. For Simmons, state power is legitimate only when subjects have 'freely consented to the exercise of such power and only where that power continues to be exercised within the terms of the consent given.' Ibid., 745. On this view, the state resembles a private association: each person within a state may choose at any time whether to become (or to remain) a member bound by its rules. In turn,

While the positivist objection threatens one-sided nonpositivist theories that reduce public law to either public authority or public justice, the objection poses no threat to theories that appeal to morality in order to delineate the distinction between public authority and public justice. The unified theory thereby offers what positivists have long insisted was impossible, a nonpositivist theory that explains how a law or a legal system might be valid even though it is unjust. One need not be a positivist to capture positivism's twin insights that what is just is not thereby valid and that what is valid is not thereby just.

The positivist objection can be overcome because it poses a false dilemma. Positivists recognize unjust laws by distinguishing between the question of a norm's validity and the question of its moral merit. Social facts dictate the answer to the former question, while morality dictates the answer to the latter. From this standpoint, a theory that purports to illuminate law through the lens of morality is suspect because valid norms are not invariably moral and moral norms are not invariably valid. Positivists therefore suppose that nonpositivist theories must flout the legal truism by making the anarchist claim that conformity to

Simmons explains that the *justification* of a state 'will typically give us moral reasons to refrain from undermining it and will typically give us moral reason to positively support that state.' Ibid., 753.

Simmons characterizes the notion of justification in terms of the justice of the state and legitimacy in terms of the state's authority over its subjects. Ibid., 746, 749–50, and 768. But his bifurcated framework departs from the structure of the unified theory in a number of respects. The first concerns Simmons's view that the state is distinguishable from its authority. For Simmons, even if an existing state can be justified, it is nevertheless incapable of imposing obligations on members who have not legitimated it through an act of consent. Ibid., 769. By contrast, the unified theory holds that the state does not exist apart from the capacity to impose coercible legal obligations on its occupants. Unlike a private association, membership in a state is not optional but is rather the condition of rightful interaction between private persons. The second concerns the relationship between the fundamental components of each theory. Whereas Simmons holds that a state can be justified (or just) even if it is illegitimate or lacking in authority, the unified theory holds that any account of the justice of the state presupposes its authority. The duty of the state to govern justly follows from its right to exercise public authority over independent persons. The third concerns the relationship that each theory envisages between the state and its inhabitants. A striking feature of Simmons's theory is that *both* justification *and* legitimacy concern the way in which private individuals should act with respect to the state. The result is that while Simmons develops a rich conceptual framework for thinking about whether a state is justified and whether it enjoys the right to rule a particular series of individuals, his framework has no resources for thinking about the duty that a justified and legitimate state might owe its inhabitants. Such an omission impoverishes the resources of institutional evaluation that the theory offers. By contrast, the principles that comprise the unified theory formulate the rights and duties of both rulers and ruled.

morality is the condition of legal validity or the quietist claim that legal validity is indicative of conformity to morality. Both possibilities flout the truism because in explaining the law in moral terms, the distinction between the question of a law's validity and the question of its morality is collapsed. The dilemma is false because the possibilities that it presents are not exhaustive. The further possibility, instantiated by the unified theory, turns on the idea that the part of morality that pertains to public law differentiates between principles of public authority and public justice and delineates the rights and duties apposite to each principle. Such a position is possible because there is no irresolvable conflict between these principles since the duties that they impose are not incumbent on the same party to the public law relationship. As I have argued, private persons must obey valid lawgiving, while public institutions must reform the existing legal order. The positivist objection is decisive only if one conceives of morality as a monolithic domain in which what one should do does not depend upon the legal relationships in which one stands. Utilitarianism – the conception of morality that the early positivists affirmed – follows this path.[56] For utilitarianism recognizes no distinction between what morality demands of private persons and what it demands of public officials. The positivist objection, however, does not establish that nonpositivists must adopt a conception of morality that is made in utilitarianism's image.

The positivist objection follows from a chronic misconception regarding the dispute between positivist and nonpositivist approaches. Legal positivists reject the view that a legal norm is validated by its moral merit or invalidated by its moral viciousness. The validity of a norm depends on its sources – that is, whether it has been enacted through the relevant law-making procedure within a particular legal system.[57] Accordingly, positivists invariably conceive of nonpositivists as defending the opposite view, which holds that a norm is legally valid not because it has been posited by the relevant institution but because of its moral merit.[58] But nonpositivist theories are not confined to this view. For, as we have seen,

[56] On the connection between utilitarian and legal positivist thought, see Martin Stone, "Legal Positivism as an Idea about Morality," *University of Toronto Law Journal* 61 (2011): 313–41.

[57] See, for example, Gardner, "Legal Positivism: 5½ Myths," 201.

[58] Joseph Raz, "Kelsen's Theory of the Basic Norm," *American Journal of Jurisprudence* 19 (1974): 100: 'Kelsen correctly points out that according to natural law theories there is no specific notion of legal validity. The only concept of validity is validity according to natural law, i.e. moral validity. Natural lawyers can only judge a law as morally valid, that is, just, or morally invalid, i.e. wrong. They cannot say of a law that it is legally valid but

the unified theory does not deny the legal positivist insight that positive law must be posited. On this central point, positivists and nonpositivists may stand in agreement, albeit for their own distinctive reasons. A positive law is not valid by virtue of some noninstitutional event or state of affairs, whether 'objective moral truth or God or the spirit of an age or the diffuse will of the people or the tramp of history through time, for example.'[59] The real disagreement between positivist and nonpositivist theories lies elsewhere.

Positivist and nonpositivist thought divides on the issue of whether the concept of law is *exhausted* by its positivity. As a nonpositivist framework, the unified theory contends that there are two respects in which the concept of law extends beyond its positivity. The first concerns the possibility of positive law. The very notion of positive law, apart from what it enjoins, raises a question about how the government of a legal system could have the authority to change the normative situation of independent persons through its enactments. I argued earlier that the public authority of a legal system is justified because persons must interact with one another on terms of equal freedom, but cannot do so in the absence of publicly authoritative institutions that impose, interpret, and enforce law. Such a justification of public authority has important implications for the identification of valid law. Since public authority is that which enables private persons to interact with one another on terms of equal freedom, any arrangement that is incompatible with such interaction cannot be publicly authoritative. All public authority must be obeyed, but as I will argue in Chapter 3 in a discussion of the barbarism of Nazi power, not every norm or condition can be publicly authoritative.

The second disagreement, which concerns the principle of justice, follows from the first. The justification of the government's authority to bind independent persons through the enactment of positive law indicates both the internal standard for assessing the adequacy of every legal system and the duty that accompanies the exercise of all public authority. Thus, the unified theory affirms what positivist theories deny,[60] that a

morally wrong. If it is wrong and unjust, it is also invalid in the only sense of validity they recognize.'

[59] Ronald Dworkin, "Thirty Years On," *Harvard Law Review* 115 (2002): 1655.

[60] But see Shapiro, *Legality*, 205–7 (arguing that from the standpoint of his planning theory of legal positivism, the substantive aim of a legal system is determined by its planners). Shapiro seeks to formulate a moral standard that is descriptively accurate of the aims that various legal systems *in fact* pursue. The unified theory instead formulates the substantive aim to which public authority, given the terms of its justification, should be directed. The principle of justice is not a fact about how public authority was exercised at a

legal system or a valid law within one can be defective on its own *internal* standard of adequacy. So conceived, public justice is not 'a brooding omnipresence in the sky,'[61] a transcendent value extrinsic to the public law relationship, but the internal moral standard for assessing the adequacy of all legal systems and all exercises of public authority. Because the unified theory of public law provides an integrated justification of public authority and public justice that retains the distinctiveness of each, it affirms what positivists have long insisted that all nonpositivist theories must deny: a law (or a legal system) may be valid even though it is not perfectly just. I draw out the implication of this point for the reformist ambitions of each theory in Chapter 4.

These theoretical departures from legal positivism culminate in a practical one. A familiar feature of legal positivist thought is its 'comprehensive normative inertness.'[62] As a theory of the ultimate basis of legal norms, positivism 'does not provide any guidance at all on what anyone should do about anything on any occasion.'[63] While positivists do not deny that the validity or invalidity of a norm may be salient from the standpoint of various moral theories, the positivist refrain that legal norms are valid by virtue of their enactment is intended to provide neither moral nor legal guidance. By contrast, the unified theory is anything but normatively inert. The principle of authority justifies the right of government to enact positive law and the corresponding duty of private persons to obey it, while the principle of justice articulates the right of private persons and the corresponding duty incumbent on government to bring the legal order into the deepest possible conformity with the independence of all who are bound by it. Such a framework provides a basis for evaluating the actions of all private persons and public officials from the moral standpoint of the public law relationship. Because private persons and public officials have distinctive rights and duties, what one should do depends upon the position that one occupies.

Once the principles of authority and justice are distinguished, questions about their compatibility might arise. Let us consider an objection from a scholar whose conception of the rule of law 'hovers over the reflections of many so-called "positivist" modern jurists.'[64] The objection

particular moment in time, but the relevant standard for assessing the moral adequacy of all exercises of public authority.

61 *Southern Pac. Co.* v. *Jensen*, 244 US 205, 222 (1917) (Holmes J, dissenting).

62 Gardner, "Legal Positivism: 5½ Myths," 203. 63 Ibid., 202.

64 Michael Oakeshott, "The Rule of Law," in *On History and Other Essays* (Oxford: Basil Blackwell, 1983), 162.

alleges that notions of public authority and public justice are not mutually implicating, as I have suggested, but mutually exclusive. In his magnificent essay "The Rule of Law," Michael Oakeshott argues that an adequate account of the authority of the rule of law precludes considerations of its justice. Oakeshott characterizes the rule of law as a 'mode of association in which *lex* (a rule understood in terms of its authenticity) and *jus* (a rule understood in terms of the "rightness" or "justice" of what it prescribes) are both recognized but not confused.'[65] As Oakeshott explains, a legal rule is authentic or authoritative if it was enacted through the appropriate public procedure.[66] Whereas the *lex* or authority of a rule concerns whether it was appropriately enacted, the *jus* or justice of a rule concerns whether it was appropriate to enact it given its moral character.[67] Since an authoritative rule may fail to be just and a just rule may fail to be authoritative, Oakeshott writes that 'the only "justice" the rule of law can accommodate is faithfulness to the formal principles inherent in the character of *lex*.[68] These formal principles include the requirements that laws be both public and prospective.[69] For if persons are to interact on the basis of common legal rules, then those rules must be publicly established at the moment of action; they can neither be secret nor retrospective. Oakeshott describes these formal principles as the '*jus* postulated in the rule of law.'[70]

Oakeshott claims that by appealing to a conception of *jus* that is external to *lex*, nonpositivist theories supplant the rule of law with anarchy. Nonpositivist theories, as Oakeshott conceives of them, are distinguished by two claims. The first is that there is a *jus* external to *lex*, a standard of right conduct that obtains independently of the promulgation of legal rules.[71] Nonpositivist theories conceive of this standard of conduct in a range of different ways: conscience, divine will, human deliberation, absolute values, inalienable rights, unconditional liberties, or a fundamental law.[72] The second is that the authority of *lex* hinges on its conformity to this external conception of *jus*.[73] Oakeshott refers to the nonpositivist view that conformity to *jus* is a prerequisite for 'the obligation to observe the conditions prescribed by *lex*' as 'the recipe for anarchy.'[74] Nonpositivism is anarchic because it renders *lex* either

65 Ibid., 136. 66 Ibid., 137–8 and 143. 67 Ibid., 141; cf. 135. 68 Ibid., 159.
69 Ibid., 140, 143, and 159. 70 Ibid., 140. 71 Ibid., 142–3.
72 Ibid., 135–6, 142, 156, and 158. 73 Ibid., 135–6, 142, and 155–6.
74 Ibid., 160; cf. 156 (referring to the 'threat of anarchy'). Here Oakeshott's argument echoes Kelsen, "The Natural-Law Doctrine before the Tribunal of Science," 488: 'If the positive law is, as all followers of the natural-law doctrine assert, valid only insofar as it

redundant or irrelevant. If *lex* conforms to *jus*, then *lex* simply echoes a norm that exists independently of it and is therefore 'redundant.'[75] Alternately, if *lex* departs from *jus*, then *lex* imposes no obligation constraining conduct and is therefore irrelevant.[76] In either case, persons are bound not by the shared standards imposed on all by legislative institutions, but by the various contested conceptions of *jus* to which persons might appeal. In the nonpositivist world that Oakeshott envisions, the only way for persons to interact on the basis of common rules of conduct would be if the opinions of a multiplicity of persons regarding the moral merits of a rule happened to converge. The nonpositivist commitment to a *jus* external to *lex*, Oakeshott concludes, cannot be reconciled with the authority of the rule of law. Expressed in the terminology of the unified theory, Oakeshott's objection alleges that the principle of justice undercuts the principle of authority.

Oakeshott's claim that nonpositivist theories are anarchic stems from a conception of nonpositivism that the unified theory does not share.[77] Unlike the nonpositivist theories that Oakeshott discusses, the unified theory neither posits a conception of justice that obtains independently of law's authority nor claims that conformity to this conception of justice is a condition of law's authority. Rather, as I have argued, the right of government to exercise public authority by imposing legal obligations on private persons must be justified. The justification of this right implicates a moral standard for assessing the adequacy of all valid legal obligations, the principle of justice. This principle cannot be – like the conceptions of *jus* that Oakeshott canvasses – extrinsic to law's authority because the ideal of equal freedom under law can neither be conceived of nor realized apart from a legal system.[78] The distinction between the principles of authority and justice further distinguishes the unified theory from the

corresponds to the natural law, any norm created by custom or stipulated by a human legislator which is contrary to the law of nature must be considered null and void. This is the inevitable consequence of the theory which admits the possibility of positive law as a normative system inferior to natural law.'

75 Oakeshott, 136 (referring to natural lawyers who 'have gone the whole hog and have declared the notion of authenticity redundant').

76 Ibid., 160.

77 For an overview of Oakeshott's account of the rule of law and its relation to positivist and nonpositivist theories, see Richard Friedman, "Michael Oakeshott and the Elusive Identity of the Rule of Law," in *The Intellectual Legacy of Michael Oakeshott*, ed. Corey Abel and Timothy Fuller (Charlottesville: Imprint Academic, 2005), 160–81.

78 I return to this point in Chapter 4 in contrasting the principle of justice with the ideal of an instrumental theory.

kinds of nonpositivist theories that Oakeshott criticizes. Whereas Oakeshott's nonpositivist theories conceive of conformity to *jus* as the condition of the authority of *lex*, the principles of public law occupy distinctive planes. As the constitutive principle of public law, the principle of authority concerns whether a given norm or social order is legally authoritative or valid. As the regulative principle of public law, the principle of justice concerns the extent of a legal norm or legal system's moral adequacy. Far from making the anarchist claim that conformity to public justice is the condition for recognizing law's authority, the unified theory holds instead that the presence of public authority is the condition for assessing the extent of its justice. Thus, the claim that a law or legal system is unjust 'must always retain the character of a complaint.'[79]

Conclusion

I have argued that public law is a juridical relationship involving mutually implicating principles.

By *relationship* I mean an association between two parties, neither of which can be considered in isolation from the other. Such relationships arise in various spheres of human life. By referring to someone as a brother or a sister, one conceives of a person as party to a relationship with another. An only child can be a boy or a girl, but cannot be a brother or a sister. The very notion of being a sibling is inherently relational because each party is situated within the context of an association. In some relationships, the parties are situated symmetrically. This is the case in relationships between siblings, friends, colleagues, and spouses. In others, the parties to the relationship are situated asymmetrically, as in the relationships between a doctor and a patient, a parent and a child, and a teacher and a student.

Public law is the asymmetric juridical relationship between a people and its government. A *people* is a plurality of persons considered as a whole insofar as its members are subject to common lawgiving. A *government* consists in the sum of institutions that subject a people to a common lawgiving. Public law is not reducible to either of these parties taken singly. In the absence of common lawgiving, one may find a crowd but one cannot find a people. In the absence of a people that is subject to lawgiving, one may witness successive acts in which persons gather in a hall, give speeches, stand up and sit down, but one cannot find a government enacting law. The relational significance of the parties cannot be eliminated.

[79] Ebbinghaus, "The Law of Humanity and the Limits of State Power," 19.

The character of the relationship between the parties is juridical. By *juridical*, I mean that the relationship is comprised of rights and corresponding duties that regard each party not as an isolated entity, but as the participants in a common association. The juridical character of this relationship can be unfolded by considering it from two interrelated standpoints. The *principle of authority* concerns the right of government to exercise public authority and the corresponding duty of private persons to obey. The *principle of justice*, by contrast, concerns the right of private persons to just governance and the corresponding duty of government to bring the existing legal system into the closest possible conformity with its own underlying justification. Public law is a juridical relationship rooted in principles of authority and justice that emerge from a conceptually sequenced exploration of the right of persons, by virtue of their dignity, to equal freedom.

The relation between these principles is one of mutual implication. Whereas the common wisdom in legal philosophy that there is no single standpoint from which the claims of authority and justice can be jointly recognized, the unified theory holds that these claims are not merely compatible but mutually implicating. The right of government to exercise public authority over independent persons implicates a duty to govern justly. The right of independent persons to just governance presupposes the presence of publicly authoritative institutions. The unified theory of public law thereby articulates a common moral standpoint from which the distinctive claims of authority and justice may each be given their due.

The unified theory of public law departs from Hart's legal positivism but redeems its original aspiration. This departure has two aspects. First, the unified theory presents public authority not as a belief that officials have in the obligation-imposing character of their own conduct, but as a juridical implication of the right of every person to independence. The second departure follows from the first. Internal to the account of public authority is the standard for assessing its adequacy. Public justice is the internal measure of the adequacy of every legal system and all public authority must be exercised in accordance with the terms on which it is justified. Because the unified theory of public law provides an integrated justification of public authority and public justice that retains the distinctiveness of each, it affirms what positivists have long insisted that all nonpositivist theories must deny: a legal system (or a particular law within it) may be valid even though it is not perfectly just. Legal positivism has no monopoly on recognizing injustice.

3

Public authority and private violence

The problem of distinguishing the public authority of a legal system from the mere infliction of private violence acquired renewed interest among legal and political philosophers in the aftermath of the Holocaust, but the problem can be traced back to Plato. Public authority imposes legal obligations upon its subjects; private violence merely compels and may be rightfully counteracted. In the *Crito*, Socrates forgoes the opportunity to escape from prison and avoid his impending execution because it is impossible for a city not to be 'destroyed if the verdicts of its courts have no force but are nullified and set at naught by private individuals.'[1] But even though Socrates recognizes that an unjust law or legal order can impose obligations on its members, he denies that public authority is unlimited. When an Athenian dictatorship demands that Socrates contribute to the murder of an innocent man, he refuses to cooperate.[2]

This chapter formulates the distinction between public authority and private violence (or what I will call *barbarism*)[3] from the standpoint of the unified theory. The standard strategy for formulating this distinction involves conceiving of barbarism as a departure from the regulative ideal of legality. Different theorists articulate this idea in different ways. Lon Fuller held that legal validity diminishes to the

[1] Plato, *Complete Works*, ed. J.M. Cooper and D.S. Hutchinson (Indianapolis: Hackett Publishing, 1997), 50a–b.

[2] *Apology* in *Complete Works*, 32a–e.

[3] I follow Kant in using the term *barbarism* to refer to lawless violence. Kant held that barbarism is 'brutishly degrading to humanity' because it subjects the rights of one or more private persons to the arbitrary force of another. See *Perpetual Peace* in *Immanuel Kant: Practical Philosophy*, trans. Mary Gregor (Cambridge: Cambridge University Press, 1996), 8:354. In *Anthropology from a Pragmatic Point of View* (Cambridge: Cambridge University Press, 2006), 330–1, Kant explains that in cases of barbarism, force prevails in the absence of law and freedom, while in cases of despotism (or what I call *injustice*), force and law prevail in the absence of freedom. Kant does not flesh out the distinction. For his discussions of barbarism, see *Doctrine of Right* 6:308, 6:337, 6:339, 6:351; and *Towards Perpetual Peace* 8:354–5, 8:357; 8:359; 8:376.

extent that a legal norm or condition deviates from the formal principles that make up the internal morality of law. Gustav Radbruch maintained that extreme injustice cannot be law. Robert Alexy argues that law forfeits its validity when it fails to make a claim to moral correctness. For each of these thinkers, barbarism follows from repudiating law's standard of moral adequacy. Thus, understanding what law ought to be is a prerequisite for distinguishing between legality and barbarism.

The unified theory breaks with this line of thought by conceiving of barbarism as a violation of public law's constitutive principle rather than its regulative one. As I argued in the prior chapter, the public law relationship between rulers and ruled has a bifurcated structure. The principle of authority *constitutes* this structure by specifying what a legal system is: a set of publicly authoritative institutions that together create the conditions under which persons can interact rightfully with one another. The principle of justice *regulates* this structure by indicating the moral ideal of a legal system: the conformity of all public authority to the dignity of each person subject to it. The violation of each of these principles generates a distinct legal pathology. A social order is *barbarous* if it violates the principle of authority by failing to maintain the conditions in which private persons can interact rightfully with one another. A legal order is *unjust* to the extent that it violates the principle of justice by failing to reconcile public authority with the freedom of each person subject to it. Each of these pathologies concerns different relations. The former pathology concerns the character of the *horizontal* interaction between private persons, while the latter concerns the character of the *vertical* interaction between the public institutions of government and the private persons bound by it.

I explore the distinction between legality and barbarism in four sections. The first explains how German legal theorists, in the aftermath of Nazism, distinguished instances of legality from instances of barbarism. I argue that by collapsing the distinction between the constitutive and regulative dimensions of public law, Radbruch and Alexy are unable to establish a workable distinction between legality and barbarism. In search of such a distinction, the second section explores the neglected framework of Julius Ebbinghaus, who rightly conceived of barbarism as the violation of a legal system's constitutive principle. The third section explains how persons in variegated contexts can distinguish instances of legality (which must be obeyed) from instances of barbarism (which may be rightfully resisted). The fourth and final section applies the framework developed in the prior sections to the circumstances of Nazi power.

3.1 Radbruch and Alexy on the limits of legality

In the aftermath of the Holocaust, German legal theorists sought to formulate a framework that would indicate the barbarism of Nazi power and guide the pursuit of justice in the postwar order. This project was undermined by the failure to draw a distinction between the constitutive and regulative dimensions of a legal system.

Radbruch's theory begins with the insight that law involves the exercise of force but is not reducible to it. Force compels but it generates no obligation to obey. To explain how law can impose obligations, Radbruch appeals to a series of legal values: certainty, purposiveness, and justice.[4] Certainty makes the positive law knowable to those who are under an obligation with respect to it. If the law is knowable, persons can adjust their conduct in light of what the law requires and thereby avoid the law's coercive sanction. Alternately, if there is no law or if what is called law is unknowable – as was the case when Emperor Caligula posted the laws in small print at the summit of a tall pillar[5] – persons cannot know what actions are permitted. The second value of law is purposiveness, which Radbruch conceives of as the benefit of the people. Since the greatest injustices of the Nazi years were alleged to be for the benefit of the people, Radbruch holds that it is not the case that what benefits the people is law; rather, 'what law is benefits the people.'[6] Law, in turn, is defined as legal certainty and the striving for justice. Radbruch conceives of justice as the equal treatment of equal persons: 'Justice means: To judge without regard to the person, to measure everyone by the same standard.'[7]

Legal certainty can be found in unjust statutes, while laws need not be enacted simply because they are just. The potential schism between legal certainty and justice prompts Radbruch to introduce his famous formula. The formula is often divided into two parts.[8] The first concerns the

4 Radbruch, "Statutory Lawlessness and Supra-Statutory Law (1946)," *Oxford Journal of Legal Studies* 26 (2006): 6.

5 Fuller, *The Morality of Law* (New Haven: Yale University Press, 1964), 93.

6 Radbruch, "Five Minutes of Legal Philosophy," *Oxford Journal of Legal Studies* 26 (2006): 14.

7 Ibid.

8 On the distinction between the two parts of Radbruch's formula, see Frank Haldemann, "Gustav Radbruch vs. Hans Kelsen: A Debate on Nazi Law," *Ratio Juris* 18 (2005): 166; Stanley L. Paulson, "On the Background and Significance of Gustav Radbruch's Post-War

distinction between unjust and invalid statutes. As Radbruch explains, the distinction between an unjust law and an invalid one concerns the *degree* that the supposed law departs from justice:

> The conflict between justice and legal certainty should be resolved in that the positive law, established by enactment and power, has primacy even when its content is unjust and improper. It is only when the contradiction between positive law and justice reaches an intolerable level that the law is supposed to give way as a "false law" [*unrichtiges Recht*] to justice. It is impossible to draw a sharper line between the cases of legalised injustice and laws which remain valid despite their false content.[9]

The positive law takes precedence even when it is unjust and unbeneficial to a people because legal certainty enables persons to conduct themselves in accordance with what is publicly known to be lawful. But because law is the will to justice, when positive law conflicts with justice to an intolerable degree, positive law forfeits its validity. The second part of Radbruch's formula is typically interpreted as an elaboration of the nature of invalid law: 'Where justice is not even aimed at, where equality – the core of justice – is deliberately disavowed in the enactment of positive law, the law is not simply "false law," it has no claim at all to legal status.'[10] A valid law is not necessarily fully just, but justice prescribes the limits of valid lawgiving. Since law is the will to justice, the repudiation of justice cannot be law.

Radbruch terms invalid lawgiving *statutory lawlessness*. Nazi lawgiving was an instance of statutory lawlessness because it renounced justice by treating equal persons unequally:

> If one applauds the assassination of political opponents, or orders the murder of people of another race, all the while meting out the most cruel and degrading punishment for the same acts committed against those of one's own persuasion, this is neither justice nor law. If laws deliberately betray the will to justice – by, for example, arbitrarily granting and

Papers," *Oxford Journal of Legal Studies* 26 (2006): 26; Thomas Mertens, "Nazism, Legal Positivism and Radbruch's Thesis on Statutory Injustice," *Law and Critique* 14 (2003): 288; Mertens, "Darker Legacies of Law in Europe: The Shadow of National Socialism and Fascism over Europe and Its Legal Traditions," *Ratio Juris* 18 (2005): 286; Robert Alexy, "A Defence of Radbruch's Formula," in *Recrafting the Rule of Law: The Limits of Legal Order*, ed. David Dyzenhaus (Oxford: Hart Publishing, 1999), 16; and Alexy, "On the Concept and the Nature of Law," *Ratio Juris* 21 (2008): 282. For an interpretation that seeks to retain the unity of the formula, see David Dyzenhaus, "The Juristic Force of Injustice," in *Calling Power to Account: Law, Reparations and the Chinese Head Tax*, ed. Dyzenhaus and Mayo Moran (Toronto: University of Toronto Press, 2005), 279–80.

[9] Quoted in Alexy, "A Defence of Radbruch's Formula," 15–16. [10] Ibid., 16.

> withholding human rights – then these laws lack validity, the people owe them no obedience, and jurists, too, must find the courage to deny them legal character.[11]

By denouncing equality as a legal value, Nazism reduced itself into an arbitrary power, which compelled but imposed no obligations. In the absence of a valid legal power, both public officials and private persons are bound by *suprastatutory law*, which consists in what justice demands regardless of whether it has been enacted in positive law.[12]

In the aftermath of Nazism, Radbruch's distinction between statutory lawlessness and suprastatutory law was repeatedly invoked by German courts. On one occasion, the Federal Constitutional Court considered the validity of the *Reich's Citizenship Law*,[13] enacted 25 November 1941, which established that Jews would lose their German nationality by taking up residence abroad. In 1968, a Jewish lawyer, who had been deported to Amsterdam in 1942 and who was presumed to have been murdered in a concentration camp, returned to Germany to establish his German nationality, which was a precondition for receiving his inheritance. The Federal Constitutional Court held that the plaintiff had never lost his citizenship because the *Reich's Citizenship Law* was invalid from the moment of its enactment. Although the *Reich's Citizenship Law* was enacted and enforced by the relevant institutions, the court denied its validity because it conflicted with 'fundamental principles of justice.'[14] Echoing the first part of Radbruch's formula, the court held that the conflict between justice and the *Reich's Citizenship Law* 'has reached so intolerable a level that' the law 'must be regarded as void from the outset.'[15]

Radbruch's claim that Nazi laws were invalid because they repudiated justice to an intolerable degree cannot stand on his account of justice. Throughout his career, Radbruch conceived of justice as formal equality: '[W]hile justice directs us to treat equals equally, unequals unequally, it does not tell us anything about the viewpoint from which they are to be deemed equals or unequals in the first place; moreover, it determines solely the relation, and not the kind, of the treatment.'[16] Justice, then, is

[11] Radbruch, "Five Minutes," 14. See also Radbruch, "Statutory Lawlessness," 8.
[12] Radbruch, "Statutory Lawlessness," 5. [13] RGB1. I. p. 722.
[14] BVerfGE 23, 98 (106). [15] Ibid.
[16] Radbruch, *Legal Philosophy* in *The Legal Philosophies of Lask, Radbruch, and Dabin*, trans. Kurt Wilk (Cambridge: Harvard University Press, 1950), 107. See also Radbruch's post-war article, "Statutory Lawlessness," 8 (defining justice as the 'equal treatment of equals').

indeterminate with respect to two issues: 'whom to consider equal or different, and how to treat them.'[17]

A problem arises with respect to each of these indeterminacies. I will consider each singly and then note their joint implication. First, justice does not determine who is an equal. Whether Aryans are equal to non-Aryans is not a question that justice addresses. Since justice does not determine who is an equal, laws that acknowledge the superiority of Aryans and the inferiority of non-Aryans cannot constitute an extreme injustice that indicates invalidity. Second, Radbruch's conception of justice merely requires that equals be treated alike but does not determine how persons are to be treated.[18] On this view, what is objectionable about Nazism was that it treated Jews and other persecuted groups differently than it treated Aryans. Nazi treatment of persons could have been just, then, if only its persecution was not limited to Jews and other persecuted groups. Thus, a perverse implication of Radbruch's account is that those who risked their lives to save the persecuted could have instead served justice by making Nazi persecution more inclusive.[19] Bringing these strands together, a Nazi could purport to act in accordance with Radbruch's conception of justice by treating his Aryan equals according to one criterion and non-Aryans according to another. Radbruch's conception of justice is simply too thin to justify the conclusion that Nazi violence was lawless.

The shortcoming in Radbruch's theory can be traced to the way that he conceptualizes the relationship between the constitutive and regulative dimensions of legality, validity, and justice, respectively. Radbruch conceives of legality as a spectrum in which justice lies at one end and

[17] Radbruch, *Legal Philosophy*, 90–1.

[18] The absurdity of conceiving of justice as mere equal treatment can be illustrated with an anecdote about the philosophy professor Sidney Morgenbesser: 'He was once asked if it was unfair that the police hit him on the head during the riot. "It was unfair but not unjust," he pronounced. Why? "It's unfair to be hit over the head, but it was not unjust since they hit everybody else over the head."' So long as Professor Morgenbesser is equal to other protesters, if the police treat protesters alike by hitting all of them on the head, then justice requires that Professor Morgenbesser be hit on the head too. See Douglas Martin, "Sidney Morgenbesser, 82, Kibitzing Philosopher, Dies," *The New York Times*, www.nytimes.com/2004/08/04/us/sidney-morgenbesser-82-kibitzing-philosopher-dies.html.

[19] On this point, see Bernard Loesener, *Legislating the Holocaust: The Bernard Loesener Memoirs and Supporting Documents*, ed. Karl A. Schleunes, trans. Carol Scherer (Boulder, Colo.: Westview Press, 2001), 95: 'Thus far, I have described the efforts and battles over a period of almost 10 years. Their goal was to influence legislation so that the largest possible number of people would, from the outset, be spared from the clutches of antisemitic legislation.' Given Radbruch's conception of justice, perhaps Loesener should have directed his efforts toward making Nazi persecution more inclusive.

invalidity at the other. When the distinction between justice and invalidity is conceptualized as one of degree rather than kind, a problem arises regardless of whether the theorist introduces a demanding or a permissive conception of justice. The more demanding a conception of justice is, the more existing conditions and norms will significantly depart from it, with the result that the validity of an extensive array of laws and legal systems will come into question. While such an approach would culminate in the desired conclusion that Nazism is barbarous, the approach would also impugn the legality of less controversial arrangements. The problem cannot be solved by formulating a more permissive conception of justice. For the more easily a conception of justice is satisfied, the more existing conditions and norms will closely conform to it. The result, instantiated by Radbruch's theory, is that the most horrific Nazi laws are deemed to be not only valid but also just. Each of these possibilities fails to satisfy Radbruch's aim of formulating a legal theory that would identify the barbarism of Nazi power and regulate the pursuit of justice in postwar Germany. By conceptualizing validity and justice as arising on a single plane, Radbruch left himself to choose between a framework that denies both the validity of Nazism but also Germany's postwar order and a framework that rightly recognizes the relative justice of Germany's postwar order but also affirms the justice of Nazi law. Each of these possibilities is equally fatal to Radbruch's theoretical ambitions.

Decades later, the German legal theorist Robert Alexy formulated an innovative conceptual framework for defending Radbruch's thesis that extreme injustice cannot be law. As a nonpositivist, Alexy defends a version of the *connection thesis*, which defines the concept of law as encompassing moral elements.[20] The connection thesis affords a number of interpretations. On one interpretation, which Alexy terms *exclusive non-positivism*, 'every moral defect yields legal invalidity.'[21] Alexy rejects this nonpositivist paradigm because its emphasis on the ideal or critical dimension of law excludes the 'factual or authoritative dimension.'[22] The

20 Alexy, *The Argument from Injustice: A Reply to Legal Positivism*, trans. Bonnie Litschewski Paulson and Stanley L. Paulson (Oxford: Clarendon Press, 2002), 4, 21 ff.; see also Alexy, "On the Concept and the Nature of Law," 285.

21 Alexy, "On the Concept and the Nature of Law," 287. See also Alexy, "Effects of Defects—Action or Argument? Thoughts about Deryck Beyleveld and Roger Brownsword's *Law as Moral Judgment*," *Ratio Juris* 19 (2006): 169–79; and Stanley L. Paulson, "Law as a Moral Judgment," *Ratio Juris* 7 (1994): 111–16.

22 Alexy, "On the Concept and the Nature of Law," 287. Alexy attributes this position to Deryck Beyleveld and Roger Brownsword, *Law as Moral Judgment* (Sheffield: Sheffield Academic, 1994), 76: '[I]mmoral rules are not legally valid.'

opposite position, *super-inclusive non-positivism*, which Alexy attributes to Kant, holds that moral defects have no bearing on legal validity.[23] Each of these positions provides a mirror image of the other's vice: exclusive non-positivism overemphasizes the ideal dimension of law at the expense of its factual dimension; super-inclusive non-positivism overemphasizes the factual dimension of law at the expense of its ideal dimension. Alexy endorses what he calls *inclusive non-positivism*, the moderate thesis that 'legal validity is lost in some cases of moral defects ... and not in others.'[24] Radbruch's formula that extreme injustice is not law is perhaps the most well-known instance of inclusive non-positivism. For Alexy, the formula captures something fundamental about the relationship between law and morality in an adequate nonpositivist framework: a legal system (or an appropriately enacted law) may impose obligations even though it is not perfectly just.[25] Such an insight cannot be accommodated by exclusive non-positivist frameworks (which deny that legal validity is compatible with even a trace of injustice) or by super-inclusive non-positivist frameworks (which assert that validity is compatible with even the most extreme injustice). This set of distinctions is familiar from the preceding chapter. Just as Hart held that an adequate theory of law must avoid anarchism and quietism by explaining how positive law could be valid but nevertheless immoral, so too Alexy seeks to develop a framework that integrates the factual and ideal dimensions of law.[26]

The basis of Alexy's inclusive-nonpositivist framework is his *theory of claim*, which holds that a legal order (or a particular law within one) necessarily makes a claim to moral correctness.[27] If the claim to moral correctness is made but unfulfilled, Alexy asserts that the legal order is defective or unjust. But if the claim to moral correctness is not made at all, then Alexy maintains that no legal order exists. Alexy illustrates how his theory of claim distinguishes between an unjust legal order and a condition of lawless violence through a series of examples. The first

[23] To my knowledge, Alexy does not discuss Kant's conception of barbarism or its significance within his broader framework.

[24] Alexy, "On the Concept and the Nature of Law," 287. Alexy also refers to this position as the weak connection thesis. See *The Argument from Injustice: A Reply to Legal Positivism*, trans. Bonnie Litschewski Paulson and Stanley L. Paulson (Oxford: Clarendon Press, 2002), 47.

[25] Alexy, "On the Concept and the Nature of Law," 282. [26] Ibid., 290 and 292.

[27] Alexy, "On the Necessary Relations Between Law and Morality," *Ratio Juris* 2 (1989): 178. On Alexy's theory of claim, see Maeve Cook, "Law's Claim to Correctness," in *Law, Rights, and Discourse: The Legal Philosophy of Robert Alexy*, ed. George Pavlakos (Oxford: Hart Publishing, 2007), 225–48.

involves a *senseless order* in which a violent group rules haphazardly by issuing 'partly contradictory, ever-changing, and partly unfulfillable single orders to the subjects.'[28] This order is not a legal system because the only general rule is that the rulers are permitted to impose violence, and no claim is made with respect to the moral correctness of this arrangement. The second example involves general rules but no claim to moral correctness. In what Alexy calls a *predatory order*, a wholly exploitative system of rules obtains in which subjects are killed for the financial benefit of the rulers.[29] Because no claim to moral correctness is made, Alexy denies that the predatory order is a legal system. In this final example, a *ruler-system*, rulers kill and exploit their subjects in light of general rules and procedures. The rulers claim, and the majority of subjects accept, that the practice is justified because it somehow serves the purpose of developing the people. Alexy concludes that the ruler-system is a legal order, albeit a highly unjust one. What makes the ruler-system a legal order is that 'a *claim to correctness* is rooted in the practice of the rulers' system and raised against everyone.'[30]

Alexy's theory of claim cannot support his conclusion that Nazism was not a legal system. As historians have noted, part of what is so troubling about Nazism was that it made a claim to moral correctness:

> The Final Solution did not develop as evil incarnate but rather as the dark side of ethnic righteousness. Conscience, originally seen to protect the integrity of the individual from the inhumane demands of the group, in the Third Reich became a means of underwriting the attacks by the strong against the weak. To Germans caught up in a simulacrum of high moral purpose, purification of racial aliens became a difficult but necessary duty.[31]

[28] Alexy, "On the Necessary Relations Between Law and Morality," 176. [29] Ibid.

[30] Ibid., 177. Alexy's examples in this passage are somewhat ambiguous. For instance, it is not clear what significance the people's acceptance of the moral claim has within Alexy's framework. In his example of the senseless order, Alexy indicates that the subjects obey only because they are afraid of coercion. In the example of the predatory order, it seems to be the case that the people deem the rules to be exploitative. Finally, in his example of the legal order of the ruler-system, Alexy indicates that the majority of rulers and ruled accept the moral claim. Does Alexy conceive of legality as involving a practice informed by general rules that is merely claimed to be morally correct by the supposed rulers? Or does legality *also* require that the claim be accepted? And if the claim must be accepted, who must accept it? Must it be accepted merely by the rulers or must it also be accepted by a majority of the ruled? If the latter, does Alexy mean to exclude the possibility that a social order that operates in accordance with general rules and makes a claim to moral correctness that is accepted by the majority of persons might nevertheless be barbaric?

[31] Koonz, *The Nazi Conscience* (Cambridge: Belknap Press of Harvard University Press, 2003), 273.

Since Nazism made a claim to moral correctness, Alexy's conclusion that Nazism was not a valid legal system cannot stand.

Alexy's argument cannot be saved by invoking a distinction between de facto and de jure claims to moral correctness. If the theory of claim is revised to hold that a valid legal system makes a claim to de facto moral correctness – that is, to what persons might suppose is morally correct – then Germany's postwar order must be a valid legal system, but Nazism must be as well. On this interpretation, Alexy's theory dovetails with Radbruch's because both conceive of barbarism in terms of a departure from a moral ideal that is easily approximated. Alternately, if Alexy's position is that a valid legal system makes a claim to de jure morality – that is, to what is actually morally correct – then Nazism would be invalid because its conception of morality was appalling. But such a position proves too much. While a standard of de facto morality culminates in an underinclusive conception of barbarism in which any social order that makes a claim to moral correctness is valid, a standard of de jure morality culminates in an overinclusive conception of barbarism because it renders invalid not only Nazism, but also any social order that appeals to an inadequate conception of morality. The attempt to salvage Alexy's position by introducing a distinction between de facto and de jure morality generates the unacceptable possibilities that any social order that makes a claim to moral correctness cannot be barbaric or that every social order that fails to make a claim with respect to the appropriate conception of morality is barbaric. Neither of these possibilities is consistent with the core insight that Alexy's inclusive non-positivism seeks to illuminate: that legal validity is lost in some cases of moral defect but not in others.

By failing to identify the problem in Radbruch's theory, Alexy resurrects it within his own. Both Radbruch and Alexy treat the question "What does it mean for law to be valid?" as derivative of the question "What does it mean for law to be just (or morally correct)?" This approach generates two equally problematic paths. The employment of a rigorous conception of justice culminates in anarchism (or what Alexy calls exclusive non-positivism), which denies the *validity* of a wide range of uncontroversial legal instances. The employment of a lax conception of justice culminates in quietism (or what Alexy calls super-inclusive non-positivism), which affirms that paradigmatic instances of barbaric violence are not only lawful but just.

3.2 The pathologies of public law

In 1953, Julius Ebbinghaus published a short article that sought to pinpoint the problem that German jurists encountered in capturing the wrongfulness of Nazi power and to sketch an alternative approach:

> When, after the last war, our German jurists sought to provide a satisfactory definition of those acts of Hitlerism, obedience to which could not rightly be demanded, they still limited themselves to the principle of justice; and they soon found themselves in the same difficulties as Locke and others like him . . . The illegality of such acts cannot properly be described as the violation of a law of justice, *but only as a violation of humanity itself in the persons of the victims*. What does this mean? How can we determine precisely the difference between such acts and simple acts of injustice? And how can it be proved that no one is obliged to comply with such acts of inhumanity by order of the state power?[32]

In this passage, Ebbinghaus does not refer to Radbruch explicitly, but his target seems clear. For the principle that Ebbinghaus attributes to Locke is that 'the right of the ruler depends upon the condition that his acts should be just.'[33] Ebbinghaus explains that in an attempt to temper the anarchist implications of such a principle, 'Locke and his followers took pains to determine the precise amount of injustice that is required to abolish the authority of a sovereign.'[34] In claiming that extreme injustice cannot be law, Radbruch's formula echoes this approach. Ebbinghaus quickly notes the 'moral confusion' that results from conceiving of fidelity to justice as the condition of law's authority and elaborates an alternative that draws a distinction in kind between two legal pathologies: injustice and inhumanity. The wrongs that characterize Nazi power, he insists, were not instances of injustice, but rather inhumanity. The distinction between these pathologies emerges from a legal theory that exhibits the bifurcated structure of the unified theory of public law, as elaborated in Chapter 2.

For Ebbinghaus, law is a system of equal freedom in which each person may engage in any action that is consistent with the freedom of others. The system secures the freedom of each person by placing reciprocal limits on conduct. Because these limits are to be determined by *general rules* that apply to *all persons*, Ebbinghaus calls this system of equal freedom the *law of humanity*.[35] He develops the law of humanity in a

[32] Ebbinghaus, "The Law of Humanity and the Limits of State Power," *Philosophical Quarterly* 3 (1953): 20.

[33] Ibid., 19. [34] Ibid. [35] Ibid., 15–6.

conceptually sequenced argument that proceeds from an account of private interaction and culminates in an account of the nature and adequacy of public authority.

The law of humanity imposes a twofold duty upon each person with respect to every other.[36] First, persons have a duty to direct their freedom toward their own self-chosen ends rather than to subordinate themselves to the choices of others. Such subordination would negate one person's freedom rather than harmonize it with the freedom of others. Second, persons have a duty to interact with others on the basis of reciprocal limits on freedom rather than on the force that each happens to possess. Whereas the first duty prohibits persons from subordinating themselves to another, the second prohibits each person from subordinating others. The twofold duty incumbent on persons is expressed in the imperative: 'Do not reduce yourself to an object of other men's arbitrary power, nor other men to objects of your own.'[37]

Even if persons discern and act in accordance with the law of humanity, so long as they remain in a lawless condition there can be no guarantee that others will do the same. In the absence of assurance that all others will act in accordance with the limits established by the law of humanity, any person who follows the law of humanity subjects their freedom to the arbitrary choices of others. But subjecting one's freedom to the arbitrary choices of others is exactly what the law of humanity forbids. Thus, the law of humanity requires that persons interact in a condition in which there is assurance that the law of humanity will be respected. The twofold duty to assert one's own freedom and to respect the freedom of others gives rise to a further duty: private persons 'must submit themselves to a common authority which has the power to impose laws upon them, and whose sole objective is the universal assurance of rights.'[38]

The justification for entering a legal condition reveals that condition's regulative principle. Public power is exercised justly when it is directed toward securing the freedom of all who are bound by it. By contrast, public power is exercised unjustly when 'the external freedom of the individual' is restricted 'in a manner which cannot be justified by the demands of a universal security of rights.'[39] So, for example, an unjust law might restrict freedom by compelling citizens to 'salute the governor's hat' or forbidding them to 'sniff the perfume of violets.'[40] Although such laws impose an unjustified constraint on the external

[36] Ibid., 16. [37] Ibid. [38] Ibid., 17. [39] Ibid., 20. [40] Ibid.

freedom of individuals, they nevertheless demand obedience. For private persons must interact with one another in a legal system in which public institutions establish, interpret, and enforce common norms of conduct, but such a system is not possible if persons retain the right to determine the norms to which their conduct must conform. Such a right would resurrect the problems of lawless interaction by subjecting each person's freedom to the arbitrary power of every other. Thus, Ebbinghaus remarks that '[w]hoever declares that he will obey only the just, expresses in reality his reluctance to obey at all. He would establish the state of nature in permanence, and surrender sovereignty to lawless liberty.'[41] Justice is the measure of law's adequacy, not the condition of its authority.

From the standpoint of the law of humanity, the problem surrounding Nazi power is not that it was *unjust* but that it was *inhuman*. Nazism sought not to constrain the freedom of persons subject to law on grounds that freedom itself did not require, but to negate the freedom of particular persons in relation to others. The persecuted were reduced from the legal status of human beings whose rights constrained the conduct of others to that of things to which others could do no wrong. For Ebbinghaus, the inhumanity of Nazi power preceded the commission of genocide and consisted in the antecedent denial that certain persons had the capacity to suffer legal wrongs:

> Those positive laws which we have accused of violating the law of humanity are laws which reduce men to the status of material things . . . The same type of violation would be involved in a law which annulled the right of specified persons to enter into contracts legally binding on others; or again, in any law which condemned men to death for their religious creed or their racial origin. For here also it is evident that such laws deny to the persons concerned all possibility of legal action. And in the latter case the denial is particularly monstrous, since what is denied is the legal possibility of life itself. Their very life is made illegal, because the acts whereby it might acquire legality are not within their power. It is as little within the power of a man's will to become convinced of what he does not believe as it is to change his racial origin. Such persons therefore are condemned to death unconditionally; for they are deprived, in principle, of any power at all to restrict the liberty of others in such a way that they could live among them.[42]

Nazi power regarded Jews as having a strange form of legal personality. On the one hand, as beings without rights, Jews imposed no duties on others

[41] Ibid., 19. [42] Ibid., 21.

and could therefore not be wronged by them.[43] On the other, Jews were regarded as possessing duties, which they violated independently of their actions. Jews could not be wronged, yet their very existence was a wrong.

This conception of the legal personality of Jews pervaded the adjudication of private disputes by Nazi courts. Contracts between Jews and Germans could be voided at the request of the latter.[44] Divorce proceedings invariably gave custody of the child to the Aryan parent despite a law that held that custody was to be awarded to the innocent partner. While the landlord–tenant law indicated that a lease could be terminated only 'if the behavior of the tenant is such that a continuation of the lease would represent an unreasonable hardship for the landlord,' Nazi courts held that the racial qualities of the tenant itself constituted such a hardship.[45] It soon became 'pointless for Jews to appeal to [courts] for the protection of their rights.'[46] Turning from the denial that Jews were capable of having rights to the Nazi conception of their duties, Nazi power sought not to prohibit particular actions but to deny the legality of particular actors by making their very existence wrongful. Laws that prohibit what one is rather than what one does cannot be followed because agents cannot abide by norms that render their very existence wrongful.[47] The inhumanity or barbarism of Nazi power consisted in the denial that Jews could be treated wrongfully by others and in the insistence that they did wrong independently of their actions.

Ebbinghaus's distinction between the law of humanity and justice parallels the bifurcated structure of the unified theory of public law. What Ebbinghaus calls *justice* is the regulative principle of public law. A state is unjust to the extent that public authority imposes constraints on the freedom of those who are bound by law that freedom itself does not require. By contrast, the law of humanity consists in the constitutive principle of public law, the principle of authority. An inhuman or barbarous arrangement or condition violates the principle of authority because it is incompatible with the right of private persons to interact with one another on terms of equal freedom. The problem with a barbaric

43 R.C. van Caenegem, *An Historical Introduction to Western Constitutional Law*, trans. David Johnston (Cambridge: Cambridge University Press, 1996), 289.

44 Ingo Müller, *Hitler's Justice* (Cambridge: Harvard University Press, 1991), 116.

45 Ibid., 117.

46 Ernst Fraenkel, *The Dual State: A Contribution to the Theory of Dictatorship* (New York: Oxford University Press, 1941), 92.

47 See Kristen Rundle, "The Impossibility of an Exterminatory Legality: Law and the Holocaust," *University of Toronto Law Journal* 59 (2009): 65–125.

regime is not that it exercises public authority in a defective manner by violating the duty of public justice owed to its inhabitants. Rather, in failing to satisfy the constitutive principle of public law, a barbaric regime does not exercise public authority at all. Since the duty of public justice attends the right to exercise public authority, where this right is absent, so too is the duty that regulates its exercise. The wrong that a barbaric regime inflicts consists not in the defective exercise of public authority, but in the perpetuation of a condition of private violence. When private violence prevails, the law of humanity imposes a fundamental obligation on every person, whether victims of violence or the supposed officials empowered to carry it out: enter into a legal condition in which an impartial public authority secures the freedom of each person in relation to every other.

The notion of barbarism does not swallow up the principle of authority. As I argued in the prior chapter, the principle of authority imposes a duty on private persons to submit themselves to the governance of a legal system. A legal system consists in the institutions and laws that secure the freedom of each individual from the arbitrary power of every other. When persons find themselves in a legal system, the principle of authority requires them to obey all valid lawgiving enacted within it, regardless of the extent to which the legal system conforms to the ideal of public justice. But when persons find themselves in a barbarous condition, the principle of authority requires the formation of a legal condition. Private persons do no wrong when they forcibly resist private violence in order to enter a condition of public law. For the principle of authority requires private persons to submit themselves to the governance of public institutions, which secures the rights of each private person in relation to every other, not to the arbitrary power of other private persons.

Ebbinghaus closes his article by emphasizing the distinction between the principles that constitute and regulate a legal system:

> It is my deep conviction that at the bottom of the moral confusion in which we find the contemporary world lies the lack of a sufficiently abstract theory. It was the law of humanity which was violated by Germans. The inevitable reaction to this violation in its turn, has become the source of seemingly insuperable difficulties about justice. The effort to distinguish and to relate these two notions which I now submit to your judgment has been intended as a contribution to the lessening of such distresses.[48]

[48] Ebbinghaus, "The Law of Humanity and the Limits of State Power," 22.

By expounding the 'profound difference between an act of injustice and act of inhumanity,'[49] Ebbinghaus's framework avoids the difficulties that arise in the theories of Radbruch and Alexy. Radbruch conceives of barbarism as the failure to treat equals equally, but leaves open the question of who is an equal and how equals are to be treated. By contrast, Ebbinghaus's framework establishes the conception of equality relevant to the existence of a legal system, the interaction of private persons on the basis of reciprocal limits on freedom. Since a legal system is that which secures the freedom of each in relation to every other, violence may be barbaric regardless of whether it targets a single person, a class of persons, or persons generally. Ebbinghaus's theory also avoids a problem that undermines Alexy's. Alexy conceptualizes the distinction between barbarism and legality in terms of how those who exercise power happen to characterize their own violent activity. Ebbinghaus instead focuses on the distinction between public authority and private violence by asking whether the activity of the supposed public authority satisfies the constitutive dimension of legality by securing the freedom of each private person in relation to every other. The juridical meaning of an act or condition is not exhausted by the disposition of the powerful toward it. Further, by distinguishing between the constitutive and the regulative dimensions of a legal system, Ebbinghaus provides a framework that enables the barbarism of Nazi power to be acknowledged without following Radbruch in denying the validity of other paradigmatic instances of legality or diluting the conception of justice apposite to assessing their adequacy.

3.3 The public meaning of the principle of authority

The unified theory of public law formulates a principle applicable to persons in all times and places: submit yourself to the public authority of a legal system, in which the freedom of each private person is secured from the arbitrary power of every other. The principle is practical insofar as it indicates how private persons must respond to public authority and private violence. Public authority must be obeyed. Private violence may be resisted with force. If private persons are to adhere to the demands that this principle makes upon their conduct, they must distinguish public authority from private violence. But on what basis are persons to draw this distinction?

[49] Ibid., 21.

The challenge that this question poses is compounded by the broad scope of the unified theory. As a general theory of public law, the unified theory's domain of application is variegated. The instances to which the theory applies extend beyond particular jurisdictions within the contemporary world to societies in distant times and places. In his 1953 article, Ebbinghaus did not explain how private persons situated in a diverse range of contexts are to distinguish public authority from private violence. His aim was simply to formulate – at a high level of abstraction – the principle that constitutes and constrains public authority and then to explain how the Nazis systematically violated it. In this section, I elaborate on Ebbinghaus's account by explaining how private persons are to bring this abstract principle to bear on their contingent circumstances.

The principle of authority has an abstract and a concrete meaning. Its *abstract meaning* consists in the injunction to submit oneself to the public authority of a legal system, which secures the freedom of each from the arbitrary power of every other. This injunction is universal: it applies wherever and whenever private persons interact with one another. Of course, the principle's abstract meaning lacks the specificity to guide the conduct of private persons in the diverse range of settings to which it applies. But this does not mean that the principle is empty. Rather, as a principle incumbent on private persons, its *concrete meaning* is immanent within the context in which their interaction occurs. This *concrete meaning* is manifested in local understandings about the authoritative or barbarous character of particular arrangements. To the extent that these understandings are shared, they form a public culture that provides a common basis for persons to distinguish public authority from private violence. The distinction between public authority and private violence has universal significance; the concrete meaning of this distinction with respect to particular arrangements varies from one context to another.

That the principle of authority gains specificity from the context to which it applies does not eliminate controversies surrounding the determination of whether an arrangement or condition is lawful or barbarous. The history of public law provides illustrations of the complexities that attend this determination.

First, private persons might occupy a shared territory without sharing a public culture. In cases in which the public cultures that persons affirm give rise to conflicting conceptions of legality, it might be impossible to construct a legal order that all would deem authoritative. When Nelson Mandela first negotiated with the Apartheid leaders for the creation of a nonracial democracy that would respect and protect the fundamental rights of all of its inhabitants, he quickly realized that they had not yet relinquished their belief in racial superiority as the organizing idea of political power. Mandela saw that so long as the public culture underwriting Apartheid persisted, it would be impossible to create a legal system that all South Africans, regardless of their racial status, could recognize as lawful.[50] The only way to create such an authority was for a rights-based public culture to supplant the race-based public culture that sustained Apartheid.[51] Every public culture draws a distinction between public authority and private violence, but not every assemblage of persons shares a public culture.

Second, a public culture may lack a disposition toward a given social arrangement. Such an arrangement may appear to occupy the world of facts given by nature rather than the world of norms governed by law. Perhaps the ancient disposition toward slavery exemplifies this possibility. For in the ancient world, slavery was typically regarded not as a justified practice but as a practice that required no justification.[52] The presence of slavery in social life was accepted by masters and slaves alike.[53] Such acceptance does not deny that slavery in the ancient world was often cruel, violent, and degrading. Yet among the Greeks, slavery

[50] Mandela, *Long Walk to Freedom: The Autobiography of Nelson Mandela* (London: Abacus, 2009), 609 ff.

[51] On the efforts to create such a public culture, see Albie Sachs, "South Africa's Unconstitutional Constitution: The Transition from Power to Lawful Power," *St. Louis University Law Journal* 41 (1997): 1252.

[52] Robert Schlaifer, "Greek Theories of Slavery from Homer to Aristotle," in *Slavery in Classical Antiquity: Views and Controversies*, ed. M.I. Finley (Cambridge: Heffer, 1964), 112: 'In the Homeric world slaves were simply accepted as facts.' Although slavery was overwhelmingly accepted in the ancient world, its acceptance was not unanimous. For example, when Aristotle canvasses opinions about slavery in his Politics, he refers to those who believe that 'the rule of a master over slaves is contrary to nature and that the distinction between slave and freeman exists by law only, and not by nature; and being an interference with nature is therefore unjust.' Alcidamas, a student of the sophist Gorgias, is known to have held this view, but it is not clear whether the view amounts to the claim that ancient slavery was barbarous. For discussion, see C.C.W. Taylor, "A Note on Ancient Attitudes Towards Slavery," *Analysis* 43 (1983): 40; Aristotle, "Politics," in Hippocrates G. Apostle and Lloyd P. Gerson, eds. and trans., *Selected Works* (Grinnell: The Peripatetic Press, 1991), 562. For a critical treatment of Aristotle's claim that slavery is natural, see Bernard Williams, *Shame and Necessity* (Berkeley: University of California Press, 2008), 103–29.

[53] William Linn Westermann, "Between Slavery and Freedom," *American Historical Review* 50 (1945): 215: 'The institution of slavery was a fact of ancient Mediterranean economic life so completely accepted as a part of the labor structure of the time that one cannot correctly speak of a slave "problem" in antiquity.'

was accepted as a fact that occasioned no 'moral horror.'[54] Among the Romans, 'those who made up the slave population, in all its diversity, were concerned with improving their lives as individuals or as members of small groups through whatever means of self-help they could find, so that it was personal, not collective, independence that was their object.'[55] In antiquity, slaves dreamt of a world in which they were masters rather than a world in which no one was a slave.[56] The ancient world contained many masters and many more slaves, but no abolitionists.[57] Of course, what is at issue here is the possible *legality* of slavery, not its conformity to the regulative principle apposite to either private or public law. From the standpoint of the unified theory, justice is not the condition of law's

[54] Westermann, "Slavery and the Elements of Freedom in Ancient Greece," in *Slavery in Classical Antiquity: Views and Controversies*, ed. M.I. Finley (Cambridge: Heffer, 1964), 32.

[55] Keith Bradley, *Slavery and Society in Rome* (Cambridge: Cambridge University Press, 1994), 130.

[56] David Brion Davis, *The Problem of Slavery in Western Culture* (Oxford: Oxford University Press, 1966), 62: '[F]rom the ancient world we find no assertion that slavery was an intolerable evil that should be eradicated by any civilized nation.'

In *The Class Struggle in the Ancient Greek World: From the Archaic Age to the Arab Conquests* (Ithaca: Cornell University Press, 1981), Ste. Croix sets out to explain and illustrate 'the value of Marx's general analysis of society in relation to the ancient Greek world.' While Ste. Croix provides a meticulous exposition of exploitation in the ancient world, it is not clear that he would disagree with the general way in which I have characterized the disposition toward slavery in the ancient world. When Ste. Croix invokes the term *class struggle*, he is explicit that the term includes the exploitation of classes and resistance toward exploitation, but need not involve any '*explicit common awareness of class* on either side, *no specifically political struggle* at all, and perhaps even *little consciousness of struggle* of any kind' (57 (emphasis in original); for similar passages, see 3, 44, 57, and 62–3). Ste. Croix provides an exposition of an exploitative practice, not of a practice that its participants regarded as exploitative, let alone incompatible with legality.

[57] The slave revolts in the ancient world are often misconceived as early abolition movements. For a succinct rebuttal, see Fábio Duarte Joly, "Spartacus Revolt," in *Encyclopedia of Antislavery and Abolition*, vol. II, ed. Peter Hinks, John McKivigan, and R. Owen Williams (Westport: Greenwood Press, 2007), 650–1: '[N]either Spartacus' revolt nor earlier slave rebellions in Sicily offered any critique of slavery as a social institution. The rebels led by Spartacus desired to leave Italy and return to their homelands. It was only in Europe in the eighteenth century as slave revolts erupted in European overseas colonies that Spartacus acquired the image of a revolutionary who had fought for universal freedom ... [Spartacus'] aim as a rebel slave-leader was not to abolish slavery, but to struggle to escape the life of a slave.' On this point, see also Bradley, *Slavery and Society in Rome*, 130: 'Rebelliousness, however, must not be confused with notions of class solidarity among slaves, and there is no indication that resistance was fuelled by ideological programmes rooted in the desire to secure radical alteration to the structure of society. There was certainly never anything at Rome comparable to the movement that led in St. Domingue to the creation of the state of Haiti.'

authority, but rather the standard for assessing its adequacy and directing its reform.

Third, recognizing the legality of slavery in ancient Greece and Rome does not entail recognizing its legality in the modern world. For slavery is not a monolithic institution with a uniform set of rights and duties, nor is its public meaning fixed. In its American incarnation, a racist form of chattel slavery operated in the shadow of a society committed to the self-evident enlightenment precepts of the *Declaration of Independence*.[58] In this context, slavery became increasingly recognized not as a mode of securing the rights and freedoms of each but as a paradigmatic instance of barbarism.[59] Frederick Douglass – who escaped slavery in the ante-bellum South and dedicated all his efforts to the 'great work of renovating the public mind, and building up a public sentiment, which should send slavery to the grave'[60] – regarded American slavery as 'a system of lawless violence' that '*never was lawful, and never can be made so* . . . '[61] Yet, Douglass also emphasized that

> [t]he idea that man cannot hold property in man, that all men are free, that human rights are inalienable, that the rights of one man are equal to those of another, that governments are ordained to secure human rights did not come all at once to the moral conscience of men, but have all come very slowly in the thoughts of the world.[62]

Fourth, even on those occasions in which a shared understanding obtains with respect to the general limits of legality within a public culture, disagreement may still remain about whether the threshold between legality and barbarism has been crossed.[63] Such ambiguity is

[58] See, for example, Thomas Paine, "African Slavery in America," 8 March 1775, *Pennsylvania Journal and the Weekly Advertiser*; and James Madison, *Records of the Federal Convention*, vol. 1, ed. Max Farrand (New Haven, Yale University Press, 1966), 135: 'We have seen the mere distinction of colour made in the most enlightened period of time, a ground of the most oppressive dominion ever exercised by man over man.'

[59] William Freehling, *The Road to Disunion: Secessionists at Bay: 1776–1854* (Oxford: Oxford University Press 1990), 124.

[60] Douglass, *Life and Times of Frederick Douglass* (New York: Cosimo, 2008), 277.

[61] "Change of Opinion Announced," May 23, 1851, *The North Star*, Reprinted in *The Liberator* (emphasis in original). See also, Douglass, "The Address of Southern Delegates in Congress to their Constituents or, the address of John C. Calhoun and Forty Other Thieves," February 9, 1849. Douglass came to conceive of American slavery as a lawless arrangement in a valid legal order.

[62] Frederick Douglass, quoted in Waldo E. Martin Jr., *The Mind of Frederick Douglass* (Chapel Hill: University of North Carolina Press, 1984), 172.

[63] For a similar discussion of ambiguities surrounding legislative limits in Lockean political philosophy, see Jeremy Waldron, *The Dignity of Legislation* (Cambridge: Cambridge

unavoidable because no public institution can provide a common authoritative judgment for all private persons indicating that they occupy a lawless condition in which public authority is absent.

Fifth, even in cases in which the legality of a critical aspect of legal ordering becomes suspect in the eyes of its public culture, it does not necessarily follow that private persons have a right to overthrow the regime in which it arises. Since private persons have a duty to submit to public authority, no one can have a right to overthrow a legal order because it contains features that would be present in any legal system that was established in its place.[64]

Sixth, the presence of a shared basis of justification does not ensure that justifications that emerge from it will arise within a fully coherent set of ideas. A public culture may contain internal inconsistencies in which the justifications offered for some institutional arrangement conflict with the justifications accepted for others.[65] In *The Subjection of Women*, John Stuart Mill criticizes his own society for failing to realize the systematic implications of its own animating principle:

> [W]hat is the peculiar character of the modern world – the difference which chiefly distinguishes modern institutions, modern social ideas, modern life itself, from those of times long past? It is that human beings are no longer born to their place in life, and chained down by an inexorable bond to the place they are born to, but are free to employ their faculties, and such favorable chances as offer, to achieve the lot which may appear to them most desirable. Human society of old was constituted on a very different principle. All were born to a fixed social position, and were mostly kept in it by law, or interdicted from any means by which they could emerge from it.[66]

University Press, 1999), 84: '[L]ocating the sense of legislative limits in political culture rather than in an authoritative institution means that we are left with the prospect of disagreement, indeterminacy, controversy among the people as to what those limits are. People will disagree about what it is for the legislature to betray its trust, or even if they agree in the abstract they will disagree about when this has happened.'

64 In the ancient world, slavery was a form of social organization for which there was no apparent alternative. See Peter Garnsey, *Ideas of Slavery from Aristotle to Augustine*, 238: 'In antebellum America, the existence of a rival free-labour system to the North forced the slave-owning South to defend itself and its way of life, first with argument, and ultimately with weapons . . . Persia and Egypt were the most advanced neighbouring civilizations of the Graeco-Roman (and Jewish) world, but they were judged to be more completely slave societies than those of the Greeks and Romans: everyone was a slave in Persia apart from the King, everyone in Egypt apart from the Pharoah. These societies lacked political institutions and the fundamental concepts of citizenship and freedom.'

65 Rawls, *Political Liberalism*, 9: 'The public political culture may be of two minds at a very deep level.'

66 John Stuart Mill, *The Subjection of Women* (New York: Dover, 1997), 16.

Although Mill accepts the fundamental conviction of the prevailing public culture, he rejects the piecemeal way in which his society has applied it. Mill sees the subjection of women as a 'monstrous contradiction to all the principles of the modern world.'[67] His aim is to spur the development of his own public culture by showing the systematic implications of its fundamental conviction. Persons who share a public culture have a common frame of reference, but may fail to consistently discern its implications.

The principle of authority is both universal and particular. It is universal because it requires private persons in all times and places to interact with one another in a legal order, that is, a condition that secures the freedom of each from the arbitrary power of every other. It is particular because the concrete meaning of this injunction is relative to local understandings, interpretations, and judgments regarding what it means to be secure from the arbitrary power of others. The principle of authority is a universal norm with variable ramifications.

I close this section by contrasting the account of barbarism that emerges from the unified theory with the account that Fuller defends. In his famous debate with H.L.A. Hart, Fuller remarked, 'To me there is nothing shocking in saying that a dictatorship which clothes itself with a tinsel of legal form can so far depart from the morality of order, from the inner morality of law itself, that it ceases to be a legal system.'[68] Fuller conceives of law as 'the enterprise of subjecting human conduct to the governance of rules.'[69] In order to subject human conduct to the governance of rules, rules must possess certain moral qualities. As Fuller explains, to govern conduct a legal rule must, at least to some extent, be (1) general, (2) public, (3) prospective, (4) clear, (5) noncontradictory, (6) possible to obey, (7) constant in time, and (8) congruent with official action.[70] These procedural principles form what Fuller calls the *internal morality of law*. A law or legal system is valid to the extent that it satisfies law's internal morality.

The unified theory contrasts with Fuller's conception of legality in two respects. First, from the standpoint of the unified theory, the principle of authority is a binary norm. It forms the relevant standpoint for distinguishing between the validity and invalidity of a legal system or a particular law. In a valid legal order, all private persons are under a

[67] Ibid., 79.

[68] "Positivism and Fidelity to Law – A Reply to Professor Hart," *Harvard Law Review* 71 (1958): 660.

[69] Ibid., 106. [70] Fuller, *The Morality of Law*, 39.

duty to obey all valid laws. In a lawless condition, private persons are under a duty to enter into a condition of public law in which public institutions secure private rights. The validity of laws and legal systems does not admit of degree. Turning from the constitutive to the regulative dimension of public law, considerations of public justice arise on a spectrum: a law or legal system may conform to its own internal standard of adequacy to a greater or lesser extent. Thus, one can sensibly say, "This law is somewhat unjust," but one can neither say, "This law is somewhat invalid" nor "This action is somewhat illegal." Fuller runs these standpoints together by framing the question of validity, of whether a law or a legal system exists, in terms of a spectrum of aspiration.[71] The more a legal system (or a particular law) conforms to the procedural morality that is internal to law, the more it can be said to exist. In Fuller's words, 'both rules of law and legal systems can and do half exist.'[72] The difficulty that this structure raises is that Fuller both conceives of law in terms of subjecting human conduct to the governance of rules *and* suggests that the validity of law diminishes to the extent that it fails to accommodate law's internal morality. In existing societies, in which one or more of the eight principles that form the internal morality of law are not fully satisfied, it is not clear whether a given norm or legal system possesses sufficient validity to bind human conduct. When confronted by the implication of his view that the validity of laws and legal systems admits of degree, Fuller emphasizes that legal systems, like any 'other complex human undertaking' may enjoy 'varying degrees of success.'[73] While I agree with Fuller that law has a regulative dimension, his attempt to capture law's constitutive and regulative dimensions on a single plane is problematic. Within Fuller's framework, the sensible claim that a particular law is not fully congruent with the internal morality of law culminates in the strange conclusions that the law is therefore only somewhat valid and its violation is therefore only somewhat prohibited.

The second difference concerns the kinds of practices that are barbarous. For Fuller, the internal morality of law is exclusively procedural.[74] Its concern is 'not with the substantive aims of legal rules, but with the ways in

[71] Ibid., 43 and 198–200. [72] Ibid., 122. [73] Ibid.; cf. 198–200.

[74] Although Fuller presents his internal morality of law as a *procedural* view, the term *formal* perhaps better captures his view. On this point, see Jeremy Waldron, "Positivism and Legality: Hart's Equivocal Response to Fuller," *New York University Law Review* 83 (2008): 1145 (distinguishing between the *form* of a legal norm and the relevant *procedure* for applying that norm); and David Dyzenhaus, *Hard Cases in Wicked Legal Systems: Pathologies of Legality* (Oxford: Oxford University Press, 2010), 251–2.

which a system of rules for governing human conduct must be constructed and administered if it is to be efficacious and at the same time remain what it purports to be.'[75] Accordingly, Fuller may deny partial (or even full) legality to practices that conflict with one or more of the procedural principles that he articulates. But in cases in which these procedural principles are fully satisfied, no objection can be raised from the standpoint of the internal morality of law. Thus, Fuller explains that the internal morality of law has 'nothing to say' about particular substantive aims that law might promote or alleviate, such as the 'subjugation of women.'[76] Because Fuller's ideal of legality is exclusively procedural,[77] he must hold that a condition in which some are subjugated to others might be not only a valid legal order but also one that fully satisfies the internal morality of law. By contrast, the unified theory conceives of barbarism as an arrangement that fails to secure independence between persons and so subjects the freedom of one or more persons to the arbitrary power of another. Such a conception of barbarism is not confined to gross violations of the procedural requirements that Fuller elaborates. A norm or condition might fully satisfy each of Fuller's procedural principles of legality and yet nevertheless fail to be valid because it subjugates the freedom of some persons to the arbitrary power of others.

3.4 The barbarism of Nazi power

In assessing the legality of Nazi power, theorists sometimes suggest that while its barbarism is apparent from the standpoint of our own public culture, its legality was equally apparent from the standpoint of its own public culture.[78] Although persecuted persons certainly recognized the barbarism of Nazi power,[79] such persons did not partake of the general

[75] Fuller, *The Morality of Law*, 97. [76] Ibid., 96.

[77] For an argument that Fuller's procedural principles of legality condition the content of enacted laws, see David Dyzenhaus, *Hard Cases in Wicked Legal Systems: Pathologies of Legality* (Oxford: Oxford University Press, 2010).

[78] See, for example, Dworkin, *Law's Empire* (Cambridge: Harvard University Press, 1986), 103–4.

[79] See Klemperer, *I Will Bear Witness: A Diary of the Nazi Years (1933–1941)*, trans. Martin Chalmers (New York: Random House, 1988), 12 ('In [World War One] I was subject to [German] military law, but subject to law nevertheless; now I am at the mercy of an arbitrary power . . . '), and 406, ('[T]oday there is no law in Germany anymore, only arbitrary power, there is also no equality anymore before arbitrary power, the Aryan pays, the Jew does time . . . '). Klemperer made the former comment in 1933 and the latter in 1941.

German public culture, which was compatible with Nazism, or, worse still, affirmed its legality.[80] In this section, I suggest that the barbarism of Nazi power was evident not merely from the standpoint of the persecuted (or from the liberal standpoint of a contemporary rights-based public culture), but that it was barbarous from the standpoint of the general German public culture. To be sure, Germany's public culture – like those of its European neighbors – displayed extraordinary prejudice toward the Jews and other persecuted minorities. But as Nazi power increasingly repudiated accepted hallmarks of legality, ordinary Germans came to recognize Nazism not as an arrangement that secured each person from the arbitrary power of others, but as an arbitrary power to which all were subject. Given the theoretical orientation of this chapter, I will not attempt to isolate the particular historical moment at which Nazism became a lawless power.

In *The Law under the Swastika*, the German legal historian Michael Stolleis rejects 'the myth that some areas [of law] remained entirely untouched by the political claims of the [Nazi] system.'[81] Earlier I

[80] The most well-known proponent of this thesis is Daniel Jonah Goldhagen, *Hitler's Willing Executioners: Ordinary Germans and the Holocaust* (New York: Alfred A. Knopf, 1996), 14: '[T]he perpetrators, "ordinary Germans," were animated by antisemitism, by a particular *type* of antisemitism that led them to conclude that the Jews *ought to die.*' For Goldhagen, at the core of Germany's public culture lay a distinctive genocidal strand of anti-Semitism that induced ordinary Germans to participate in systematic slaughter. Goldhagen's thesis has been decisively refuted by Holocaust historians. For overviews of the controversy between Goldhagen and his critics, see A.D. Moses, "Structure and Agency in the Holocaust: Daniel J. Goldhagen and His Critics," *History and Theory* 37 (1998): 194–9; and István Deák, "Holocaust Views: The Goldhagen Controversy in Retrospect," *Central European History* 30 (1997): 295–307.

If Nazi barbarism cannot be attributed to a peculiarly virulent strain of German anti-Semitism, as Goldhagen alleges, then why did so many ordinary Germans participate in genocide? In *Ordinary Men: Reserve Battalion 101 and the Final Solution in Poland* (New York: HarperPerennial, 1993), Christopher Browning constructs a more nuanced account. Ordinary Germans participated in the genocide for a series of reasons of varying weight: careerism, deference to authority, the circumstances of war, dehumanization of the victims, anti-Semitic propaganda, and the pressure to conform to the group. Whereas Goldhagen traces genocide to a virulent strain of anti-Semitism peculiar to Germany's public culture, Browning emphasizes general psychological and sociological phenomena common to all human beings. Historians prefer Browning's explanation because it sheds light on why soldiers from across Europe who were not socialized in Germany were so willing to participate in violent acts against Jews as well as members of other groups and why German soldiers were, at least initially, hesitant to do so. Browning's explanation, however, is deeply disturbing because it suggests that under the appropriate circumstances, human beings are capable of committing barbarous acts.

[81] Stolleis, *The Law under the Swastika: Studies on Legal History in Nazi Germany*, trans. Thomas Dunlap (Chicago: University of Chicago Press, 1998), 9 [hereinafter: *The Law under the Swastika*].

illustrated Ebbinghaus's account of inhumanity with a discussion of how Nazism distorted private law by resolving private disputes on the basis of the racial identity of the disputants. Nazi power, however, did not merely subject the freedom of German Jews to the arbitrary power of German non-Jews. Nazism rejected private law itself as liberal, individualistic, Roman, and Jewish and sought to replace it with its own German brand of fascism.[82] Consequently, even the legal disputes among German non-Jews were to be resolved in accordance with the perceived requirements of Nazi ideology. As the German-born political scientist and constitutional theorist Karl Loewenstein observed in 1936,

> The first principle of free access to the ordinary courts is to a large extent repudiated by the National Socialist regime. During the first two years of the regime numerous breaches of the existing civil law were committed in forcing the new political order on business life. Obligations of contract, vested rights, the right to dispose freely of property, were superseded by political coordination. Legal titles were voided and property confiscated under the pressure of party members and officials. The courts, invoked for redress of grievances, or for damages, were frequently bound to decide, according to existing laws, in favor of the dispossessed claimants. As such action taken by the courts threatened to frustrate the political results of the revolution in business life, a law of December 13, 1934, empowered the Minister of the Interior at his discretion to withdraw all civil claims from the ordinary courts even after they had become *res judicata*, and to settle them in the interests of the state without permitting appeal. The effect of the law was to deprive private individuals of the right to bring their cases before the ordinary courts. Compensation for damages incurred through the revolution became a matter of arbitrary decision of the ministry.[83]

By subjecting all private interaction to the impulses of Nazi ideology, Nazism displaced familiar features of private law, including the rights of property and contract, the right to bring one's case before an impartial judiciary, and the right to a remedy proportional to the wrong.[84] Persons were thereby denied a stable and calculable order in which to interact with one another.[85]

Just as Nazism sought to remove the constraints that legality imposed on private interaction, so too Nazism ignored or dismantled any legal arrangement that constrained the conduct of power. As a matter of criminal law, the Nazi regime meted out punishment for the violation of secret, vague, and retrospective laws, separated the notion of a wrong

[82] Ibid., 51.
[83] Karl Loewenstein, "Law in the Third Reich," *Yale Law Journal* 45 (1936): 807.
[84] Ibid., 782. [85] Ibid., 780.

from an action, and, as early as 1934, engaged in the widespread murder of political opponents without criminal sanction.[86] As a matter of administrative law, the regime routinely denied the jurisdiction of administrative courts to review police action.[87] Finally, as a matter of constitutional law the Nazis transformed the parliamentary system into a dictatorship, disbanded the political parties through terror, violated the separation of powers by ruling through executive decree, purified the civil service of perceived political opponents and racial inferiors, and brought an end to German federalism (even though this violated the constitution).[88]

Enrst Fraenkel famously characterized Nazi governance in terms of a tension between, on the one hand, the normative state directed toward safeguarding the legal order through statutes, judicial decisions, and administrative oversight, and, on the other, the prerogative state consisting of 'unlimited arbitrariness and violence unchecked by any legal guarantees.'[89] As Nazism increasingly divested itself of all legal constraints on the exercise of power, the dual character of Nazi governance collapsed into a merely prerogative state that retained a single aspect of legality, force.[90] What the Nazis called *law* was an instrument through which power could be exercised but that recognized no constraints on the exercise of power. The result was that the exercise of power failed to adhere to public law's constitutive dimension. Power was not generally directed toward securing the freedom of each private person from the arbitrary power of others.

The refusal to recognize the limits of legality culminated in the violence that characterized the Nazi years.

To be sure, the German public culture in that time was certainly anti-Semitic, but its anti-Semitism did not underwrite the most extreme acts of Nazi violence. Holocaust historians distinguish between the traditional anti-Semitism prevalent in Germany and other European states, and the

86 Stolleis, *The Law under the Swastika*, 2 and 20. On the Nazi distortions of criminal law – including the use of retroactive laws, punishment by analogy, and the abandonment of the fundamental criminal law principle *nullum crimen sine legal, nulla poëna sine lege* – see Henry Lunau, "The Threat of Nazi Law to All Fundamental Legal Principles," *Proceedings of the American Foreign Law Association* 23 (1942): 6.

87 Stolleis, *The Law under the Swastika*, 2 and 134. On the unlimited power of the police to bypass judicial oversight, see van Caenegem, *An Historical Introduction to Western Constitutional Law*, 289.

88 Stolleis, *The Law under the Swastika*, 12.

89 Fraenkel, *The Dual State: A Contribution to the Theory of Dictatorship*, xiii.

90 Stolleis, *The Law under the Swastika*, 13.

radical brand of anti-Semitism that fuelled Nazi violence. As Claudia Koonz explains,

> Seen against the enormity of Nazi savagery, it is easy to imagine that German collaborators in persecution shared the seething paranoia of Adolf Hitler and his closest comrades. Extreme outcomes, it would seem, must result from extreme beliefs. But careful investigation of public opinion in Nazi Germany reveal that, while most Germans shared the "polite" or "cultured" anti-Semitism common in Western Europe and North America, they disapproved of diehard Nazis' coarse racist diatribes and pogrom-style tactics.[91]

This distinction between Germany's cultured anti-Semitism and Nazi ideology is echoed by Saul Friedländer and Ian Kershaw. Friedländer notes that the prevailing culture of anti-Semitism legitimated economic and social forms of discrimination, but maintains that the majority of Germans 'shied away from widespread violence against [Jews], urging neither their expulsion from the Reich nor their physical annihilation.'[92] Similarly, Ian Kershaw emphasizes that the culture of anti-Semitism was sympathetic to discrimination but not to violence:

> Very many, probably most, Germans were opposed to the Jews during the Third Reich, welcomed their exclusion from the economy and society, saw them as natural outsiders to the German "National Community", a dangerous minority against who it was legitimate to discriminate. Most would have drawn the line at physical maltreatment. The Nazi Mayor of Mainstockheim . . . no doubt spoke for many when, in preventing violence and destruction by SA and Party fanatics during the pogrom of November 1938, he reportedly said: "You don't have to have anything to do with the Jews. But you have got to leave them in peace." Such an attitude was not violent. But it was discriminatory. And such "mild" anti-Semitism was clearly quite incapable of containing the progressive radical dynamism of the racial fanatics and deadly bureaucratization of the doctrine of race-hatred.[93]

91 *The Nazi Conscience*, 11.

92 *Nazi Germany and the Jews: The Years of Persecution, 1933–1939*, vol. I (New York: Harper Collins Publishers, 1997), 3–4.

93 *Popular Opinion and Political Dissent in the Third Reich: Bavaria 1933–1945* (Oxford: Oxford University Press, 1983), 371. See also Saul Friedländer, "From Anti-Semitism to Extermination: An Historiographical Study of Nazi Policies Toward the Jews and an Essay in Interpretation," *Yad Vashem Studies* 16 (1984): 33; and especially Richard J. Evans, *The Third Reich in History and Memory* (Oxford: Oxford University Press, 2015), 116–17: 'Both in the pogrom of November 1938 and later on, during the war, the majority of people, rather than being indifferent, disapproved of violence and murder towards the Jews. But they felt unable to do anything concrete because of fear of this violence being

As the Nazi program transitioned from discrimination to mass murder, the Nazis increasingly concealed their activity. The reason why the Nazis chose to carry out their most extreme acts of violence in secrecy was that they were aware that the public would be appalled by their actions.[94] When it became known that 70,000 disabled persons had been gassed in the Nazi euthanasia program, 'public disquiet' erupted.[95] The program was subsequently cancelled because the '"German people" was not yet "mature" enough for this kind of inner self-cleansing. It simply was not progressive enough yet to surrender responsibility for the apparently quite conservative dimensions of the social right of existence to a handful of scientifically prominent experts.'[96] Nevertheless, before the end of the war, a further 70,000 patients were killed through a covert program involving 'starvation, drugs, and neglect.'[97]

Following the leak of the euthanasia program, Hitler sought to keep the extermination of the Jews 'absolutely secret.'[98] The systematic slaughter of European Jewry was executed 'without the German people being told and without any legislative text being issued.'[99] The order to exterminate issued from an oral command delivered by Hitler, most likely, to Goering, Himmler, and Heydrich.[100] In a letter dated July 11, 1943, Bormann – the Head of the Nazi Party – wrote that the Führer demanded that '[w]here the Jewish Question is brought up in public, there may be

turned against themselves by the regime and its agents, because of fear of arrest and prosecution, or sanctions of other kinds ... What we have to recognise in this context, hard though it may be, is the absolute centrality of violence, coercion and terror to the theory and practice of German National Socialism from the very outset ... It is impossible to understand the terror vented by the Nazis upon people in the regions they conquered ... and upon the Jews across the whole of the occupied areas of the Continent, unless we grasp the fact that they had already vented it upon large sectors of their own people before 1939: and not merely on despised and tiny minorities of social outcasts, but on millions of their fellow citizens, indeed at one level or another, to one degree or another, on the great majority of them.'

94 For an account of the difficulties that the Nazis encountered in gauging public opinion in the repressive environment they created, see Aryeh L. Unger, "The Public Opinion Reports of the Nazi Party," *The Public Opinion Quarterly* 29 (1966): 565.

95 Arthur L. Caplan in "How Did Nazi Medicine go so Wrong?" in *When Medicine Went Mad: Bioethics and the Holocaust*, ed. Caplan (New Jersey: Humana Press, 1992), 85.

96 Götz Aly and Karl Heinz Roth, "The Legalization of Mercy Killings in Medical and Nursing Institutions in Nazi Germany from 1939 until 1941," *International Journal of Law and Psychiatry* 7 (1985): 162.

97 Caplan, "How Did Nazi Medicine go so Wrong?" 87.

98 Friedländer, "From Anti-Semitism to Extermination: An Historiographical Study of Nazi Policies Toward the Jews and an Essay in Interpretation," 13.

99 Van Caenegem, *An Historical Introduction to Western Constitutional Law*, 290.

100 Ibid.

no discussion of a future overall solution (*Gesamtlösung*).'[101] Similarly, in a secret speech delivered to the elite SS Gruppenführer on October 4, 1943, Himmler insisted that the SS must not discuss the extermination of the Jews: 'This was an unwritten and never to be written page in our history.'[102] In a subsequent speech to state and district leaders that occurred days later, Himmler lamented that even 'respectable and decent National Socialist people all know their decent Jew.'[103] If the number of petitions submitted to Nazi authorities was any indication, Himmler suggested that there must have been more decent Jews in Germany than the number of Jews in the whole country. The disposition of the public toward Nazi violence necessitated the secrecy of the extermination program.[104] In Ernst Fraenkel's words, Nazism sustained itself 'by veiling its true nature.'[105]

The barbarism of Nazi power was evident in relation to the public culture that prevailed in Germany during the decline of the Weimar Republic and extended into the Nazi years. In a 1951 case, Germany's Supreme Federal Court considered whether those who organized and carried out the deportation of Jews to death camps in Poland had aided and abetted murder. Although a lower court held that the mens rea of the offense had not been established because it was the duty of the accused to perform government policies, the Supreme Federal Court held that the lower court had erred because the authority of the state is not unlimited. The court supported this statement by appealing to 'certain maxims of human conduct regarded as inviolable which in the course of time have

[101] "Hitler Bans Public Reference to the 'Final Solution of the Jewish Question,' July 11, 1943," in *Documents on the Holocaust: Selected Sources on the Destruction of the Jews of Germany and Austria, Poland, and the Soviet Union*, ed. Yitzhak Arad, Israel Gutman, and Abraham Margaliot, trans. Lea Ben Dor (Lincoln: University of Nebraska Press, 1999), 342.

[102] Richard Breitman, "Secrecy and the Final Solution," in *New Perspectives on the Holocaust*, ed. Rochelle L. Millen (New York: New York University Press, 1996), 78. See also, Kershaw, *Popular Opinion and Political Dissent in the Third Reich: Bavaria 1933–1945*, 371: 'Our examination of popular opinion on the Jewish Question has shown that in its anti-Jewish policies the Nazi regime acted not in plebiscitary fashion, but with increasing autonomy from popular opinion until the extermination policy in the east was carried out by the SS and SD as a "never to be written glorious page of our history," as Himmler put it . . . '

[103] Himmler, "A Secret Speech on the Jewish Question," in *The Jew in the Modern World*, ed. Paul R. Mendes-Flohr and Jehuda Reinharz (Oxford: Oxford University Press, 1995), 514.

[104] Kershaw, *Popular Opinion and Political Dissent in the Third Reich: Bavaria 1933–1945*, 371.

[105] Fraenkel, *The Dual State: A Contribution to the Theory of Dictatorship*, 39.

come to be recognized by all civilized nations on the basis of common ideas of morality and which are held to be legally obligatory, regardless of whether the laws of some particular nation permit them to be disregarded.'[106] State power lacks the authority to violate fundamental normative principles by authorizing arbitrary arrest and deportation. The court went on to argue that the defendants must have been aware of the limits of state power given the public culture in which they were socialized. Edgar Bodenheimer summarized the judgment of the court: 'It cannot be assumed . . . that the defendants, all of whom had received their education and moral upbringing in the period preceding National Socialist rule, were unaware of these general principles basic to human life in society.'[107] Having been socialized in a decent democratic society, knowledge of these principles could be imputed to the defendants.

On another occasion, the court engaged in detailed historical analysis to demonstrate that ordinary citizens understood Nazism to be a lawless power.[108] In a well-known case involving a grudge informer who denounced her husband to the Nazi authorities so that she could continue her adulterous relationships, both the Supreme Court and a jury accepted as a 'matter of common knowledge' that

> [t]here was, despite the warped judgment of wide circles during the Nazi period, a lively awareness in the population that administrative and legal authority could be abused for the purpose of intimidation and suppression of opposition views. Sentences, which served the purpose of political terror rather than the realisation of the law, had actually led to a heightened popular sense of right and wrong rather than stifling it.[109]

As Nazism increasingly jettisoned every right, principle, institutional arrangement, and, in general, every legal constraint by which persons could distinguish lawful power from the mere imposition of lawless violence, the arbitrary character of its power became increasingly apparent. Instead of securing each person from the arbitrary power of all others, Nazism had itself become a lawless power to which all were subject. I have suggested that the barbarism of Nazism was evident from the standpoint of the actual public culture in which it arose.

[106] Edgar Bodenheimer, "Significant Developments in German Legal Philosophy since 1945," *American Journal of Comparative Law* 3 (1954): 390 (quoting from BGSt 2, 237 (1951)).

[107] Ibid., 391.

[108] H.O. Pappe, "On the Validity of Judicial Decisions in the Nazi Era," *Modern Law Review* 23 (1960): 273.

[109] Ibid., 267–8.

Turning from actuality to possibility, one might ask whether Nazism *could* be lawful. In other words, could there be a public culture so constituted that it might deem the practices characteristic of Nazism to be a lawful mode of securing the freedom of each private person from the arbitrary power of every other? It is difficult to conceive of a public culture in which persons would understand the extinguishment of their capacity for rights, the imputation of wrongs that bear no relation to their conduct, and ultimately their own systematic extermination as a way of securing their freedom from the arbitrary power of others. Throughout this chapter, I have drawn attention to various historical examples involving societies that draw the distinction between lawful and arbitrary power in different ways. Socrates denied that one could have a legal obligation to participate in the murder of an innocent person; Caligula's supposed subjects denied that secret laws could impose obligations; and Frederick Douglass rejected the legality of racial chattel slavery in the antebellum South. As Nazism shook off every vestige of legality except force, its violence ran afoul of each of these standards. The barbarism of Nazi power would therefore be evident not simply in the context of the public culture in which it arose – a modern European state with a sophisticated albeit prejudiced public culture – but also in a diverse array of public cultures scattered across the distances of space and time.

Conclusion

The unified theory provides an alternative to the prevailing tendency in conceptualizing the distinction between legality and barbarism. Radbruch, Alexy, and Fuller conceive of barbarism as a departure from the regulative ideal of legality, whether conceived of in terms of justice as the equal treatment of equals, a claim to moral correctness, or as the aspirational principles that make up the internal morality of law. By contrast, I have presented the distinction between legality and barbarism in terms of the violation of public law's constitutive principle rather than its regulative one. Such an approach provides the resources to vindicate two theses that each of these thinkers endorse: public authority must be obeyed, but there are limits to what can be publicly authoritative.

4

Toward public justice

One of the defining features of contemporary political and legal philosophy is its progressive aspiration. Whereas earlier theories sought *either* to justify the adequacy of existing societies *or* to formulate the nature of a perfectly just one, contemporary theorists seek to articulate a framework for thinking about how existing societies can be brought into ever-deeper conformity with the demands of justice. This chapter explores how a theory must be structured to make good on this progressive aspiration.

A progressive theory must integrate three components into a coherent whole: (1) an underlying subject, for example political societies or legal systems; (2) a moral standard for critically assessing the adequacy of instances of the underlying subject, that is, a conception of justice; and (3) a framework for articulating what is required of instances of the underlying subject that are defective in relation to the relevant moral standard. Each of these components is indispensable. In the absence of an underlying subject, the theory would fail to delineate a domain of inquiry. In the absence of a moral standard, the theory would lack a standpoint for determining the adequacy of instances of the underlying subject and assessing whether alternative arrangements would be preferable. Finally, in the absence of a framework that articulates what is required of defective instances of the underlying subject, the theory would offer no guidance for thinking about how the defects that it identifies are to be addressed.

That a progressive theory must integrate these kinds of components might seem obvious. However, I will argue that the leading theories in political and legal philosophy fail to provide an integrated account of these components, and, consequently, cannot make good on their progressive aspiration. While a variety of theories could be canvassed, I will confine my remarks to what I take to be the leading paradigms in political and legal philosophy: John Rawls's justice as fairness and H.L.A. Hart's legal positivism, respectively. Once the difficulties that these theories encounter are in view, I present the unified theory of public law in terms of the components that make up a progressive theory. Finally,

I defend the unified theory from a series of objections that target the relationship between the abstract conception of justice that it affirms and the particularity of the legal systems to which it applies.

A note of clarification is in order before I begin. Philosophic theories that invoke the notion of progress are often accused of harboring a naïve belief in its inevitability.[1] This chapter does not offer a philosophy of history that looks for patterns in the past to make predictions about the future, but an exploration of an approach to legal and political philosophy rooted in the view that the 'limits of the possible are not given by the actual, for we can to a greater or lesser extent change political and social institutions, and much else.'[2] On the view that I will defend, progress is conceived of 'not as an inevitable sequence of improvements but as aspiration and compelling obligation.'[3]

4.1 Rawls on ideal and nonideal theory

At first glance, justice as fairness seems to fulfill the tripartite structure of a progressive theory. The underlying subject of justice as fairness is the *basic structure* of a modern constitutional democracy. The conception of justice appropriate for the basic structure is set out in what Rawls calls *ideal theory*. Lastly, the transitional framework for reforming defective instances of the basic structure forms a corresponding *nonideal theory*. In what follows, I briefly unpack each of these components, as presented in *Justice as Fairness: A Restatement*, and argue that the *relationship* between these components raises a critical difficulty that undercuts the progressive orientation of the theory.

The first component, the basic structure of a well-ordered society, is the 'primary subject' of justice as fairness and its unifying idea.[4] The

[1] See, for example, Bertrand Russell, *Unpopular Essays* (New York: Routledge, 2009), 9. For a defense of Enlightenment thinkers from this accusation, see Jonathan Israel, *A Revolution of the Mind: Radical Enlightenment and the Intellectual Origins of Modern Democracy* (Princeton: Princeton University Press, 2009), 3–4 (arguing that the widespread criticism of Enlightenment naïvety about human perfectibility is a 'complete myth conjured up by early twentieth-century scholars unsympathetic to [Enlightenment] claims'); and Susan Neiman, *Moral Clarity: A Guide for Grown-up Idealists* (New York: Harcourt, 2008), 120 (suggesting that what unites Enlightenment thinkers is not the acceptance of the view that progress is inevitable, but the rejection of the view that stagnation and regress are inescapable).

[2] Rawls, *Justice as Fairness: A Restatement* (Cambridge: Harvard University Press, 2001), 5.

[3] Gabriel A. Almond, Marvin Chodorow, and Roy Harvey Pearce, "Progress and Its Discontents," *Bulletin of the American Academy of Arts and Sciences* 35 (1981): 23.

[4] *Justice as Fairness*, 10.

basic structure 'is the way in which the main political and social institutions of society fit together into one system of social cooperation, and the way they assign basic rights and duties and regulate the division of advantages that arises from social cooperation over time.'[5] Justice as fairness focuses on the basic structure because of the deep and wide-ranging impact that a system of coercive institutions that assigns rights and duties and that allocates advantages and disadvantages has on the lives of citizens, from their attitudes and aspirations to their prospects and opportunities.[6]

The second component, *ideal theory*, sets out the conception of justice that is to regulate the basic structure of a well-ordered society. Rawls arrives at this conception by appealing to the

> public political culture of a democratic society, and to the traditions and interpretations of its constitution and basic laws, for certain familiar ideas that can be worked up into a conception of political justice. It is assumed that citizens in a democratic society have at least an implicit understanding of these ideas as shown in everyday political discussion, in debates about the meaning and ground of constitutional rights and liberties, and the like.[7]

The public political culture is a 'fund of implicitly shared ideas and principles'[8] that is latent in the basic structure of a constitutional regime and interpreted by the judiciary, political parties, statesmen, and jurists.[9] These include the idea of society as a fair system of intergenerational social cooperation and its companion ideas of citizens as free and equal persons engaged in social cooperation and of a well-ordered society in which the basic structure is regulated by a public conception of justice.[10] Rawls formulates justice as fairness as the answer to a question raised by the presence of the fundamental ideas that characterize a modern constitutional democracy. If we acknowledge that society is a fair system of social cooperation between free and equal citizens, what would it mean for society to be well-ordered?[11]

The final component, *nonideal theory*, concerns the realization of the aim formulated in ideal theory:

> Non-ideal theory asks how this long-term goal might be achieved, or worked toward, usually in gradual steps. It looks for policies and courses of action that are morally permissible and politically possible as well as

[5] Ibid., 10; *Political Liberalism* (New York: Columbia University Press, 1996), 11.
[6] *Justice as Fairness*, 10. [7] Ibid., 5. [8] *Political Liberalism*, 14.
[9] *Justice as Fairness*, 5–6 and 19. [10] Ibid., 5 and 25. [11] Ibid., 39.

> likely to be effective. So conceived, non-ideal theory presupposes that ideal theory is already on hand. For until the ideal is identified . . . non-ideal theory lacks an object, an aim, by reference to which its queries can be answered.[12]

Rawls divides nonideal theory into two subparts, each of which corresponds to an assumption within his ideal theory.[13] The assumption of strict compliance – that persons and institutions act in conformity with the obligations set out by justice as fairness – gives rise to a branch of nonideal theory concerned with partial or noncompliance. The assumption of favorable conditions – that historical, social, and economic conditions are conducive to the realization of a well-ordered society – yields a branch of nonideal theory responsive to the unfavorable conditions that frustrate the pursuit of a well-ordered society.

Although Rawls pioneered and popularized the distinction between ideal and nonideal theory, he did not develop a nonideal theory of domestic justice.[14] In *A Theory of Justice*, Rawls acknowledges that the problems of nonideal theory are 'pressing and urgent,' but confines his discussion almost entirely to ideal theory because it provides 'the only basis for the systematic grasp of these more pressing problems.'[15] Reflecting on that work, Rawls wrote, 'The serious problems arising from existing discrimination and distinctions on gender and race are not on its agenda, which is to present certain principles of justice and then to check them against only a few of the classical problems of political justice as these would be settled within ideal theory.'[16] When Rawls considers nonideal theory, he focuses on nonideal principles appropriate for private individuals rather than public officials.[17] Rawls all but ignores the distinction between ideal and nonideal theory in *Political Liberalism*,[18] and *The Law of Peoples* confines its extensive discussion

[12] Rawls, *The Law of Peoples* (Cambridge: Harvard University Press, 1999), 89–90.

[13] On the subparts of nonideal theory, see Rawls, *A Theory of Justice* (Cambridge: Harvard University Press, 1971), 246; and Rawls, *Law of Peoples*, 5 and 90. See also A. John Simmons, "Ideal and Nonideal Theory," *Philosophy & Public Affairs* 38 (2010): 5–36; and Gopal Sreenivasan, "Non-ideal Theory: A Taxonomy with Illustration," in *Global Justice and Bioethics*, ed. Joseph Millum and Ezekiel J. Emanuel (Oxford: Oxford University Press, 2012), 135–52.

[14] *Justice as Fairness*, 66. [15] *A Theory of Justice*, 9.

[16] *Justice as Fairness*, 66; cf. *Political Liberalism*, xxviii: 'Among our most basic problems are those of race, ethnicity, and gender. These may seem of an altogether different character calling for different principles of justice, which *Theory* does not discuss.'

[17] Rawls discusses two cases involving unjust laws, civil disobedience and the conscientious refusal to serve in an unjust war. See *A Theory of Justice*, 371–82.

[18] In *Political Liberalism*, the term appears in passing on 18 and 285.

of nonideal theory to international relations.[19] Finally, in *Justice as Fairness*, Rawls again indicates that he will focus his inquiry on ideal theory because it engages the 'current conflict in democratic thought,' which asks 'what conception of justice is most appropriate for a democratic society under reasonably favorable conditions.'[20] For Rawls, the problems of a nonideal theory of domestic justice may be pressing and urgent, but insofar as nonideal theory presupposes an ideal to be pursued, nonideal theory remains an area of subsequent concern.

Rawls's distinction between ideal and nonideal theory has become the focal point for debates in political philosophy about progressive theorizing. In spite of the extensive literature that his distinction has generated,[21] there remains no systematic formulation of a Rawlsian nonideal

19 *Law of Peoples*, 89–120. 20 *Justice as Fairness*, 13.

21 For discussions of Rawls's conception of the distinction between ideal and nonideal theory, the value of the distinction, and analogous distinctions in other philosophic frameworks, see Elizabeth Anderson, *The Imperative of Integration* (Princeton: Princeton University Press, 2010); Elizabeth Anderson, "Toward a Non-Ideal, Relational Methodology for Political Philosophy: Comments on Schwartzman's *Challenging Liberalism*," *Hypatia* 24 (2009): 130–45; Katherine Eddy, "Against Ideal Rights," *Social Theory and Practice* 34 (2008): 463–81; Colin Farrelly, "Justice in Ideal Theory: A Refutation," *Political Studies* 55 (2007): 844–64; Joel Feinberg, "Duty and Obligation in the Non-Ideal World," *Journal of Philosophy* 70 (1973): 263–75; Pablo Gilabert, "Global Justice and Poverty Relief in Nonideal Circumstances," *Social Theory and Practice* 34 (2008): 411–38; Lisa L. Fuller, "Burdened Societies and Transitional Justice," *Ethical Theory and Moral Practice* (2011): 369–86; Robert E. Goodin, "Political Ideals and Political Practice," *British Journal of Political Science* 25 (1995): 37–56; Burke A. Hendrix, "Where Should We Expect Social Change in Non-Ideal Theory," *Political Theory* 41 (2013): 116–43; Christine M. Korsgaard, "The Right to Lie: Kant on Dealing with Evil," *Philosophy & Public Affairs* 15 (1986): 325–49; Andrew Mason, "Just Constraints," *British Journal of Political Science* 34 (2004): 251–68; Charles W. Mills, "'Ideal Theory' as Ideology," *Hypatia* 20 (2005): 165–84; Liam Murphy, *Moral Demands in Nonideal Theory* (Oxford: Oxford University Press, 2000); Michael Phillips, "Reflections on the Transition from Ideal to Non-Ideal Theory," *Noûs* 19 (1985): 551–70; Margaret Jane Radin, "Lacking a Transformative Social Theory: A Response," *Stanford Law Review* 45 (1993): 409–24; Anthony R. Reeves, "Judicial Practical Reason: Judges in Morally Imperfect Legal Orders," *Law and Philosophy* 30 (2011): 319–52; Ingrid Robeyns, "Ideal Theory in Theory and Practice," *Social Theory and Practice* 34 (2008): 341–62; Tamar Schapiro, "Compliance, Complicity, and the Nature of Nonideal Conditions," *Journal of Philosophy* 100 (2003): 329–55; David Schmidtz, "Nonideal Theory: What It Is and What It Needs To Be," *Ethics* 121 (2011): 772–96; Amartya Sen, "What Do We Want From a Theory of Justice?" *Journal of Philosophy* 103 (2006): 215–38; George Sher, *Approximate Justice: Studies in Non-Ideal Theory* (Lanham: Roman & Littlefield, 1997); A. John Simmons, "Ideal and Nonideal Theory," 5–36; Gopal Sreenivasan, "Health and Justice in Our Non-Ideal World," *Politics, Philosophy & Economics* 6 (2007): 218–36; Sreenivasan, "Non-ideal Theory: A Taxonomy with Illustration"; Zofia Stemplowska, "What's Ideal About Ideal Theory?" *Social Theory and*

theory of domestic justice.[22] Accordingly, those who accept Rawls's distinction and are eager to bring justice as fairness to bear on nonideal instances of domestic justice seek to 'take up where Rawls left off' by articulating nonideal principles for societies that are not well-ordered.[23] Such societies include those in which the arrangement of background institutions that make up the basic structure 'are unjust or do not exist at all' and in which the public political culture is mired in racism, sexism, and other forms of prejudice inimical to the realization of a well-ordered society.[24] What I want to suggest is that the fundamental problem in formulating justice as fairness as a progressive paradigm lies not in Rawls's omission of a nonideal theory of domestic justice, as is often supposed, but in a feature of Rawls's ideal theory.

Recall that Rawls generates his ideal theory by appealing to fundamental ideas that are 'deeply embedded' within the public culture of a modern constitutional democracy and working them up into a conception of justice.[25] In Rawls's words,

> A political conception of justice is formulated so far as possible solely in terms of fundamental ideas familiar from, or implicit in, the public political culture of a democratic society: for example, the idea of society as a fair system of cooperation and the idea of citizens as free and equal. That there are such ideas in their public culture is taken as a fact about democratic societies.[26]

Rawls does not offer justice as fairness as a *general* conception of justice appropriate for assessing the basic structure of society in all times and places. Justice as fairness is a conception of justice appropriate 'for the *special case* of the basic structure of a modern democratic society,' that is, a constitutional democracy in which citizens endorse, at least implicitly, certain fundamental ideas about the social order that they occupy.[27] This

Practice 34 (2008): 319–40; Adam Swift, "The Value of Philosophy in Nonideal Circumstances," *Social Theory and Practice* 34 (2008): 363–87; Laura Valentini, "On the Apparent Paradox of Ideal Theory," *Journal of Political Philosophy* 17 (2009): 332–55.

22 Robeyns, "Ideal Theory in Theory and Practice," 348: '[T]he literature on theories of justice remains remarkably silent on what, then, precisely is needed in order to make the transition from ideal theory to nonideal theory and action design and implementation . . . To the best of my knowledge, there is no systematic and comprehensive account of what a nonideal theory of justice entails, or on which methodology it would rest. There are some scattered contributions to the question of how we could go about developing nonideal theory, and also some insightful work within nonideal theorizing about justice, yet this body of literature remains far removed from a systematic account of nonideal theory.'

23 Fuller, "Burdened Societies and Transitional Justice," 370.

24 Ibid.

25 *Justice as Fairness*, 5 and 25.

26 Ibid., 27.

27 Ibid., 14 (my emphasis).

is not to say that societies that are not constitutional democracies or in which citizens do not accept the fundamental ideas from which justice as fairness springs are adequate, but rather that justice as fairness does not provide the standard for assessing their adequacy. As Rawls explains, 'justice as fairness is framed for a democratic society. Its principles are meant to answer the question once we view a democratic society as a fair system of social cooperation between citizens regarded as free and equal, what principles are most appropriate to it?'[28] The argument takes the form of a conditional: *if* a given society falls within the special case, *then* these principles of justice obtain.

That Rawls's ideal theory applies solely to instances of the special case of a modern constitutional democracy has important implications for the formulation of any corresponding nonideal theory. For Rawls, ideal theory provides principles for assessing the adequacy of the basic structure of a modern constitutional democracy. Since his ideal theory applies only to the special case of the basic structure of a modern constitutional democracy, it provides no resources for deeming societies that are not constitutional democracies (or in which one or more of the fundamental ideas is not present in the public political culture) to be defective. But if the ideal theory of justice as fairness provides no basis for deeming such societies defective, then nonideal theory lacks its condition of application. The problem with treating justice as fairness as a general theory of political development is not that it lacks a nonideal theory and that it is therefore incomplete. For even if such a theory were to materialize, it would not be applicable to societies that are not instances of the special case. The narrowness of Rawls's ideal theory of justice limits the domain to which any corresponding nonideal theory could apply to defective instances of the special case. A nonideal theory of domestic (as opposed to international) justice would not be applicable to what Rawls calls decent hierarchical societies because they do not conceive of persons as free and equal citizens.[29] It would not apply to burdened societies because they 'lack the political and cultural traditions to be well-ordered.'[30] It would not apply to benevolent absolutisms because even though they respect at least some human rights, they lack democratic institutions and traditions.[31] Finally, it would not apply to outlaw states because they are

[28] Ibid., 39. The passage continues, 'Alternatively: which principles are most appropriate for a democratic society that not only professes but wants to take seriously the idea that citizens are free and equal, and tries to realize that idea in its main institutions?'

[29] *Law of Peoples*, 66. [30] Ibid., 106. [31] Ibid., 4, 63, and 92.

not democratic and fail to honor human rights.[32] Since each of these societies falls beyond the special case, they cannot be defective with respect to the ideal that justice as fairness elaborates.

Burton Dreben, Rawls's interlocutor and defender, considered it a strength of justice as fairness that it made no attempt to justify modern constitutional democracy, but instead appealed to fundamental features of modern constitutional democracy to justify a conception of justice:

> It is very important to understand that Rawls is a good enough thinker not to argue against those who do not believe in liberal constitutional democracy. Neither in *A Theory of Justice*, nor surely in *Political Liberalism*, nor in any of the other works, is he engaged in the kind of struggle that, say, Locke was engaged in. The outcome of that struggle he takes for granted, just as I think any sensible person should today. You do not argue in political philosophy over the benefits of constitutional liberal democracy; what you try to do is see what that concept leads to, what it entails, what it demands . . . You do not argue for it. You do not ground it. You see what it leads to.[33]

Dreben overlooks a problem latent within Rawls's strategy for generating his ideal theory. Because Rawls does not provide a justification of liberal constitutional democracy, his ideal theory cannot explain why societies that are not liberal constitutional democracies are defective on their own internal standard of adequacy. And in the absence of such an explanation, a Rawlsian nonideal theory could not apply to them. The reason that a progressive theory must attempt a justification of liberal constitutional democracy is not, as Dreben imagines, to convince fools and fascists who do 'not see the virtue of that ideal.'[34] Rather, an account of why liberal constitutional democracy alone is adequate may shed light on two sets of issues. First, it may shed light on the kinds of constitutional norms, institutional arrangements, and legal doctrines that are appropriate for a liberal constitutional democracy. I return to this point in the subsequent chapters. Second, and more significantly for the present chapter, such an account would avoid the tension between the theory of justice that Rawlsians affirm and the kinds of judgments that they make about obvious cases of injustice. Dreben rejects the adequacy of all alternatives

32 Ibid., 80–1, 94–5, and 105–6.

33 "On Rawls and Political Liberalism," in *The Cambridge Companion to Rawls*, ed. Samuel Freeman (Cambridge: Cambridge University Press, 2003), 323.

34 Ibid., 328–9. Dreben continues, '[S]ometimes I am asked, when I go around speaking for Rawls, What do you say to an Adolph Hitler? The answer is [nothing]. You shoot him. You do not try to reason with him. Reason has no bearing on that question.'

to constitutional democracy,[35] but nevertheless clings to a conception of justice that offers no resources for illuminating their inadequacy. Similarly, Rawls asserts that 'we may assume that any actual society is more or less unjust – usually gravely so,'[36] even though many actual societies are not instances of the special case, which means that justice as fairness provides no basis for deeming them unjust.

The difficulty that undermines the progressive aspiration of justice as fairness is suggestive. Considered as a progressive theory, justice as fairness goes off the rails at its initial step by identifying its underlying subject as the basic structure of a modern constitutional democracy. Such an underlying subject culminates in an ideal theory that is too narrow to fulfill its progressive aspiration because it is inapplicable to societies that are not modern constitutional democracies. Perhaps the problem that justice as fairness encounters can be avoided by beginning with a broader underlying subject – political societies in general or legal systems as such – and relating it to an appropriate conception of justice. With this strategy in mind, I now turn to consider a leading approach to progressive theorizing in contemporary legal philosophy.

4.2 Hart's reformist project

Unlike Rawls, who constructed his progressive theory from particular features of modern constitutional democracies and the public political culture that supports them, H.L.A. Hart sought to formulate a general jurisprudence that was 'not tied to any particular legal system or legal culture.'[37] For Hart, the development of a general theory of law is not merely a theoretical achievement, but is integral to the practical aim of reforming laws and legal systems. As in my discussion of Rawls, I will confine my discussion of Hart to the aspects of his framework that are relevant to its progressive aspiration. From this standpoint, Hart's legal positivism raises a mirror image of the problem encountered in Rawls: justice as fairness is progressive but not general; Hart's legal positivism is general but not progressive.

In rejuvenating analytic jurisprudence, Hart emphasized that legal positivism offered more than a defensible thesis about the concept of law. Hart's claim was that legal positivism cultivated moral attitudes

[35] Ibid.
[36] "Political Liberalism: Reply to Habermas," *Journal of Philosophy* 92 (1995): 154.
[37] Hart, *The Concept of Law* (Oxford: Clarendon Press, 1994), 239.

conducive to the reform of defective laws and legal systems. As Hart explained, the founders of analytic jurisprudence, Bentham and Austin, 'were not dry analysts fiddling with verbal distinctions while cities burned, but were the vanguard of a movement which laboured with passionate intensity and much success to bring about a better society and better laws.'[38] For Hart, as for his predecessors, the separation of law and morals was integral to the reformist project. By distinguishing the question of whether a particular norm is a valid law from the question of whether it is just, legal positivism yields the twin insights that what is law is not thereby just and that what is just is not thereby law. The validity of a legal norm depends not on its justice but on whether it was enacted in accordance with the appropriate social rule. Armed with these insights, positivist reformers are able to identify valid laws, assess their moral adequacy, and insist that morally defective laws yield to the enactment of progressive alternatives. The conceptual separation of law and morals provides positivist reformers with the intellectual clarity required to bring law and morals together by repealing unjust laws and enacting just ones.

When assessing whether legal positivism is a progressive theory of law, it is important to distinguish between the projects of particular legal positiv*ists*, on the one hand, and the theory of legal positiv*ism*, on the other. Although some positivists have pursued an agenda of progressive reform, positivism is not itself a progressive paradigm. Positivism is the thesis that the concept of law is exhausted by its positivity. Accordingly, positivism holds that one can provide a comprehensive account of the concept of law without recourse to the endless controversies of morality.[39] Indeed, part of positivism's widespread attraction is that the separation of law and morals enables its proponents to agree about the concept of law even when they disagree about the demands of morality. While proponents of positivism assert that it is 'a *radical* theory of law, one unfriendly to the *status quo*,'[40] critics point out that the 'banners of legal positivism' have marched both with those who sought to uproot an unjust status quo and those who sought to preserve it.[41] But if the concept of law that the

[38] "Positivism and the Separation of Law and Morals," *Harvard Law Review* 71 (1958): 596.
[39] Brian Leiter, "Why Legal Positivism?" University of Chicago, Public Law Working Paper (10 December 2009), http://ssrn.com/abstract=1521761.
[40] Brian Leiter, "The Radicalism of Legal Positivism," University of Chicago, Public Law Working Paper 303, http://ssrn.com/abstract=1568333.
[41] Ronald Dworkin, "Law's Ambition for Itself," *Virginia Law Review* 71 (1985): 175. See also Robert Cover, *Justice Accused: Antislavery and the Judicial Process* (New Haven: Yale University Press, 1975), 1.

positivist endorses is compatible with a variety of views about morality, some progressive and others regressive, then positivism *as such* is not a progressive theory. For whether positivism is progressive or regressive depends on something *extrinsic* to the concept of law that positivists endorse, namely, an independent conception of morality. Of course, a positivist might reply that positivism can and must be coupled with an *appropriate* critical morality, but this simply restates the problem. How can positivism purport to be a progressive theory of law if it can be coupled with an inappropriate (or uncritical) morality? If it is a virtue of positivism that it can be coupled with a progressive conception of morality, then it is surely a vice if it can just as easily be coupled with a regressive conception.

Perhaps the positivist wishes to retreat to a more moderate claim about positivism's virtues. Because the concept of law is compatible with a variety of views about morality, positivism is not progressive as such, as its proponents have asserted, but, for the same reason, neither is it regressive as such, as its critics have alleged.[42] Rather, the positivist might insist that insofar as positivism is *compatible* with a progressive approach to morality, it provides an alternative to regressive theories and this is something to be celebrated. With this claim, a classification emerges. A theory can be progressive, regressive, or morally variable. Theories of the first type would involve an underlying subject – whether legal systems or societies of a certain kind – that implicated a progressive moral standard for assessing the adequacy of its instances and directing their reform. Theories of the second type would mirror the first by offering an underlying subject that implicated a regressive moral standard. Quietist theories exemplify this possibility by holding that the features of an existing legal system (or society) form the standard by which its adequacy is to be assessed, which means that no existing instance can fail to be fully adequate. Quietist theories are not progressive because, as Bentham once remarked, 'if nothing is ever to be found fault with, nothing will ever be mended.'[43] Theories of the third type would involve an underlying subject, in Hart's case, legal systems, that was not tethered to any particular conception of morality and was, consequently, compatible with both progressive and regressive conceptions of morality.[44]

42 On the conflict between those who conceive of positivism as progressive or regressive, see David Dyzenhaus, *Hard Cases in Wicked Legal Systems: Pathologies of Legality* (Oxford: Oxford University Press, 2010), 1.

43 *A Fragment on Government* (Cambridge: Cambridge University Press, 2001), 10.

44 For the sake of completeness a further branch could be added to this classification: a theory that is dismissive of morality.

The problem that Hart encounters in formulating a progressive theory can be contrasted with the problem, discussed earlier, that arises in justice as fairness. Hart formulates a *general* theory applicable to legal systems as such, but this theory is *morally variable* rather than progressive. Rawls offers a *progressive* framework for the special case of a modern constitutional democracy, but the theory lacks generality. What I wish to consider in the next section is what a theory that was *both* general *and* progressive might look like.

4.3 Public justice as an ideal and as a duty

A theory that is both general and progressive must bear a certain kind of structure. If the theory is to be general, the underlying subject of the theory must be legal systems or political societies as such, rather than those distinguished by some contingent feature, as in Rawls's account of the special case. Further, if the theory is to be progressive, it must appeal to some feature of the underlying subject to generate a conception of justice apposite to all of its instances. Such an approach would follow Hart (but not Rawls) in formulating a general theory rather than a theory of the special case. And it would follow Rawls (but not Hart) in formulating a theory that is progressive rather than morally variable.

The challenge of formulating such a theory lies in the relationship between its general and its progressive aspects. On one side lies Hart's theory, which holds that when one understands law as a general concept in abstraction from particular laws or legal systems, one sees that law has no necessary connection to morality. The generality of Hart's approach culminates in its moral variability. On the other lies Rawls's theory, which holds that the moral standard appropriate for assessing the adequacy of a particular political society or a legal community depends on facts about its practices. Justice as fairness retains its progressive orientation by confining the application of this approach to the special case of a modern constitutional democracy, thereby sacrificing the theory's generality. A theory that is *both* general *and* progressive must defend a position not found in either of these theories: that a legal system (or a political order) as such contains its own internal standard of moral adequacy.

In what follows, my strategy is to draw on the unified theory of public law to identify a feature that is constitutive of legal systems in general. Internal to this feature, I will argue, is the standard for critically assessing the adequacy of legal systems and directing the reform of legal systems that are defective on their own internal standard of adequacy. I call the former the *ideal* of public justice and the latter the *duty* of public justice.

The unified theory is a general theory of public law, the branch of law that concerns the relationship between the individual and the state. As a general theory, its underlying subject is legal systems as such rather than legal systems distinguished by democratic institutions, rights protecting constitutional norms, or the commitments of the public culture. The unified theory identifies public authority as the constitutive feature of a legal system. Public authority creates the parties to the public law relationship, a government comprised of public institutions and a people comprised of private persons bound by its lawgiving.

The right of government to exercise public authority over free and equal persons must be justified. As I argued in Chapter 2, the justification of public authority is premised on human dignity or what I call independence or equal freedom, the right to determine and pursue one's purposes in a manner compatible with the right of all others to the same. The right of government to exercise public authority can be justified because persons cannot interact with one another on terms of equal freedom in the absence of publicly authoritative institutions that establish, interpret, and implement legal obligations.

Since the public authority of government is justified on the basis of the right of every person to independence, internal to the justification of the constitutive feature of a legal system is the standard for critically assessing the adequacy of its instances. Public justice is the ideal of a legal system that fully conforms to the terms of its justification. A legal order consists in a set of public institutions that make the conduct of each person accountable to the independence of every other. In a *just* legal order, the arrangements that render persons accountable to one another are themselves fully compatible with the independence of each person who is bound by them. A legal system exemplifies this ideal to the extent that the procedures through which laws are enacted and the content of enacted laws are compatible with the independence of everyone among the people. In a just legal order, the members of a people are not passive citizens bound by laws of another's making but active citizens who, through their representatives, collectively author the laws by which all are bound. Turning from the procedure for enacting law to its content, the ideal of public justice involves a system of positive law that each could consent to as an independent member of the legal order. The ideal of public justice is satisfied when the legal order that citizens collectively enact accords with the right of every person to equal freedom under law.

Alternately, a legal system is defective or unjust to the extent that it fails to conform to the terms of its justification by securing the independence of all who are bound by its lawgiving.

The ideal of public justice is a *system of law* in which each particular feature of the legal order is directed toward the realization of the internal aim of the whole, the equal freedom of persons under law. Such an ideal encompasses the entire legal system from its fundamental norms to the institutions through which those norms are made effective and from the issuance of positive law to the construction of legal doctrine. A just legal order consists neither in a particular just law nor in the independence of a particular person. Such arrangements would not exclude the possibility that other laws might treat other persons in a manner unbefitting of their independence, and, consequently, that the legal system as a whole would fail to conform to the terms of its justification.

That the principle of justice requires government to realize an ideal to the greatest possible extent does not mean that the unified theory of public law is an instrumental theory. Consider how the unified theory departs from, for example, the utilitarianism of Jeremy Bentham. Bentham roots his theory in an ideal that exists apart from legal concepts, legal forms of reasoning, or legal institutions: 'Nature has placed mankind under the governance of two sovereign masters, *pain* and *pleasure*.'[45] On Bentham's view, an action is adequate to the extent that it produces utility, conceived of as pleasure and the absence of pain.[46] Thus, Bentham writes that a 'measure of government (which is but a particular kind of action, performed by a particular person or persons) may be said to be conformable to or dictated by the principle of utility, when in like manner the tendency which it has to augment the happiness of the community is greater than any which it has to diminish it.'[47] For Bentham, as for instrumental theories generally, a legal system is simply a tool for realizing something that is of value apart from it. Proponents of instrumental theories differ about the particular value that legal systems should pursue but agree that if legal systems are of value, it is because they have a propensity to further the realization of some extrinsically valuable end.[48] Unlike the ideal of an instrumental theory, the ideal of public

45 Jeremy Bentham, *An Introduction to the Principles of Morals and Legislation* (Oxford: Clarendon Press, 1879), 1 (c. I., 1st para.).

46 Ibid., 1 (c. I, 2nd para.). 47 Ibid., 3 (c. I, 7th para.).

48 For an elaboration of this distinction between instrumental and noninstrumental legal theories, see Ripstein, *Force and Freedom* (Cambridge: Harvard University Press, 2009), 7–11 and 255–6.

justice is not conceivable apart from a legal system. Public justice consists in an adequate relationship between the parties to the public law relationship, a people – a multitude of private persons subject to common lawgiving – and its government, the publicly authoritative institutions that represent the people as a whole. When publicly authoritative institutions are absent, so too are the parties to this juridical relationship. Consequently, questions about the adequacy of the relationship that obtains between the parties cannot arise. The internal ideal of a legal system is neither valuable nor conceivable apart from one.

The ideal of public justice forms the internal standard for assessing the adequacy of every existing legal system and every conceivable legal system. A legal system is adequate to the extent that it conforms to and defective to the extent that it deviates from its internal ideal of public justice. So conceived, the ideal of public justice does not follow from some contingent fact about a particular legal system, such as the textual provisions found in a written constitution, its democratic form of lawgiving, or the convictions that make up its public political culture. Rather, the ideal of public justice follows from an inherent feature of the public law relationship instantiated by all legal systems. The ideal of public justice is internal to legal systems not because it stems from some contingent feature that each happens to share, but because the ideal arises from the constitutive feature of a legal system as such, the right of government to exercise public authority over private persons. Public justice is the internal ideal of every legal system simply by virtue of being a legal system. The ideal of public justice can of course be recognized by a publicly authoritative act – for example, the promulgation of constitutional norms recognizing the human dignity of all who are subject to law's authority – but the ideal can neither be established nor displaced by such an act.

The distinction between what a legal system is and what an ideal legal system would be explains how an existing legal system could be defective on its own internal standard of adequacy. Accordingly, we must ask what public justice requires of defective legal systems.

The *ideal* of public justice and the *duty* of public justice draw out different implications of the justification of public authority. The *ideal* of public justice delineates the features of a legal system that fully conforms to the terms of its justification by uniting authority with the independence of its members. The *duty* of public justice is the requirement that government exercise public authority in accordance with the terms of its justification. As we saw in Chapter 2, the right to exercise public authority is accompanied by an obligation to bring the existing legal system into the deepest possible approximation of the ideal of public justice. The basis of this obligation lies in the justification of public authority: because the right of government to exercise public authority presupposes the right of every private person to independence, government cannot deny the right of persons to independence without thereby denying the justificatory ground of its own authority. Since the right of persons to independence grounds both the right of government to exercise authority over private persons and the right of private persons to just governance, every unjust exercise of public authority involves a moral incoherence.

The *ideal* of public justice must not be confused with the *duty* to realize it. The *ideal* of public justice is a legal system that fully conforms to the terms of its justification. Existing legal systems are adequate to the extent that they approximate this ideal. When we assess how just a legal system is, whether one legal system is more just than another, or whether a possible reform would improve existing arrangements, the ideal of public justice forms the relevant measure. By contrast, the *duty* of public justice requires government to direct the exercise of public authority toward bringing the legal order as a whole into the deepest possible conformity with its own internal ideal. At issue is not the degree of conformity between the existing legal system and the ideal of public justice at a particular moment, but the extent to which the existing legal system has engaged in progressive reform within a discrete period of time. Regardless of how closely a legal system approximates the ideal of public justice, it must exercise public authority in accordance with the duty of public justice.

The distinction between the ideal of public justice and the duty to approximate it forms a fundamental part of political discourse. Consider Abraham Lincoln's understanding of the *Declaration of Independence*, which famously proclaims the inherent right of equal persons to life, liberty, and the pursuit of happiness, and that government must secure these rights:

> [The Founders] meant simply to declare the *right*, so that the *enforcement* of it might follow as fast as circumstances should permit. They meant to set up a standard maxim for free society, which should be familiar to all, and revered by all; constantly looked to, constantly labored for, and even though never perfectly attained, constantly approximated, and thereby constantly spreading and deepening its influence . . .[49]

[49] "The Dred Scott Decision: Speech at Springfield, Illinois, June 26, 1857," in *Abraham Lincoln: His Speeches and Writings*, ed. Roy P. Basler (New York: Da Capo Press, 1990), 361. See also Gary J. Jacobsohn, "Abraham Lincoln 'On this Question of Judicial

Lincoln conceived of the Founders as encapsulating an ideal conception of public justice internalized by the American people, or as he described it, 'a philosophical cause . . . entwining itself more closely about the human heart.'[50] This ideal forms the 'standard maxim for a free society,' which persons may look to in assessing the adequacy of the existing legal order. The duty of an existing society is not to do the impossible by perfectly instantiating this standard, but to approximate this standard 'as fast as circumstances should permit.'

Correlative to the duty of public justice is the right of everyone among the people to just governance. Government is not to regard members of the people as beings who have a duty to obey its authority but who have no right to justice. Nor are members of the people to regard themselves as having a right to ideal justice. The former position overlooks that the right to exercise public authority is always accompanied by a duty to govern justly. The latter overlooks that a person may raise a claim to just governance only as a member of a legal system, in which every person subject to public authority has an equal claim. The duty incumbent on government is to exercise public authority in a justifiable manner by creating a legal system that as a whole approximates the ideal of public justice to the greatest possible extent. Public authority must be exercised in a manner that brings the entire system of positive laws, institutional arrangements, constitutional norms, and legal doctrines into the highest possible degree of agreement with the ideal of public justice.

The duty of public justice does not require government to address each of its defects at once. When circumstances obtain in which the reform of a *particular* injustice would counteract the duty to bring the legal system as a *whole* into the deepest possible conformity with the ideal of public justice, government is justified in temporarily delaying that reform. The delay is justified because the duty of public justice requires government to realize the ideal of public justice to the fullest possible extent by reforming the legal system as a whole, not to frustrate the reform of the whole for the sake of reforming a particular aspect of it. But because the duty of public justice is unremitting, once circumstances ripen, the justification

Authority': The Theory of Constitutional Aspiration," *Western Political Science Association* 36 (1983): 65. On the Declaration as a prescription for rather than a description of American society, see Giovanni Sartori, *Democratic Theory* (New York: Frederick A. Praeger: 1965), 53.

50 Lincoln, "Fragment on the Constitution and Union," in *The Collected Works of Abraham Lincoln*, vol. IV, ed. Roy Basler (New Brunswick: Rutgers University Press, 1977), 169.

for postponing reform dissolves and any further delay simply perpetuates injustice.[51]

Similarly, government may introduce temporary programs that do not themselves conform to the ideal of public justice but are required to bring the existing legal order as a whole into closer approximation of it. Consider how Jonathan Wolff conceptualizes the justification of affirmative action:

> [A] world which includes affirmative action is not an ideal one. As a long-term policy, affirmative action is undesirable, and in certain respects unjust. People should be treated on their individual merits, as critics of affirmative action claim. But without a temporary policy of affirmative action it will be much harder to create a world in which affirmative action is unnecessary: in which people are treated on their individual merits. So we should see affirmative action as a transitional policy in a step towards a more just world.[52]

Wolff's remark maps onto the structure of the unified theory. His point is that given the unjust conditions of an existing society, affirmative action may be required by the duty of public justice as a temporary measure designed to bring the existing legal system into closer approximation with the ideal of public justice, of which affirmative action is not a part. The internal aim of public law is not to create a world without affirmative action, but a world in which such measures are no longer necessary because equality of opportunity has been transformed from rhetoric into reality. Affirmative action may be integral to the creation of such a world, but it has no place within it.

The duty of public justice is unremitting and transformative. The duty is unremitting because it accompanies the presence of public authority. Accordingly, the duty cannot be discharged through the performance of the very acts that it necessitates or through its violation. The duty is transformative because it requires government to formulate, implement, and refine a program for the progressive reform of an existing legal system. By acting in conformity with its duty, an existing society brings the compulsion of public authority into accord with the demands of public justice.

What hope can we have for public law given the broad expanse that lies between existing societies and the ideal of public justice? The hope is that

51 I elaborate on the nature of this justification in the context of Kant's theory of public right in "Permissive Laws and the Dynamism of Kantian Justice," *Law and Philosophy* 33 (2013): 105–36.

52 *An Introduction to Political Philosophy* (Oxford: Oxford University Press, 1996), 209.

by acting in accordance with the duty of public justice, progressive reforms will create the conditions for further progress, and equal degrees of reform will occur in shorter and shorter successive intervals. That legal systems may be capable of reforming themselves at increasing rates is not a mere conceptual possibility but a familiar feature of legal experience. The maturation of a public culture, the increasing inclusivity of representative institutions, and the formulation of constitutional norms that tie the exercise of public authority to the realization of public justice ready the path for further ameliorative measures. Frederick Douglass captured this hope when he observed: 'Unlike the movement for the abolition of slavery, the success of the effort for the enfranchisement of the freedmen was not long delayed. It is another illustration of how any advance in pursuance of a right principle prepares and makes easy the way to another.'[53] Even if existing societies depart markedly from the ideal of public justice, perhaps equal steps toward the ideal can be taken in successively shorter durations.

The unified theory departs from Rawls and Hart by holding that a legal system is defective on its own internal standard of moral adequacy to the extent that it fails to realize a system of equal freedom. Unlike Hart's legal positivism, which conceives of morality as extrinsic to the concept of law, the unified theory holds that a legal system as such contains its own internal morality: the justification of the constitutive feature of a legal system – the right of government to exercise authority on independent persons – implicates a distinctive moral standard for the critical assessment of all legal systems. Thus, the unified theory retains the generality of Hart's approach, while eschewing its moral variability. Further, unlike Rawls's justice as fairness, which seeks to formulate a moral standard internal to a particular kind of political order by appealing to its contingent features, the unified theory draws on the constitutive feature of a legal system to formulate a moral standard internal to legal systems generally. The unified theory thereby provides a standpoint for explaining why a legal system is defective on its own internal standard of adequacy to the extent that it fails to create a condition of equal freedom. Justice as fairness maintains that a liberal legal or political order must govern in a liberal way; the unified theory provides resources for thinking about why a legal or political order must become liberal.

[53] Douglass, *Life and Times of Frederick Douglass* (New York: Cosimo, 2008), 277.

4.4 Progress and particularity

The unified theory of public law is a liberal theory: its principles of authority and justice emerge from an exploration of the right of every individual to equal freedom. Liberalism leads a double life. On the one hand, it forms the backbone of a tradition that extends from Enlightenment thought to the emergence of modern constitutional states that makes the dignity of their members the purpose and constraint of all exercises of public authority. On the other, liberalism is increasingly subject to the 'old objections of formalism, emptiness, abstractness and absence of historical and cultural connections.'[54] Because the unified theory of public law arrives at a conception of justice by reflecting on what a legal system is rather than on contingent features of particular legal systems, the unified theory may appear vulnerable to these old objections. The purpose of this section is to explicate the connection between the progressive orientation of the unified theory and the concrete particularity of existing legal systems. I will consider two objections that seek to sever this connection.

The first objection begins with the observation that the progressive development of an existing society arises within a particular context distinguished by legal, political, historical, and sociological features. These features make up both the setting in which reform must occur and the circumstances to which reform must respond. However, when the realization of a just society is given theoretical expression, what is typically imagined is not the reform of an existing society's defects, but rather the creation of a perfectly just society from scratch. As Ronald Dworkin formulates the objection,

> The great classics of political philosophy . . . study social justice from the point of view of people committed in advance to no government or constitution, who are free to create the ideal state from first principles. So they imagine people living in a prepolitical state of "nature" writing social contracts on blank slates. But real people in ordinary politics act within a political structure as well as on it. Politics, for us, is evolutionary rather than axiomatic; we recognize, in working toward a perfectly just state, that we already belong to a different one.[55]

In the theories that Dworkin describes, progressive development is presented in terms of the transition from the absence of a political order to the creation ex nihilo of a perfectly just one. In turn, governance involves

[54] Robert Alexy, "Discourse Theory and Human Rights," *Ratio Juris* 9 (1996): 210.
[55] Ronald Dworkin, *Law's Empire* (Cambridge: Harvard University Press), 164.

the maintenance of a perfectly just political order in which public institutions and laws are perfectly adequate and fully endorsed by all who are bound by them. In actuality, progressive development takes a very different shape. The point of departure for progressive development is not a blank slate but an existing society. Governance, at best, involves not the maintenance of a perfectly just social order but the ongoing approximation of one. Further, this approximation must be carried out by imperfect public institutions in circumstances characterized by unjust laws and a public culture with suspect commitments. Surely, the objection concludes, such theories distort the nature of legal and political reform.

Versions of this objection have been raised in a variety of contexts. In his prewar writings, Gustav Radbruch raised this criticism against theories of natural law, which he conceived of as affirming a formal ideal of legality while eschewing the matter or particularity of historically situated legal systems:

> The theory of natural law assumes that the resisting power of the matter against the idea may be put at zero. It completely volatilizes the matter of the law. In its view, the material of the legal idea is not a definite historical situation but the state of nature; and that state of nature is depicted not as a sociological relationship but rather as an unsociable side-by-sidedness of individuals; the first creation of social relations between them being reserved to the legal idea, unhampered by any pre-existing sociological ties.[56]

Thus, Radbruch repudiates natural law for failing to integrate the rational form of law with the variability of legally, politically, historically, and sociologically determined content. The same skepticism about the capacity of theory to engage with the contingent circumstances to which reform responds can be found in Bruce Ackerman's constitutional theory. Ackerman insists that the American constitutional order defies theoretical illumination because it is the product of piecemeal reforms undertaken in response to successive historical crises rather than the wholesale implementation of a discrete philosophic program:

> The modern [American] Constitution does not express a timeless philosophy of right revealed in the Declaration of Independence or some Herculean labor of philosophical reflection. It is the product of ongoing political struggle – generation after generation mobilizing itself to critique

[56] Radbruch, *Legal Philosophy* in *The Legal Philosophies of Lask, Radbruch, and Dabin*, trans. Kurt Wilk (Cambridge: Harvard University Press, 1950), 121.

> and reconstruct large chunks of the received constitutional understanding. The guiding image should be Neurath's Boat, not Kant's Critique. In the aftermath of Civil War, Americans ripped gaping holes in the traditional structure, replacing them with new planks that didn't fit the old design. The question was whether the ship would keep sailing during such a shattering reconstruction, not whether its overall design would survive a philosophy seminar.[57]

For Ackerman, as for Dworkin and Radbruch, reform is an ongoing process that takes place within and responds to the contingencies of a particular context. Accordingly, any theory that conceives of reform in terms of a transition from a featureless condition to a fully just one fails to illuminate its subject.

The unified theory's central distinction between public authority and public justice enables it to sidestep this objection. The principle of authority is constitutive of public law because its satisfaction culminates in the creation of the parties to the public law relationship, a government and a people comprised of those bound by its lawgiving. By contrast, public justice is the *regulative* principle of public law. It concerns the right of all who are subject to public authority to just governance and the corresponding obligation incumbent on government. In the absence of a legal system, the principle of justice lacks its condition of application because neither of the parties to the public law relationship is present, and so questions about the adequacy of their relationship cannot arise. It is the existing legal system, in all its contingent particularity, that forms the point of departure from which the ideal of public justice must be pursued.

What the duty of public justice requires in a particular legal system cannot be specified in abstraction from the circumstances that obtain within it. The duty of public justice requires the public authority to identify the ways in which the existing legal system is defective in relation to its own internal ideal, to reflect on how these defects can be addressed, and to implement a program of reform that brings the legal system as a whole into the closest possible conformity with its own internal ideal. Within the unified theory, politics – conceived of as a justifiable practice – is the art of drawing on experiential knowledge to direct the exercise of public authority toward the realization of public justice. The duty of public justice and

57 Ackerman, "Rooted Cosmopolitanism," *Ethics* 104 (1994): 520. For a further formulation of the criticism that attacks the capacity of social contract theories to illuminate constitutional transitions, see Jacob T. Levy, "Not So *Novus* an *Ordo*: Constitutions without Social Contracts," *Political Theory* 37 (2009): 192.

the practice of politics are inextricably bound. The specification of the duty of public justice requires political knowledge of the contingent features of an existing legal system. The practice of politics involves bringing knowledge about the contingent features of an existing legal system to bear on the exercise of public authority, which, given its justification, must be exercised in accordance with the duty of public justice. As the Swiss jurist Johann Caspar Bluntschli remarked, 'All politics must be realistic; all politics should be idealistic. Both principles are true if they complement one another. Both principles are wrong if they exclude one another.'[58] That politics must be directed toward the realization of the ideal of public justice does not mean that the contentious character of politics must fall away. Intense disagreements may persist about whether a particular practice is compatible with the ideal of public justice, or about the order in which government should address its various defects, or about the ameliorative arrangements that government should enact in their place.

Once the relationship between the particularity of existing legal systems and the duty of public justice is expounded, a further objection arises. Although the duty of public justice applies only within the concrete setting of an existing legal system, if legal systems are to approximate the ideal of public justice, they must divest themselves of their distinctive particularity. Thus, the objection alleges that the 'colorful variety of the legal views of different ages and nations' are to be repudiated as so many instances of 'error' to be supplanted with uniformity.[59] Since the particularity of an existing legal system must be cast aside to approximate the ideal of public justice, the unified theory must be hostile to all forms of particularity after all. Just legal systems may be distinguished by the territories that they occupy, but not by the content of their laws.

That the ideal of public justice is the internal aim of every legal system does not entail legal uniformity. The ideal of public justice is satisfied when the laws, institutional arrangements, and legal doctrines through which public power is exercised are compatible with the independence of all who are subject to them. Since the ideal of public justice is a capacious norm rather than a fine-grained blueprint, it may be satisfied by a variety of arrangements. Public justice directs but does not predetermine the practice of public law.[60] Insofar as the practice of public law involves the

[58] Bluntschli, *Politik als Wissenschaft* (Stuttgart: Verlag der J.G. Cotta'schen Buchhandlung, 1876), I, 4, 32.

[59] Radbruch, *Legal Philosophy*, 60.

[60] For an analogous argument in the private law context, see Ernest J. Weinrib, *The Idea of Private Law* (Cambridge: Harvard University Press, 1995), 204–29.

exercise of public authority over independent persons, it must be directed toward the creation of a system of law that – to the greatest possible extent – conforms to this standard. Because different kinds of institutional arrangements, positive laws, and legal doctrines can contribute to the realization of this standard, it can be concretized through different arrangements.[61] I will return to this point in formulating the constitutional and doctrinal dimensions of human dignity in the subsequent chapters.

Some may detect an air of paradox in this account of the ideal of public justice. On the one hand, the ideal is implicated by the justification of public authority and as such is incumbent on government in all times and places. On the other, the way in which the ideal of public justice is conceptualized reflects contingent features of particular legal systems at particular times. Thus, one might object that the ideal of public justice is incoherent: it is both beyond history and within it, universal and yet particular. These claims, however, occasion no contradiction. The ideal of public justice is a normative concept and as such is not established by the occurrence of a particular event at a specific moment in time. While the ideal of public justice is unchanging, the way in which particular societies in particular moments understand that ideal and extend it to particulars is, of course, subject to historical forces, and may deepen with time, experience, and reflection as a legal system seeks to justify its coercive activity to all members of the legal order. When a society's conception of the ideal of public justice is refined, further discrepancies between the existing contours of public authority and the demands of public justice may become evident and the duty incumbent on the public authority may become

[61] See, for example, Dieter Grimm, "Freedom of Speech in a Globalized World," in *Extreme Speech and Democracy*, ed. Ivan Hare (Oxford: Oxford University Press, 2009), 11–22. After noting that freedom of speech is an integral aspect of 'individual self-determination and personal dignity' and a necessary feature of democratic self-government, Grimm observes that while freedom of expression is recognized around the world, 'a consensus can be found only on a very high level of abstraction.' Ibid., 12 and 20. Even in the West, a variety of conceptions of freedom of expression obtain. Grimm illustrates this variability by contrasting the way in which the French and German legal systems conceptualize freedom of expression, its relation to public discourse, the role of the media in discussing issues of public importance, and how freedom of expression relates to other rights, such as the right to privacy. While the approach of each of these legal systems must be assessed on their merits, Grimm emphasizes 'that when it comes to concretizing the right [of freedom of expression] and balancing it against other rights or interests, a variety of national solutions are compatible with the basic guarantee. Universal recognition of freedom of speech does not require uniform legal solutions or interpretation.' Ibid., 22.

correspondingly heightened.[62] Within the unified theory, it is not the ideal of public justice that must undergo development, but the way in which particular societies conceive of it. Thus, the unified theory of public law is progressive, but not in the Hegelian sense. The duty of public justice incumbent on public authority is correlative to the right of the people, not to World Spirit. In turn, the ideal of public justice is not developing in history, say, as World Spirit comes to know itself as free. Rather, the ideal of public justice is a public norm that arises in a sequenced juridical argument that proceeds from the right of every person to equal freedom. The ideal is unchanging, but its public significance within particular societies can develop in accordance with a learning process that is responsive to, but not determined by, historical events.[63]

The idea of a public political culture plays a different role in the unified theory than it plays in justice as fairness. For Rawls, the institutional

[62] For an illustration, see Germany's *Life Imprisonment Case*, BVerfGE 45, 187 (1977). An English translation of excerpts can be found in Donald P. Kommers and Russell A. Miller, *The Constitutional Jurisprudence of the Federal Republic of Germany* (Durham: Duke University Press, 2012), 363–9. In 1949, Germany adopted a new constitution that made the inherent dignity of the human person the purpose and constraint of all public power. Given Germany's experience of Nazi barbarism, the new constitution explicitly prohibited the death penalty, which was widely perceived to be incompatible with the state's duty to respect and protect human dignity. Consequently, as of 1949, life imprisonment became the most severe penal sanction in Germany. While the constitutionality of life imprisonment was not questioned at the time, a generation later, a constitutional complaint prompted the Federal Constitutional Court to consider whether life imprisonment was itself consistent with the constitutional commitment to dignity. The court noted that it 'was not until the furor over the death penalty had subsided that scientists in the late 1960s began to concern themselves with the problem of life imprisonment.' Scientists then learned that imprisonment without hope of reintegration into society is deeply destructive of human personality. In its judgment, the court wrote, 'Since the adoption of the Basic Law, our understanding of the content, function, and effect of basic rights has deepened. Additionally, the medical, psychological and sociological effects of life imprisonment have become better known. Current attitudes are important in assessing the constitutionality of life imprisonment. New insights can influence and even change the evaluation of this punishment in terms of human dignity and the principles of a constitutional state . . . ' Thus, the court interpreted the constitutional commitment to dignity to require the state to create the legal conditions in which those who had atoned for their crimes and were no longer a danger to society could be reintegrated. Underlying the court's decision is the view that as the internal aim of the legal order becomes more deeply understood, arrangements previously deemed unproblematic may be recognized to be unjust, and the duty that accompanies public power may therefore become more demanding. In time, a deeper appreciation of the institutional implications of human dignity may indicate the inadequacy of the requirements that the court set out in the *Life Imprisonment Case*.

[63] Pauline Kleingeld, "Kant, History, and the Idea of Moral Development," *History of Philosophy Quarterly* 16 (1999): 59–80.

structure and public culture of a modern constitutional democracy form the materials for justifying principles of justice that are appropriate for such a society. Rawls's theory of justice emerges from this question: What conception of justice would be appropriate for a modern constitutional democracy given its institutional framework and the convictions that are embedded in its public culture? The difficulty that this approach raises is that the materials from which Rawls justifies his conception of justice are not themselves justified. Consequently, as I noted earlier, justice as fairness has no resources to explain why states must adopt the constitutional norms and institutional arrangements of a modern constitutional democracy. Similarly, justice as fairness has no resources to explain why a public culture must endorse the fundamental ideas on which justice as fairness rests and why it would be defective to the extent that it fails to do so.

The public culture plays a different role within the unified theory. Instead of treating the convictions that form a particular public culture as justifying a conception of justice, the unified theory holds that the nature of the public culture is itself bound up with the relevant conception.[64] The duty of public justice ultimately requires the realization of a democratic system of government in which the people rules itself in accordance with norms of equal freedom. If the people is to govern itself in this manner, then it must develop a public culture that has internalized the principles of public law. By this I mean that the public culture must, on the one hand, be capable of distinguishing those arrangements that are merely authoritative from those that are just, and, on the other, be committed to bringing the sum of authoritative arrangements into conformity with the demands of public justice. The refinement of the public culture is a condition for the performance of the duty of public justice incumbent on the people. Thus, instead of following Rawls in appealing to the public culture to develop a conception of justice, the unified theory appeals to a conception of justice to regulate the ongoing development of the public culture.

The unified theory of public law presents an alternative to both acontextual theories that bypass the particular circumstances of existing societies and quietist theories eager to embrace the adequacy of the status quo. While the unified theory holds that public justice is an ideal common to legal systems as such, it is not an 'ideal that is everywhere everlastingly the

64 Here I follow a distinction developed in Onora O'Neil, "Constructivism in Rawls and Kant," in *The Cambridge Companion to Rawls*, ed. Samuel Freeman (Cambridge: Cambridge University Press, 2003), 360.

same.'[65] The approximation of the ideal of public justice requires the ongoing eradication of injustice, not the elimination of particularity.

Conclusion

The leading paradigms in contemporary political and legal philosophy share a progressive aspiration to provide a theoretical standpoint for criticizing existing societies and directing their reform. The purpose of this chapter has been to explore three central questions about progressive theorizing.

First, how would a theory have to be structured in order to make good on this progressive aspiration? I have argued that a progressive theory must integrate three components: (1) an underlying subject, (2) a moral standard for assessing the moral adequacy of instances of the underlying subject, and (3) a norm articulating what is required of instances of the underlying subject that are defective in relation to their own internal standard of adequacy.

Second, do the leading political and legal theories possess such a structure? Rawls's theory fails to make good on its own progressive aspiration because even though it encompasses all three components, the theory conceives of the first and second components in a manner too narrow to apply to the range of instances relevant to the third. The result is a theory of justice that is progressive but not general. Hart's theory raises the opposite problem: it is general insofar as its underlying subject is legal systems as such, but it is morally variable insofar as the conception of legality is compatible with a variety of different conceptions of morality, some progressive and others regressive.

Third, what would a theory look like that is both general and progressive? The unified theory is general insofar as its underlying subject is legal systems as such, but it is not morally variable. The fundamental idea that integrates its general and progressive components is that a legal system involves the right of government to exercise public authority over independent persons. The justification of this right indicates both the internal ideal of a legal system as such and what is required of a legal system that is defective in relation to its own internal ideal. While such an approach departs significantly from the theories canvassed earlier, it retains one of Rawls's most basic ideas: 'that the correct regulative principle for anything depends on the nature of that thing.'[66]

[65] Radbruch, *Legal Philosophy*, 121. [66] *A Theory of Justice*, 29.

PART II

The constitutional dimension

5

The modern constitutional state

In the world of constitutional law, theory and practice are moving in opposite directions. As a matter of *constitutional practice* since the end of World War II, an extensive and growing literature produced by lawyers, judges, and political scientists acknowledges the emergence of a groundbreaking constitutional paradigm. In states as diverse as Germany, South Africa, and Canada, this modern constitutional paradigm integrates (1) a constitution that exhaustively establishes the conditions for the valid exercise of all public authority, (2) a constitutionally entrenched bill of rights that delineates the right of persons, by virtue of their inherent dignity, to just governance, and (3) a politically independent judicial body to which any individual can bring a constitutional complaint challenging the validity of any exercise of public authority on the grounds that it violates a constitutional right. The emergence of this modern constitutional paradigm has been described as 'the most important public law event of the twentieth century,'[1] 'a constitutional and civil rights revolution,'[2] and as the 'full realization' of democracy.'[3]

As a matter of *constitutional theory*, the modern constitutional paradigm remains enigmatic. Proponents of modern constitutionalism typically argue that 'the question whether or not a country should entrench a bill of rights and subject it to judicial oversight is not one of principle, but one of pragmatics. It requires a balancing of benefits

[1] Juan Colombo Campbell, "Constitutional Court Judges' Roundtable," *International Journal of Constitutional Law* 3 (2005): 545 (citing Louis Favoreu, "Justicia y Jueces Constitucionales," *Revista de Derecho Publico* 61 (1999): 10–16).

[2] Mauro Cappelletti, "Repudiating Montesquieu? The Expansion and Legitimacy of 'Constitutional Justice'," *Catholic University Law Review* 35 (1986): 28 [hereinafter "Constitutional Justice"].

[3] *United Mizrahi Bank Ltd., et al.* v. *Migdal Cooperative Village, et al.* [1995] 49 P.D. 221, para. 47.

and costs ... [E]ach country has to find its own solution.'[4] Ronald Dworkin's final treatment of constitutional governance is emblematic of this approach. Distancing himself from his earlier view that judicial review of constitutional rights makes an essential contribution to a well-ordered regime by elevating the level of public debate[5] and generating just outcomes,[6] Dworkin maintained in *Justice for Hedgehogs* that the appropriateness of judicial review hinges on considerations 'that vary from place to place.'[7] These considerations include a country's track record in protecting individual and minority rights, as well as 'the strength of the rule of law, the independence of the judiciary, and the character of the constitution judges are asked to enforce.'[8] In a world in which the judicial review of constitutional rights has solidified as a central feature of constitutional governance, Dworkin refrained from formulating its principled justification.

The pragmatism of proponents of constitutional governance can be contrasted with the principled objections of its opponents. While opponents need not be hostile to notions of individual rights, they share the view that the legal and institutional structure through which modern constitutional states make constitutional rights justiciable is objectionable. By empowering the judiciary to strike down legislation, a modern constitutional state imposes an illegitimate constraint on the democratic right of a majority (or plurality) to enact its preferences into law.[9] This view accepts that a legal system should respect the rights of individuals, but rejects the institutional framework through which modern constitutional states enable individuals to vindicate their rights.[10] Confronted by principled opponents but lacking a principled defense, modern constitutionalism has had to develop without and in opposition to an established theoretical framework.

The purpose of this chapter is to offer a principled defense of the modern constitutional state by setting out the connection between its

[4] Dieter Grimm, "Constitutional Adjudication and Democracy," *Israel Law Review* 33 (1999): 196. While Grimm's view is that 'more arguments speak for, than against judicial review,' he conceives of the arguments both for and against as pragmatic in nature.

[5] Ronald Dworkin, *Freedom's Law: The Moral Reading of the American Constitution* (Cambridge: Harvard University Press, 1996), 345 [hereinafter *Freedom's Law*].

[6] Ibid., 34.

[7] Dworkin, *Justice for Hedgehogs* (Cambridge: Harvard University Press, 2011), 398.

[8] Ibid.

[9] Jeremy Waldron, "The Core of the Case Against Judicial Review," *Yale Law Journal* 115 (2006): 1375 and 1388–9.

[10] Ibid., 1366.

normative commitment to the inherent dignity of each of its inhabitants, on the one hand, and its distinctive legal and institutional structure, on the other. I proceed in four sections.

The first formulates the moral problem between rulers and ruled to which the legal and institutional structure of a modern constitutional state systematically responds. The problem – common to all precursors of modern constitutionalism – is not that rulers *necessarily* exercise public authority in a manner that violates the inherent dignity and fundamental rights of the ruled, but that in the event of a violation one or more persons are left without legal recourse. In legal systems in which public authority is exercised by the few, as in autocratic or oligarchic forms of government, the many are left without legal recourse. Conversely, in legal systems in which public authority is exercised by the many, as in majoritarian democracies, it is the few who stand vulnerable. In each of these legal systems, there exists no legal and institutional structure that makes the dignity and fundamental rights of each person justiciable. I call this the *problem of accountability*.

The second section presents the fundamental innovation of modern constitutional states through an exposition of the legal and institutional structure of Germany, South Africa, and Canada. In contrast to earlier forms of government, modern constitutionalism is systematically designed to make the exercise of public authority accountable to neither the preferences of the many nor the few, but – for the first time in the long history of public law – to the justiciable right of each and every person to governance that conforms to the demands of dignity. This accountability is evident in the distinctive features of a modern constitutional state: a written constitution that establishes the conditions for the valid exercise of public authority, a constitutionally entrenched bill of rights premised on the inherent dignity of each person subject to public authority, and a politically independent judicial body to which any individual (and, in some cases, representative or surrogate actors) may bring a constitutional complaint. Through its legal and institutional structure, a modern constitutional state transforms the right of each person within the legal order to just governance from a mere moral imperative into a justiciable legal right. So conceived, a modern constitutional state addresses a problem that arises in every legal system, but that no legal system can address apart from the distinctive legal and institutional structure of a modern constitutional state.

The third section assesses the adequacy of a competing constitutional model, the commonwealth model instantiated by the United Kingdom.

On the one hand, I argue that the commonwealth model should not be regarded as a constitution ideal to which legal systems should aspire, because the problem of accountability persists within it. On the other, I argue that the commonwealth model should not be cast aside, because it offers legal systems that cannot presently realize modern constitutionalism with a way of approximating its approach to rights protection. Although the commonwealth model is not the ideal constitution, there are contexts in which its adoption represents a step in the right direction.

The fourth section defends this model of governance from a leading critic, Jeremy Waldron. Waldron raises two lines of objection. First, he criticizes theorists who, like Dworkin, justify the judicial review of legislation by appealing to the desirable outcomes that the practice might produce, for example, elevated levels of public debate or just decisions. Waldron argues that such justifications do not succeed because legal experience reveals both that judicial review might fail to produce these outcomes and that these outcomes might be produced by legal systems that lack judicial review. The position that I advance is not vulnerable to this line of objection because it does not defend judicial review as an arrangement for producing outcomes that could, in principle, be achieved without it. As I argue in the second section, the problem of accountability cannot be addressed apart from the legal and institutional structure of a modern constitutional state. Waldron's second line of objection attacks the practice directly by arguing that insofar as it imposes constraints on majority rule, it is undemocratic and therefore illegitimate. I respond by explaining that even though modern constitutionalism is not majoritarian, it is nonetheless a democratic form of governance. It is democratic insofar as citizens exercise political rights and thereby govern themselves through their representatives. It is not majoritarian insofar as it creates a legal framework in which the legislative power of the citizenry is accountable to the inherent dignity and fundamental rights of each person bound by it.

Two clarifications are in order from the outset.

My defense of modern constitutionalism does not offer a detailed blueprint of the totality of constitutional norms and institutional arrangements appropriate for legal systems in general. Instead, the purpose of the defense is to articulate a moral problem inherent in the public law relationship between rulers and ruled and then to explain how the general legal and institutional structure of modern constitutional states addresses this problem. So conceived, modern constitutionalism is a versatile form of legal ordering that can be filled with a variety of different kinds of arrangements: unitary or federal, unicameral or bicameral, common law or civil law, presidential or parliamentary in its system of government, and centralized or decentralized in its system of judicial review. The purpose of the constitutional theory that I elaborate is to set out a general moral framework that offers resources for distinguishing between admissible and objectionable instances of legal variation.

Further, in offering a principled defense of modern constitutionalism, I do not deny that pragmatic considerations have a role to play. Principles neither answer to pragmatic considerations nor exclude them. Rather, pragmatic considerations are relevant to the determination of how principles, in a particular context, are to be effectuated. If it can be established as a matter of principle that each legal system must enact reforms to address the problem of accountability, and that the concrete features of an existing legal system present opportunities for and obstacles to reform, the question of what a particular legal system must do cannot be raised in abstraction from its concrete circumstances. Every legal system must bring itself into the deepest possible conformity with the modern constitutional paradigm. But because different legal systems present distinctive opportunities and obstacles to reform, the duty to create an accountable legal order may call for different reforms in different legal systems. I return to this point in the third section, in discussing constitutionalism in the United Kingdom.

5.1 The problem of accountability

The problem of accountability emerges from a particular understanding of the public law relationship between rulers and ruled.

In expounding the normative dimension of public law in the preceding chapters, I defended the view that public law is constituted and regulated by two distinct but mutually implicating juridical principles. The principle of authority constitutes public law: a legal system consists in the public institutions of government that impose, interpret, and enforce law upon a plurality of private persons. The principle of justice regulates public law: public authority is exercised adequately to the extent that it is directed toward bringing the existing legal order into conformity with the right of each person bound by it to public justice or equal freedom under law. Thus, the justification of the right of government to exercise public authority implicates the relevant moral standard for assessing the adequacy of its exercise. The right of government to exercise public authority enters the world accompanied by a duty to reconcile law's authority with the dignity of each free and equal person subject to it.

Once the right of government to rule is understood to be accompanied by a duty of just governance owed to each person subject to law's authority, the problem of accountability materializes. The problem is not that rulers necessarily violate the right of the ruled to just governance, but that in event of a violation, one or more persons is left without legal recourse. The right of government to exercise public authority is always accompanied by a duty to govern justly, but persons subject to public authority have no legal mechanism that enables them to stand on their right to just governance and hold the exercise of public authority to the terms of its justification. This problem, I will argue, is a common feature of all precursors to modern constitutionalism.

The problem of accountability is a distinctive feature of the public law relationship between rulers and ruled. In private law, which concerns the rights and duties apposite to the interaction of private persons, the problem of accountability is addressed by the presence of public institutions. A person who suffers a wrong at the hands of another private person can bring his or her case before the impartial authority of a judge and demand to be made whole by the wrongdoer. A different structure, however, obtains in the public law relationship between rulers and ruled. When one suffers a wrong at the hands of the public authority, the public authority is both a party to the dispute and judge in its own cause. Accordingly, the public authority might ignore one's grievance, deny that the grievance amounts to a wrong, or even concede the commission of a wrong but withhold a corresponding remedy. Every person subject to public authority has a right to just governance, but whether that right will be respected depends on the very party that is under an obligation with respect to it. Publicly authoritative institutions make private persons accountable to one another, but they also generate a problem of accountability whenever the legal system is organized in such a way that persons susceptible to public wrongs are left without legal recourse.

The problem of accountability is *conceptual*, not *causal*. Alexander Hamilton makes a causal claim in his remark, 'Give all the power to the many, they will oppress the few. Give all the power to the few, they will oppress the many.'[11] Hamilton's remark is causal because it suggests that if there is a discrepancy between those who exercise power and those on

[11] *Debates on the Adoption of the Federal Constitution*, ed. Jonathan Elliot (New York: Burt Franklin, 1888), 203.

whom power is exercised, it is probable that the former will oppress the latter. The problem of accountability, by contrast, is deeper because it arises not from the *likelihood* that public authority will be exercised unjustly, but from the mere *possibility* that persons susceptible to unjust governance could be left without legal recourse. The problem would therefore arise even if circumstances were so fortuitously arranged that public authority had always been exercised justly because those entitled to just governance would nevertheless remain incapable of standing on their right to just governance. The problem persists in any legal system in which there is a disjuncture between those who are subject to public authority and those who have the legal standing to constrain the exercise of public authority to the terms of its justification.

The history of the theory and practice of public law is a testament to the pervasiveness of the problem of accountability. When Aristotle surveyed the constitutions of the ancient world, he discerned that the 'governing body is the authoritative element' and 'that the authoritative element [must] be either one or a few or the many.'[12] Each of these modes of exercising public authority shares a common defect: the failure to address the problem of accountability. The problem is inescapable so long as public authority rests in the hands of a single person (as in a monarchy), a few persons (as in an aristocracy), or many persons (as in a majoritarian democracy). A monarchy is unaccountable to every person bound by its lawgiving, while an aristocracy is unaccountable to the many. A majoritarian democracy is sometimes described as an accountable form of government because it makes those who exercise public authority answer to the preferences of the majority of adult citizens, as registered periodically during elections.[13] But from the standpoint of the problem of accountability, majoritarian democracy is defective in three respects.

First, majoritarians typically conceive of public authority as an instrument for realizing *popular preferences*.[14] The majoritarian view is premised on the capacity of rational persons to formulate their own

[12] Aristotle, *Politics* in *Selected Works*, trans. Hippocrates G. Apostle and Lloyd P. Gerson (Iowa: Peripatetic Press, 1991), III.7, 1279a27.

[13] See, for example Francis Fukuyama, *The Origins of the Political Order* (New York: Farrar, Straus, and Giroux, 2011), 321–2 and 420.

[14] See, for example, Robert Alan Dahl, *Polyarchy: Participation and Opposition* (New Haven: Yale University Press, 1971), 1 (assuming that 'a key characteristic of a democracy is the continuing responsiveness of the government to the preferences of its citizens, considered as political equals').

preferences about how public authority should be exercised.[15] Since persons are capable of formulating their own preferences regarding the exercise of public authority, the state should not subjugate persons to the preferences of rulers, but should instead create the conditions in which citizens can guide the exercise of public authority toward the fulfillment of their shared preferences. Because it is unrealistic to suppose that citizens will invariably agree about what preferences public authority should serve, a procedure is required that both recognizes the capacity of citizens to formulate their own preferences and that affords each citizen an equal say in determining what preferences public authority should pursue. Majoritarian democracy is that procedure. In a majoritarian democracy, preferences are legitimated not by the merit of their content, which might culminate in disagreement, but by attracting the assent of the many, that is, a majority or plurality of adult citizens at the ballot box. The popular assent of the many transforms any preference from a private wish into a public purpose. In this social calculus of unconstrained preferences, 'My preferences about how you lead your life . . . count as much as yours.'[16] Such a framework is not necessarily opposed to directing public authority toward the fulfillment of the right of each person to just governance. For the purpose to which law's authority is directed depends upon the preferences that persons happen to have. But that is exactly the problem. The aggregation of the unconstrained preferences of the many might culminate in outcomes that are incompatible with the right of the few to just governance. When such outcomes arise, the few are without legal recourse.

Second, majoritarian democracy holds that government is accountable to the *people* when it is answerable to the preferences of the majority of its adult citizens. By contrast, to address the problem of accountability, a legal system must make the exercise of public authority answerable to the right of every person within it to just governance. This includes all adult citizens, and also children, prisoners, tourists, immigrants, refugees, and guest workers. Such an inclusive conception of accountability is puzzling to majoritarians. If government is accountable to preferences and different persons affirm incompatible preferences, then it is impossible for government to be accountable to the preferences of every person subject to its lawgiving. The next best thing would be for government to be

15 For an overview of this conception of democracy, see Gregory H. Fox and George Nolte, "Intolerant Democracies," *Harvard International Law Journal* 36 (1995): 14–16.

16 Dworkin, "Law's Ambitions for Itself," *Virginia Law Review* 71 (1985): 186.

accountable, in the words of Justice Oliver Wendell Holmes, to the 'right of a majority to embody their opinions in law.'[17] However, if the duty of government is not to impose the particular purposes affirmed by 'the dominant forces of the community' upon all others,[18] but to subject freedom to a set of reciprocal constraints so that each person can exercise purposiveness in a manner compatible with the right of others to the same, then the problem of incompatible purposes dissolves.[19]

Third, in a majoritarian democracy government is held accountable *from time to time* through elections. The problem of accountability is not addressed by such an intermittent mechanism. In addition, a legal system must create the conditions in which every person bound by law's authority can stand on his or her right to just governance, regardless of whether an election has just concluded, is presently occurring, or will soon transpire.

Prior to their respective transitions to modern constitutionalism, Germany, South Africa, and Canada illustrate that whether public authority is exercised by a single person, a minority of persons, or by the majority of adult citizens, its exercise remains unaccountable to the inherent dignity of all those who are bound by it. In Germany, public authority was exercised (at least for a time) by one and was unaccountable to all; in South Africa, public authority was exercised by the few and unaccountable to the many; and, in Canada, public authority was exercised by the many and unaccountable to the few. Following the descent of Weimar into Nazism, the Führer exercised power in accordance with the totalitarian slogan *Du bist nichts, dein Volk ist alles!* ('You are nothing; your nation is everything!'). The Führer determined how persons were to be treated in accordance with his perception of the objectives of the nation. Whereas in Nazi Germany power was exercised by one and was unaccountable to all,[20] Apartheid South Africa placed state power in the

[17] *Lochner* v. *New York*, 198 U.S. 45, 75–76 (1905) (Holmes, J., dissenting). For an exploration of the judicial philosophy that animates Holmes's approach to the First Amendment, see Steven J. Heyman, "The Dark Side of the Force: The Legacy of Justice Holmes for First Amendment Jurisprudence," *William & Mary Bill of Rights Journal* 19 (2011): 661–723.

[18] *Gitlow* v. *New York*, 268 U.S. 652, 673 (1925) (Holmes, J., dissenting).

[19] On the distinction between conceiving of freedom as the right to do whatever one wishes and in terms of a set of reciprocal limits on conduct, see Arthur Ripstein, *Force and Freedom: Kant's Legal and Political Philosophy* (Cambridge: Harvard University Press, 2009), 16–17.

[20] I argue in Chapter 3 that Nazism ultimately deteriorated into a condition of lawless violence. The same may be true of Apartheid South Africa, but I cannot pursue this issue here.

hands of the few, a white minority that could enact law 'without a need to justify even to those governed by the law.'[21] Those who were excluded from contributing to the enactment of law 'were treated as not having inherent worth; as objects whose identities could be arbitrarily defined by those in power . . . In short they were denied recognition of their inherent dignity.'[22] Although the majority of the population was denied political rights, the judiciary 'accepted that parliament could make laws that, expressly or by necessary implication, sanctioned discrimination and the deprivation of rights.'[23] Unlike South Africa, in which the few exercised power in a manner unaccountable to the many, Canada presented the opposite problem: the many exercised public authority in a manner that was unaccountable to the few. Prior to the enactment of the *Charter of Rights and Freedoms* in 1982, persons enjoyed the right to ask the legislature to govern in a manner compatible with their human dignity and fundamental rights. However, 'Canada's constitutional order protected these norms only in the interstices of its parliamentary system of government and its federal structure.'[24] So long as the federal and provincial branches of government acted *intra vires*, public power could be directed toward the 'discriminatory denial of employment opportunities and the franchise; the removal of the right of citizens, natural born and naturalized, to remain in Canada; restrictions on basic political rights and social benefits.'[25] In sum, the problem of accountability pervaded the disparate modes of governance in Germany, South Africa, and Canada prior to their transitions to modern constitutionalism. In each case the legal order was arranged in such a way that individuals subject to law's authority lacked the legal standing to vindicate their basic right to just governance.

It is crucial to distinguish an *accountable* legal order from a perfectly *just* one. A legal order is accountable if each person subject to law's authority can stand on his or her right to just governance. Thus, even if 'there is no human institution – political or social, judicial or ecclesiastical – that can guarantee that legitimate (or just) laws are always enacted

[21] Etienne Mureinik, "A Bridge to Where? Introducing the Interim Bill of Rights," *South African Journal on Human Rights* 10 (1994): 32.

[22] *Prinsloo* v. *van der Linde*, 1997 (3) SA 1012 (CC), para. 31.

[23] Arthur Chaskalson, "From Wickedness to Equality: The Moral Transformation of South Africa Law," *International Journal of Constitutional Law* 1 (2003): 592.

[24] Lorraine Eisenstat Weinrib, "Canada's Constitutional Revolution: From Legislative to Constitutional State," *Israel Law Review* 33 (1999): 14.

[25] Ibid., 16.

and just rights always respected,'[26] the question of how a legal order could be designed to make the right of persons to just governance justiciable persists. Here, an analogy with legal relationships in private law is helpful. By recognizing, interpreting, and enforcing private rights, a legal system makes private persons accountable to one another in their conduct by enabling each private person to stand on his or her own rights in relation to every other. Of course, this does not mean that private persons never commit injustices against one another or that the judiciary is infallible in recognizing and remedying private wrongs. Rather, it means that persons who have suffered a private wrong have the legal recourse to bring the supposed wrongdoer before an authoritative body empowered to recognize wrongs and impart remedies. An accountable legal order extends legal recourse from the domain of private law relationships to the public law relationship between a state and its members. A legal system is accountable if it creates the conditions under which the inherent dignity of the human person forms a justiciable constraint on the exercise of all public authority. An accountable legal order is not one devoid of public injustices, but one in which these injustices are themselves justiciable.

The problem of accountability raises a fundamental question about legal ordering: How would a legal system be designed in order to make public authority accountable neither to the preferences of the many nor to the few, neither during this election nor the next, but to the unceasing right of each inhabitant of the legal order to just governance?

5.2 A new form of government

Modern constitutionalism is a mode of legal organization that is systematically designed to address the problem of accountability by transforming the right of each person to just governance from 'a mere guideline of a political, moral, or philosophical nature' into a justiciable constraint on all public authority.[27] A legal system designed to make the exercise of public authority accountable to the inherent human dignity of all who are bound by it would have a distinctive legal and institutional structure. First, to constrain the exercise of public authority, a legal system would

[26] John Rawls, "Political Liberalism: Reply to Habermas," *The Journal of Philosophy* 92 (1995): 166.

[27] Mauro Cappelletti, "The Expanding Role of Judicial Review in Modern Societies," in *The Role of Courts in Society*, ed. Simon Shetreet (Dordrecht: Martinus Nijhoff Publishers, 1988), 89.

have to establish conditions for the valid exercise of public authority by any branch of government, whether the legislature, executive, or judiciary. Second, these legal conditions would have to reflect the right of each person, as a bearer of dignity, to just governance. Third, the legal order would have to create an institution that empowered any individual to challenge the validity of an exercise of public authority on the basis of its nonconformity with his or her right to just governance.

In what follows, I argue that this is exactly what a modern constitutional state provides by integrating constitutional supremacy, constitutional rights, and judicial review. I will elaborate on the role of each of these components by explaining how the constitutional orders in Germany, South Africa, and Canada addressed the problem of accountability that obtained in the preceding regime. I will then argue that if even one of these legal or institutional components is absent, the problem of accountability persists. Because every legal system must address the problem of accountability, and the problem cannot be addressed apart from the general legal and institutional framework of a modern constitutional state, every legal system must ultimately adopt some version of this framework.

A modern constitution *constitutes* government by establishing the conditions for the valid exercise of public authority within a given legal system. Since the constitution is exhaustive in establishing these conditions, all public authority descends from it: there can be no 'extra-constitutional mode of exercising public power.'[28] Further, because the constitution determines the conditions of the valid exercise of public authority within a given legal system, the constitution denies the validity of any act of government – legislative, executive, or judicial – that conflicts with constitutional standards. Thus, Germany's Basic Law indicates that the rights and duties that it recognizes bind the legislature, the executive, and the judiciary.[29] Similarly, the *Constitution of the Republic of South Africa* holds that 'law or conduct inconsistent with it is invalid, and the obligations imposed by it must be fulfilled.'[30] Because the

[28] Dieter Grimm, "The German and American Constitutionalism: A Comparison," *The Berlin Journal* 7 (2003): 8. See also Grimm, "The Achievement of Constitutionalism and Its Prospects in a Changed World," in *The Twilight of Constitutionalism*, ed. Petra Dobner and Martin Loughlin (Oxford: Oxford University Press, 2010), 9.

[29] Basic Law of the Federal Republic of Germany, 1949, articles 1(3) and 20(3). On constitutional supremacy in Germany, see Jutta Limbach, "The Concept of the Supremacy of the Constitution," *Modern Law Review* 64 (2001): 1.

[30] *Constitution of the Republic of South Africa*, 1996, s. 2; Chaskalson, "From Wickedness to Equality: The Moral Transformation of South African Law," 599; and Lourens W.H.

Constitution is the supreme law, a court 'must declare that any law or conduct that is inconsistent with the Constitution is invalid to the extent of its inconsistency.'[31] In the Canadian context, the *Constitution Act, 1982*, declares that the 'Constitution of Canada is the supreme law . . . any law that is inconsistent with the provisions of the Constitution is, to the extent of the inconsistency, of no force or effect.'[32] As the Supreme Court of Canada stated unanimously in one of its most important judgments: 'The Constitution binds all governments, both federal and provincial . . . They may not transgress its provisions: indeed, their sole claim to exercise lawful authority rests in the powers allocated to them under the Constitution, and can come from no other source.'[33] Since the constitution alone empowers government, no branch of government may exercise the authority that the constitution affords while ignoring the duties that it imposes.

In making the right of persons to just governance the constitutional condition for the valid exercise of all public authority, a modern constitutional state makes a fundamental break from earlier forms of government. In precursors to modern constitutionalism, public authority could of course be directed toward the enactment and enforcement of just laws that fulfill the right of persons to just governance. But in the event of this right's violation, those who suffer public wrongs could be left without legal recourse. By contrast, the modern constitutional state reorients the relationship between the right of government to exercise public authority and the right of persons to just governance by, on the one hand, recognizing that every person within the legal order – by virtue of his or her inherent dignity – imposes a duty on all public authority, and, on the other, establishing that compliance with this duty is a constitutional condition for the valid exercise of public authority. Thus, article 1 of Germany's Basic Law declares, 'Human dignity shall be inviolable. To respect and protect [human dignity] shall be the duty of all state authority.'[34] That the state must *respect* human dignity precludes the state from

Ackermann, "The Legal Nature of the South African Constitutional Revolution," *New Zealand Law Review* (2004): 643.

31 *Constitution of the Republic of South Africa*, 1996, s. 172(1)(a).

32 *Constitution Act, 1982*, s. 52(1), being Schedule B to the *Canada Act 1982* (UK), 1982, c. 11 [hereinafter *Charter*].

33 *Reference re Secession of Quebec*, [1998] 2 SCR 217, 258.

34 Basic Law of the Federal Republic of Germany, 1949, article 1(1) [hereinafter Grundgesetz]. See Eckart Klein, "Human Dignity in German Law," in *The Concept of Human Dignity in Human Rights Discourse*, ed. David Kretzmer and Eckart Klein (The Hague: Kluwer Law International 2002), 146 ('The dignity of man is the legitimizing basis

interfering with persons in a manner unbefitting of their dignity. That the state must *protect* human dignity requires the state to create the conditions in which all persons within the legal order may live in dignity under law.[35] In South Africa, the 'touchstone of the new political order' is the recognition of the inherent dignity of all South Africans, which the Apartheid regime denied.[36] Thus the South African Constitution is premised on the values of 'human dignity, equality and freedom.'[37] In the words of Justice Sachs of the Constitutional Court of South Africa, 'The test, whether majoritarian or minoritarian positions are involved, must always be whether the measure under scrutiny promotes or retards the achievement of human dignity, equality and freedom.'[38] Although Canada's *Charter of Rights and Freedoms* does not explicitly entrench human dignity, it holds that the rights and freedoms that it guarantees are grounded in the values of a 'free and democratic society.'[39] Chief Justice Dickson elucidated both the aim and the foundation of such a society: 'A free society is one which aims at equality with respect to the enjoyment of fundamental freedoms . . . Freedom must surely be founded in respect for the inherent dignity and the inviolable rights of the human person.'[40] In a modern constitutional state, the exercise of public authority is to be answerable neither to the preferences of the few nor of the many, but to the equal right of every inhabitant of the legal order to just governance.

By recognizing that the *inherent* dignity of human persons forms the purpose and constraint of all public power, a modern constitutional state repudiates any arrangement that ties the right of persons to just governance or their capacity to hold public power accountable to characteristics that some possess but others lack, whether a particular gender, race, religious worldview, class, or favorable standing with respect to the

of the State and its legal order. The State's respect for and protection of human dignity constitute its purpose').

35 Donald P. Kommers and Russell A. Miller, *The Constitutional Jurisprudence of the Federal Republic of Germany* (Durham: Duke University Press, 2012), 60. On the affirmative duty to protect human dignity, see Dieter Grimm, "The Basic Law at 60 – Identity and Change," *German Law Journal* 11 (2010): 43–4; and David P. Currie, "Positive and Negative Constitutional Rights," *University of Chicago Law Review* 53 (1986): 864.

36 *S.* v. *Makwanyane and Another* (1995) 3 SA 391, para. 329.

37 *Constitution of the Republic of South Africa*, 1996, ss. 1 and 7.

38 *Minister of Home Affairs* v. *Fourie*, 2006 1 SA 524 (CC), para. 94.

39 *Canadian Charter of Rights and Freedoms*, s. 1, Part I of the *Constitution Act, 1982*, being Schedule B to the *Canada Act 1982* (U.K.), 1982, c. 11.

40 *R.* v. *Big M Drug Mart Ltd.*, [1985] 1 SCR 295, 336.

dominant forces of the community. As Ernst Benda, a former president of Germany's Federal Constitutional Court, explained,

> The most important sentence in the Basic Law will always be Article 1 . . . The founding fathers and mothers of the Basic Law purposely did not refer to the state or state authority, or to the nation, in this opening sentence. On the contrary, it concerns the human person and the dignity of the individual. It is an explicit rejection of every ideology which sacrifices human life or life chances to a supposedly higher cause. And it is a rejection, too, of every form of discrimination on grounds of origin, colour, creed or conviction. Article 1 does not say: "The dignity of the German people shall be inviolable". Nor does it refer to the dignity of the healthy or wealthy. It is a clear commitment to the inviolability of *human* dignity. This is not an abstract philosophical concept, but a binding obligation and an enduring mission for all those who bear political responsibility in our democratic and social state under the rule of law.[41]

The general constitutional duty to respect and protect human dignity is concretized by a set of constitutional rights that specify the relationship between the free individual and the coercive state. Germany's Basic Law sets out the relationship between human dignity and constitutional rights in article 1. In this article, the recognition that human dignity is 'inviolable' is immediately followed by the statement that the 'German people therefore [*darum*] acknowledge inviolable and inalienable human rights as the basis of every community, of peace and of justice in the world.'[42] Accordingly, persons possess a set of basic rights, including the general right to liberty, which entitles each person to the free development of his or her personality in concert with others in the legal order.[43] The rights contained in the Basic Law are 'not mere proclamations or slogans' as they were under the Weimar Constitution,[44] but rather are 'directly applicable law' that binds all branches of government.[45] As Dürig observes, 'In earlier times (including Weimar) the basic rights were

[41] Ernst Benda, "Foreword by the Federal President," in *Basic Law for the Federal Republic of Germany* (Berlin: Bundestag, 2000), 5–6.

[42] Grundgesetz, articles 1(1) and 1(2) (my emphasis). For discussions of the relationship between dignity and constitutional rights, see Klein, "Human Dignity in German Law," 146 ff.; and Edward J. Eberle, "The German Idea of Freedom," *Oregon Review of International Law* 10 (2008): 16–17.

[43] Grundgesetz, article 2(1).

[44] Dürig, "An Introduction to the Basic Law of the Federal Republic of Germany," in *The Constitution of the Federal Republic of Germany*, ed. Ulrich Karpen (Baden-Baden: Nomos Verlagsgesellschaft, 1998), 13.

[45] Grundgesetz, article 1(3).

only valid subject to the laws; today the laws are only valid subject to the basic rights.'[46]

This conception of the relationship between the inherent dignity of the human person and constitutional rights is echoed by the constitutional orders of South Africa and Canada. In South Africa, human dignity is not only a foundational value of the legal order[47] but also a justiciable right.[48] Dignity 'informs the content of all the concrete rights' that the constitution delineates.[49] Similarly, Canada's *Charter* grounds the rights and freedoms it elaborates in the values of a free and democratic society, which include the 'inherent dignity of the human person.'[50] This inherent dignity 'is at the heart of individual rights in a free and democratic society.'[51] Within the modern constitutional paradigm, constitutional rights are not – as proponents of the majoritarian conception of accountability would assert – simply a catalog of past agreements enacted into law, but an elaboration of the more general duty that each person, as a being free and equal in dignity, imposes on public authority.

A constitution that makes the duty to govern justly the condition for the valid exercise of public authority is necessary to render government accountable to each of its members, but it is not sufficient. It is necessary because it enables a distinction to be drawn between valid exercises of public authority (which conform to the right of persons to just governance) and mere exercises of power (which violate the constitutional condition for the valid exercise of public authority). It is not sufficient because it leaves persons who believe that this right has been violated without legal recourse. If government is to be accountable to the human dignity of each person subject to its authority, there must be an institution capable of assessing constitutional complaints on their merits, providing a public determination of the constitutionality of state action (or

46 Dürig, "An Introduction to the Basic Law of the Federal Republic of Germany," 13.

47 *Constitution of the Republic of South Africa*, 1996, s. 7. See Francois Venter, *Constitutional Comparison: Japan, Germany, Canada and South Africa as Constitutional States* (The Hague: Kluwer Law International, 2000), 139–47.

48 *Constitution of the Republic of South Africa*, 1996, s. 10.

49 Arthur Chaskalson, "Human Dignity as a Foundational Value of Our Constitutional Order," 204. See also Arthur Chaskalson, "Human Dignity as a Constitutional Value," in *The Concept of Human Dignity in Human Rights Discourse*, 136.

50 *R.* v. *Oakes*, [1986] 1 SCR 103, 136. On the relations between human dignity and constitutional rights in Canada, see Wilson J.'s concurring opinion in *R.* v. *Morgentaler*, [1988] 1 SCR 30, 166.

51 See, for example, *Egan* v. *Canada*, [1995] 2 SCR 513, 543; and *Hill* v. *Church of Scientology of Toronto*, [1995] 2 SCR 1130, 1179.

inaction), invalidating state action (or inaction) that violates constitutional standards, and imparting remedies to those who have suffered public wrongs.[52] Further, to perform this role, the relevant institution would have to possess legal expertise in constitutional interpretation and rights adjudication. Finally, this institution would have to be politically independent so that complaints would be considered on their legal merits rather than in reference to the preferences of the government of the day.

The judiciary (or a specialized constitutional court) is uniquely suited for this role. The legal expertise of the judiciary enables it to interpret constitutional law and adjudicate rights claims. The political independence of the judiciary insulates it from political pressure and thereby enables it to assess constitutional complaints against the government in accordance with the normative framework established by the constitution. Further, unlike the legislature, which owes a duty of just governance to each person in the constitutional order but is accountable only to a majority (or plurality) of adult citizens at election time, judicial review enables any person to bring a constitutional complaint at any time challenging the validity of any instance of government conduct. The right of each person to bring a constitutional complaint before a politically independent judicial body empowered and obligated to effectuate constitutional norms reflects the most basic commitment of the modern constitutional paradigm: that each person subject to public authority must enjoy the legal capacity to respond to a public wrong by standing on his or her right to just governance.

Following the horrors of Nazism and the failure of Weimar to make constitutional norms 'judicially enforceable,'[53] Germany created a constitutional court to transform constitutional norms into a constitutional reality: 'In the spirit of "Never again" the framers were convinced that a constitution, as good as it may be, is of little value if it is not accompanied by an independent institution that enforces constitutional law . . . So a court with a very wide range of powers was foreseen in the Basic Law . . . '[54] The Basic Law states, 'Should any person's rights be violated by public authority, he may have recourse to the courts.'[55] In turn, the *Constitution of South Africa* affirms that 'Everyone has the right

[52] Mauro Cappelletti, "The Expanding Role of Judicial Review in Modern Societies," 89.
[53] Kommers and Miller, *The Constitutional Jurisprudence of the Federal Republic of Germany*, 44.
[54] Grimm, "Values in German Constitutional Law" (on file with author).
[55] Grundgesetz, articles 19(4) and 93(1)(4a). On the contrast between the justiciability of constitutional rights under the Weimar Constitution and the Grundgesetz, see Donald P.

to have any dispute that can be resolved by the application of law decided in a fair public hearing before a court or, where appropriate, another independent and impartial tribunal or forum.'[56] Similarly, Canada's *Charter* establishes that 'Anyone whose rights or freedoms, as guaranteed by this Charter, have been infringed or denied may apply to a court of competent jurisdiction to obtain such remedy as the court considers appropriate and just in the circumstances.'[57] As Chief Justice Dickson explained the provision,

> Of what value are the rights and freedoms guaranteed by the *Charter* if a person is denied or delayed access to a court of competent jurisdiction in order to vindicate them? How can the courts independently maintain the rule of law and effectively discharge the duties imposed by the *Charter* if court access is hindered, impeded or denied? The *Charter* protections would become merely illusory, the entire *Charter* undermined.[58]

The legitimacy of judicial review of legislation hinges on the conception of accountability that one endorses. On a majoritarian conception of accountability, articulated above, judicial review is a suspect practice insofar as it involves judges, who are accountable to no one, dismissing the preferences that the people's representatives have enacted into law while imposing their own preferences upon the people. The conception of accountability that stems from the unified theory casts judicial review in a different light. Neither the legislature nor the judiciary enjoys an unconstrained right to exercise public authority by enacting its preferences into law. The legislature must enact laws that fulfill the right of every person to just governance, while the judiciary must ensure that the exercise of constitutional authority adheres to constitutional standards. To this end, the judiciary must assess constitutional complaints on their merits. And when legislative or executive power is found to depart from the constitutional conditions of its exercise, the judiciary must declare its invalidity. As Justice Iacobucci explained in a landmark decision of the Supreme Court of Canada,

> It is suggested that this appeal represents a contest between the power of the democratically elected legislatures to pass the laws they see fit, and the power of the courts to disallow those laws, or to dictate that certain

Kommers, "German Constitutionalism: A Prolegomenon," *Emory Law Journal* 40 (1991): 853.

56 *Constitution of the Republic of South Africa*, 1996, ss. 34 and 165(2).

57 *Canadian Charter of Rights and Freedoms*, s. 24 (1).

58 *B.C.G.E.U.* v. *British Columbia (Attorney General)*, [1988] 2 SCR 214, 229.

> matters be included in those laws. To put the issue in this way is misleading and erroneous. Quite simply, it is not the courts which limit the legislatures. Rather, it is the Constitution, which must be interpreted by the courts, that limits the legislatures. This is necessarily true of all constitutional democracies. Citizens must have the right to challenge laws which they consider to be beyond the powers of the legislatures. When such a challenge is properly made, the courts must, pursuant to their constitutional duty, rule on the challenge.[59]

While proponents of the majoritarian view of accountability call for a passive judiciary deferential to legislative power, a judiciary that fails to hold government to constitutional standards would both violate its own constitutional duty and resurrect the problem of accountability, which the modern constitutional state exists to address.

Now a proponent of majoritarian democracy might object that far from addressing the problem of accountability, the modern constitutional state simply raises it in a new form. For in a majoritarian democracy, the legislature is elected and accountable to the people, while in a modern constitutional state the judiciary is 'unelected and unaccountable.'[60] The objection is successful if the relevant conception of accountability refers to the intermittent capacity of a majority or plurality of adult citizens to make the exercise of public authority answerable to their preferences. On this conception of accountability, a majoritarian democracy is inherently accountable and a modern constitutional state is inherently unaccountable. But if the relevant conception of accountability for a regime of public law concerns the ongoing right of each inhabitant within the legal order to challenge any exercise of public authority on the basis that it violates his or her inherent dignity, then the positions of the two regimes are reversed: a modern constitutional state is inherently accountable, while a majoritarian democracy is inherently unaccountable.

The modern constitutional project is not exhausted by the performance of the judicial role. Even if the judiciary fulfills its role by assessing the constitutionality of state action on the basis of the legal merit of the complaint rather than considerations of political expedience, the separation of powers prevents the judiciary from enforcing its determinations on the legislature or the executive.[61] The modern constitutional project

59 *Vriend* v. *Alberta*, [1998] 1 SCR 493, para. 56.

60 Jeremy Waldron, *Law and Disagreement* (Oxford: Oxford University Press, 1999), 293.

61 See, for example, Grimm, "Constitutional Adjudication and Democracy," 109 ('the courts have no means to enforce respect for the constitution vis-à-vis the rulers. There is no bailiff for constitutional matters'); Kommers and Miller, *The Constitutional Jurisprudence of the Federal Republic of Germany*, 37 ('the Constitutional Court's rulings are exclusively

cannot succeed if the legislature does not internalize constitutional norms and seek to further their realization through its lawgiving or if the executive fails to carry out the judgments of the judiciary and the laws enacted by the legislature. It is crucial to note, however, that even though the modern constitutional state cannot exclude the possibility of these injustices occurring, it is a legal order that makes their occurrence a violation of its supreme law. In turn, the legal order makes the violation of its supreme law a basis for legal recourse. As I noted earlier, insofar as justice and accountability are not synonymous notions, a legal order can be accountable even if it is not fully just.

To sum up, the legal and institutional structure of a modern constitutional state systematically addresses the problem of accountability. The integration of constitutional supremacy, constitutional rights, and judicial review enables each individual within the legal order to challenge the validity of an exercise of public authority on the grounds that it violates his or her right to just governance. Within this framework, the judiciary must answer neither to the many (which would regenerate the problem of accountability) nor to a higher authority (which, in turn, would have to answer to a higher authority ad infinitum), but solely to the supreme norms of the constitutional order.

I will now make the case that the problem of accountability cannot be addressed apart from the legal and institutional structure of a modern constitutional state. If any of the building blocks of a modern constitutional state – constitutional supremacy, constitutional rights, or judicial review – are absent, the problem of accountability persists.

Suppose that a legal system integrates constitutional supremacy and constitutional rights but lacks judicial review of legislation. This was the situation in Weimar immediately following the enactment of the Weimar Constitution of 1919.[62] In these circumstances, the constitution may recognize the 'inviolable' liberty of the person,[63] but the problem of accountability nevertheless remains. In the absence of judicial review, individuals lack the legal capacity to vindicate the rights that the

declaratory'); and Mauro Cappelletti, "Judicial Review in Comparative Perspective," *California Law Review* 58 (1970): 1053 ('The theoretical power of the judge of constitutionality is awesome, yet in the end he has neither sword nor purse and must depend on others to give his decisions meaning').

62 For an account of the subsequent piecemeal introduction of judicial review, see Carl Joachim Friedrich, "The Issue of Judicial Review in Germany," *Political Science Quarterly* 43 (1928): 188; and J.J. Lenoir, "Judicial Review in Germany under the Weimar Constitution," *Tulane Law Review* 14 (1940): 361.

63 Weimar Republic, 1919, article 114.

constitution acknowledges. This does not mean that constitutional rights will be routinely violated, but it does mean that bearers of rights are at the mercy of government, the very entity that constitutional rights place under an obligation. As the political scientist Carl Joachim Friedrich observed in 1928, 'If the German National Assembly may decide at will whether its statutes conform to the Constitution or not, the Bill of Rights and Duties is in large part robbed of all protection.'[64]

Now suppose that a legal system integrates constitutional supremacy and judicial review but lacks constitutional rights. This was the situation in Canada prior to the enactment of the *Charter of Rights and Freedoms.* Within this legal setting, individuals could challenge the validity of legislation for failing to meet constitutional standards. However, since those standards concerned a division of powers between the federal and provincial governments rather than constitutional duties incumbent on both, the right to challenge the constitutionality of a publicly authoritative act did not track the right of persons, by virtue of their inherent equal dignity, to just governance. So long as the federal or provincial legislatures acted 'within their allotted jurisdiction,' they 'were subject to no overarching laws, bound by no substantive principles, and constrained by no guarantees of individual or collective rights.'[65] Bora Laskin, who later became Chief Justice of Canada, observed that within this legal framework, the 'basic constitutional question was which jurisdiction [federal or provincial] should have the power to work the injustice, not whether the injustice should be prohibited.'[66] In the absence of a scheme of constitutional rights, the exercise of public authority remains unaccountable to the inherent dignity of all who are subject to it.[67]

64 "The Issue of Judicial Review in Germany," 194. For a similar remark in the context of pre–World War I Germany, see Otto von Gierke, "German Constitutional Law in Its Relation to the American Constitution," *Harvard Law Review* 23 (1910): 284–5: '[I]t is a fundamental deficiency of our public law that there exists no protection of constitutional principles by an independent court of justice ... In Europe the conviction of the omnipotence of legislature prevails, so that the judges are obliged to obey every legislative measure enacted in legal form. Thus as against a "Reichgesetz" no appeal to any court can bring help in the case of violation of constitutional rights.'

65 Lorraine Eisenstat Weinrib, "'Do Justice to Us!' Jews and the Constitution of Canada," in *Not Written in Stone: Jews, Constitutions, and Constitutionalism in Canada*, ed. Daniel J. Elazar, Michael Brown, and Ira Robinson (Ottawa: University of Ottawa Press, 2003), 33.

66 Quoted in Irwin Cotler, "Jewish NGOs and Religious Human Rights: A Case Study," in *Religious Human Rights in Global Perspective*, ed. John Witte, Jr. and Johan D. van der Vyver (The Hague: Kluwer Law International, 1996), 254.

67 On the fragility of common law rights in a parliamentary supremacy, see Sir John Laws, "The Good Constitution," *Cambridge Law Journal* 71 (2012): 569–70.

The final possibility involves a legal system that lacks constitutional supremacy. Such a legal system does not necessarily exercise public authority unjustly, but it necessarily fails to address the problem of accountability. For in the absence of constitutional supremacy, rights cannot have constitutional status. When rights do not have constitutional status, conformity to rights cannot be a justiciable condition of the valid exercise of public authority. I return to this point below in discussing the adequacy of the commonwealth constitutional model.

The problem of accountability, then, cannot be addressed in the absence of the legal and institutional structure of a modern constitutional state. Accordingly, a *principled* defense of the legal and institutional structure of a modern constitutional state comes into view. Every legal system must address the problem of accountability. But no legal system can address the problem apart from the legal and institutional structure of a modern constitutional state. Therefore, every legal system must bring its arrangements into accord with the parameters of modern constitutionalism.

The modern constitutional paradigm can be contrasted with Phillip Pettit's constitutional ideal: contestatory democracy. Recognizing that even a democratic government might dominate its citizens, he defends a conception of democracy in which all government action is contestable. A contestatory democracy includes multiple forums for contestation, including the 'opportunity of writing to your Member of Parliament, the capacity to require an ombudsman to make an inquiry, the right to appeal against a judicial decision to a higher court, and less formal entitlements such as those involved in rights of association, protest, and demonstration.'[68]

Modern constitutionalism makes two fundamental departures from Pettit's constitutional vision. The first concerns the justification of judicial review. Pettit conceives of judicial review as an instrument, among others, for bringing about contestation. For him, the question of which instruments a particular legal system should adopt is an empirical question about how best to promote contestability.[69] By contrast, I have argued not that it is *possible* to bring about contestation through judicial review, but that the problem of accountability cannot be addressed apart

[68] Phillip Pettit, *Republicanism: A Theory of Freedom and Government* (Oxford: Oxford University Press, 2010), 193.

[69] Ibid.

from it. Thus, judicial review is a *necessary* component of a legal system that addresses the problem of accountability.

The second discrepancy concerns the relationship between judicial review and democratic governance. On Pettit's view, the role of contestation is to influence the democratic will, not to subject it to legal constraints. Thus, Pettit explains that in a contestatory democracy the democratic process enjoys primacy over contestatory mechanisms and substantive constitutional constraints. As he puts it, 'everything is up for grabs.'[70] In my view, contestatory democracy perpetuates the problem it purports to solve. In a contestatory democracy, one's right to be free from the arbitrary domination by government is contingent on one's capacity to wield political influence, even though one's lack of political influence is a central reason that one is susceptible to such domination in the first place. Accordingly, I defend a conception of constitutionalism in which the constraints binding public authority are legal rather than merely political. A modern constitutional state creates the conditions in which any person may challenge the validity of any exercise of public authority on the grounds that it violates his or her right to just governance. Challenges should, of course, influence the formation of the democratic will, but insofar as the challenges concern the validity of legislative and executive action, the legal impact of a challenge is not simply a product of its political influence.

Modern constitutionalism is a groundbreaking paradigm in public law. Its innovation consists in creating the legal and institutional conditions in which public authority is accountable neither to the preferences of the few nor to the preferences of the many, but to the right of every person to just governance. This innovation is made possible by reorienting the relationship between the two pillars of public law: public authority and public justice. In all precursors to modern constitutionalism, the practice of public law is defective because even though each member of the legal order has a right to just governance, the legal order is arranged in such a way that one or more persons subject to its governance are incapable of vindicating their most basic public right. The modern constitutional state is a systematic attempt to constrain the exercise of public authority to the terms of its justification by establishing a supreme positive law that makes the satisfaction of this right the condition for the valid exercise of public authority, specifying what this right demands through a set of constitutional rights that flesh out the appropriate

[70] Ibid., 201.

relationship between the freedom of the individual and the power of government, and rendering these rights justiciable before a politically independent judicial forum so that any person within the constitutional order may challenge the validity of a publicly authoritative act by raising a constitutional complaint. The constitutional norms and institutional framework of the modern constitutional state culminate in a legal order in which each individual has standing to insist that public authority adhere to the strictures of public justice.

5.3 Assessing commonwealth constitutionalism

This section contrasts modern constitutionalism with a competing model: commonwealth constitutionalism. I argue that because this model fails to address the problem of accountability, it should be rejected as a constitutional ideal. However, while the commonwealth model should not be considered an ideal that legal systems as such should strive to realize, it may nevertheless be appropriate in circumstances in which the full realization of modern constitutionalism is not yet possible.

Commonwealth constitutionalism is an innovative and distinctive model that works to reconcile parliamentary sovereignty with rights protection.[71] Its leading proponent, Stephen Gardbaum, explains that the model has three 'essential and defining features':

> (1) [A] legalized bill or charter of rights; (2) some form of enhanced judicial power to enforce these rights by assessing legislation (as well as other governmental acts) for consistency with them that goes beyond traditional presumptions and ordinary modes of statutory interpretation; and (3), most distinctively, notwithstanding this judicial role, a formal legislative power to have the final word on what the law of the land is by ordinary majority vote.[72]

The United Kingdom is the paradigmatic instance of commonwealth constitutionalism. Section 1 of the *Human Rights Act* of 1998 incorporates the *European Convention on Human Rights* (Convention) into

[71] See, for example, Stephen Gardbaum, "The New Commonwealth Model of Constitutionalism," *American Journal of Comparative Law* 49 (2001): 707–60; Stephen Gardbaum, "Reassessing the New Commonwealth Model of Constitutionalism," *International Journal of Constitutional Law* 8 (2010): 167–206; Stephen Gardbaum, "The Case for the New Commonwealth Model of Constitutionalism," *German Law Journal* 14 (2013): 2229–48.

[72] Gardbaum, "Reassessing the New Commonwealth Model of Constitutionalism," 169.

domestic law.[73] Section 3 of the Convention imposes a duty on the judiciary to interpret legislation '[s]o far as it is possible to do so' in accordance with its enumerated rights.[74] Section 4 establishes that in the event that a legislative provision cannot be reconciled with a Convention right, higher courts may issue a declaration of incompatibility. Because Convention rights do not have the status of higher law, a declaration of incompatibility 'does not affect the validity' of the legislative provision.[75] The result is that Parliament can respond to the declaration by amending the relevant legislative provision.[76] The commonwealth model therefore departs from two familiar paradigms. Unlike systems of legislative supremacy, the commonwealth model offers an effective scheme of rights protection by making Convention rights subject to judicial oversight in domestic courts. Unlike systems of constitutional supremacy, the commonwealth model does not subject the democratic will of Parliament to a judicial veto or to the imposition of judicial remedies.[77] The result, Gardbaum claims, is a model that recognizes that it is 'possible to have what is essential to both: judicial protection of fundamental rights *and* the legislature retaining the right to have the last word on what is the law of the land.'[78]

The adequacy of the commonwealth model can be considered from the standpoint of the problem of accountability. Recall that the problem calls for a legal and institutional structure in which an individual can challenge the validity of an exercise of public authority on the grounds that it violates his or her right to just governance. While the commonwealth model enables individuals to raise a complaint alleging that a legislative provision violates Convention rights, those rights lack the status of supreme law. The result is that even in cases in which the provision cannot be interpreted to accord with Convention rights, the provision's validity is unaffected. Of course 'the normal result of a declaration [of incompatibility] will be amendment or repeal,' but the *Human Rights Act* 'does not *require* remedial action by government and Parliament in response to a declaration.'[79] Thus, in the aftermath of a declaration of

[73] *Human Rights Act*, 1998 (c. 42), s. 1. [74] Ibid., s. 3(1). [75] Ibid., s. 4(6).

[76] Ibid., s. 10. But see Gardbaum, "The New Commonwealth Model of Constitutionalism," 733: 'Once a declaration [of incompatibility] has been made, [the *Human Rights Act*] creates no legal duty on either Parliament or the government to respond in any way, but it does empower the relevant minister to make a "remedial order" . . . [The *Human Rights Act*] obviously did not need to empower Parliament to amend or repeal such legislation since the power clearly already exists.'

[77] Gardbaum, "The New Commonwealth Model of Constitutionalism," 739.

[78] Ibid., 741. [79] Ibid., 738.

incompatibility, the government remains at liberty 'to refuse to take steps to remedy the incompatibility if it deems it appropriate to do so.'[80] In such cases, the government is both the party that is found to have violated a Convention right *and* the party that determines whether to amend the provision in question. In the event that an amendment is not forthcoming, domestic law offers no legal recourse to those whose rights have been publicly acknowledged to have been violated. Even if rights are invariably protected in the commonwealth model, the problem of accountability nevertheless persists.

Although the commonwealth model fails to address the problem of accountability, it need not be rejected completely. Gardbaum defends the commonwealth model in two different ways. First, he argues that the commonwealth model is superior to the available alternatives because it integrates their respective virtues – as he understands them – while eschewing their respective vices.[81] I reject this view. Because the problem of accountability is inescapable within the commonwealth model, it does not form an ideal appropriate for legal systems in general. Gardbaum's second defense is more modest. He asserts that the commonwealth model may be appropriate for a particular legal system because of contingent circumstances that obtain within it.[82] Thus, when Gardbaum describes the constitutional debate surrounding the *Human Rights Act* in the United Kingdom, he emphasizes both that the existing model of legislative supremacy was unacceptable because of its legacy of rights violations and that constitutional supremacy was unachievable because of deep-rooted commitments to parliamentary sovereignty. In his words, the United Kingdom was confronted by 'the following traditional conundrum: on the one hand, an ordinary statute bill of rights would likely provide insufficient legal protection for them; on the other, more protection than this was problematic if not *impossible* under the British constitution and its central doctrine of parliamentary sovereignty.'[83] Thus, Gardbaum presents the commonwealth model not as a 'universally appropriate model of constitutionalism,' but merely as a possibility that should be acknowledged in the catalog of constitutional options.[84] I am sympathetic to this proposal, but for my own reasons.

80 K.D. Ewing, "The Human Rights Act and Parliamentary Democracy," *Modern Law Review* 62 (1999): 92.
81 Gardbaum, "The Case for the New Commonwealth Model of Constitutionalism," 81.
82 Gardbaum, "Reassessing the New Commonwealth Model of Constitutionalism," 206.
83 See "The New Commonwealth Model of Constitutionalism," 732 (my emphasis).
84 Gardbaum, "Reassessing the New Commonwealth Model of Constitutionalism," 205–6.

If legal systems have a duty to bring themselves into the deepest possible conformity with the legal and institutional structure of a modern constitutional state, a question arises about the types of arrangements that should be adopted when the undiminished realization of such a regime is impossible. The commonwealth model offers an intermediary point between legislative supremacy and modern constitutionalism. This model takes an important step beyond legislative supremacy by enabling the judicial oversight of Convention rights. The model falls short of modern constitutionalism because Convention rights lack the status of supreme law and so do not invalidate legislative provisions that violate them. Commonwealth constitutionalism should be regarded not as a constitutional ideal that is obligatory for legal systems as such to realize, but as a way for legal systems in which parliamentary sovereignty is presently inescapable to approximate the rights protection of a modern constitutional regime. On this view, the commonwealth model does not itself instantiate the ideal of constitutionalism, but may in certain contexts represent a significant step toward it.

Turning from considerations of justification to ones of fit, a further problem emerges as Gardbaum claims other jurisdictions as instances of his model. While he regards Canada's constitutional arrangements as the 'pioneer' of the commonwealth model,[85] a deep antagonism obtains between the former and the latter. This antagonism stems from the fact that in Canada, rights enjoy the status of supreme law. As such, rights cannot be amended through ordinary lawgiving. Further, the judiciary is empowered not only to determine whether ordinary laws conform to constitutional rights, but also to invalidate laws that do not. Finally, far from providing the legislature with plenary power to override the *Charter*, the notwithstanding clause, established in s. 33, does not apply to all constitutional rights, is temporary, and has become so politically toxic that it fails to temper 'the countermajoritarian difficulty posed by an unlimited power of judicial review.'[86] Gardbaum responds to these discrepancies by arguing that to the extent that the Canadian constitutional practice departs from the model, the former is a defective instance of the latter.[87]

[85] Gardbaum, "The New Commonwealth Model of Constitutionalism," 719.
[86] Ibid., 727.
[87] Gardbaum, "Reassessing the New Commonwealth Model of Constitutionalism," 183: 'In sum, I view Canada as part of the new model because of section 33 . . . but as suffering from a serious practical problem due to the apparent near-convention against its use. The problem is less that the override power is rarely exercised per se than that this convention

The constitutional theory that I develop offers an alternative possibility: Canada is not a defective instance of the commonwealth model, but a generally successful instance of the modern constitutional model. Within the modern constitutional model, any individual can challenge the validity of any exercise of public authority on the grounds that it violates his or her constitutional rights.

Some might take issue with my account of Canada as a modern constitutional state. After all, s. 33 of the *Charter* empowers the legislature temporarily to override a range of constitutional rights. And surely such a provision indicates that many of the duties that the *Charter* imposes on the legislature are defeasible. While I cannot provide a full response to this objection here, I will say this. As a matter of constitutional theory, the problem of accountability requires every legal system to bring its arrangements into conformity with the parameters of a modern constitutional state. This duty has important implications in a range of legal contexts. On the one hand, this duty provides a program for constitutional reform in legal systems that lack the legal and institutional structure that render the exercise of public authority accountable to the right of each person to just governance. On the other, this duty binds legal systems that possess this legal and institutional structure to develop practices that are conducive to the realization of its constitutional aspirations. To this end, a modern constitutional state must develop conventions against employing arrangements that are inimical to the realization of a just and accountable legal order. The override clause is such an arrangement insofar as it could be employed to sidestep many of the rights and freedoms that the *Charter* exists to secure. Accordingly, so long as the clause remains in force, a modern constitutional state would have a duty to develop a convention against its use – regardless of whose rights happened to be at stake. As a matter of constitutional practice, this is arguably what has happened in Canada. In the context of a legal culture that is in principle hostile to overriding rights, the override does not subvert the accountability of the legal order.

Alon Harel's insightful book *Why Law Matters*[88] offers an alternative justification of the commonwealth model. Harel's theory shares the noninstrumentalism of the unified theory, but generates an opposing conclusion about the adequacy of commonwealth constitutionalism. I

seems largely to exclude the sort of political discussion about rights called for by the ideal working of the new model.'

88 (Oxford: Oxford University Press, 2014).

will identify the point of divergence and trace its broader implications for questions of constitutional design. My account articulates a general problem about the public law relationship between rulers and ruled. I then argue that the legal and institutional structure of a modern constitutional state is required to address this problem. On this view, constitutional supremacy, constitutional rights, and judicial review are all required for the same reason. By contrast, Harel offers one justification for constitutional rights and another for judicial review. Although both of these justifications are noninstrumental, they introduce conflicting standards of justification that undermine his defense of the commonwealth model. I will consider each justification in turn and then note the discrepancy that obtains between them.

Harel's justification of constitutional rights proceeds from the conviction that in the enjoyment of their rights, individuals should not be 'at the mercy' of the legislature.[89] On the basis of this conviction, he argues that a legal system is defective if the enjoyment of rights within it depends upon legislative discretion. This leads Harel to identify a 'non-contingent' defect of majoritarian democracies: 'Even if the legislature is highly enlightened and is devoted to the protection of rights and justice, the mere fact that [individual] rights are "at its mercy" is a deficiency that needs to be addressed.'[90] On this point, Harel and I are in agreement.

But as the focus of Harel's argument shifts from individual rights to institutional deliberation, his original conviction is supplanted by an alternative justificatory standard. Judicial review is justified, he argues, because it constitutes the right to a hearing. This right consists of three components. The state must (1) 'provide an opportunity for a person to challenge its decision,' (2) 'be willing to engage in meaningful deliberation,' and (3) 'be willing to reconsider the decision, to change it if the deliberation triggered by the individual grievance exposes that the decision is wrong.'[91]

The difficulty that undermines Harel's account is that the two justificatory standards that he introduces are incompatible. Consider his treatment of the commonwealth model (which he refers to as a system of weak judicial review).[92] Such a model is justified, Harel argues, because it is compatible with each of the components that comprise a right to a hearing:

> [U]nder the British Human Rights Act, the petitioner can raise a grievance and she is entitled to a full account of whether her rights have been

[89] Ibid., 148. [90] Ibid., 189. [91] Ibid., 221. [92] Ibid., 220.

> violated (a declaration of incompatibility). But the reconsideration is left to the legislature and its good will and in principle the legislature is not obliged to rely in its decision on the particularities of the case.[93]

For Harel, the distinctive feature of commonwealth constitutionalism is that it transfers the 'task of reconsideration' – the third component of the right to a hearing – from the judiciary to the legislature.[94] Such a transfer is permissible, Harel explains, because meaningful reconsideration remains possible: a legislature can 'take seriously the hearings conducted by courts even if they are not obliged to accept their judgments.'[95]

This makes the conflict between the disparate justifications that run through Harel's constitutional theory apparent. On the one hand, his justification of constitutional rights holds that a legal system is defective if the freedom of any individual within it is 'contingent on the good will of the legislature.'[96] On the other, Harel's justification of judicial review holds that the commonwealth model is acceptable even though it leaves the task of determining whether to conform with right 'to the legislature and its good will.'[97] Because the justificatory standards that Harel develops do not cohere, his theory culminates not in an integrated justification of constitutional rights and judicial review, but in a dilemma. Either the rights of individuals must not be placed at the mercy of the legislature (in which case the commonwealth model is unacceptable for the same reason as majoritarian democracy) or individuals merely have the right to a hearing – a right which can be fulfilled by any branch of government, including the legislature[98] (in which case the commonwealth model would be acceptable, but so would majoritarian democracy). Since Harel seeks to justify the commonwealth model while rejecting majoritarian democracy, each of these possibilities is fatal to the ambitions of his theory. Such a dilemma can be avoided by generating each of the components of a modern constitutional state from a common noninstrumental justificatory basis. This chapter follows that strategy.

93 Ibid., 222. 94 Ibid. 95 Ibid., 223. 96 Ibid., 7. 97 Ibid., 222.

98 Ibid., 213–4: 'The right-to-a-hearing justification for judicial review does not require review by courts or judges. It merely requires guaranteeing that grievances be examined *in certain ways* and *by using certain procedures* and *modes of reasoning*, but it tells us nothing of the identity of the institutions in charge of performing this task. Thus, in principle, the right to a hearing can be protected by any institution, including perhaps the legislature.'

5.4 A reply to Waldron

I have argued that there is a connection between the duty of a legal system to respect and protect human dignity, on one hand, and the legal and institutional structure of a modern constitutional state, on the other. Precursors to modern constitutionalism raise the problem of accountability because they render one or more persons subject to public authority incapable of constraining its exercise to the terms of its justification. Insofar as a state is defective to the extent that it fails to address the problem of accountability and modern constitutionalism alone addresses this problem, every state must adopt modern constitutional arrangements.

In this section, I will defend the legal and institutional structure of a modern constitutional state from its leading critic, Jeremy Waldron. As a liberal, Waldron holds that 'minorities are entitled to a degree of support, recognition, and insulation that is not necessarily guaranteed by their numbers or by their political weight.'[99] As a critic of constitutionalism, Waldron holds that rights protection is not advanced by enabling the judiciary (or a special constitutional court) to invalidate legislation. Waldron offers two kinds of arguments against the judicial review of constitutional rights.[100] The first claims that judicial review does not produce better outcomes than majoritarian arrangements. The second claims that regardless of the outcomes that judicial review produces, the procedure is itself objectionable because it is undemocratic. If both objections are successful, then Waldron can conclude that the benefits that judicial review offers are uncertain, but the injustice it perpetrates in constraining the will of the majority is inescapable.[101] I respond to each objection in turn.

The most prominent strategy for justifying rights-based constitutionalism involves identifying some beneficial outcome and then arguing that constitutional arrangements contribute to its realization. Proponents of this strategy appeal to a range of different desirable outcomes, but share the conviction that if such a form of constitutional governance is justifiable, it is because it contributes to the achievement of outcomes that are themselves desirable. According to this outcome-oriented justification,

[99] Waldron, "The Core of the Case Against Judicial Review," 1364. [100] Ibid., 1353.

[101] Jeremy Waldron, "A Rights-Based Critique of Constitutional Rights," *Oxford Journal of Legal Studies* 13 (1993): 50. On this point, see also Jeremy Waldron, "Judicial Review and the Conditions of Democracy," *Journal of Political Philosophy* 6 (1998): 352.

constitutionalism is an instrument: its value lies in what it brings, not in what it is.[102]

Ronald Dworkin's initial defense of rights-based constitutionalism is representative of the outcome-based approach. In *Freedom's Law*, Dworkin explains that when considering issues of constitutional design, in general, and rights protection, in particular, he sees 'no alternative but to use a result-driven rather than a procedure-driven standard for deciding them.'[103] Accordingly, when Dworkin reflects on whether constitutional rights should be protected through judicial review, he turns his attention to the kinds of outcomes that this arrangement generates. For Dworkin, judicial review is justified because it produces a welcomed benefit by improving the quality of public debate:

> When an issue is seen as constitutional . . . and as one that will ultimately be resolved by courts applying general constitutional principles, the quality of public argument is often improved, because the argument concentrates from the start on questions of political morality . . . When a constitutional issue has been decided by the Supreme Court, and is important enough so that it can be expected to be elaborated, expanded, contracted, or even reversed by future decisions, a sustained national debate begins, in newspapers, and other media, in law schools and classrooms, in public meetings and around dinner tables. That debate better matches [the] conception of republican government, in its emphasis on matters of principle, than almost anything the legislative process on its own is likely to produce.[104]

As Dworkin explains, judicial review improves the quality of public debate by framing issues of public importance not in terms of their popularity or expediency (as legislatures too often do), but as questions of political morality.[105] Once questions of public importance are framed in this way, the judiciary responds by selecting 'the best answers.'[106]

Those who join Dworkin in defending rights-based constitutionalism typically share his presupposition that questions concerning the appropriateness of a legal regime should be addressed in reference to the benefits it brings and the burdens it alleviates. For example, Aileen Kavanagh holds that the 'ultimate standard by which we judge political institutions is their likelihood of achieving good substantive

[102] For a classification and criticism of five prominent instrumental justifications of judicial review, see Alon Harel and Tsvi Kahana, "The Easy Core Case for Judicial Review," *Journal of Legal Analysis* 2 (2010): 4–12.

[103] Dworkin, *Freedom's Law*, 34. [104] Ibid., 345. [105] Ibid., 344. [106] Ibid., 34.

outcomes.'[107] Accordingly, the 'justification for constitutional review must depend ultimately on empirical assumptions about the likelihood that courts will succeed in protecting rights.'[108] Kavanagh recognizes that the success of courts in protecting rights may vary in different contexts. She therefore argues that scholars should support constitutional arrangements when they would be effective in protecting rights and oppose them when they would be ineffective.[109]

While Kavanagh defends constitutionalism by focusing on the benefits that it might bring, Samuel Freeman calls attention to the burdens that it might alleviate. Freeman conceives of constitutional democracy as an expedient for safeguarding equal rights in social and historical circumstances in which legislative power might be used to 'subvert the public interest in justice and to deprive classes of individuals of the conditions of democratic equality.'[110] For Freeman, as for Kavanagh and Dworkin, the justification of judicial review 'is contingent upon the extent to which these procedures serve the ends in virtue of which they are found appropriate.'[111] Judicial review is appropriate when it is conducive to the promotion of the best outcomes in relation to the complex matrix of factual circumstances at hand. As circumstances fluctuate within a given legal system, judicial review may be rightly adopted as beneficial and subsequently forsaken as detrimental or vice versa.[112]

Outcome-based justifications do not establish that rights-based constitutionalism is, as a matter of principle, preferable to other modes of governance. On the one hand, each of the advantageous outcomes to which these justifications appeal can be realized by other kinds of legal systems. On the other, the various advantages that rights-based constitutionalism supposedly generates might fail to materialize. Thus, Waldron has responded to Dworkin by cataloging instances in which public debate has flourished in majoritarian democracies and floundered in rights-based constitutional regimes.[113] If rights-based constitutionalism is simply an instrument for the promotion of outcomes that it might

[107] "Constitutional Review, the Courts, and Democratic Scepticism," *Current Legal Problems* 62 (2009): 134.

[108] Ibid., 104. [109] Ibid., 123–5.

[110] Samuel Freeman, "Constitutional Democracy and the Legitimacy of Judicial Review," *Law and Philosophy* 9 (1990): 345.

[111] Ibid., 361.

[112] Kavanagh, "Constitutional Review, the Courts, and Democratic Scepticism," 108.

[113] Waldron, "Judicial Review and the Conditions of Democracy," 339–40; and Waldron, "The Core of the Case Against Judicial Review," 1349 (contrasting the quality of debates over the 'liberalization of abortion law, the legalization of homosexual conduct among

fail to produce and that could be realized in its absence, then why is it valuable?

To this, a proponent of the outcome-based approach might reply that we value rights-based constitutionalism not because it provides advantages that other forms of government are incapable of offering, but rather because it realizes the same kinds of advantages as other forms of legal ordering to a greater extent. Thus, Dworkin holds that the American experiment with judicial review of constitutional rights has been justified because the 'United States is a more just society than it would have been had its constitutional rights been left to the conscience of majoritarian institutions.'[114] His claim is not that legislatures, unlike courts, are incapable of protecting rights, but that if the United States lacked judicial review, then the United States would be less rights-protecting than it is today.

This claim is more problematic than Dworkin acknowledges. The claim takes the form of a counterfactual: *If it was not the case that A, then the result would not have been B.* As Waldron has rightly observed, counterfactual claims are 'extraordinarily difficult to assess.'[115] To verify Dworkin's claim that in the absence of judicial review the United States would be less just than it is today, one would have to determine the overall balance of just and unjust outcomes that have accumulated in the history of American constitutional jurisprudence.[116] One would then have to weigh this determination against the sum of just and unjust outcomes that *would have* occurred in the range of possible alternative legal systems. The former determination is perhaps incalculable; the latter is unknowable. To be sure, the problem with Dworkin's counterfactual claim is not that he is wrong in asserting that if the United States lacked judicial review of constitutional rights, then it would be less just. Indeed, he might be correct. However, since the veracity of his claim seems 'impossible to verify,' his justification of constitutionalism dissolves into mere assertion.[117] Thus Waldron concludes that it remains 'an open question whether judicial review has made the United States (or

consenting adults, and the abolition of capital punishment' in states that are and are not constitutionalized) and 1384–5.

114 Dworkin, *Law's Empire* (Cambridge: Harvard University Press, 1986), 356.

115 Waldron, "Judicial Review and the Conditions of Democracy," 337.

116 Ibid., 337–8 (explaining that verifying Dworkin's counterfactual would require weighing just judicial decisions like *Brown* v. *Board of Education*, 347 U.S. 483 (1954), against unjust decisions, such as those that struck down progressive labor legislation during the *Lochner* era).

117 Waldron, *Law and Disagreement*, 288.

would make any society) more just than it would have been without that practice.'[118]

So long as this problem of verification persists, we cannot elevate rights-based constitutionalism over other forms of government by pointing to its superior outcomes. Instead, the outcome-based justification yields the more modest conclusion that there might be circumstances in which constitutional arrangements are compatible with the realization of desirable outcomes. If this is all that can be said in favor of constitutionalism, then those who have described the modern constitutional paradigm as a 'fundamental innovation' in governance[119] must be mistaken. The innovation of modern constitutionalism is hardly *fundamental* if it is just another means of achieving desirable outcomes that could be brought about without it. Further, modern constitutionalism is not *innovative* if it, like other modes of governance, might fail to bring about the outcomes by which it is justified.

This chapter offers a different way of thinking about rights-based constitutionalism by rejecting the unstated assumption of its proponents and critics: any justification of constitutional arrangements must be outcome-based.[120] Unlike Dworkin and his followers, I have not argued that modern constitutionalism is justified because of some benefit that it might bring that could, in principle, be achieved in its absence, such as debates of high quality or just outcomes. Instead, just as majoritarians defend their conception of democracy by appealing to the moral significance of its procedures, so too a parallel strategy is available to justify the legal and institutional structure of a modern constitutional state. Modern constitutionalism is a systematic response to a moral problem that confronts every legal system – the problem of accountability. Addressing this problem is what modern constitutionalism does, and what cannot be done in its absence. Precursors to modern constitutionalism may, as Waldron illustrates, enjoy high levels of public debate. They may even succeed in enacting just laws. There is, however, one problem that precursors to modern constitutionalism cannot address: the problem of accountability. A modern constitutional state alone makes the inherent dignity of each individual a 'justiciable and enforceable *right* that must be

118 Ibid., 355. For a detailed classification of the kinds of 'consequentialist calculations' that would have to be balanced to verify Dworkin's counterfactual claim, see Wojciech Sadurski, "Judicial Review and the Protection of Constitutional Rights," *Oxford Journal of Legal Studies* 22 (2002): 275.

119 Cappelletti, "Constitutional Justice," 6.

120 Harel and Kahana, "The Easy Core Case for Judicial Review," 27.

respected and protected.'[121] If every state must make the exercise of public authority accountable to the right of each of its inhabitants to just governance, and accountability of this kind is impossible apart from the legal and institutional structure of a modern constitutional state, then every state must – as a matter of principle – adopt modern constitutional arrangements. Modern constitutionalism, then, is required not because of the welcomed benefits that it might bring, but because of what it is: a form of legal ordering that transforms the inherent equal human dignity of each person subject to law's authority into a justiciable legal norm.

The legal and institutional structure of a modern constitutional state is not an *instrument* for bringing about the morally desirable end of accountable government. The structure of a modern constitutional state is itself morally valuable because accountable government is not possible apart from it. What it means for a legal system to be accountable is for it to be a modern constitutional state.

Such a justification of modern constitutionalism departs from the outcome-based strategy in two respects. First, it establishes that the transition to modern constitutionalism is itself morally *necessary* for a legal system rather than merely *compatible* with the achievement of some extrinsically desirable outcome. Second, it justifies modern constitutionalism on the basis of a fundamental moral problem common to legal systems instead of on the basis of cultural, historical, or political circumstances found in some legal systems but absent in others. Once the problem to which modern constitutionalism systematically responds is in view, we can abandon outcome-based justifications without abandoning modern constitutionalism.

Whereas Waldron's first line of criticism targets the justifications that constitutional theorists have advanced to support judicial review, his second criticism attacks judicial review from the standpoint of a majoritarian democratic theory. For Waldron, a legitimate political order is democratic, a democratic political order is majoritarian, and a constitutional regime is undemocratic and therefore illegitimate because it departs from majoritarian arrangements. He makes this point in a variety of ways.

In one formulation, Waldron claims that the entrenchment of constitutional norms imposes a disability on the legislature, which hinders its 'normal function of revision, reform, and innovation in the law.'[122] He is

[121] *Dawood, Shalabi and Thomas* v. *Minister of Home Affairs*, 2000 3 SA 936 (CC), para. 35.
[122] Waldron, *Law and Disagreement*, 221.

correct that the entrenchment of constitutional norms imposes a disability on the legislature insofar as it denies the legislature the legal power to abrogate certain features of the constitutional order, such as its commitment to respect and protect the inherent dignity and fundamental rights of persons. But it need not follow that this constrains the legislature's normal function. If the public authority of government must always be directed toward the fulfillment of the inherent dignity of each individual within the legal order, then modern constitutionalism does not impose a new constraint on the legislature, but instead recognizes a duty implicit in any legal system. The modern constitutional state introduces a novel legal and institutional framework to make this duty justiciable, but the duty accompanies the exercise of all public authority.

In another formulation of the objection from democracy, Waldron suggests that constitutionalism diminishes democratic rights by placing 'issues of high principle' in the judicial domain, while leaving the people's elected representatives the less important task of sorting out 'interstitial matters of social and economic policy.'[123] I reply that modern constitutionalism does not relegate the legislature to mundane matters. As we saw earlier in this chapter, the constitutional duty to realize a legal order that to the greatest possible extent unites the authority of law with the dignity of each person bound by it is incumbent on all branches of government, including the legislature. While the legislature does not have the final say on issues of constitutional interpretation, this does not mean that issues of high principle are the preserve of the judiciary alone. All branches of government are bound by constitutional norms. Such an approach neither degrades the legislature nor idealizes the judiciary. The legislature must give laws that fulfill the right of each person to just governance. The judiciary must hold the government to constitutional standards in its exercise of constitutional authority.

On other occasions, Waldron formulates the objection from democracy in this way: the problem with judicial review is that it excludes citizens from participating in important decisions regarding their own rights. Citizens will rightly feel 'slighted' by this exclusion because the constitutional order, in effect, says to them that they are not up to the task of making important decisions regarding their own governance.[124] I do not know if Waldron is correct in asserting that judicial review makes citizens feel slighted. If he is, then the global proliferation of modern constitutionalism is all the more puzzling. There is another possibility,

[123] Ibid., 213. [124] Ibid., 239.

which I offer not as a claim about how persons actually feel about modern constitutional norms and practices, but rather how it would be reasonable for them to feel. When people see that they live in a legal order that acknowledges the inherent dignity of each of its members, entrenches as its highest law the duty of all public institutions to extend just governance to each member of the legal order, and creates the conditions in which any person who believes that his or her right to just governance has been violated may hold public power to account by raising a legal complaint in a politically independent forum that is both empowered and obligated to render judgment on the legal merits, the constitutional order may be recognized as a form of legal organization that takes seriously the right of each person to just governance. No one should feel slighted by arrangements that render the legal system accountable to each person subject to its authority.

Finally, Waldron sometimes challenges proponents of judicial review by noting that like legislators, judges often disagree about rights. When disagreements arise in multi-judge appellate courts, a decision-procedure is required to resolve them and the 'decision-procedure most often used is simple majority voting.'[125] With this observation in place, Waldron accuses defenders of judicial review of having an incoherent outlook toward majority voting. On the one hand, defenders of judicial review reject majority voting as a decision procedure for cases in which *legislators* disagree about rights. On the other, defenders of judicial review affirm majority voting as a decision procedure for cases in which *judges* disagree about rights. Thus, Waldron asks, 'Why is [majority decision] an appropriate principle to use in an institution that is supposed to be curing or mitigating the effects of majoritarianism?'[126] As I have argued, proponents of judicial review need neither reject the claim that the legislature should make determinations about rights nor the claim that in cases of disagreement it should employ majority voting. Instead, they may insist that every legal system, democracies included, must address the problem of accountability. The assessment of the constitutionality of legislation by an impartial judicial body is an integral feature of a legal system that is accountable to the right of each of its inhabitants to just governance. As Waldron notes, there are judicial procedures for resolving disagreement that do not involve majority voting,[127] but majority

125 Waldron, "The Core of the Case Against Judicial Review," 1364.

126 Jeremy Waldron, "Five to Four: Why Do Bare Majority Rule on Courts?" *Yale Law Journal* 123 (2014): 1694.

127 Ibid.

voting in the judiciary does not diminish the accountability of the legal order.

Conclusion

Modern constitutionalism is a practice in search of a theoretical justification. In countries around the world, modern constitutionalism has become the preeminent response to the full range of pathologies of public law, from the inhumanity of failed states to the unaccountability of autocratic, oligarchic, and majoritarian forms of government. At the same time, modern constitutionalism is increasingly subject to criticism from theorists committed to earlier models of governance, which are incapable of addressing the problem of accountability. While critics dismiss modern constitutionalism as wrong in principle, its defenders are content to offer pragmatic defenses. These defenses fail to illuminate the fundamental innovation of modern constitutionalism or articulate why practitioners regard modern constitutionalism as a fundamental advance over earlier forms of legal ordering.

This chapter has formulated a principled defense of the legal and institutional structure of a modern constitutional state. Modern constitutionalism is a form of governance that is systematically designed to address the problem of accountability. While earlier legal systems succeeded in making public authority accountable to the preferences of the few or the many, the modern constitutional state creates the legal conditions in which the exercise of public authority is accountable to the ongoing right of each member of the legal order to just governance. States must bring themselves within the parameters of modern constitutionalism because all legal systems must make the exercise of public authority accountable to the right of each person bound by it to just governance and such accountability is impossible apart from the legal and institutional structure of a modern constitutional state.

PART III

The doctrinal dimension

6

Constitutional reform

Constitutional theorists often agonize over the question of how difficult it should be to amend a constitution.[1] Some argue that when constitutional norms are difficult to amend, subsequent generations might find themselves constrained by the dead hand of the past, unable to reform defective arrangements and address emerging challenges.[2] In such circumstances, the constitution is in danger both of losing its 'legal relevance and of being circumvented.'[3] But others argue that when constitutional norms are easy to amend, subsequent generations might find the constitutional order degraded 'from a warrantor of democratic freedom into an instrument of authoritarian or totalitarian domination.'[4] The constitutional design of the amending power raises a dilemma because a danger arises regardless of whether the amending formula is demanding or permissive.[5]

1 Christopher L. Eisgruber, *Constitutional Self-Government* (Cambridge: Harvard University Press, 2001), 20: 'How Much Constitutional Obduracy Is Optimal?' See also James Wilford Garner, *Introduction to Political Science* (New York: American Book Company, 1910), 405–6; Rosalind Dixon, "Constitutional Amendment Rules: A Comparative Perspective," in *Comparative Constitutional Law*, ed. Tom Ginsberg and Rosalind Dixon (Cheltenham: Edward Elgar, 2011), 102; Stephen Holmes and Cass R. Sunstein, "The Politics of Constitutional Revision in Eastern Europe," in *Responding to Imperfection: The Theory and Practice of Constitutional Amendment*, ed. Sanford Levinson (Princeton: Princeton University Press, 1995), 275 and 283; Hugh Evander Willis, *Constitutional Law of the United States* (Bloomington: Principia Press, 1936), 116.

2 Eisgruber, *Constitutional Self-Government*, 11; and Donald Lutz, "Toward a Theory of Constitutional Amendment," in *Responding to Imperfection: The Theory and Practice of Constitutional Amendment*, 240; and especially Thomas Paine, *The Rights of Man* in *Rights of Man, Common Sense, and Other Political Writings* (Oxford: Oxford University Press, 1998), 92.

3 Dieter Grimm, "The Basic Law at 60 – Identity and Change," *German Law Journal* 11 (2010): 33.

4 Ulrich K. Preuss, "The Implications of 'Eternity Clauses': The German Experience," *Israel Law Review* 44 (2001): 435. See also Holmes and Sunstein, "The Politics of Constitutional Revision in Eastern Europe," 295.

5 Theorists appraise the likelihood of these dangers emerging and their seriousness in different ways and thereby arrive at different conclusions about how the amending power of a constitution should be calibrated or about how to interpret the rigor of a

The practice of modern constitutional states rejects the assumption that generates this debate. The assumption is that if a constitutional order may be amended, then it must be open to amendments of any kind, whether the amendment ameliorates injustice or occasions it. Modern constitutional states raise an alternative approach. They authorize amendments that seek to ameliorate constitutional defects, but preclude amendments that would exacerbate them.

To appreciate this radical innovation, consider the difference between the amending power in the Weimar Constitution and in Germany's postwar Basic Law. The Weimar Constitution could be amended by a supermajority consisting of two-thirds of the legislature.[6] In its day, jurists understood the legal constraints on constitutional amendments as wholly procedural in nature. A legislative supermajority enjoyed an 'unlimited mandate' for constitutional amendment.[7] The enemies of the constitutional order enacted amendments suspending constitutional rights, authorized legislation by executive decree, and centralized all governmental authority. It soon 'became a cause of regret that there were no explicit substantive limits to the extent to which the constitution could be amended.'[8]

Following the collapse of Nazism in 1945, the German political scientist Arnold Brecht articulated a groundbreaking innovation in the constitutional design of amending powers: 'For preventing the possibility the majority rule will be abused to authorize barbaric measures . . . it would be advisable for the new German Constitution (and for any other democratic constitution to be enacted in the future) to contain certain sacrosanct principles and standards [which] . . . could not be impaired even by

particular constitution's amending formula. For a defense of the rigid approach that prevails in the United States, see Eisgruber, *Constitutional Self-Government*, 11–12. For criticism suggesting that it is overly rigid, see Stephen M. Griffin, "Constitutionalism in the United States: From Theory to Politics," in *Responding to Imperfection: The Theory and Practice of Constitutional Amendment*, 60. For criticism that it is not rigid enough, see William L. Marbury, "The Limitations upon the Amending Power," *Harvard Law Review* 33 (1919): 224 (objecting to the imposition of the Federal Woman's Suffrage Amendment on unwilling states). For interpretations of the American constitutional order that reduce the rigidity of the constitution by suggesting the possibility of modes of constitutional reform that take place outside of article V, see Bruce Ackerman, "Higher Lawmaking," in *Responding to Imperfection*, 63–87; and Akhil Reed Amar, "Popular Sovereignty and Constitutional Amendment," in *Responding to Imperfection*, 88–115.

6 Weimar Republic, 1919, article 76.

7 Grimm, "The Basic Law at 60 – Identity and Change," 34.

8 David P. Currie, *The Constitution of the Federal Republic of Germany* (Chicago: University of Chicago Press, 1994), 7–8.

constitutional amendments.'[9] Four years later, Germany enacted a Basic Law that systematically addressed the vulnerabilities of its constitutional predecessor. With regard to amendments, the central problem with the Weimar Constitution was not the number of times it was amended, but rather the kind of amendments that it permitted.[10] The Basic Law responded in article 79(3), known as the *eternity clause*, which explicitly indicates that certain kinds of constitutional amendments 'shall be inadmissible.'[11] These include amendments that would 'undermine or corrode' the core commitments of the constitutional order,[12] including human dignity, democracy, the rule of law, and federalism. Amendable features of the constitutional order can be varied or repealed by a legislative supermajority,[13] but there is no lawful procedure for abrogating these constitutional essentials, even by 'a 100 percent majority.'[14] The result is a constitution that is comparatively easy to amend,[15] but that denies the legality of amendments that would diminish the cornerstones of the constitutional order.

In the decades since the Basic Law was enacted, eternity clauses have become a 'new reality' in postwar constitutional practice.[16] This chapter draws on the unified theory of public law to expound the nature and justification of this new reality. In so doing, I set out a conception of

[9] Yaniv Roznai, "Unconstitutional Constitutional Amendments – The Migration and Success of a Constitutional Idea," *American Journal of Comparative Law* 61 (2013): 668 (citing Arnold Brecht, *Federalism and Regionalism in Germany—The Division of Prussia* (New York: Oxford University Press, 1945), 138).

[10] Nicolas Nohlen, "Germany: The Electronic Eavesdropping Case," *International Journal of Constitutional Law* 3 (2005): 684: 'It is true that the Basic Law itself has been amended more than fifty times since 1949. However, the constitutional problem of the Weimar Republic was not the number of constitutional amendments, but the intensity. The practice of the constitutional legislator within this time came to be known as "breaking through the constitution" (*Verfassungsdurchbrechung*).'

[11] Basic Law of the Federal Republic of Germany, 1949 [hereinafter Grundgesetz].

[12] Donald P. Kommers and Russell A. Miller, *The Constitutional Jurisprudence of the Federal Republic of Germany* (Durham: Duke University Press, 2012), 46.

[13] Grundgesetz, article 79(2).

[14] Dieter Grimm, "German and American Constitutionalism: A Comparison," *Berlin Journal* 7 (2003): 11.

[15] In well over 200 years, the American Constitution has been amended a total of either 26 or 27 times. For discussion, see Laurence Tribe, *The Invisible Constitution* (Oxford: Oxford University Press, 2008), 2–3. By contrast, Germany's Basic Law was amended a total of fifty-eight times in its first sixty-one years. See Lech Garlicki and Zofia A. Garlicka, "External Review of Constitutional Amendments? International Law as a Norm of Reference," *Israel Law Journal* 44 (2011): 353.

[16] Claude Klein, "Introduction," *Israel Law Review* 44 (2011): 320. See also Roznai, "Unconstitutional Constitutional Amendments," 714.

constituent power, the public authority to establish, modify, or repeal constitutional norms.

I proceed in four sections.

The first describes the emergence of eternity clauses in modern constitutional states around the world. I distinguish the character of eternity clauses in modern constitutional states from those that appeared in earlier forms of constitutionalism. I then provide an overview of eternity clauses, both express and implied, in constitutional jurisdictions around the world.

The second section considers the adequacy of the dominant justification of eternity clauses, the *basic structure doctrine*. This doctrine distinguishes between two kinds of constitutional moments. The first involves the original establishment of a constitutional order, while the second concerns the subsequent enactment of constitutional amendments. According to the doctrine, these moments stand in a hierarchical relationship: amendments must conform to the identity of the established constitutional order. I argue that this doctrine is objectionable because it focuses on the wrong consideration. Instead of focusing on how constituent power should be exercised, the doctrine focuses on the order in which successive exercises of constituent power occur. The result is that the original exercise of constituent power establishes the parameters for all future constitutional reform. The problem with this doctrine is that it is only as adequate as the constitutional context in which it happens to be applied. When applied within a modern constitutional state, the doctrine could be deployed to invalidate amendments that would undermine the constitution's protection of human dignity and fundamental rights. But the doctrine could just as easily be applied in the context of a wicked regime to deny the legality of amendments that would establish a legal and institutional framework that protected human dignity and fundamental rights.

The third section formulates an alternative justification of eternity clauses. The justification unpacks the ramifications of the legal structure of a modern constitutional state for its amendment power. In Chapter 5, I argued that the duty of just governance requires legal systems to adopt, maintain, and refine a modern constitutional form of governance. Further, within a modern constitutional state, this duty forms a justiciable condition of the valid exercise of all public authority. Since an amendment to the constitutional order is a paradigmatic exercise of public authority, it follows that amendments that violate the duty of just governance cannot be valid. Because this duty demands that modern constitutional states maintain and refine their arrangements, any amendment that undermines the cornerstones of a modern constitutional state cannot be valid. This justification of eternity clauses proceeds from the legal structure of a modern constitutional state and does not apply to others kinds of legal systems. This means that unlike the basic structure doctrine, the justification cannot be employed to perpetuate or resurrect defective alternatives to the modern constitutional state.

The fourth and final section responds to critics of *constituent power*. In the eyes of its critics, constituent power is a paradoxical and dangerous idea. Constituent power is paradoxical when invoked to ground the authority of a legal order: in imagining the people acting to establish a legal order, proponents of constituent power overlook that a people cannot act as a whole in the absence of such an order. Constituent power is *dangerous* because it immunizes the constitutional arrangements that a people adopts from moral scrutiny. I respond to these objections by arguing that within the unified theory, constituent power is neither paradoxical nor dangerous. It is not paradoxical because constituent power concerns not the legitimating basis of public authority but the mode through which government must address its constitutional defects. It is not dangerous because if constituent power is a paradigmatic instance of public authority, public justice provides the appropriate standard for assessing the adequacy of its exercise.

A couple of clarifications are in order from the outset.

First, eternity clauses are sometimes dismissed as being hopelessly misconceived. After all, placing certain constitutional arrangements behind the shield of an eternity clause does not establish their perpetuity.[17] It 'is simply a fact about political power as such' that 'in the long run a strong majority of the electorate can eventually make the constitution conform to its political will . . . There is no way around this fact, not even by entrenchment clauses that try to fix permanently the basic democratic guarantees.'[18] For example, particular constitutional

[17] Garlicki and Garlicka, "External Review of Constitutional Amendments? International Law as a Norm of Reference," 352: '[T]he list of unamendable provisions may be modified or abridged if this is the will of the supermajority of parliament. Moreover, these norms can disappear entirely from the text when the whole constitution is replaced by a new one. The insertion of "unamendable constitutional provisions" into the original text of a constitution therefore offers only limited protection against future action of new parliamentary supermajorities that enjoy the support of the electorate. No constitution is eternal, and no constitution is able to vest its norms with an eternal guarantee of stability.'

[18] John Rawls, *Political Liberalism* (New York: Columbia University Press, 1996), 233. For Rawls's argument for implied eternity clauses, see section 6.2 below.

provisions might be ignored or the whole constitutional order might be uprooted in an act of revolutionary violence. However, if the purpose of an eternity clause is not to establish that the enactment or repeal of certain constitutional provisions is forever impossible as a matter of *fact*, but rather to establish that the enactment or repeal of certain constitutional provisions is inadmissible as a matter of *law*, then these concerns recede. As eternity clauses play an increasing role in a variety of constitutional settings around the world, the present chapter explores the justificatory basis of this legal inadmissibility.

Second, eternity clauses are sometimes criticized for empowering the judiciary to overturn legal norms enacted through a democratic procedure.[19] In the prior chapter, I explored different versions of this objection in providing a justification of the legal and institutional structure of a modern constitutional state, including the judicial review of the constitutionality of all exercises of public authority. Rather than pass over the same ground again, the present chapter considers the implications of this legal and institutional structure for issues surrounding constitutional reform.

6.1 The rise of eternity clauses

Although theorists from across the political spectrum disagree about the purposes to which amendments should be directed, they often affirm Alexander Hamilton's view of the amending power: the people can 'alter or abolish the established Constitution, whenever they find it inconsistent with their happiness.'[20] Thus, Robert Bork argues that the American people may amend the constitution to subject judicial review to the will of the legislative majority,[21] Michael Walzer maintains that people can use the amending process to 'disestablish' the constitutional order,[22] and – as

[19] See, for example, *The Supreme Court Versus the Constitution*, ed. Pran Chopra (New Delhi: Sage Publications, 2006).

[20] Alexander Hamilton, "The Federalist No. 78," in Hamilton, John Jay, and James Madison, *The Federalist: A Commentary on the Constitution of the United States* (Philadelphia: J.B. Lippincott, 1864), 580. For contemporary restatements of this idea, see Jed Rubenfeld, *Freedom and Time: A Theory of Constitutional Self-Government* (New Haven: Yale University Press, 2001), 174 (arguing that 'the principle of self-government over time-requires that a nation be able to reject any part of a constitution whose commitments are no longer the people's own'); and Eisgruber, *Constitutional Self-Government*, 120 (arguing that because 'constitutions must leave people free to govern themselves, any constitution – no matter how good – must leave people free to enact bad provisions').

[21] Robert Bork, *Slouching Towards Gemorrah: Modern Liberalism and American Decline* (New York: HarperCollins, 1996), 319.

[22] Michael Walzer, "Philosophy and Democracy," *Political Theory* 9 (1981): 392.

I discuss below – Bruce Ackerman notes that the American people may amend the constitution to repeal the rights that it protects.[23] According to this understanding of the amending power, the only constraints on its exercise are procedural. As Martin Loughlin encapsulates this conception, constituent power is 'an expression of the open, provisional, and dynamic aspects of constitutional ordering.'[24] Constituent power is a procedure that may be directed toward any aim.

This conception of constituent power now stands in stark contrast with the constitutional practice of states that acknowledge both procedural *and* substantive constraints on the amending power. Within modern constitutional states, constitutional essentials such as inherent dignity, fundamental (including democratic) rights, and judicial review are conceived of not as mere preferences that the people might affirm in one generation only to relinquish in the next, but as features that the legal order must adopt and that it may not relinquish through law. These substantive constraints on the amending power might appear expressly in the constitution or be implied by its overarching constitutional structure. Germany provides the leading example of the former, India of the latter.

6.1.1 Express eternity clauses

In the history of express eternity clauses, three approaches can be roughly distinguished. The classification that I offer here is conceptual, not chronological.

The first involved express eternity clauses of a 'sweeping' and 'open-ended' nature.[25] Article 112 of the Constitution of Norway (1814) stipulates that amendments 'must never . . . contradict the principles embodied in this Constitution, but solely relate to modifications of particular provisions which do not alter the spirit of the Constitution.'[26] Similarly, the Greek Constitution of 1864 indicated that the constitution as a whole could not be revised, and that only provisions that were not fundamental could be amended.[27] Although explicit, such eternity clauses do not

23 Bruce Ackerman, "Rooted Cosmopolitanism," *Ethics* 104 (1994): 517; and Ackerman, *We the People: Foundations* (Cambridge: Harvard University Press, 1991), 13–15.

24 Martin Loughlin, "The Concept of Constituent Power," *European Journal of Political Theory* 13 (2014): 219. See also Loughlin, *The Idea of Public Law* (Oxford: Oxford University Press, 2003), 113.

25 Eivind Smith, "Old and Protected? On the 'Supra-Constitutional' Clause in the Constitution of Norway," *Israel Law Journal* 44 (2011): 373.

26 Norway, 1814, article 112.

27 See Roznai, "Unconstitutional Constitutional Amendments," 689.

themselves indicate which constitutional provisions are fundamental or what kinds of amendments accord with the spirit of the constitution.[28]

The second approach introduced 'specific prohibitions' identifying arrangements immune from constitutional amendment.[29] The distinctive feature of this approach is its piecemeal character: prohibitions were conceived of as isolated constraints rather than a set of specifications reflecting a more general constitutional ideal. The amendment power of the 1884 French Third Republic placed only the 'republican form of government' beyond the amendment power.[30] The eternity clause of the Mexican Constitution of 1824 was more comprehensive, but protected both liberal and illiberal features of the constitutional order. It protects the republican form of government, the separation of powers, and liberty of the press, but also the official state religion, which 'is, and will be perpetually, the Roman Catholic Apostolic. The Nation will protect it by wise and just laws, and prohibit the exercise of any other whatever.'[31]

The third approach emerged following the moral horrors of World War II. In Germany, the 'drafters of the Basic Law, traumatized by the near-defenseless collapse of the Weimar Republic and the unprecedented crimes of the Nazi regime, took great pains to avoid the weaknesses of the Weimar Constitution and to fortify the Basic Law against a repeat of this experience.'[32] In 1949, a 'bold experiment in constitutional engineering' culminated in the Basic Law.[33] Article 79(3) places the fundamental commitments of the constitutional order beyond the bounds of constitutional reform. Among the commitments that cannot be repudiated through law are the 'dignitarian principles of Article 1' and the 'basic structural principles of the constitutional order set forth in Article 20 (i.e. federalism, separation of powers, rule of law, and the social welfare state).'[34] These constitutional commitments are eternal in the sense that the constitution

[28] On the attempt to discern the historical and contemporary meaning of Norway's eternity clause, see Smith, "Old and Protected? On the 'Supra-Constitutional' Clause in the Constitution of Norway," 378 ff.

[29] Garlicki and Garlicka, "External Review of Constitutional Amendments? International Law as a Norm of Reference," 349 (referring to the first application of 'the technique of enumerated prohibitions').

[30] Klein, "Introduction," 319. A similar provision appears in Portugal's Constitution of 1911. See Roznai, "Unconstitutional Constitutional Amendments," 677.

[31] Mexico, 1824, articles 3 and 171.

[32] Preuss, "The Implications of 'Eternity Clauses': The German Experience," 439.

[33] Donald P. Kommers, "The Basic Law: A Fifty Year Assessment," in *Fifty Years of German Basic Law: The New Departure for Germany* (Baltimore: Johns Hopkins University Press, 1999), 3.

[34] Ibid.

acknowledges the ongoing duty of the state to uphold these arrangements and denies the legality of any amendment that would diminish or abolish them.

Germany's eternity clause departs from its predecessors. In contrast to the vagueness of the first approach, Germany's eternity clause identifies specific provisions of the constitution that are unamendable. In contrast to the fragmentary character of the second approach, Germany's eternity clause reaffirms the duty that human dignity imposes on all public authority and elaborates the legal and institutional conditions of its fulfillment. As Dieter Grimm puts the point, human dignity forms 'the unalterable foundation of Germany's constitutional order.'[35]

Germany's eternity clause indicates that the constitutional order is reducible neither to the *proceduralism* that forms the dominant understanding of the American Constitution nor to the opposing tendency, which Bruce Ackerman refers to as *rights-foundationalism.*[36] Consider the way in which Ackerman contrasts the American Constitution and the German Basic Law. The difference, he explains, lies in the relationship that each system establishes between democratic procedures and substantive rights. The United States is a *proceduralist* constitutional order because it renders substantive commitments to rights protection subordinate to democratic procedures. Germany is a *rights-foundationalist* constitutional order because it renders democratic procedures subordinate to the protection of substantive rights. Ackerman's distinction, however, relies on a selective interpretation of both constitutions. When reading the American Constitution, Ackerman notes that rights are not protected from amendment and assumes that procedures must therefore trump rights (although democratic procedures are also not protected from amendment). When reading Germany's Basic Law, Ackerman notes that rights are placed beyond the power of amendment and assumes that rights must therefore trump democracy (although democratic procedures are also placed beyond the power of amendment). Ackerman's distinction between proceduralist and rights-foundationalist constitutional orders cannot be exhaustive because modern constitutional states like Germany fall in neither camp. In Germany, the foundational value is neither fundamental rights nor democratic procedures. Rather, both fundamental rights and democratic procedures are valued

[35] Dieter Grimm, "Human Rights and Judicial Review in Germany," in *Human Rights and Judicial Review*, ed. David M. Beatty (Dordrecht: Martinus Nijhoff Publishers, 1994), 270.

[36] *We the People: Foundations*, 13–15.

because of the state's commitment to realize a legal order adequate to the dignity of its members. Insofar as amendments involve an exercise of public authority, and the constitution indicates that no exercise of public authority can be valid if it is incompatible with dignity, the constitution establishes that both democracy and fundamental rights are insulated from amendments that would dilute or dissolve them.

Germany's eternity clause is not an isolated occurrence. The Constitution of Portugal (1976) contains 'the most detailed' eternity clause in the world.[37] The clause protects fourteen components of the constitutional order from amendment, including the republican form of government, the separation of church and state, the rights and freedoms of citizens and of workers, the separation of powers, democracy, and an independent judiciary empowered to review the constitutionality of authoritative actions and omissions.[38] While Portugal's Constitution was influenced by the German model, the Constitution of Brazil was influenced by the Portuguese.[39] The Constitution of Brazil contains an eternity clause precluding the consideration of amendments tending to the abolition of the federal form of the state, the democratic ordering of the state, the separation of powers, and 'individual rights and guarantees.'[40] Similar eternity clauses can also be found in the constitutions of Greece,[41] the Czech Republic,[42] and Turkey.[43]

37 Roznai, "Unconstitutional Constitutional Amendments," 677–8.

38 Portugal, 1976, article 288.

39 Roznai, "Unconstitutional Constitutional Amendments," 679.

40 Brazil, 1988, article 60(4).

41 Greece, 1975, article 110(1), referring to articles 2(1), 4(1), 4(4), 4(7), 5(1), 5(3), 13(1), and 26 (indicating the constitutional provisions that are not subject to revision, including the 'primary obligation' of the state to respect and protect human dignity, equality before the law, freedom of religion, freedom to develop one's personality in society, inviolability of personal liberty, rejection of titles of nobility, and eligibility criteria for the public service).

42 Czech Republic, 1993, article 9(2) (rendering inadmissible any amendment that alters the 'fundamental attributes of the democratic state governed by the rule of law'). For discussion of the constitutional jurisprudence surrounding the Czech Republic's eternity clause, see Roznai, "Legisprudence Limitations on Constitutional Amendments? Reflections on the Czech Constitutional Court's Declaration of Unconstitutional Constitutional Act," *Vienna Journal on International Constitutional Law* 7 (2014): 29–57.

43 Turkey, 1982, articles 1–4 (indicating that provisions establishing Turkey as a republic and as a 'democratic, secular and social state governed by the rule of law; bearing in mind the concepts of public peace, national solidarity and justice; respecting human rights; loyal to the nationalism of Atatürk, and based on the fundamental tenets set forth in the Preamble.' The eternity clause also encompasses the Turkish language, flag, and the national anthem.) For a brief discussion of Turkey's non-amendment constitutional jurisprudence, see Aharon Barak, "Unconstitutional Constitutional Amendments," *Israel Law Review* 44 (2011): 322–5.

6.1.2 *Implied eternity clauses*

Substantive constraints on the amending power can arise independently of the directives of a constitutional text.

While on a visit to India in 1965, the German comparative law professor Dietrich Conrad delivered a lecture entitled "Implied Limitations of the Amending Power." Conrad prefaced his remarks by stating that it 'is the duty of the jurist . . . to anticipate extreme cases' and suggesting that 'sometimes only extreme tests reveal the true nature of a legal concept.'[44] Conrad then proceeded to explore the concept of a constitutional amendment by conjuring a series of hypothetical amendments, as if duly enacted in accordance with the procedures set out in article 368 of the Constitution of India:

> Could a constitutional amendment abolish Article 21, to the effect that forthwith a person could be deprived of his life or personal liberty without authorisation by law? Could the ruling party, if it sees its majority shrinking, amend Article 368 to the effect that the amending power rests with the President acting on the advice of the Prime Minister? Could the amending power be used to abolish the Constitution and reintroduce, let us say, the rule of a moghul emperor or of the Crown of England? I do not want, by posing such questions, to provoke easy answers. But I should like to acquaint you with the discussion which took place on such questions among constitutional lawyers in Germany in the Weimar period – discussion, seeming academic at first, but suddenly illustrated by history in a drastic and terrible manner.[45]

In the years that followed this lecture, a series of constitutional crises prompted the Supreme Court to consider whether the Indian Constitution contained an implicit eternity clause that constrained its amending power. The result is a jurisprudence on constitutional amendments that is 'unrivalled' in the contemporary world.[46] In the discussion that follows, I focus on the disparate forms of reasoning that emerge in two particularly significant cases.

In *Golaknath* v. *State of Punjab*,[47] the Indian Supreme Court, in a 6–5 decision, determined that constitutional rights constrain the amending

44 A.G. Noorani, "Behind the 'Basic Structure Doctrine': On India's Debt to a German Jurist," *Frontline* 18 (2001), www.hinduonnet.com/fline/ fl1809/18090950.htm (last visited July 10, 2015).

45 Ibid.

46 Gary Jeffrey Jacobsohn, "An Unconstitutional Constitution? A Comparative Perspective," *International Journal of Constitutional Law* 4 (2006): 462.

47 [1967] 2 SCR 762 [hereinafter *Golaknath*].

power. At issue was the constitutionality of the seventeenth amendment to the Indian Constitution, which empowered the state to extinguish property rights. The majority found the amendment to be unconstitutional because it violated article 13(2) of the Indian Constitution: 'The State shall not make any *law* which takes away or abridges the rights conferred by this Part and any law made in contravention of this clause shall, to the extent of the contravention, be void.'[48] The majority reasoned that the power of Parliament to amend the constitution, established in article 368, must be exercised in accordance with the fundamental rights that article 13(2) recognizes as binding Parliament.[49] Insofar as the constitutional amendment that Parliament enacted denied the constitutional right to property, it must be void. Within the Indian constitutional order, fundamental rights enjoy a 'transcendental character': they can be guaranteed by the constitution, but they cannot be revoked through its amending power.[50] However, the majority did not invalidate the amendment. It acknowledged the impact of the amendment on 'the social and economic affairs of our country and the chaotic situation that may be brought about by the sudden withdrawal at this stage of the amendments from the Constitution.'[51] It then restricted its decision to a prospective overruling, upholding the validity of the amendment at issue, while declaring that 'Parliament will have no power from the date of this decision to amend any provisions' of the Bill of Rights 'so as to take away or abridge the fundamental rights enshrined therein.'[52]

In the years that followed, Parliament enacted a series of amendments to systematically dismantle *Golaknath*. One of these amendments established, in general, that Parliament's power to establish, modify, or repeal constitutional provisions was unlimited and, in particular, that the amending power contained in article 368 was unconstrained by the fundamental rights acknowledged in article 13. In *Kesavananda Bharati* v. *State of Kerala*, the court responded with a landmark decision consisting of eleven opinions spanning over 700 pages.[53] Justice Khanna's majority opinion overturned *Golaknath*, but proceeded to invalidate the amendments on the basis of a new constitutional doctrine constraining the amendment

[48] Constitution of India, 1949, article 13(2) (my emphasis). [49] *Golaknath*, 789 and 804.
[50] Ibid., 792. [51] Ibid., 814.
[52] Ibid., 815. For a critical discussion of the majority's ruling, see Sudhir Krishnaswamy, *Democracy and Constitutionalism in India: A Study of the Basic Structure Doctrine* (New Delhi: Oxford University Press, 2009), 5–24.
[53] (1973) 4 S.C.C. 225 (hereinafter *Kesavananda*).

power. On the one hand, Khanna rejected *Golaknath* by restricting the application of article 13(2), which denies validity to *laws* that fail to conform to fundamental rights, to ordinary legislation but not to amendments enacted through article 368. On the other, Khanna held that the very notion of a constitutional amendment introduces constraints on its exercise. Echoing a passage from an article written by Dietrich Conrad,[54] Khanna formulated the basic structure doctrine:

> The word "amendment" postulates that the old Constitution survives without loss of its identity despite the change and continues even though it has been subjected to alterations. As a result of the amendment, the old Constitution cannot be destroyed and done away with; it is retained though in the amended form. What then is meant by the retention of the old Constitution? It means the retention of the basic structure or framework of the old Constitution . . . Although it is permissible under the power of amendment to effect changes . . . and to adapt the system to the requirements of changing conditions, it is not permissible to touch the foundation or to alter the basic institutional pattern. The words "amendment of the Constitution" with all their wide sweep and amplitude cannot have the effect of destroying or abrogating the basic structure or framework of the Constitution. It would not be competent under the garb of amendment, for instance, to change the democratic government into dictatorship or hereditary monarchy . . .[55]

According to the basic structure doctrine, any amendment to the constitution must preserve its underlying identity. Thus Khanna agrees with the *Golaknath* majority that the constitutional order imposes limits on the amendment power that the judiciary must oversee. But he departs from its reasoning by denying that these limits are constituted by fundamental rights. Since constitutional rights are simply the product of positive law, they 'can be abridged or taken away by amendment of the Constitution.'[56]

Although the *Golaknath* and *Kesavananda* decisions split the Indian judiciary, the Supreme Court consolidated the basic structure doctrine in later cases. It is now an established feature of Indian constitutional jurisprudence. While serious disagreement persists about how to identify features of the basic structure,[57] there is general agreement that the basic structure encompasses secularism, democracy, the rule of law,

[54] Ibid., para. 1485 (citing Conrad): 'Any amending body organised within the statutory scheme, howsoever verbally unlimited its power, cannot by its very structure change the fundamental pillars supporting its constitutional authority.'

[55] Ibid., para. 1480. [56] Ibid., para. 1509.

[57] See Krishnaswamy, 131–63; and Richard Albert, "Nonconstitutional Amendments," *Canadian Journal of Law and Jurisprudence* 22 (2009): 22.

federalism, and judicial review and independence.[58] The doctrine has even been invoked to invalidate an amendment that purported to overturn the basic structure doctrine itself by explicitly removing all constraints on the amendment power.[59] The doctrine has influenced many of India's neighbors, including Nepal, Bangladesh, and Pakistan.[60] In South Africa, where the constitution empowers the Constitutional Court to 'decide on the constitutionality of any amendment to the Constitution,' but includes no explicit clause imposing specific constraints on the amendment power,[61] the court has referred to the doctrine without express affirmation or repudiation.[62]

Finally, while the Supreme Court of Canada has not pronounced on India's amendment jurisprudence, it may have expressed openness to the basic structure doctrine. In one of its most important opinions, the unanimous court characterized the constitution as a 'global system of rules and principles which govern the exercise of constitutional authority.'[63] Because the written text of the constitution contains gaps, it does not exhaust this system. Accordingly, the court stipulated that it will fill these gaps by looking to the 'vital unstated assumptions upon which the text is based.'[64] These assumptions or 'underlying principles' include federalism, democracy, constitutionalism and the rule of law, and respect for minorities.[65] Insofar as these principles form the 'internal architecture' or the 'basic constitutional structure' of Canadian constitutionalism,[66] they impose constraints on the pursuit of fundamental constitutional revision.

58 Soli Sorabjee, "The Ideal Remedy: A Valediction," in *The Supreme Court Versus the Constitution*, 204. For an alternative account suggesting that the basic structure doctrine includes (1) constitutional supremacy, (2) republicanism and democracy, (3) secularism, (4) the separation of powers, and (5) federalism, see *Kesavananda*, para. 316–8. Departing from the reasoning that flows through Justice Khanna's majority, Chief Justice Sikri suggests that these features are unified by the 'dignity and freedom of the individual,' which 'are easily discernible not only from the preamble but the whole scheme of the Constitution.'

59 *Minerva Mills* v. *Union of India* (1981) SCR 206.

60 See Gábor Halmai, "Unconstitutional Constitutional Amendments: Constitutional Courts as Guardians of the Constitution?" *Constellations* 19 (2012): 187–8; and Roznai, "Unconstitutional Constitutional Amendments," 694–701.

61 *Constitution of the Republic of South Africa*, 1996, s. 167(4)(d).

62 *Premier of Kwazulu-Natal and Others* v. *President of the Republic of South Africa and Others*, 1996 (1) SA 769 (CC). For discussion, see Roznai, "Unconstitutional Constitutional Amendments," 705–7. See also *United Democratic Movement* v. *President of the Republic of South Africa*, 1996 (1) SA 769 (CC).

63 *Reference re Secession of Quebec* [1998] 2 SCR 217, para. 148.

64 Ibid., para. 49.

65 Ibid., para. 32.

66 Ibid., para. 50. See also *Reference re Senate Reform* [2014] 1 SCR 704, para. 60 and 97.

The nature of this constraint has not been fully explicated, but in the particular case the court set out some institutional and procedural rules for the secession of Quebec from Canada.

The amending powers of a diverse and growing body of legal systems operate under the constraint of eternity clauses, both express and implied. The prevalence of these constraints raises the questions: Can eternity clauses be justified? On what constitutional theory would such a justification rest? The next section considers how leading constitutional theorists have responded to these questions.

6.2 Against the basic structure doctrine

Eternity clauses purport to impose perpetual constraints on a constitution's amending power. A theoretical exposition of eternity clauses must explain why such constraints cannot themselves be discarded through the exercise of that power. In the case of an *explicit* eternity clause, why may the amendment power not be used, initially, to weaken or even repeal an eternity clause, and then, subsequently, to enact an amendment that the former eternity clause would have precluded?[67] In the case of an *implied* eternity clause, why may the amendment power not be used to enact a constitutional provision establishing that the amendment power is unconstrained and thereby overturn the basic structure?[68]

This section expounds the standard approach that theorists employ to justify constraints on a constitution's amending power. This strategy, known as the *basic structure doctrine*, holds that such constraints can be justified because subsequent amendments must conform to the fundamental commitments of the existing constitutional order. I present the doctrine through its most prominent proponents and critics and argue that the doctrine is only as adequate as the legal context in which it is raised. Although its proponents often present the doctrine as a bulwark of liberal democratic constitutionalism, the doctrine could just as easily

[67] Smith, "Old and Protected? On the 'Supra-Constitutional' Clause in the Constitution of Norway," 375. See also Carl J. Friedrich, "Rebuilding the German Constitution, II," *American Political Science Review* 43 (1949): 719 (noting that Germany's eternity clause both forbids amendments and 'would seem to be itself subject to amendment').

[68] See, for example, *Minerva Mills* v. *Union of India* (1981) SCR 206, 239 (in which the Indian Supreme Court invalidated a constitutional amendment declaring that 'there shall be no limitation whatever on the constituent power of Parliament to amend by way of addition, variation or repeal the provisions of this Constitution . . . ').

defend an unjust constitutional order from liberal and democratic reforms.

In *We the People: Foundations*, Bruce Ackerman articulates a theory of the American Constitution that stands in direct opposition to the basic structure doctrine. Whereas proponents of the doctrine hold that constitutional amendments to a legal order are constrained by its essential features, Ackerman holds that it is through the establishment and amendment of constitutional norms that the essential features of a legal order are determined. He illustrates his position by raising a 'hypothetical case' of a 'morally disastrous' amendment to the American Constitution:

> Suppose that the religious revival now prominent in the Islamic world is the first wave of a Great Awakening that envelops the Christian West. A general revulsion against godless materialism yields mass political mobilization that finally results in a successful campaign for partial repeal of the First Amendment. With the dawn of the new millennium, Amendment XXVII is proclaimed throughout the land: Christianity is established as the state religion of the American people, and the public worship of other gods is hereby forbidden.[69]

Ackerman notes that such an amendment would 'deeply offend' his 'commitment to freedom of conscience,'[70] but insists that its constitutionality is unassailable. This position reflects Ackerman's understanding of the American Constitution as founded upon self-government: 'Fundamental rights have constitutional status only if they have their source in a deliberate and mobilized affirmation of principle by the American people. Our constitution is democratic first, rights-respecting second.'[71] It follows that the same democratic procedure that established constitutional rights may be deployed to repeal them.[72]

In *Political Liberalism*, John Rawls responded to Ackerman's hypothetical amendment involving the partial repeal of the First Amendment. Rawls claimed that the procedural hurdles contemplated in article V of the American Constitution were necessary conditions for enacting a valid constitutional amendment, but he denied that they were sufficient. Echoing a long line of political and constitutional thought,[73] Rawls elaborated on the meaning, function, and limits of the amendment power:

69 Ackerman, *We the People: Foundations* (Cambridge: Harvard University Press, 1991), 14.
70 Ibid. 71 Bruce Ackerman, "Rooted Cosmopolitanism," *Ethics* 104 (1994): 517.
72 Ibid., 531–2.
73 For a nineteenth-century antecedent of Rawls's argument, see Thomas M. Cooley, "The Power to Amend the Federal Constitution," *Michigan Law Journal* 2 (1893): 118 (arguing that 'an amendment . . . must be in harmony with the thing amended . . . ').

> [A]n amendment is not merely a change. One idea of an amendment is to adjust basic constitutional values to changing political and social circumstances, or to incorporate into the constitution a broader and more inclusive understanding of those values. The three amendments related to the Civil War all do this, as does the Nineteenth Amendment granting women the vote; and the Equal Rights Amendment attempted the same. At the Founding there was the blatant contradiction between the idea of equality in the Declaration of Independence and the Constitution and chattel slavery of a subjugated race; there were also property qualifications for voting and women were denied the suffrage altogether. Historically those amendments brought the Constitution more in line with its original promise. Another idea of amendment is to adapt basic institutions in order to remove weaknesses that come to light in subsequent constitutional practice. Thus, with the exception of the Eighteenth, the other amendments concern either the institutional design of government, witness the Twenty-second, which allows the president to serve only two terms; or certain basic matters of policy, witness the Sixteenth, which grants Congress the power to levy income taxes. Such has been the role of amendments.[74]

Rawls's argument distinguishes between the unconstrained power to *change* a constitution and the narrower power to *amend* it. An amendment involves a particular kind of change, one that preserves the existing constitution's identity and fulfills its aspirations. For Rawls, amendments may further the realization of constitutional values or address constitutional defects that experience has exposed. Ackerman's hypothetical amendment instantiates neither of these possibilities, so it cannot be characterized as a constitutional amendment. Rawls concludes,

> [A]n amendment to repeal the First Amendment and replace it with its opposite fundamentally contradicts the constitutional tradition of the oldest democratic regime in the world. It is therefore invalid. Does this mean that the Bill of Rights and the other amendments are entrenched? Well, they are entrenched in the sense of being validated by long historical practice. They may be amended in the ways mentioned above but not simply repealed and reversed. Should that happen, and it is not inconceivable that the exercise of political power might take that turn, that would be constitutional breakdown, or revolution in the proper sense, and not a valid amendment of the constitution.[75]

[74] Rawls, *Political Liberalism*, 238–9.

[75] Ibid., 239. For discussion of this passage, see Charles L. Kelbley, "Are There Limits to Constitutional Change? Rawls on Comprehensive Doctrines, Unconstitutional Amendments, and the Basis of Equality," *Fordham Law Review* 72 (2004): 1510.

Rawls invokes the basic structure doctrine to defend the liberal core of American constitutionalism from illiberal amendments, but the doctrine can be formulated in abstraction from liberal (or illiberal) commitments. Consider the following passages, in which constitutional scholars describe the basic structure doctrine:

> [E]very constitutional arrangement is based upon a set of core principles which cannot be changed and which can be regarded as intrinsic to its specific identity: this explains the tendency in many constitutional arrangements to identify a set of supraconstitutional provisions which the constitution's text itself, or even more frequently the courts (by induction), state cannot be amended or suppressed.[76]
>
> [E]very constitution has an implied eternity clause according to which its basic structure cannot be changed other than by the establishment of a new constitution. The provisions on the amendment of the constitution cannot authorize a change in the basic structure of the constitution . . .[77]
>
> The authority to "amend the constitution," granted by constitutional legislation, means that other constitutional provisions can substitute for individual or multiple ones. They may do so, however, only under the presupposition that the identity and continuity of the constitution as an entirety is preserved. This means the authority for constitutional amendment contains only the grant of authority to undertake changes, additions, extensions, deletions, etc., in constitutional provisions that preserve the constitution itself. It is not the authority to establish a new constitution, nor is it the authority to change the particular basis of this jurisdiction for constitutional revisions . . . *Constitutional amendment, therefore, is not constitutional annihilation.*[78]

These passages appeal to a shared conviction about the relationship between a constitution and its amendment power: any exercise of the amendment power must be consistent with the fundamental commitments of the existing constitutional order in which it arises. Because an existing constitution might be characterized by liberal or illiberal arrangements, it is not surprising that both defenders and critics of liberalism have appealed to this doctrine to preserve their own preferred arrangements.

[76] Carlo Fusaro and Dawn Oliver, "Towards a Theory of Constitutional Change," in *How Constitutions Change – A Comparative Study*, ed. Carlo Fusaro and Dawn Oliver (Oxford: Hart Publising, 2013), 428.

[77] Barak, "Unconstitutional Constitutional Amendments," 337. Barak attributes this position to the Indian Supreme Court.

[78] Schmitt, *Constitutional Theory*, trans. Jeffrey Seitzer (Durham: Duke University Press, 2008), 150.

The American liberal constitutional lawyer Laurence Tribe echoes Rawls in claiming that 'it may well be that *some* properly adopted formal amendments could themselves be deemed "unconstitutional" because of their radical departure from premises too deeply embedded to be repudiated without a full-blown revolution.'[79] Tribe's example of an amendment that 'might well be deemed void regardless of its process of adoption' involves repealing the guarantee of a republican form of government in article IV and replacing it with a provision that ties membership in Congress to hereditary privilege rather than electoral success.[80]

Tribe's argument generates a liberal conclusion, but the argument on which he relies might, in different circumstances, be directed toward defending deeply illiberal features of the constitutional order from reform. Consider the conclusion that the Southern secessionist John C. Calhoun drew from the basic structure doctrine. Calhoun conceived of antebellum slavery not as an evil to be tolerated but as a 'positive good.'[81] He argued that since slavery was woven into the fabric of the American constitutional order, it could not be abolished through a constitutional amendment.[82] Amendments that 'would radically change the character of the Constitution, or the nature of the system' are null and void.[83]

By focusing on the relation of fit that obtains between an existing constitution and a proposed amendment to it, the basic structure doctrine overlooks the moral significance of the proposed modification. Accordingly, the doctrine can be invoked, as Rawls and Tribe propose, to maintain the constitutional essentials of a liberal democracy or, as Calhoun illustrates, to perpetuate racial slavery. A doctrine that perpetuates the identity of the existing constitutional order is only as good as the context in which it happens to be raised.

[79] Tribe, *The Invisible Constitution* (Oxford: Oxford University Press, 2008), 33.

[80] Ibid., 33–4.

[81] John C. Calhoun, "Slavery a Positive Good," February 6, 1837, http://teachingamerican-history.org/library/document/slavery-a-positive-good/.

[82] For an alternate reading of the American Constitution, which draws on the basic structure doctrine to establish the legal invalidity of antebellum slavery, see Walter F. Murphy, "*Slaughter-House*, Civil Rights, and Limits on Constitutional Change," *American Journal of Jurisprudence* 32 (1987): 1–22.

[83] "A Discourse on the Constitution and Government of the United States," in *John C. Calhoun: Selected Writings and Speeches*, ed. H. Lee Cheek Jr. (Washington: Regnery Publishing, 2003), 165.

Among the theorists who defend the basic structure doctrine, Carl Schmitt alone seems aware of its indifference to liberal democracy. He notes that the Weimar Republic could deploy its amendment power to modify particular constitutional provisions, but could not change the constitution as a 'whole' by eliminating the 'fundamental political decisions that constitute the substance of the constitution.'[84] This means that the Weimar Republic 'cannot be transformed into an absolute monarchy or into a Soviet republic through a two-thirds majority decision of the Reichstag.'[85] However, Schmitt is quick to point out that the reverse is also true. The basic structure doctrine preserves a democracy from amendments that would destroy it, but it also preserves other forms of government from democratic reforms. Thus, Schmitt holds that while there are no 'legal means' for transforming a democracy into a monarchy, it 'is exactly the same in the opposite case': a monarchy cannot be lawfully transformed into a democracy.[86] That Schmitt would endorse a doctrine that is indifferent to liberal democracy is hardly surprising. What is surprising is that leading proponents of liberal democracy would endorse such a doctrine.

The majority decision in *Kesavananda* implicitly follows Schmitt in conceiving of India's amendment power as constrained not by moral considerations apposite to constitutional reform, but by the identity of the existing constitution. In his formulation of the doctrine, Justice Khanna holds that the basic structure of the Indian constitutional order shields its democratic and secular character from amendments that would destroy them.[87] But he is also adamant that these commitments do not stand for a more general normative principle embodied by the constitution. In interpreting article 368 of the Indian Constitution, Khanna maintains that the court should not follow the 'dictionary meaning of the word "amend,"' which encompasses notions of correction, reform, and improvement.[88] An amendment is nothing more than a change, and '[c]hange can be for the better as well as for the worse.'[89] Accordingly, whether a particular amendment affirms or effaces fundamental rights makes no constitutional difference.[90]

[84] Schmitt, *Constitutional Theory*, 79. [85] Ibid. [86] Ibid., 151.
[87] *Kesavananda*, para. 1480. [88] Ibid., para. 1490.
[89] Ibid., para. 1495. In its value neutrality, the formulation of the basic structure doctrine in *Kesavananda* is quite different from the formulation that appeared in *Golaknath*. In the latter, Chief Justice Rao, in *obiter dictum*, framed the basic structure doctrine as restricting parliament to the enactment of amendments that operate 'within the framework of the original instrument for its better effectuation.'
[90] Ibid., para. 1489.

The fundamental problem with the basic structure doctrine is that it focuses on the wrong consideration. The doctrine posits a hierarchical relationship between successive exercises of constituent power. An exercise of constituent power that amends the existing constitutional order must conform to the antecedent exercise of constituent power that established it. Thus the doctrine focuses on the order in which exercises of constituent power occur rather than how constituent power should be exercised. The result is that proponents of the doctrine hold that the aspirations of the existing constitutional order can be elaborated and refined, but not supplanted through law. If constitutional amendments must preserve the underlying identity of the existing constitution, then in cases in which the identity of the existing constitution is unjust or unaccountable, the doctrine precludes the lawful transition to a just constitutional order.[91] Thus, for example, the doctrine would have prevented new democracies, such as Hungary and Poland, from adopting constitutional amendments that 'deliberately destroyed' the communist 'identity of the original constitution.'[92]

[91] Someone might object that, with respect to Rawls, my criticism of the basic structure doctrine is unfair. For Rawls, unlike Schmitt, deploys the doctrine in the context of a theory confined to the special case of a liberal constitutional democracy, not a general theory of the state. To the extent that my criticism explores the implications of Rawls's argument outside of its intended context, the criticism is unfair.

My aim in this section was merely to show the illiberal implications of the doctrine to which Rawls appeals. Nevertheless, I believe that even in the special case of a liberal constitutional democracy, Ackerman's hypothetical amendment raises a serious challenge for Rawls's theory. As I observed in Chapter 4, Rawls's mature theory of justice takes the form of a conditional: *if* this society is an instance of the special case, *then* justice as fairness provides the appropriate conception of justice for it. See Rawls, *Justice as Fairness: A Restatement* (Cambridge: Harvard University Press, 2001), 39. In turn, the special case is characterized as a constitutional democracy in which citizens affirm a series of fundamental ideas about their social order. These include the idea that citizens are free and equal, which means that each citizen is capable of understanding and being motivated by claims of justice and that each has the capacity to formulate, pursue, and revise a conception of the good. Now, Ackerman's hypothetical amendment involving the establishment of a state religion is clearly objectionable from the standpoint of this fundamental idea because it stands in direct opposition to the capacity to formulate one's own conception of the good. However, once such an amendment is enacted through the onerous amendment procedure that prevails in the United States, does justice as fairness even apply? What clearer indication could there be than a constitutional amendment to establish that a fundamental idea that forms the condition of application for Rawls's theory of justice is no longer affirmed? And if this fundamental idea is not affirmed, then it is incorrect to say that the amendment is objectionable from the standpoint of justice as fairness. Rather, one must say that the society at hand is no longer an instance of the special case and that, consequently, justice as fairness no longer provides the appropriate theory of justice for it.

[92] See Garlicki and Garlicka, "External Review of Constitutional Amendments? International Law as a Norm of Reference," 353.

From the standpoint of a constitutional theory committed to the realization of liberal democratic modes of governance, the basic structure doctrine provides a mirror image of Ackerman's framework. The former recognizes no limits on the kinds of injustices that may be shielded from lawful reforms. Thus, as illustrated earlier, Calhoun relies on the basic structure doctrine to ground his claim that slavery is a perpetual feature of American constitutionalism. The latter recognizes no limits on the kinds of injustices that may be lawfully introduced. Thus, Ackerman claims that even the First Amendment could be lawfully repealed. These constitutional theories offer a stark choice between the view that any arrangement, however unjust, could be protected by an eternity clause or that no arrangement, however just, could be.

In the next sections of this chapter, I formulate an alternative to each of these one-sided approaches. In contrast to theorists who are hostile to the very notion of an eternity clause, I offer a justification that protects the constitutional essentials of a modern constitutional state from amendments that would diminish or destroy them. In contrast to theorists committed to the view that any arrangement could be safeguarded by an eternity clause, I argue that eternity clauses that undergird injustice cannot bind. The result is a constitutional theory that jointly departs from both Ackerman's framework and the basic structure doctrine by explaining why eternity clauses constrain constitutional amendments in some cases but not others.

6.3 Eternity clauses: a justification

The unified theory recognizes that every legal system has an ongoing duty to establish, maintain, and refine a modern constitutional form of governance. If eternity clauses, whether explicit or implied, are to cohere to this duty, then they must bind in certain types of legal systems but not in others. On the one hand, the justification must explain why eternity clauses constrain constitutional amendments that would dilute or dissolve the substantive commitments and institutional arrangements of a modern constitutional state. In this respect, the justification must depart from constitutional theories that conceive of the constraints on the amending power as wholly procedural in nature. On the other, the justification must be compatible with the duty of legal systems to enact amendments to bring themselves into ever-deeper accord with the modern constitutional paradigm. In this respect, the justification must depart from the basic structure doctrine, which binds future exercises of the amending power to the original grant of constituent power, however just or unjust its character.

In Chapter 5, I argued that a modern constitutional state resembles its precursors in one respect but makes a fundamental departure from them in another. A modern constitutional state shares the normative structure of earlier forms of government: the right to exercise public authority, given the terms of its justification, must be directed toward bringing the existing legal order into the deepest possible conformity with the ideal of public justice. A modern constitutional state departs from its precursors by introducing legal and institutional structures that raise this duty from a mere moral imperative into a justiciable constraint on all public authority. The *legal structure* of a modern constitutional state makes the satisfaction of this duty a condition of the valid exercise of all public authority. The *institutional structure* of such a state establishes that any individual within the legal order may bring a constitutional complaint to an impartial judicial institution challenging the validity of an exercise of public authority on the ground that it violates the duty of just governance. The legal and institutional structure of a modern constitutional state has significant ramifications for its amendment power.

As a matter of its legal structure, a modern constitutional state lacks the authority to exercise its amendment power in a manner that violates its duty of public justice. After all, within a modern constitutional state, the satisfaction of this duty forms the condition for the valid exercise of all public authority. Since a constitutional amendment is a paradigmatic instance of public authority, it follows that exercises of the amending power that violate this duty must be invalid. And since this duty requires a modern constitutional form of governance to be established, refined, and maintained, exercises of the amending power that seek to diminish or dissolve the legal and institutional architecture of a modern constitutional state cannot be valid. Thus, the legal structure of a modern constitutional state implies an eternity clause that protects its essential features.

As a matter of its institutional structure, a modern constitutional state must make amendments to the constitutional order justiciable. The basic idea that animates this institutional structure is that public authority is to be accountable neither to the preferences of the many nor to the few, but to the equal right of each individual to just governance. Accordingly, individuals must be able to bring a constitutional complaint before an impartial judicial forum, alleging that an exercise of public authority violates the right to just governance. Insofar as constitutional amendments involve an exercise of public authority, they too must be justiciable. Thus, the validity of constitutional amendments is adjudicated in courts around the world, including Germany, India, the Czech Republic, and Brazil. Where constitutional amendments violate the government's duty of just governance, it is the constitutional duty of the judiciary to declare them invalid. I return to this point below.

The justification of eternity clauses that emerges from the unified theory does not replicate the error of the basic structure doctrine. As I explained in the prior section, the basic structure doctrine justifies constraints on the amending power by subordinating the power to amend a constitution to the antecedent exercise of constituent power that created the constitutional order. The result is that *every* constitutional order has an implied eternity clause that protects its basic structure from amendment. The doctrine thereby solidifies the established constitutional order, regardless of the extent to which it conforms to or departs from the demands of public justice. The unified theory takes a different approach by conceiving of eternity clauses as an implication of the legal structure that distinguishes a modern constitutional state from earlier forms of government. This structure establishes that a modern constitutional state simply lacks the legal authority to degrade the fundamental norms and institutional arrangements that address the problem of accountability. Because this legal incapacity follows from the legal structure that distinguishes a modern constitutional state from alternative forms of governance, the unified theory justifies only those eternity clauses that safeguard the constitutional essentials of a modern constitutional state. Accordingly, the duty of alternative forms of government to engage in constitutional reforms to bring themselves into accordance with modern constitutionalism remains intact. Every modern constitutional state has an implied eternity clause protecting its basic structure. Every precursor to modern constitutionalism must engage in constitutional reform.

Such a justification sheds light on a perennial controversy about the kinds of institutional norms and institutional arrangements that an implied eternity clause encompasses. To make the exercise of public authority accountable to the right of each person to just governance, the modern constitutional state integrates constitutional supremacy, constitutional (including democratic) rights, and judicial review. As I argued in Chapter 5, each of these elements must be present to render the exercise of public authority accountable to the right of each person to just governance. So too, as I noted in Chapter 2, the realization of just governance presupposes certain structures that distinguish public authority from private power, including the rule of law and the separation of powers. Insofar as the principle of justice requires legal systems to address the problem of accountability, and this problem cannot be addressed in the absence of these arrangements, a modern constitutional state that enacts amendments that dissolve or dilute these constitutional essentials thereby violates this principle. And since the satisfaction of this principle forms the condition for the valid exercise of public authority in a modern constitutional state, such amendments cannot stand.

An implied eternity clause protects the constitutional essentials of a modern constitutional state from an amendment that would diminish or dissolve them, but does not place them beyond the bounds of amendment. An amendment that *refines* provisions within the constitutional text to bolster their strength, extend their reach, or clarify their interrelation may be admissible if it conforms to the duty of just governance. In the language of the German Constitutional Court, the eternity clause precludes the abandonment or surrender of constitutional principle (*prinzipielle Preisgabe*),[93] not the mere refinement of the text through which that constitutional principle is presently, but perhaps imperfectly, formulated.[94]

Eternity clauses do not simply deny validity to certain kinds of constitutional amendments. They also provide a framework for the future of constitutional reform. As the German Constitutional Court explained in the landmark *Southwest* case, 'Taken as a unit, a Constitution reflects certain overarching principles and fundamental decisions to which individual provisions of the Basic Law are subordinate.'[95] Eternity clauses posit a hierarchy between the perpetual and the provisional features of the constitutional order. A feature of the constitutional order must be regarded as *perpetual* if it is demanded by the principle of justice. For in a modern constitutional state, arrangements demanded by the principle of justice cannot be lawfully repudiated. The entire constitutional order is beholden to its most basic norm, that the dignity of human persons forms the purpose of all public authority and the constraint upon its exercise. By contrast, a feature of the constitutional order must be regarded as

[93] See BVerfGE 30, 1 (1970). Here I defend the legality of amendments that refine the text of constitutional provisions protected by an eternity clause, not the amendment at issue in the case cited.

[94] On this point, see also *Golaknath*, 815: 'We have not said that the provisions of the Constitution cannot be amended but what we have said is that they cannot be amended so as to take away or abridge the fundamental rights.' For the opposing view that the 'Eternity Clause prohibits the constitutional legislator from even affecting' the provisions that it enumerates, see Nohlen, "Germany: The Electronic Eavesdropping Case," 684.

[95] BVerfGE 1, 14 (1951).

provisional if it presently forms part of the supreme law, but violates the demands of public justice. Examples of provisional features include injustices that deny the freedom of persons, for example, by imposing a state religion upon them, or that deny equality by elevating some to the level of a noble, while degrading others to the rank of a passive citizen bound by laws of another's making.

If every modern constitutional state has an implied eternity clause, then what should we make of modern constitutional states that *also* have an express eternity clause?

First, the constraints specified in an express eternity clause may fail to exhaust the constraints binding the amendment power. For if the legal structure of a modern constitutional state implies an eternity clause that protects its constitutional essentials, then the implied limitations must apply to cases in which the expressed eternity clause is underinclusive.[96] For example, the Italian Constitution of 1947 contains an express eternity clause establishing that a constitutional amendment may not change the state's republican form.[97] The Italian Constitutional Court understands the constraints on the amending power to be more expansive than the explicit wording of its eternity clause might suggest.[98] The court interprets the Italian Constitution as containing 'some supreme principles that cannot be subverted or modified in their essential content,' including 'principles that, although not expressly mentioned among those not subject to the principle of constitutional revision, are part of the supreme values on which the Italian Constitution is based.'[99] Scholars understand these supreme values to include democracy, the inviolable character of rights, and constitutional supremacy.[100]

Second, express eternity clauses stand as a public testament to the mandatory nature of modern constitutionalism. The adoption of a modern constitutional form of governance is not optional. Just as states are under an obligation to adopt a modern constitutional form of governance, so too the same obligation requires modern constitutional states to maintain themselves. Although eternity clauses cannot 'prevent revolutions,' they publicly acknowledge the wrongfulness and illegality of

[96] Barak, "Unconstitutional Constitutional Amendments," 337.
[97] Italy, 1947, article 139. [98] Here I follow Roznai, 686.
[99] Corte Const. judgment no. 1146 of Dec. 15, 1988, quoted in Lois F. del Duca and Patrick del Duca, "An Italian Federalism? The State, Its Institutions and National Culture as Rule of Law Guarantor," *American Journal of Comparative Law* 54 (2006): 801.
[100] Víctor Ferreres Comella, *Constitutional Courts and Democratic Values: A European Perspective* (New Haven: Yale University, 2009), 106–7.

amendments that would unravel the modern constitutional order and resurrect the problem of accountability.[101] In recognizing this wrong, they provide the possibility of a remedy.

Third, express eternity clauses reinforce the judicial role with respect to constitutional amendments. Within a modern constitutional state, the judiciary serves as the guardian of the constitutional order by responding to constitutional complaints alleging that public authority has violated the right of persons to just governance. Insofar as constitutional amendments involve an exercise of public authority, the judicial role must not end where constitutional amendments begin.[102]

Fourth, express eternity clauses may indicate the local significance of particular constitutional arrangements that are not encompassed by an implied eternity clause. Germany's eternity clause, for example, establishes that the federal structure is a permanent feature of the constitutional order. This does not mean that federalism should be regarded as a constitutional essential in every modern constitutional state. I noted in the prior chapter that the duty of just governance neither requires nor precludes the transition to a federal system of government. And yet, within the context of German constitutionalism, federalism is integral to the performance of this duty. Federalism is understood to provide a bulwark against the centralization of power that culminated in the barbarism of the Nazi years. As a *never again* constitution, federalism is understood to be an indispensable safeguard of the free democratic order created by the Basic Law. While the duty of public justice does not require federalism, federalism may nonetheless play a crucial role in stabilizing a state committed to this duty's ongoing satisfaction.

6.4 Defending constituent power

Constituent power consists in the public authority to establish, modify, or repeal constitutional norms. Since the unified theory holds that each legal

101 Günter Dürig, "An Introduction to the Basic Law of the Federal Republic of Germany," in *The Constitution of the Federal Republic of Germany*, ed. Ulrich Karpen (Nomos Verlagsgesellschaft, Baden-Baden, 1998), 16.

102 For an alternate view of the nature of amendments and the judicial role with respect to them, see *Coleman* v. *Miller*, 307 U.S. 433, 456 (1939) (in which Justice Black argues that the process of an article V amendment is '"political" in its entirety, from submission until an amendment becomes part of the Constitution, and is not subject to judicial guidance, control or interference at any point'). See also Justice Khanna's judgment in *Kesavananda*, 1490 (arguing that the question of whether an amendment is an improvement is not justiciable).

system must engage in constitutional reform to bring itself into accordance with the modern constitutional paradigm, the theory relies on the concept of constituent power. In recent years, this concept, apart from the way in which it is exercised in one context or another, has come under heavy fire with one commentator even suggesting that the idea of constituent power should be abandoned.[103] From the perspective of its critics, constituent power is a paradoxical and dangerous idea.[104] Constituent power is paradoxical when invoked to ground the authority of a legal order. In imagining the people acting to establish an authoritative legal order, proponents of constituent power fail to notice that a people cannot act as a whole in the absence of such an order. Constituent power is dangerous because it invites the conclusion that whatever arrangement *We the People* enact is unassailable. I take up each of these challenges to the notion of constituent power in turn. My aim in this section is not to establish that constituent power is an unproblematic notion, but to show that the problems that critics attribute to it do not arise within the unified theory.

The classic exposition of the distinction between constituent power and constituted power appeared in the twilight of France's *Ancien Régime*. In 'What is the Third Estate?' the Abbé Sieyès defined *constituted power* as the ordinary authority of government to rule in accordance with the legal framework set out in the constitution. In turn, *constituent power* consists in the extraordinary capacity of the nation to establish a constitutional framework for governance.[105] For Sieyès, constituent power is the answer to the question of how constituted power is possible. The nation's past exercise of constituent power is the sole legitimating basis of government's constituted power. Because the French nation had not authorized the constituted power of the *Ancien Régime*, Sieyès denounced the supposed constituted power as lacking legal authority. To create a genuine constituted power, the nation must exercise its constituent power and, in so doing, act as 'the origin of all legality.'[106]

Sieyès' account of constituent power is paradoxical. The paradox emerges from the different roles that the nation plays in his argument. On the one hand, Sieyès holds that the constituted power of government

[103] David Dyzenhaus, "Constitutionalism in an Old Key: Legality and Constituent Power," *Global Constitutionalism* 1 (2012): 229 and 253.

[104] Ibid., 230–1, 233–4, and 237.

[105] Emmanuel Joseph Sieyès, "What is the Third Estate?" in *Political Writings*, trans. Michael Sonenscher (Indianapolis: Hackett, 2003), 136.

[106] Ibid., 137.

can be generated only by a nation's antecedent exercise of constituent power.[107] The nation creates the constituted power of government through its choice. On the other, Sieyès, at least at times, rightly recognizes that for an aggregate of private persons to act as a unified entity, its members must be represented by a public institution.[108] The constituted power of government creates the nation. Thus, the nation plays two incompatible roles within Sieyès' framework: the nation is both the effect that follows the establishment of government and its prior legitimating cause. Each of these possibilities is problematic. If the nation is an effect of government, then the nation cannot legitimate government through a prior act. And if the nation is the legitimating cause of government, then Sieyès owes his readers an account of how there can be a nation (as opposed to a multitude of private wills) capable of acting as a unified whole prior to being represented by public institutions.[109]

But even if the prior act of the nation could *somehow* legitimate the constituted power of government, a further objection remains. Proponents of constituent power often hold that a legal order is sanctified not by the moral merits of its arrangements and aspirations, but by a prior decision undertaken by the nation (or *We the People*) that establishes it.[110] In the eyes of its liberal critics, the danger of constituent power is not that the nation will invariably choose arrangements that are inimical to the dignity of free and equal persons, but that the idea of constituent power legitimates whatever arrangements the nation happens to adopt.[111] For these critics, constituent power is objectionable because it places liberal democracy on an equal footing with all other forms of government, whether despotic or ecclesiastical.[112] Even if the

[107] Ibid., 134.

[108] Ibid., 97: 'What is a nation? It is a body of associates living under a *common* law, represented by the same *legislature*, etc.' But at other points, Sieyès suggests that a nation consists in a 'number of isolated individuals seeking to unite' (134), is 'formed solely by natural law' (136–7), and that a 'nation never leaves the state of nature' (139).

[109] On the distinction between the action of multitude of individuals and a people, see Thomas Hobbes, *De Cive* (New York: Appleton-Century-Crofts, 1949), 70–1.

[110] Dyzenhaus, "Constitutionalism in an Old Key: Legality and Constituent Power," 230–1.

[111] Walter F. Murphy, "Consent and Constitutional Change," in *Comparative Constitutional Law*, ed. Vicki C. Jackson and Mark Tushnet (New York: Foundation Press, 1999), 253 (criticizing consent as the legitimating basis of constitutional amendments because it 'posits no limitations whatever on the people who confer it . . . other than what the people themselves choose to impose').

[112] Kumm, "The Best of Times and the Worst of Times: Between Constitutional Triumphalism and Nostalgia," in *The Twilight of Constitutionalism*, ed. Petra Dobner and Martin Loughlin (Oxford: Oxford University Press, 2010), 210.

nation succeeds in adopting a liberal democratic constitution, the nation retains the constituent power to subsequently degrade this arrangement.[113] As Sieyès puts the point, whatever constitutional arrangements happen to prevail, 'the Nation would still be the master to change them.'[114]

Each of these lines of objection concerns the relationship between constituent power and constituted power. The first challenges the idea that the constituted power of government can be legitimated by a nation's prior act of constituent power. The second argues, in the alternative, that if legal authority can be legitimated by a prior act of constituent power, then the nation's choice insulates the resulting regime from moral criticism. Taken together, the objections hold that once one admits the claim that all legitimate power originates in the nation, then one is consigned to concluding *either* that no arrangement can be legally authoritative (because if a nation is the effect of government's authority it cannot be its legitimating cause) *or* that every legally authoritative arrangement is unobjectionable (because the nation chose it). The former possibility is anarchism, the latter quietism. Thus, for its critics, constituent power brings with it the problems of the reductionist theories of public law explored in Chapter 2 and revisited in Chapter 3. In what follows, I explain how the unified theory offers a constitutional framework that integrates the idea of constituent power without collapsing into anarchism or quietism.

The idea of constituent power plays a fundamentally different role within the unified theory than it does within Sieyès's framework. Sieyès appeals to the idea of a nation exercising constituent power in explaining how constituted power is possible, that is, how government could possess public authority. Accordingly, the question of whether a particular government possesses constituted power is to be answered by looking backwards to a historical event. Government possesses constituted power in those cases in which it was authorized by the nation's prior act. By contrast, within the unified theory the public authority of government (or what Sieyès calls constituted power) follows not from a *historical fact* about how the legal order came about, but from a *norm*, the principle of authority. According to this principle, private persons must submit

[113] Dyzenhaus, "Constitutionalism in an Old Key: Legality and Constituent Power," 237.

[114] Sieyès, 141. For Sieyès, however, unlike later proponents of constituent power, there are certain arrangements to which the nation is incapable of giving its assent. His examples involve features of the *Ancien Régime*, including minority rule and hereditary privilege. Ibid., 142.

themselves to the public authority of a legal system, in which each private person can enjoy his or her independence in relation to every other.

The unified theory avoids the anarchism of Sieyès's framework by departing from it in two respects. The first is that within the unified theory, the justification of public authority is not paradoxical. Unlike Sieyès's framework, the unified theory does not hold that the people somehow precedes and acts to legitimate the public authority of government. Instead, as I argued in Chapter 2, the unified theory holds that the basis of public authority lies in the obligation of private persons to submit themselves to a condition that enables rightful interaction between them. From the standpoint of the unified theory, the people do not create the legal order. Rather, the legal order creates the people by subjecting a plurality of individuals to common legislative, executive, and adjudicative institutions. Thus, the authority of government does not rest on the paradoxical claim that a people can act as a whole prior to being represented by public institutions. The second distinction follows from the first. Because the authority of the legal order is not premised on a historical event in which the nation exercised constituent power, it persists even in cases in which no such event occurred.[115] Because the principle of authority is a norm rather than a historical fact, whether one occupies a lawful condition or a lawless one depends on whether public institutions are present that by establishing, interpreting, and enforcing legal norms create the conditions in which persons can interact with one another rightfully. Where such institutions are present, private persons are bound by them. Because their authority follows from a normative principle rather than from the history of their origin, their authority cannot be denied because of the way that they, as a matter of fact, came into the world.

If the unified theory does not assign constituent power to the role of underwriting the public authority of government, then what role does it play? I defined constituent power, earlier, as the public authority to establish, modify, or repeal constitutional norms. Because public authority does not exist outside of a legal system, neither does constituent power. Within the unified theory, constituent power concerns not the

115 Kumm, 208: 'In some constitutional jurisdictions there was simply no procedure underlying its coming into force that could plausibly be interpreted as the will of We the People. Think . . . of the German Constitution, both when it was first enacted and in the context of reunification . . . It would appear highly contrived to locate the authority of the German constitution in an original constitutive act either 1949 or 1990.' See also Dyzenhaus, "Constitutionalism in an Old Key: Legality and Constituent Power," 259.

possibility of a legal system's constituted power or public authority, as Sieyès and his followers hold,[116] but the reform of that power. In terms of the central distinction of the unified theory, constituent power concerns the regulative rather than the constitutive principle of public law.

This brings me to the second objection. Whereas the first objection challenges the idea that legal authority or constituted power results from the people's prior exercise of constituent power, the second challenges the idea that what makes a constitution rightful is that the nation happened to enact it. Such a view is objectionable because it insulates the choices that emerge through an exercise of constituent power from moral criticism.[117] The unified theory incorporates the notion of constituent power while eschewing this quietist implication. Chapters 2 and 4 argued that in any legal system, the right to exercise public authority implicates an internal standard of moral adequacy, equal freedom under law. All exercises of public authority must be directed toward bringing the legal system as a whole into the deepest possible conformity with this ideal. This duty follows not from contingent facts present in some legal systems while absent in others, but from what a legal system is – a set of coercive institutions governing human beings with dignity and rights. Insofar as constituent power involves establishing, modifying, or repealing constitutional norms, it is an instance of public authority and is therefore always accompanied by the duty of just governance. Thus, constituent power is not a moment of 'openness without any necessary end,'[118] as is often suggested. Rather, like all public authority, the exercise of constituent power must always be directed to the realization of public justice. In the words of the Bavarian Constitutional Court, 'There are fundamental constitutional principles, which are of so elementary a nature and so much the expression of a law that precedes the Constitution, that the maker of the Constitution himself is bound by them.'[119] On a subsequent occasion, the court elaborated on the nature of these principles and their relation to public authority: '[T]he constitution-maker is bound by what is right, which means that he has to serve

[116] See, for example, Loughlin, *The Idea of Public Law*, 99 (describing constituent power as the 'source of modern political authority').

[117] Gottfried Dietze, "Unconstitutional Constitutional Norms? Constitutional Development in Postwar Germany," *Virginia Law Review* 42 (1956): 18–19.

[118] Ilan rua Wall, "Notes on an 'Open' Constituent Power," *Law, Culture and the Humanities* (2013): 1.

[119] Dietze, 16 (citing Judgment of 4 April 1950, 2 Verwaltungs-Rechtsprechung No. 65 (1950)).

the ethical and moral values of human dignity and justice and, thereby, freedom. All state power and therefore also that of the constitution-maker is limited by the idea of right from the very beginning.'[120]

The objection that constituent power is a quietist notion can be reformulated as a criticism of eternity clauses. In the prior sections, I focused on eternity clauses that are directed toward shielding the essentials of a modern constitutional state from amendments that violate the duty of public justice. But eternity clauses could, of course, be directed toward perpetuating injustice. The point can be illustrated without recourse to hypothetical cases. Consider a Hungarian law enacted in 1741, which established that the privileges of noblemen are 'unalterable,' or the Mexican Constitution of 1824, which states, 'The Religion of the Mexican Nation is, and shall be perpetually, the Roman Catholic Apostolic' and prohibits the exercise of other religions.[121] As these provisions illustrate, eternity clauses can be dangerous. The binds that they impose might preserve just arrangements, but by the same token they might perpetuate injustice.

The unified theory diffuses this objection by providing a critical standpoint from which to differentiate perpetual features of a legal order from transient ones. The overarching duty of government is to transform the existing legal order from an aggregate of inherited customs and traditions into a system of equal freedom in which all public authority is directed toward and constrained by the dignity of all persons subject to it. Accordingly, those who exercise public authority must continually distinguish between what public authority has established and what public justice demands. What is perpetual in public law is not the contingent features of the existing order, but the unremitting duty of government to bring its arrangements into the deepest possible approximation of the ideal of public justice. Accordingly, an eternity clause that accords with the demands of public justice simply reinforces the overarching duty that accompanies all exercises of public authority by specifying its implications for the amending power. But an eternity clause that bolsters unjust features of the existing legal order calls upon the state to violate the duty that accompanies the exercise of all public authority.

[120] Ibid., 17 (citing Judgment of March 14, 1951, Die Öffentliche Verwaltung 471 (1951)).

[121] I take these examples from Roznai, "Unconstitutional Constitutional Amendments," 661 (citing Zoltan Szente, "The Historic Origins of the National Assembly in Hungary," *Historia Constitutional* 9 (2007): 239), and 666 (citing The Constitution of the Mexican United States, Title 1(3) and 171 (providing that the religion of the Mexican Nation 'can never be reformed')).

Since such a duty cannot be discharged through its violation, the duty persists and binds government to repeal the unjust eternity clause and reform the very arrangements that the clause sought to entrench.

By distinguishing what a legal system is from what a legal system must become, the unified theory makes sense of a basic conviction: existing constitutions are not 'free from imperfections'[122] and 'Amendments therefore will be necessary.'[123] The familiar idea of amending a defective constitution is unintelligible to both anarchists and quietists. In Chapter 2, I characterized *anarchism* as the view that what is unjust cannot be authoritative and *quietism* as the view that what is authoritative cannot be unjust. For anarchists, reforming a defective constitution is impossible. If what is unjust cannot be authoritative, then there is nothing to reform.[124] For quietists, reforming a defective constitution is similarly impossible. If the existing constitution is authoritative, then it is thereby just. A constitutional order can be altered, but it cannot be reformed. By contrast, the unified theory accommodates the idea of constitutional reform by recognizing that an existing constitution may satisfy the principle of authority but nevertheless fall short of the ideal of public justice.[125]

[122] Letter of George Washington to Bushrod Washington, November 10, 1787, in *The Writings of George Washington*, ed. J.C. Fitzpatrick, vol 29 (Washington: Government Printing Office, 1944), 311.

The full passage reads, 'The warmest friends and the best supporters the Constitution has, do not contend that it is free from imperfections; but they found them unavoidable and are sensible, if evil is likely to arise therefrom, the remedy must come hereafter; for in the present moment, it is not to be obtained; and, as there is a Constitutional door open for it, I think the People (for it is with them to Judge) can as they will have the advantage of experience on their Side, decide with as much propriety on the alterations and amendments which are necessary [as] ourselves.'

[123] George Mason, *The Records of the Federal Convention of 1787*, ed. Max Farrand (New Haven: Yale University Press, 1937), 1:202–3 (cited in Sanford Levinson, "Introduction: Imperfection and Amendability," in *Responding to Imperfection*, 3).

[124] For the danger of a constitutional conception in which constitutional norms cannot be valid unless they conform to some normative ideal, see Schmitt, 89: *Constitutional Theory*, 'For political reasons, that which is designated as a "true" or "genuine" constitution often only corresponds to a particular ideal of the constitution. A consequence of the manner of speaking typical of political conflict is that every struggling party recognizes as a true constitution only the constitution corresponding to their political demands.' Schmitt attributes this view to the liberal bourgeoisie and, ultimately, to Kant and Hegel. Ibid., 92.

[125] Here I follow Dieter Grimm's characterization of an existing constitution as 'a set of legal norms,' rather than 'a philosophical construct. The norms emanate from a political decision rather than some pre-established truth.' Grimm, "The Achievement of Constitution and Its Prospects in a Changed World," 9. For the opposing view that constitutional norms that depart from the demands of political morality cannot be valid, see Kumm, 212–3: 'At the heart of modern constitutionalism ... is the idea that the

Some constitutional orders impose arbitrary restrictions on freedom, restrictions that freedom itself does not require. Others fail to make the exercise of public authority accountable to the right of each person to just governance. Since the duty of government is to bring the legal order as a whole into the deepest possible conformity with the ideal of public justice, where the constitution is itself defective in relation to its own internal ideal, it stands in need of constitutional reform. However, if we were to give up on the idea of constituent power, such reform would be impossible.

Conclusion

Joseph Raz has argued that legal systems claim not simply to have authority, but to have '*unlimited* authority.'[126] This claim follows, for Raz, from a legal system's disposition toward all actual and possible lawgiving. On the one hand, a legal system makes a claim to the authority of the laws that it has actually enacted. On the other, a legal system 'provides ways of changing the law and of adopting any law whatsoever.'[127] And when possible laws are made actual, the legal system makes a claim to their authority too. Raz illustrates his position by noting that in the United Kingdom, Parliament possesses the authority to 'make and unmake any law, on any matter, and to any effect whatsoever.'[128] This unlimited authority is not a peculiarity of 'English constitutional theory'; even in the United States, where Congress is limited by the Constitution, the Constitution 'itself may be changed by law.'[129] Thus Raz concludes that regardless of whether the constitution constrains legislative power, legal systems claim unlimited authority.

Raz's conceptual claim about legal systems is defied by modern constitutional practice. Modern constitutional states do not claim unlimited authority. What they claim is that conformity to the demands of just governance forms the condition for the valid exercise of all public authority. This claim has implications for understanding the

exercise of legitimate public authority is not unlimited and requires a certain kind of justification. Legitimate public authority is circumscribed and has to justify itself before a *higher law*. In order to be legitimate, all exercise of public authority has to be derived from and shown to be compatible with that higher law ... That new higher law insists that all posited law must be conceivable by those whom it addresses *as the result of a deliberate collective choice of free and equal individuals.*'

126 *The Morality of Freedom* (Oxford: Oxford University Press, 1986), 76 (my emphasis).

127 Ibid., 77. 128 Ibid., 76. 129 Ibid.

constitutional limits of both legislation and constitutional amendments. Laws that violate the duty of public justice cannot be valid. Nor is the authority of a modern constitutional state to vary its constitutional arrangements unlimited. Insofar as constitutional amendments involve an exercise of public authority, amendments that violate the duty of public justice are invalid. A modern constitutional state lacks the legal authority to diminish or dissolve the core commitments of the constitutional order. This does not mean that these commitments will last forever. Rather, it means that legal systems are incapable of repudiating these arrangements through law. The purpose of this chapter has been to expound the nature and justification of this incapacity.

7

The moral structure of proportionality

In articulating the guiding principles of constitutional adjudication in post-Apartheid South Africa, Justice Albie Sachs remarked, 'If I were to be stranded on a desert island and allowed to take only two constitutional elements with me, I would take human dignity and proportionality.'[1] This chapter elucidates the connection between these elements.

The doctrine of proportionality consists in a set of conditions that a government must satisfy to justify a law that limits a constitutional right.[2] In the Canadian formulation of the doctrine, to initiate the proportionality analysis, government must demonstrate that the impugned law pursues an objective that is pressing and substantial in a free and democratic society. To satisfy the proportionality analysis, government must demonstrate (1) that the means that the law employs are rationally connected to the relevant objective, (2) that the law pursues this objective in a manner that minimally impairs the right, and (3) that 'the benefits which accrue from the limitation are proportional to its deleterious effects as measured by the values underlying the [*Canadian Charter of Rights and Freedoms*].'[3] In delineating the limits of constitutional rights, legal systems around the world are increasingly turning to proportionality.[4]

1 Albie Sachs, *The Strange Alchemy of Life and Law* (Oxford: Oxford University Press, 2009), 203.

2 Aharon Barak, *Proportionality: Constitutional Rights and Their Limitations* (Cambridge: Cambridge University Press, 2012), 3.

3 *Thomson Newspapers Co.* v. *Canada (Attorney General)* [1998] 1 SCR 877, para. 125. See also *R.* v. *Oakes* [1986] 1 SCR 103; *Dasgenais* v. *Canadian Broadcasting Corp.* [1994] 3 SCR 835.

4 Proportionality originated in the Prussian administrative courts in the late nineteenth century, reemerged in postwar Germany in the late 1950s in the *Lüth Case* BVerfGE 7, 198 (1958), and has since migrated to the European Court of Human Rights, Canada, South Africa, Israel, the United Kingdom, New Zealand, Australia, India, Turkey, Switzerland, Spain, Portugal, Latin America, Brazil, Hong Kong, South Korea, Hungary, and Poland. Dieter Grimm describes proportionality as Germany's most significant constitutional export. Grimm, "The Basic Law at 60 – Identity and Change," *German Law*

The doctrine raises challenging questions. If constitutional rights are specifications of the overarching duty that human dignity imposes on all state authority, how could the limitation of a constitutional right ever be justified? More broadly, what does it mean to *justify* the limitation of a constitutional right? Why does the justification consist of these conditions? Does each condition play a distinctive role in the justification, or are some conditions redundant? What is the significance of the order in which the conditions typically appear? What is the meaning of the requirement that concludes the analysis (proportionality *stricto sensu*)? What is its connection to notions of balancing? Who should bear the onus of demonstrating that the conditions that precede and comprise the doctrine are satisfied?

If there is one point on which defenders and critics of proportionality converge, it is that there is no 'generally accepted canonical formulation' of the doctrine.[5] When proportionality is invoked by courts and explored by theorists, subtle discrepancies emerge. This chapter formulates and defends a particular conception of proportionality. This conception is not an invention, but an exposition of an understanding latent in a strand of jurisprudence from different constitutional jurisdictions. Instead of defending the doctrine as practiced in a particular jurisdiction, I will instead weave together elements from different jurisdictions into a dignitarian conception. The integrating idea of this conception is that proportionality is a doctrinal distillation of the demanding set of conditions under which government is morally justified in limiting a right

Journal 11 (2010): 42. On the convergence of constitutional states on the doctrine of proportionality, see Barak, *Proportionality: Constitutional Rights and Their Limitations*, 145–210; Moshe Cohen-Eliya and Iddo Porat, "Proportionality and the Culture of Justification," *American Journal of Comparative Law* 59 (2011): 463–90; and Grimm, "Proportionality in Canadian and German Constitutional Jurisprudence," *University of Toronto Law Journal* 57 (2007): 384. On the historical origins of proportionality, see David P. Currie, *The Constitution of the Federal Republic of Germany* (Chicago: University of Chicago Press, 1994), 307 ff.; Madhav Khosla, "Proportionality: An Assault on Human Rights?: A Reply," *International Journal of Constitutional Law* (2010): 298; Matthias Kumm, "Political Liberalism and the Structure of Rights: On the Place and Limits of the Proportionality Requirement," in *Law, Rights, and Discourse*, ed. George Pavlakos (Oxford: Hart Publishing, 2007), 132–3; and especially Alec Stone Sweet and Jud Mathews, "Proportionality Balancing and Global Constitutionalism," *Columbia Journal of Transnational Law* 47 (2008): 98 ff.

5 See Grant Huscroft, Bradley W. Miller, and Grégoire Webber, "Introduction," in *Proportionality and the Rule of Law: Rights, Justification, Reasoning*, ed. Grant Huscroft, Bradley W. Miller, and Grégoire Webber (Cambridge: Cambridge University Press, 2014), 3; and Kai Möller, "Proportionality: Challenging the Critics," *International Journal of Constitutional Law* 10 (2012): 710–1.

through law. When the conditions that form the doctrine are satisfied, the duty of public justice that human dignity imposes on all public authority necessitates the limitation of a constitutional right.

I develop and defend this conception of proportionality in four sections. The first formulates the moral problem to which proportionality systematically responds. The problem is that once constitutional rights are interpreted as incidents of the overarching duty of government to respect, protect, and fulfill human dignity, rights inevitably come into conflict with other incidents of this duty. Accordingly, modern constitutional states require a doctrine that determines the duty of government when such conflicts arise. The second section presents a conception of proportionality and explains how its stages form a sequenced set of conditions that, when satisfied, indicate that government is morally required to limit a constitutional right through law. The third distinguishes this conception from the one developed by Robert Alexy. Whereas Alexy defends the view that proportionality abstracts from considerations of substantive moral and political theory, I develop the contrasting view that proportionality is both generated by and responsive to such considerations. Further, I argue that once the moral structure of proportionality comes into view, the stock objections alleging that proportionality is immoral and irrational dissolve. The fourth and final section explores the theory that critics typically invoke as an alternative to proportionality: Ronald Dworkin's rights as trumps model. I argue that this model is not an alternative to proportionality, but an inchoate version of it. Thus, critics of proportionality must look to some other theory of rights for support.

There are two objections that are sometimes directed at proportionality that I will not consider here. The first is that proportionality exhibits a pathological tendency 'to skew the pitch' toward a liberal understanding of the rightful relationship between collective force and individual freedom.[6] Insofar as this objection concerns the purpose to which public authority should be directed, it engages the normative dimension of public law, discussed in Chapter 2 and revisited in Chapter 4. The second objection is that proportionality is illegitimate insofar as it enables courts to strike

6 See Bradley W. Miller, "Proportionality's Blind Spot: 'Neutrality' and Political Philosophy," in *Proportionality and the Rule of Law: Rights, Justification, Reasoning*, 384 and 389–90; Francisco J. Urbina, "A Critique of Proportionality," *American Journal of Jurisprudence* 57 (2012): 75–6; and Luc B. Tremblay, "An Egalitarian Defense of Proportionality-Based Balancing," *International Journal of Constitutional Law* 12 (2014): 864–90.

down the 'democratically justifiable conclusions of the legislature.'[7] This objection concerns the constitutional dimension of public law insofar as it questions the institutional arrangements appropriate for a constitutional regime. This objection is considered at length in Chapter 5. Because this chapter explores the doctrinal dimension of public law, I refrain from discussing objections that engage the preceding dimensions.

The final stage of the proportionality analysis is often described in terms of balancing a right against a limitation. Like the word *dignity*, the word *balancing* has a historical meaning that departs from its contemporary significance in modern constitutional practice. Balancing emerged in American jurisprudence '[a]s a methodology for bringing pragmatic instrumentalism to constitutional doctrine.'[8] Thus, early critics rejected balancing as 'a technique for watering down constitutional guarantees.'[9] These associations cast balancing in opposition to the constitutional project that this book defends. In connecting the normative and constitutional dimensions of dignity to the doctrine of proportionality, I develop an account of proportionality *stricto sensu* that coheres with the absolute duty of the state to realize a regime adequate to the dignity of all who are subject to its authority. On this view, proportionality does not introduce exceptions to the duty of public justice, but formulates what this duty requires in cases in which conflicts arise between its specifications.

7.1 Constitutional conflicts

The protections that constitutional rights afford should reflect the point of having constitutional rights. From this simple conviction springs the problem that the doctrine of proportionality addresses. This section

[7] Alison L. Young, "Proportionality is Dead: Long Live Proportionality," in *Proportionality and the Rule of Law: Rights, Justification, and Reasoning*, 52–5. See also Miller, "Proportionality's Blind Spot: 'Neutrality' and Political Philosophy," 378–9; Timothy Endicott, "Proportionality and Incommensurability," in *Proportionality and the Rule of Law: Rights, Justification, and Reasoning*, 326 and 340–2; Stavros Tsakyrakis, "Proportionality: An Assault on Human Rights," *International Journal of Constitutional Law* 7 (2009): 472; Urbina, "A Critique of Proportionality," 75; Neomi Rao, "On the Use and Abuse of Dignity in Constitutional Law," *Columbia Journal of European Law* 14 (2008): 232; Grégoire C.N. Webber, *The Negotiable Constitution: On the Limitation of Rights* (Cambridge: Cambridge University Press, 2012), 106; Grant Huscroft, "Proportionality and Pretense," *Constitutional Commentary* 29 (2014): 229–56.

[8] T. Alexander Aleinikoff, "Constitutional Law in the Age of Balancing," *Yale Law Journal* 96 (1987): 962.

[9] Ibid., 1004.

presents the problem. The subsequent section explains how proportionality responds.

A constitutional right is a legal norm that is, at once, general and particular. It is general when considered in relation to its instances. It must be general because norms that are to guide and constrain state conduct must be broader than the particular instances to which they apply. Thus constitutional rights are formulated in the language of 'majestic generalities'[10] recognizing, for example, the right of every person to the 'free development of his personality,'[11] or the right 'not to be treated or punished in a cruel, inhuman or degrading way.'[12] Such pronouncements do not themselves exhaustively specify the particular arrangements that they prohibit or require. For example, Germany's Basic Law does not indicate whether the right to the free development of one's personality includes the right to ride horses through a public forest,[13] nor does the *Constitution of the Republic of South Africa* set out a blueprint elaborating what it means for an arrangement to be 'cruel, inhuman or degrading.'[14] General constitutional rights must be related to their instances through interpretation.

While constitutional rights are more general than the particular instances to which they apply, they are in turn more particular than the normative abstraction that they specify. In a modern constitutional state, constitutional rights are concretizations of the general right that each person, by virtue of his or her dignity, has to public justice. By delineating this general right into a set of constitutional rights, the normative abstraction of inherent human dignity gains sufficient determinacy for public officials to apply it to particulars. So conceived, constitutional rights occupy an intermediary position between the abstraction of inherent human dignity and the particulars to which it applies. Because constitutional rights relate an abstract norm to particulars, they can be neither wholly general (like the normative abstraction that they specify) nor wholly particular (like the instances to which they apply).

Consider the relationship between human dignity and the constitutional rights that flow through Germany's Basic Law. Article 1(1) of the Basic Law recognizes the inviolability of human dignity and proclaims

10 *Fay* v. *New York*, 332 US 261, 282 (1947) (Jackson, J.).

11 Basic Law of the Federal Republic of Germany, 1949, article 2(1) [hereinafter Grundgesetz].

12 Constitution of the Republic of South Africa, 1996, s. 12(1)(e).

13 BVerfGE 80, 137 (1989).

14 *S.* v. *Makwanyane and Another* (1995) 3 SA 391 (CC), para. 8.

the duty of all state authority to respect and protect it.[15] Having recognized the duty that human dignity places on all state authority, article 1(2) ties the idea of human dignity to constitutional rights: 'The German people therefore [*darum*] acknowledge inviolable and inalienable human rights as the basis of every community, of peace and of justice in the world.'[16] Because human dignity imposes a duty on all state power, and the recognition of dignity involves a commitment to respect and protect rights, article 1(3) establishes that the rights entrenched in the Basic Law themselves impose a duty on all state power: 'The following basic rights shall bind the legislature, the executive and the judiciary as directly applicable law.'[17] The articles that follow concretize the idea of human dignity by elaborating the constitutional rights that it encompasses: 'all basic rights are specific manifestations of the human dignity principle.'[18] Although the notion of human dignity does not appear in the text of Canada's *Charter*, within Canadian constitutional jurisprudence human dignity is 'inextricably bound' to the rights that the *Charter* explicitly guarantees.[19] The inherent dignity of human persons is conceived of as 'a concept which underlies all the *Charter* rights.'[20] In both Canada and Germany, constitutional rights are understood as an elaboration of the more general duty that the legal order owes to each person subject to its authority.[21]

If constitutional rights are specifications of human dignity, then the concrete protections that particular constitutional rights afford must cohere to that norm. Thus, Justice Dieter Grimm explains that Germany's Federal Constitutional Court

> understands constitutional rights as legal expressions of values, and these values guide the determination of the meaning of a legal norm. However, the purpose ought to be fulfilled in the real world, and this world is constantly changing. The goal of interpretation is to fulfil the purpose of the norm to the utmost extent under changing conditions. This means

15 Grundgesetz, art 1(1). 16 Ibid., 1(2). 17 Ibid., 1(3).

18 BVerfGE 93, 266 (1995), 293. See also Grimm, "Proportionality in Canadian and German Constitutional Jurisprudence," *University of Toronto Law Journal* 57 (2007): 387.

19 *Blencoe* v. *British Columbia (Human Rights Commission)* [2000] 2 SCR 307, para. 76.

20 *Hill* v. *Church of Scientology of Toronto* [1995] 2 SCR 1130, para. 120. See also *R.* v. *Morgentaler* [1988] 1 SCR 30, 166; *Egan* v. *Canada* [1995] 2 SCR 513, 543; *R.* v. *Oakes*, 136; and *R.* v. *Big M Drug Mart Ltd.* [1985] 1 SCR 295, 336.

21 For an overview of the role and nature of human dignity in Canadian and German constitutional jurisprudence, see Dierk Ullrich, "Concurring Visions: Human Dignity in the Canadian Charter of Rights and Freedoms and the Basic Law of the Federal Republic of Germany," 3 *Global Jurist Frontiers* 1 (2003).

> that the segment of social reality in which a constitutional norm shall take effect must be taken into account. It becomes an integral part of interpretation. The consequence is a three-dimensional understanding of constitutional norms: text plus purpose plus context. Analysis of the social reality to which a norm applies is part of the determination of its meaning.[22]

A similar approach to the interpretation of constitutional rights has emerged in other constitutional states, including Canada. The Supreme Court of Canada conceives of the *Charter* as 'a purposive document. Its purpose is to guarantee and to protect, within the limits of reason, the enjoyment of the rights and freedoms it enshrines. It is intended to constrain governmental action inconsistent with those rights and freedoms.'[23] Accordingly, the court maintains that interpretation of a constitutional right should be 'a generous rather than a legalistic one, aimed at fulfilling the purpose of a guarantee and securing for individuals the full benefit of the Charter's protection.'[24] Through interpretation, enduring constitutional norms are applied 'to meet new social, political, and historical realities often unimagined by its framers.'[25] As determinations of the more basic right of each inhabitant of the legal order to just governance, constitutional rights must be interpreted in a manner that relates abstract notions surrounding human dignity to the concrete features of the existing legal order.[26]

Purposive interpretation determines the protections that constitutional rights afford from the standpoint of the basic right of each person to just governance. The aim of such a mode of interpretation is to provide individuals with 'the full measure of the fundamental rights and freedoms' entrenched in the constitution.[27] If particular constitutional rights are to be interpreted in reference to the overarching norm that they instantiate, they will often require a broad interpretation. But if constitutional rights are interpreted broadly, conflicts inevitably emerge between particular constitutional rights and competing instances of the overarching norm that rights instantiate.[28]

[22] Grimm, "The Basic Law at 60 – Identity and Change," 44.

[23] *Hunter et al.* v. *Southam Inc.*, [1984] 2 SCR 145, 156.

[24] *R.* v. *Big M Drug Mart Ltd.*, 344. [25] *Hunter et al.* v. *Southam Inc.*, 155.

[26] See also Barak, *Proportionality: Constitutional Rights and Their Limitations*, 70–1: 'The language of the constitutional text protecting rights . . . should be interpreted in a way that realizes the reasons underlying the right itself.'

[27] *Minister of Home Affairs* v. *Fisher* [1980] A.C. 319, 328.

[28] Moshe Cohen-Eliya and Iddo Porat, "Proportionality and the Culture of Justification," 481; and Barak, *Proportionality: Constitutional Rights and Their Limitations*, 81–2.

A *constitutional conflict* consists in a clash between competing specifications of the ideal of public justice or human dignity under law. Specifications stand in conflict when each must be realized, and the full realization of one precludes that of the other. Constitutional conflicts arise between a constitutional right, on one hand, and what I will call an *obligatory objective*, that is, an objective integral to the maintenance and refinement of a legal order committed to respecting and protecting the human dignity of all who are subject to its authority. These objectives include, inter alia, public safety, public health, public order, and the state's duty to uphold the 'rights and freedoms of others.'[29] Thus, one's right to free expression might conflict with the state's duty to protect another's right to privacy, reputation, or a fair trial. Alternately one's right to privacy might conflict with the state duty with respect to public safety or national security, just as political rights might be exercised in a manner that conflicts with the state's duty to maintain the free democratic order. Such conflicts are ubiquitous within a modern constitutional state.

Constitutional conflicts may not be avoided by repudiating the purposive interpretation of constitutional rights. Modern constitutional states, as I have argued, seek to transform the right of every person to just governance into an effective constraint on the exercise of public power. Because this right must be specified if it is to be brought to bear on legal particulars, the modern constitutional state delineates a set of particular constitutional rights and interprets each to secure the normative purpose underlying its entrenchment. Of course, constitutional conflicts might be avoided by rejecting purposive interpretation and thereby diminishing the protections that particular constitutional rights afford. While this strategy could succeed in avoiding constitutional conflicts, it does so by severing the connection between the general right of each person to just governance and the protections that particular constitutional rights afford. In the resulting scheme, rights would have absolute strength, but the protections that rights afford their bearers would be arbitrary.

Since the modern constitutional state is committed to purposive interpretation of constitutional rights, and purposive interpretation generates constitutional conflicts, a modern constitutional state requires a doctrine that identifies cases of conflict and determines the constitutionality of state action with respect to them. I will now explain how the conditions

[29] See, for example, UN Commission on Human Rights, *The Siracusa Principles on the Limitation and Derogation Provisions in the International Covenant on Civil and Political Rights*, September 28, 1984, E/CN.4/1985/4.

that precede and comprise the doctrine of proportionality perform this role.

7.2 Proportionality as a justificatory sequence

The meaning of a constitutional right indicates what it would mean to justify its infringement. Because constitutional rights are specifications of human dignity, their infringement is justified when consonant with the overarching duty of which the right is an instance. Proportionality consists in the set of justificatory conditions that government must satisfy to establish that an infringement coheres to this duty.

The justification proceeds in three sequenced stages. The first stage, which precedes the proportionality analysis, asks whether the impugned law pursues the kind of objective that could justify the limitation of a constitutional right. The second stage, which comprises the rational connection and minimal impairment requirements, focuses on the relationship between the obligatory objective that the law pursues and the rights-infringing means that the law employs. Whereas the first stage concerns the objective of the law and the second concerns the relationship between the objective that the law pursues and the rights-infringing means that it employs, the third considers the extent to which the right is infringed and the objective is furthered and asks whether the duty to realize the ideal of public justice necessitates the infringement.

These justificatory conditions form a conceptual sequence. The first stage asks whether a constitutional conflict is *possible*, the second asks whether a constitutional conflict is *actual*, and the third asks whether it is *necessary* for the government to respond to the conflict by limiting a constitutional right.[30] As I will argue, each of these stages is increasingly demanding: if a prior stage has not been satisfied, no subsequent stage

[30] The category of necessity is often aligned with the minimal impairment requirement, not proportionality *stricto sensu*. See, for example, Barak, *Proportionality: Constitutional Rights and Their Limitations*, 317–39. To satisfy the minimal impairment requirement, government must establish the following conditional: If the objective is to be achieved, then the right must be infringed to a given extent. Thus, one could say that in cases in which the objective cannot be achieved in the absence of the infringement, the infringement is *necessary* to achieve the objective. However, it is important to note that this necessity is conditional insofar as it applies only *if* the objective ought to be achieved. The question of whether the objective – with its attending rights infringement – should be achieved concerns *moral* (as opposed to *conditional*) necessity. In what follows, I will explicate proportionality *stricto sensu* in terms of the condition under which government is morally necessitated to justify the infringement of a constitutional right.

can be. In the absence of an actual constitutional conflict between a constitutional right and an obligatory objective, the limitation of the constitutional right cannot be necessitated by the duty of public justice. In turn, if the impugned law does not pursue the kind of objective that makes a constitutional conflict possible, an actual constitutional conflict cannot result. Because each stage presupposes the satisfaction of the preceding stages, the failure to establish a particular link in the chain of justification indicates not only that the infringement of the right cannot be justified, but also that no subsequent link in the chain of justification can be forged.

7.2.1 The possibility of a constitutional conflict: the obligatory objective condition

Not all objectives are capable of justifying the limitation of a constitutional right. A limitation is justifiable only if it is consonant with the overarching duty of government to bring the existing legal order into the deepest possible conformity with the ideal of public justice or human dignity under law. If the objective for a limitation was *antagonistic* toward this ideal, then the limitation would constrain a particular determination of this ideal for the sake of violating another. Alternately, if the objective was *indifferent* toward this ideal, then the limitation would constrain a particular determination of this ideal without furthering another. Since the realization of the ideal of public justice is not deepened by measures that simply constrain one (or more) of its determinations, considerations of just governance must underlie all justified limitations. Conversely, limitations that do not pursue an obligatory objective are necessarily unjustified.[31]

An illustration of the obligatory objective requirement arises in *R.* v. *Big M Drug Mart*. At issue was the constitutionality of the *Lord's Day Act*, which prohibited persons from engaging in 'work, business, or labour' on Sunday.[32] After interpreting the 'freedom of conscience and

[31] In holding that objectives that do not advance an obligatory objective are incapable of justifying the limitation of a constitutional right, I depart from the prevailing approach in Germany, where 'any lawful purpose' can, in principle, justify the infringement of a constitutional right. Thus, rights cannot be limited for the sake of objectives that are *discordant* with the constitution's most basic principle, but *trivial* purposes may advance into the proportionality analysis. On the German approach, see Grimm, "Proportionality in Canadian and German Constitutional Jurisprudence," 388–9.

[32] *Lord's Day Act*, R.S.C. 1970, c. L13, s. 4.

religion' provisions entrenched in Canada's *Charter* purposively as reflecting the 'valuation of human dignity,'[33] the Supreme Court of Canada held that the *Act* violated the right of each Canadian to be free of compulsion that reflects a sectarian purpose. The problem with the legislation was that – as Chief Justice Dickson would put the point on a subsequent occasion – the infringement of a constitutional right may not be justified by 'objectives which are *trivial or discordant with the principles of a free and democratic society* . . . It is necessary, at a minimum, that an objective relate to concerns which are pressing and substantial in a free and democratic society before it can be characterized as sufficiently important.'[34] By affirming 'religious values rooted in Christian morality and, using the force of the state' to impose them on 'believers and non-believers alike,'[35] the *Lord's Day Act* subordinated a right that was integral to a free and democratic society to an objective that is 'fundamentally repugnant' to that ideal.[36]

Public justice forms the moral basis that underwrites all constitutional rights and all justified limitations.[37] Since considerations of policy, preference, tradition, utility, and administrative convenience are extrinsic to this ideal, they might *violate* rights, but cannot *justify* their limitation. Against considerations of this kind, rights are absolute. I return to this point below in defending proportionality from the objection alleging that the doctrine is immoral because it permits rights to be infringed for the sake of pernicious objectives.

[33] R. v. *Big M Drug Mart Ltd.*, 346. [34] R. v. *Oakes*, 138–9 (my emphasis).
[35] R. v. *Big M Drug Mart Ltd.*, 337.
[36] Ibid., 352.
This approach to the obligatory purpose requirement can also be found in the constitutional jurisprudence of South Africa. In *National Coalition for Gay and Lesbian Equality*, Justice Ackermann considered the constitutionality of offences that criminalized private acts of sodomy between consenting adult males. After exploring how the offence severely limits the constitutional rights of gay South Africans to equality, privacy, dignity, and freedom, Justice Ackermann turns to consider the purpose of the limitation: 'No valid purpose has been suggested. The enforcement of the private moral views of a section of the community, which are based to a large extent on nothing more than prejudice, cannot qualify as such a legitimate purpose. There is accordingly nothing, in the proportionality enquiry, to weigh against the extent of the limitation and its harmful impact on gays. It would therefore seem that there is no justification for the limitation.' *National Coalition for Gay and Lesbian Equality and Another* v. *Minister of Justice and Others*, 1999 (1) SA 6 (CC), para. 37.
[37] *Canada (Human Rights Commission)* v. *Taylor*, [1990] 3 SCR 892, 916. See also Barak, "Proportional Effect: The Israeli Experience," *University of Toronto Law Journal* 57 (2007): 382 ('human rights and the limitations on them derive from the same source. They reflect the same values').

That a rights-infringing law pursues an obligatory objective establishes the *possibility* that a constitutional conflict obtains between determinations of the ideal of public justice. The subsequent stages, which form the doctrine of proportionality, determine whether that conflict is *actual*, and whether it is morally *necessary* for the government to respond by limiting a constitutional right.

7.2.2 The actuality of a constitutional conflict: the rational connection and minimal impairment requirements

The initial steps of the proportionality analysis establish the actuality of a constitutional conflict by considering the relationship between the rights-infringing means that the law employs and the obligatory objective that the law pursues. These steps include the rational connection and minimal impairment requirements.

To satisfy the rational connection requirement, the government must establish that the rights-infringing means that the law employs are conducive to the realization of the law's objective.[38] If the government fails to satisfy this condition, the impugned law cannot be justified because it limits a constitutional right for the sake of realizing an objective that the rights-infringing means do not advance. In such cases, the justification for limiting the constitutional right fails because no matter how integral the objective is to the realization of public justice, the objective is not advanced by the means that the law employs.[39] The actuality of a constitutional conflict is not established by the mere assertion that a law pursues an obligatory objective.

An example of the failure to satisfy the rational connection requirement arises in Germany's *Falconer Hunting License* case.[40] An amendment to

[38] Barak, *Proportionality: Constitutional Rights and Their Limitations*, 315; Patrick Quirk, "An Australian Looks at German 'Proportionality,'" *University of Notre Dame Australia Law Review* 1 (1999): 42 (' . . . the appropriateness requirement strikes at a lack of *causal connection* between chosen means and the desired end').

[39] See Denise Réaume, "Limitations on Constitutional Rights: The Logic of Proportionality," Oxford Legal Studies Research Paper No. 26/2009, http://papers.ssrn.com/sol3/papers.cfm?abstract_id=1463853: 'The proffered objective might well be important, but *it* does not ground the impugned provision; it therefore cannot transfer its justificatory power to that provision.'

[40] See BVerfGE 55, 159 (1980). English synopses of this case can also be found in Grimm, "Proportionality in Canadian and German Constitutional Jurisprudence," 389; Quirk, "An Australian Looks at German 'Proportionality,'" 42–3; and Donald P. Kommers and Russell A. Miller, *The Constitutional Jurisprudence of the Federal Republic of Germany* (Durham: Duke University Press, 2012), 404.

the *Federal Hunting Act* required falconers to demonstrate both 'technical knowledge' of guns and 'proficiency on a firing range' in order to obtain a falconry license. A falconer raised a constitutional complaint alleging that the amendment was unconstitutional because it violated his right to the free development of his personality.[41] The Federal Constitutional Court held that even though government may regulate hunting for the sake of public safety, the amendment was unconstitutional because falconry does not involve the use of guns to hunt falcons but the use of falcons to hunt other animals. Accordingly, the requirement that falconers pass a test demonstrating knowledge of and proficiency with guns was an arbitrary restriction on their freedom that did nothing to advance the objective of public safety. In the words of the court, 'No apparent reason can be found for the amendment ... It is not justifiable to establish barriers completely extraneous to the exercise of falconry.'[42]

The presence of a rational connection between the rights-infringing means that the law employs and the obligatory objective that the law pursues is not sufficient to justify the limitation of a constitutional right. Even when a rational connection has been established, it remains possible that the objective could be achieved through legislative means that are less injurious of the right. To satisfy the minimal impairment requirement, government must demonstrate the absence of alternative means that would achieve the objective of the impugned law to the same extent while imposing a lesser infringement on the right.[43] When a variety of means are equally effective in achieving an obligatory objective, government must employ the means that are least intrusive of the right.[44] The

41 Quirk, "An Australian Looks at German 'Proportionality,'" 42.

42 BVerfGE 55, 159 (1980) ('Für die Gesetzesänderung lasse sich kein einleuchtender Grund finden ... Es sei aber nicht gerechtfertigt, völlig sachfremde Barrieren gegen die Ausübung der Beizjagd zu errichten').

43 *R.* v. *Big M Drug Mart Ltd.*, 352; *R.* v. *Oakes*, 139.

44 In practice, the Supreme Court of Canada has at times effaced this requirement. For a particularly egregious formulation, see *Multani* v. *Commission scolaire Marguerite-Bourgeoys* [2006] 1 SCR 256, para. 50 (per Charron J.): 'The limit, which must minimally impair the right or freedom that has been infringed, need not necessarily be the least intrusive solution.' On the 'obvious tension' separating notions of *reasonable impairment* from *minimal impairment*, see Tom Hickman, "Proportionality: Comparative Law Lessons," *Judicial Review* 12 (2007): 40–5.

Stone Sweet and Matthews, *Proportionality Balancing and Global Constitutionalism*, 105 (quoting Rupprecht von Krauss, *Der Grundsatz der Verhältnismässigkeit in seiner Bedeutung für die Notwendigkeit des Mittels in Verwaltungsrecht* (1955), 25. [hereinafter *Verhältnismässigkeit*]: '[I]t would be a contradiction to raise personal freedom to the leading state principle and at the same time to permit unnecessary restrictions of this freedom by the state to be considered lawful ... ').

failure to do so violates the duty of just governance because no matter how integral the obligatory objective is to the realization of public justice, a law that is not minimally impairing needlessly infringes a right. Government cannot purport to bring the legal order into the deepest possible conformity with its own internal ideal when it gratuitously infringes an aspect of it.

The justificatory sequence cannot conclude with the satisfaction of the minimal impairment requirement. If the proportionality analysis concluded with minimal impairment, then it would be possible that 'a quite negligible public interest could lead to a severe rights infringement, without being unlawful.'[45] Grimm provides an example of such a possibility. Suppose that a law 'allows the police to shoot a person to death if this is the only means of preventing a perpetrator from destroying property.'[46] The protection of property is the kind of objective for which a constitutional right could be limited. There is a rational connection between killing perpetrators and protecting property. And the minimal impairment requirement is also satisfied insofar as the law specifies that shooting is permitted only in cases in which there are no other means of protecting property. If the proportionality analysis concluded with the minimal impairment requirement, then any obligatory objective could justify the limitation of any constitutional right to any extent. But as Grimm's example illustrates, even a minimally impairing rights-infringement can have grave implications for rights bearers. The reason why the minimal impairment requirement cannot conclude the justificatory sequence is that minimal impairment, like rational connection, simply concerns the relationship between the means that the law employs and the objective that the law pursues. Since the minimal impairment requirement focuses on whether there is a way of achieving the relevant objective to a comparable extent that is less rights-infringing, the availability of an alternative that is less rights-infringing but that achieves the relevant objective to a lesser extent is without significance at this stage in the analysis. As Justice Aharon Barak observes, '[o]nly if it is possible to realize the objects of the statute by less drastic means does this step grant protection to human rights.'[47]

The satisfaction of the minimal impairment requirement establishes the actuality of a constitutional conflict. The conflict consists in a clash

45 Ibid., 106 (citing Krauss, *Verhältnismässigkeit*, 15).
46 Grimm, "Proportionality in Canadian and German Constitutional Jurisprudence," 396.
47 Barak, "Proportional Effect: The Israeli Experience," 373.

between determinations of the ideal of public justice, each of which must be realized, but that cannot be jointly realized in full. If the right is not limited, the objective cannot be achieved in full. If the objective is to be achieved in full, the right must be limited. Since the right and the objective cannot both be realized undiminished, a modern constitutional state must determine the duty of government with respect to the conflict. This determination forms the final stage of the proportionality analysis.

7.2.3 The necessity of limiting a constitutional right: the proportionality stricto sensu *requirement*

To satisfy the proportionality *stricto sensu* requirement, government must establish that the limitation of a constitutional right coheres with its duty to bring the legal order as a whole into the deepest possible conformity with the ideal of public justice. It is in this sense that the doctrine of proportionality *justifies* the limitation of a constitutional right. When the conditions that make up the doctrine of proportionality are satisfied, the duty of public justice necessitates the limitation of a constitutional right.

The term 'proportionality *stricto sensu*' was coined by the German administrative law scholar Rupprecht von Krauss, who conceived of it in terms of 'relating two or more quantities that can be set against a common yardstick.'[48] These quantities consist in the constitutional right and the competing obligatory objective. Within the unified theory, the yardstick against which these quantities are set is the ideal of public justice or human dignity under law, which, as we have seen, forms the basis of both constitutional rights and the purposes for which they can be justifiably limited. The right and the competing purpose can be conceived of as quantities because each can be realized to varying extents. The infringement of a right can be slight or significant, as can the extent to which a limitation furthers an obligatory objective. Proportionality *stricto sensu* considers these quantities from the shared standpoint that each instantiates and asks whether the limitation is required to bring the legal order into the deepest conformity with its internal ideal.

Consider Chief Justice Dickson's majority opinion in *R.* v. *Keegstra*,[49] which concerned the constitutionality of a provision of the *Criminal*

[48] Stone Sweet and Matthews, *Proportionality Balancing and Global Constitutionalism*, 105 (citing Krauss, *Verhältnismässigkeit*, 14).

[49] [1990] 3 SCR 697.

Code that prohibited public acts that willfully promoted hatred against identifiable groups.[50] James Keegstra, a former high school teacher, was charged under this provision for anti-Semitic teachings, which claimed that Jews were 'inherently evil,' hostile to Christians, and responsible for all the evils of the world, whether moral, political, or economic.[51] The Chief Justice held that Keegstra's constitutional right to freedom of expression was infringed and that the provision pursued a pressing and substantial purpose by promoting dignity, equality, and multiculturalism and opposing racial, ethnic, and religious hatred. Having determined that a constitutional conflict was present, he proceeded to consider the rights and limits that comprised it from the standpoint of their normative basis, what Canadian constitutional jurisprudence terms the values of a free and democratic society. Beginning with the relationship of these values to freedom of expression, he noted that the kind of expressive activity that the provision prohibits involves the willful and public promotion of hatred against members of identifiable groups. Since the objective of such expression is to establish that 'members of identifiable groups are not to be given equal standing in society, and are not human beings equally deserving of concern, respect and consideration,'[52] the Chief Justice held that the prohibited expression runs 'directly counter to the values central to a free and democratic society.'[53] While the expression at issue is 'only tenuously connected with the values underlying the guarantee of freedom of speech,'[54] the limitation is of 'enormous importance' when considered from the standpoint of these same values.[55] The limitation seeks to diminish racism and 'bolster the notion of mutual respect necessary in a nation which venerates the equality of all persons.'[56] Thus, the limitation pursues an objective that is 'central to the concept of a free and democratic society.'[57] As the conflict involves an expressive activity that is 'wholly inimical' to the values of a free and democratic society and a limitation that is central to their realization, the Chief Justice concluded that the limitation is justified.[58] The 'commonality' of values[59] that underlies both freedom of expression and the countervailing objective demands the right's limitation.

Alternately, cases might arise in which the justification fails because of the significant extent to which a constitutional right is infringed and the comparatively marginal extent to which the obligatory objective

[50] Criminal Code, R.S.C. 1985, c. C-46, s. 319(2). [51] *R.* v. *Keegstra*, 714. [52] Ibid., 756.
[53] Ibid. [54] Ibid., 787. [55] Ibid. [56] Ibid., 756. [57] Ibid., 787. [58] Ibid., 764.
[59] Ibid., 736.

contributes to the ideal of public justice. This possibility is illustrated by Grimm's example, discussed earlier, of a law that licenses the use of lethal force to protect property.[60] Or a justification might fail because of the availability of alternative means that do not fully achieve the obligatory objective, but are nevertheless more conducive to the realization of the ideal of public justice because they infringe rights to a far lesser extent.[61] Such means would not undermine the government's justification at the minimal impairment stage as they do not fully achieve the objective.[62]

Because proportionality *stricto sensu* has played a small role within Canadian constitutional jurisprudence, scholars sometimes suggest that the condition is a redundant stage in the proportionality analysis. As the Canadian constitutional lawyer Peter Hogg puts the point,

> If the objective is sufficiently important, and the objective is pursued by the least drastic means, then it must follow that the effects of the law are an acceptable price to pay for the benefit of the law. I conclude, therefore, that an affirmative answer to the first step - sufficiently important objective - will always yield an affirmative answer to the fourth step - proportional effect.[63]

The charge of redundancy overlooks a fundamental distinction between the obligatory objective condition and proportionality *stricto sensu*. The

60 Grimm, "Proportionality in Canadian and German Constitutional Jurisprudence," 396. For parallel examples, see Bernard Schlink, "Proportionality in Constitutional Law: Why Everywhere but Here?" *Duke Journal of Comparative and International Law* 22 (2012): 293; and BVerfGE 16, 194 (1963).

61 For example, see HCJ 2056/04 *Beit Sourik Village Council* v. *Israel* [2004] IsrSC 58(5) 807. When the Israeli government planned to build a separation fence to prevent terrorist attacks, West Bank residents brought a complaint to the Israeli Supreme Court alleging that the separation fence - much of which was built on West Bank land - posed a severe infringement of their rights, including their rights to property, freedom of movement, and freedom of occupation. Applying the proportionality doctrine, the court determined that the government acted pursuant to an appropriate objective (security), that a rational connection obtained between the means (the building of the separation fence) and the objective, and that there were no alternative means that realized the same degree of security while impairing the rights of West Bank residents to a lesser extent. Nevertheless, the court held that the government had not satisfied the proportionality *stricto sensu* requirement because, as Justice Barak later put it, an alternative route was available that 'provided slightly less security and much more protection of human rights.' Barak, "Proportional Effect: The Israeli Experience," 376.

62 For a discussion of this point in the context of Israeli and Canadian proportionality jurisprudence, see Sara Weinrib, "The Emergence of the Third Step of the Oakes Test in *Alberta* v. *Hutterian Brethren of Wilson Colony*," *University of Toronto Faculty of Law Review* 68 (2010): 77–97.

63 P.W. Hogg, *Constitutional Law of Canada*, vol. II (Toronto: Thomson Carswell, 2007), 153.

former asks: Is this the kind of consideration for which rights can be limited in a free and democratic society? The latter asks: Given the relative extents to which the right is infringed and the competing objective is realized, is the limitation necessitated by the government's duty to bring the legal order into the deepest possible conformity with the ideal of a free and democratic society? The charge of redundancy overlooks that the obligatory objective condition concerns the *kind* of purpose that can justify the limitation of a constitutional right, while the proportionality *stricto sensu* requirement concerns issues of *degree*. Insofar as questions of kind and degree are irreducible, the charge of redundancy fails.[64]

One of the reasons that the doctrine of proportionality is so troubling for legal and constitutional theorists is that it emerges at the intersection of two sets of issues that they typically prefer to separate. The first issue concerns the objectives that government may legitimately pursue. The second concerns the means that government may legitimately employ. If one thinks about each of these issues in isolation from the other, then one is led to the conclusion that state action is unobjectionable so long as it employs legitimate means in pursuit of a legitimate end. This is exactly what the proportionality *stricto sensu* requirement denies. A law that pursues an obligatory objective by employing means that are both rationally connected to that purpose and minimally impairing of an infringed constitutional right may nevertheless be unjustified because, given the severity of the rights-infringement and the extent to which the limitation realizes (or is likely to realize) an obligatory objective, the realization of public justice is not optimized by the limitation.

Proportionality *stricto sensu* constitutes the final link in a chain of increasingly demanding justificatory conditions that form the doctrine of proportionality. Because each condition is more demanding than the one

[64] Like Hogg, Alan Brudner conceives of the proportionality *stricto sensu* as a redundant stage in the analysis that repeats the purpose requirement. See Brudner, "What Theory of Rights Best Explain the *Oakes* Test?" in *The Limitation of Charter Rights: Critical Essays on R.* v. *Oakes*, ed. Grégoire C.N. Webber and Luc Tremblay (Montreal: Les Editions Themis, 2009), 59–74. Brudner defends a pluralist-paradigm theory of proportionality rooted in a Hegelian account of the relationship between individual autonomy and the common good. After disqualifying competing theories for failing to illuminate the practice of proportionality, Brudner concedes that within his own framework 'no further justificatory work is left' for the proportionality *stricto sensu* condition. Ibid., 73. By contrast, I have suggested that the overarching justification that traverses the doctrine of proportionality cannot end with minimal impairment. Minimal impairment merely establishes that there is no way of pursuing the relevant purpose without infringing a constitutional right. It does not address the question of whether the realization of public justice within the constitutional order is advanced by the limitation.

that preceded it, the failure to satisfy a single condition renders it impossible to satisfy any of the subsequent ones. Government cannot satisfy the proportionality *stricto sensu* condition if the minimal impairment condition remains unsatisfied because to the extent that the rights infringement is gratuitous, the duty of public justice does not necessitate the right's limitation. Government cannot satisfy the minimal impairment condition if the rational connection condition that precedes it remains unsatisfied because if the rights-infringing means do not further the realization of the objective, then to the extent that the objective could be achieved without limiting a right, the impugned law cannot be minimally impairing. Finally, government cannot satisfy the rational connection condition by establishing that the rights-infringing means contribute to the realization of an obligatory objective if the law does not pursue one. Because each stage of the justificatory sequence raises a condition that presupposes the satisfaction of any earlier stage, the failure to satisfy a single stage culminates in the failure to satisfy all subsequent ones. In any failed justification, the proportionality *stricto sensu* condition remains unsatisfied.

Although proportionality *stricto sensu* is the most demanding stage in this justificatory sequence, the doctrine is not reducible to it, as is sometimes claimed.[65] Because this stage concerns the duty of government with respect to an actual constitutional conflict, it presupposes a series of prior determinations. On the one hand, there must be a right that has been infringed. On the other, the law must pursue an obligatory objective through means that are both rationally connected to that purpose and minimally impairing of the right. These prior determinations enable the judiciary to deliberate on whether the proportionality *stricto sensu* has been satisfied by considering both the extent of the rights infringement and the extent to which the obligatory objective is furthered from the standpoint of the common moral ideal that each instantiates. The determination of whether the proportionality *stricto sensu* condition has been satisfied cannot be carried out in abstraction from the preceding stages of the justificatory sequence that it concludes.

At each stage of this sequence, the onus lies upon the government to justify the limitation of a constitutional right.[66] The placement of the

65 Tsakyrakis, "Proportionality: An Assault on Human Rights," 474.

66 *R.* v. *Oakes*, 136–7 ('The onus of proving that a limit on a right or freedom guaranteed by the *Charter* is reasonable and demonstrably justified in a free and democratic society rests upon the party seeking to uphold the limitation'). See also *S.* v. *Makwanyane and Another*, para. 102.

onus reflects the normative and constitutional dimensions of public law. Modern constitutionalism is a form of legal organization in which conformity to the demands of human dignity is a condition for the valid exercise of all public authority. Since constitutional rights are determinations of dignity, the validity of a law that infringes a constitutional right is immediately called into question. Accordingly, if the government seeks to defend the law's validity, it must displace the presumption of invalidity by demonstrating that the infringement is consonant with its duty to govern within dignity's parameters. The failure of such a demonstration would indicate that the impugned law is not only unjust, but that it thereby fails to satisfy the constitution's standard of legal validity. Alternately, if government could uphold the validity of legislation that infringes a constitutional right without establishing that the legislation is compatible with its duty to govern justly, modern constitutionalism would not be true to its animating idea that the satisfaction of the duty of public justice is the condition for the valid exercise of all public authority. I return to this point below in explaining how proportionality accommodates the idea that rights enjoy priority over competing objectives.

7.3 Alexy and his critics

Robert Alexy is perhaps the foremost defender of proportionality. The distinguishing feature of his conception is the claim that proportionality is a formal structure that can be captured in abstraction from a substantive moral theory. In this section, I explain why his structural conception culminates in the objections that proportionality is immoral and irrational. My aim is neither to criticize Alexy's view nor to refute the objections that are raised against it, but to show that these objections stem from the structural character of his conception. Because the conception developed in the prior section emerges from the substantive moral commitments of the unified theory, the objections raised against Alexy's conception are inapplicable to it.

In *A Theory of Constitutional Rights*, Alexy develops 'a general legal theory of the constitutional rights of [Germany's] Basic Law.'[67] The theory is *general* insofar as its purpose is not to consider 'specific problems of specific rights,' but to explore 'problems common to all

[67] Alexy, *A Theory of Constitutional Rights*, trans. Julian Rivers (Oxford: Oxford University Press, 2002), 5.

constitutional rights.'[68] The theory is *legal* insofar as it engages with the 'evaluative questions which have been left open by the authoritative materials at hand.'[69] These materials include the constitutional rights entrenched in Germany's Basic Law.[70] This focus distinguishes Alexy's project from those who offer historical theories of constitutional rights valid in prior ages and those who offer philosophic theories of constitutional rights 'independent of positive law.'[71] The general, legal, and constitutional aspects of Alexy's project enable him to raise a broad question about particular constitutional cases: Given a certain factual and legal context, what is the morally correct decision?[72]

The basis of Alexy's theory lies in a distinction between two kinds of norms: *principles* and *rules*:

> The decisive point in distinguishing rules from principles is that *principles* are norms which require that something be realized to the greatest extent possible given the legal and factual possibilities. Principles are *optimization requirements*, characterized by the fact that they can be satisfied to varying degrees, and that the appropriate degree of satisfaction depends not only on what is factually possible but also on what is legally possible. The scope of the legally possible is determined by opposing principles and rules.
>
> By contrast, *rules* are norms which are always either fulfilled or not. If a rule validly applies, then the requirement is to do exactly what it says, neither more nor less. In this way rules contain *fixed points* in the field of the factually and legally possible. This means that the distinction between rules and principles is a qualitative one and not one of degree. Every norm is either a rule or a principle.[73]

The distinction between principles and rules turns on the respective conditions of their satisfaction. A principle is satisfied when it is optimized, that is, realized to the greatest extent possible. Whereas a principle can be satisfied to varying extents, a rule is a binary norm: it is either satisfied or unsatisfied.

[68] Ibid., 10. [69] Ibid., 8 [70] Ibid., 5. [71] Ibid., 3. [72] Ibid., 8.

[73] Ibid., 47–8. Alexy's distinction between rules and principles echoes Ronald Dworkin, *Taking Rights Seriously* (Cambridge: Harvard University Press, 1978), 24. Dworkin argues that rules 'are applicable in an all-or-nothing fashion.' If a rule is valid and the facts that it stipulates are given, then the outcome that the rule requires must be accepted. By contrast, principles do not require a certain outcome in a certain context, but rather are reasons that carry weight. Alexy, like Dworkin, holds that valid rules cannot conflict and that conflicts between principles are to be resolved by considering their relative weight. See Lorenzo Zucca, *Constitutional Dilemmas: Conflicts of Fundamental Legal Rights in Europe and the USA* (Oxford: Oxford University Press, 2007), 11.

Alexy deepens his distinction between rules and principles by setting out what each kind of norm requires in cases of conflict. Given the binary structure of a rule, a conflict between rules can be resolved only by declaring one of the rules invalid or by narrowing the scope of one of the rules by reading an exception into it.[74] In Alexy's example, the rule requiring students to remain in class until the bell rings conflicts with the rule requiring students to leave the class at once when the fire alarm sounds. Since one cannot both remain in class until the bell rings and leave before the bell rings, one must *either* read an exception into the former rule by requiring persons to remain in class until the bell rings unless the fire alarm sounds *or* declare that one of the rules is invalid. By contrast, when principles come into conflict, the conflict is resolved by asking which principle, in the context of the prevailing circumstances, outweighs the other.[75] A principle must yield when it is confronted by a competing principle that, in the situation at hand, carries greater weight.[76]

Alexy's 'central thesis' is that 'constitutional rights are principles and that principles are optimization requirements.'[77] As optimization requirements, conflicts between principles are to be resolved in terms of balancing the competing principles on the basis of their weight in the relevant instance. Alexy formulates this weighing of principles in terms of what he calls the *Law of Balancing*: 'The greater the degree of non-satisfaction of, or detriment to, one principle, the greater must be the importance of satisfying the other.'[78] He claims that the *Law of Balancing* is 'identical' to the final stage of proportionality analysis, proportionality *stricto sensu*.[79]

Alexy's conception of proportionality is 'structural.'[80] It offers a systematic exposition of what it means to balance principles, while abstracting from questions of 'substantive moral and political theory.'[81] Thus, the conception offers no resources for evaluating the weight that particular

[74] *A Theory of Constitutional Rights*, 49. [75] Ibid., 50. [76] Ibid., 58. [77] Ibid., 388.
[78] Ibid., 401. [79] Ibid.
[80] Ibid., 13. On the structural character of Alexy's framework, see Mattias Kumm, "Constitutional Rights as Principles: On the Structure and Domain of Constitutional Justice. A Review Essay on *A Theory of Constitutional Rights*," *International Journal of Constitutional Law* 2 (2004): 574, 575–6 (hereinafter "Constitutional Rights as Principles"), and 590; Kai Möller, "Balancing and the Structure of Constitutional Rights," *International Journal of Constitutional Law* 5 (2007): 458 and 467; David Bilchitz, "Does Balancing Adequately Capture the Nature of Rights?" *South African Public Law* 25 (2010): 423–44; and Zucca, *Constitutional Dilemmas: Conflicts of Fundamental Legal Rights in Europe and the USA*, 21.
[81] Robert Alexy, "Thirteen Replies," in *Law, Rights and Discourse: The Legal Philosophy of Robert Alexy*, ed. George Pavlakos (Oxford: Hart Publishing, 2007), 341.

constitutional rights possess or for identifying objectives that are incapable of justifying the limitation of constitutional rights.[82] For Alexy, the doctrine of proportionality is a formal structure that must be supplemented by some extrinsic moral theory. In his words, proportionality 'essentially depends on premises provided from the outside.'[83]

Alexy's critics allege that the conception of proportionality that he defends is immoral and irrational. Each of these objections targets the structural character of his conception.

The claim that proportionality is immoral takes a variety of forms, each of which turns on the idea that the doctrine fails to take rights seriously. Because Alexy's conception admits no constraints on the kinds of objectives that might be placed opposite rights in the balance, critics lament that rights might be subordinated to pernicious objectives.[84] Further, critics claim that instead of affording rights priority over competing interests, Alexy's conception makes rights compete with all other interests on a common plane.[85] Finally, critics allege that his conception does 'violence to the idea of a constitution.'[86] After all, constitutions entrench rights in order to identify and prohibit unacceptable state action. If rights may be justifiably limited, then anything that the constitution prohibits may, in actuality, be permitted: 'Whatever the constitution does, proportionality can undo.'[87] Once the doctrine of proportionality is admitted into the constitutional order, 'everything,

[82] Ibid.

[83] Ibid., 344. See also Matthias Klatt, "An Egalitarian Defense of Proportionality-Based Balancing: A Reply to Luc B. Tremblay," *International Journal of Constitutional Law* 12 (2014): 899.

[84] See, for example, Webber, *The Negotiable Constitution: On the Limitation of Rights*, 105; Urbina, "A Critique of Proportionality," 65; Tsakyrakis, "Proportionality: An Assault on Human Rights," 488. Of course, Alexy might respond that such objectives, however identified, could be afforded a low value (or even a value of zero) so that they would be incapable of outweighing any other principle. See Alexy, "Thirteen Replies," 341 and 344. But it is not clear how an objective could be characterized as an optimization principle and yet have a value of zero.

[85] Webber, *The Negotiable Constitution: On the Limitation of Rights*, 104; Tsakyrakis, "Proportionality: An Assault on Human Rights," 474; and Jürgen Habermas, *Between Facts and Norms: Contributions to a Discourse Theory of Law and Democracy* (Cambridge: MIT Press, 1999), 259.

[86] Grégoire C.N. Webber, "Proportionality, Balancing, and the Cult of Constitutional Rights Scholarship," *Canadian Journal of Law and Jurisprudence* 23 (2010): 198.

[87] Webber, *The Negotiable Constitution: On the Limitation of Rights*, 100. See also Habermas, *Between Facts and Norms: Contributions to a Discourse Theory of Law and Democracy*, 258–9.

even those aspects of our life most closely associated with our status as free and equal, is, in principle, up for grabs.'[88]

Underlying these iterations of the charge of immorality is the structural character of Alexy's approach. In the words of a leading critic of proportionality, a structural or formal conception 'does not purport (at least explicitly) to struggle with the *moral* correctness, goodness or rightness of a claim but only with its *technical* weight, cost or benefit.'[89] Such an approach is misguided because an amoral conception offers resources that are unsuited for thinking about morally fraught questions concerning the nature and limits of constitutional rights.[90] If the problem that undermines Alexy's account is its failure to engage with considerations of substantive morality, then the alternative is clear. We must 'aspire to struggle more explicitly with the moral and political reasoning inherent to all rights.'[91]

Once proportionality is understood as calling for a right to be balanced against an unrestricted range of interests, a further objection arises. The objection alleges that proportionality cannot be rational. For only commensurable elements can be rationally balanced. In turn, elements are commensurable if there is a common criterion for assessing the relative degree of their interference or satisfaction.[92] And Alexy's framework, the objection alleges, fails to offer such a criterion.

In drawing on the substantive commitments of the unified theory of public law, I develop a conception of proportionality that departs from Alexy's structural approach. In what follows, I explain why this

[88] Tsakyrakis, "Proportionality: An Assault on Human Rights," 489. For Alexy's account of how his conception accommodates categorical claims, see "Thirteen Replies," 344.

[89] Webber, *The Negotiable Constitution: On the Limitation of Rights*, 90. See also Tsakyrakis, "Proportionality: An Assault on Human Rights," 487.

[90] Webber, *The Negotiable Constitution: On the Limitation of Rights*, 105.

[91] Ibid., 115. On this point, see also Urbina, "A Critique of Proportionality," 80: 'An appropriate method for deciding cases of human rights limitations would have to respond to sound moral reflection regarding what are the morally relevant considerations that ought to bear on the different kinds of human rights claims, and go some way toward expressing those considerations through legal categories able to guide the judge to a reasonable solution. None of the conceptions of proportionality fulfils these requirements.'

[92] Like proportionality, commensurability is a contested concept. Here I rely on the conception that appears in Virgílio Afonso da Silva, "Comparing the Incommensurable: Constitutional Principles, Balancing, and Rational Decision," *Oxford Journal of Legal Studies* 31 (2011): 278. See also Webber, *The Negotiable Constitution: On the Limitation of Rights*, 90; Urbina, "A Critique of Proportionality," 51.

conception is not vulnerable to the charges that the doctrine is immoral and irrational.

Instead of arguing with Alexy and other defenders of proportionality that the doctrine is *amoral*[93] or with critics who claim that it is instead *immoral*, I defend the view that proportionality is a *moral* doctrine for assessing the constitutionality of government conduct in cases of conflict. Such a conception (1) denies that rights may be balanced against pernicious objectives, (2) acknowledges the priority of rights over competing considerations, and (3) maintains the categorical constraints that a rights-based constitution imposes on state power. I take up each of these points in turn.

First, while Alexy's structural conception of proportionality is 'not in a position' to identify illicit objectives and exclude them from balancing,[94] the conception that I defend is preceded by the obligatory objective condition. The condition precedes the proportionality analysis because the doctrine of proportionality applies solely to cases in which there is a possible conflict between determinations of the ideal of public justice. When a right is confronted by a consideration that is extrinsic to this ideal, no constitutional conflict arises and justification is therefore impossible. Thus, certain kinds of considerations are incapable of justifying the limitation of a constitutional right, regardless of their degree or intensity.[95]

Second, within the conception of proportionality that emerges from the unified theory, rights enjoy priority over all competing objectives. Rights have *absolute* priority over considerations that do not satisfy the obligatory objective condition. If an objective is illegitimate, it cannot justify even a negligible rights infringement. But even with respect to objectives that satisfy this condition, rights enjoy a relative priority.

Consider what Alexy calls a *stalemate situation*, in which a constitutional right is confronted by a countervailing principle of equal weight.[96] For Alexy, a right can be displaced by any principle that possesses equal or greater weight. Thus, if the constitutional right and the countervailing

[93] See, for example, D.M. Beatty, *The Ultimate Rule of Law* (Oxford: Oxford University Press, 2004), 170. Beatty claims that proportionality makes controversies surrounding, for example, abortion or discrimination entirely dependent 'on the factual details of each case.' Within the conception of proportionality that I defend, the doctrine is not a factual inquiry that displaces moral considerations, but a moral inquiry that establishes the relevance of certain factual considerations.

[94] Alexy, "Thirteen Replies," 341.

[95] On this point, see Khosla, "Proportionality: An Assault on Human Rights?: A Reply," 305; and Möller, "Proportionality: Challenging the Critics," 718.

[96] Alexy, *A Theory of Constitutional Rights*, 410–12.

principle weigh equally in the balance, he concludes that government enjoys the discretion to infringe the right by enacting legislation or to refrain from doing so. The unified theory takes a different approach. As I have argued, a modern constitutional state makes conformity to the duty of public justice the condition for the valid exercise of public authority. Constitutional rights are instances of this duty. Thus, a law that infringes a right is presumed to be invalid. If the government seeks to displace the presumption of invalidity, it bears the onus of justifying the infringement. To this end, government must demonstrate that the infringement accords with the duty of public justice by satisfying the demanding set of conditions that precede and comprise the doctrine of proportionality. In the stalemate situation that Alexy envisages, the government necessarily fails to justify the infringement. For if the right and the limit would contribute equally to the realization of the ideal of public justice, then government has not discharged its justificatory burden.[97] Accordingly, the presumption of the law's invalidity becomes conclusive. The priority of rights is evident in the very structure of constitutional adjudication: a right prevails unless government can demonstrably justify its infringement.

Third, although Alexy's conception of proportionality is criticized for dissolving the categorical constraints that a constitution imposes on state power, I have argued that the doctrine has a categorical core. Proportionality reflects the absolute duty of government to bring the existing legal order into the deepest possible conformity with human dignity. Far from forming an exception to this duty, proportionality determines what this duty requires in cases of constitutional conflict.

[97] Competing conceptions of proportionality often fail to appreciate the significance of the burden. Mattias Kumm, for example, presents proportionality as an institutionalization of a Socratic process of public reasoning about whether a coercive act might reasonably be accepted by the free and equal citizens affected by it. See Kumm, "The Idea of Socratic Contestation and the Right to Justification: The Point of Rights-Based Proportionality Review," *Law & Ethics of Human Rights* 4 (2010): 141–75. While Kumm's Socratic analogy captures an aspect of the rationality to which proportionality aspires, it fails to capture a crucial feature that underlies proportionality analysis. The parties to a Socratic debate, being equal citizens, enter the debate on symmetrical terms: no party carries an argumentative burden that the other parties to the debate lack. The public law context of constitutional adjudication is different because the burdens that each party must discharge are determined by the position that each occupies in the public law relationship. Within this relationship, private persons have a right to just governance that imposes a corresponding obligation on all public power. Since the modern constitutional state makes the satisfaction of this obligation the condition for the valid exercise of public power, when government has infringed a constitutional right, government bears the onus of justification. What counts as an adequate engagement in public reasoning is determined by the juridical structure of the relationship that obtains between the parties.

To justify the limitation of a constitutional right, government must demonstrate that the law limiting a constitutional right is necessitated by the very normative ideal that the right instantiates. At issue in proportionality is whether government has responded to a constitutional conflict in a manner that is consistent with the duty of public justice, not whether an exception should be made to the duty's demands.

Once the connection between proportionality and the moral commitments of a modern constitutional state comes into view, the remaining objection, which alleges that proportionality is irrational because it involves balancing incommensurable considerations, dissolves. Proponents of proportionality often respond to this objection by granting that proportionality involves balancing incommensurable considerations and then devising intricate arguments to forestall the conclusion that the doctrine is therefore irrational.[98] I do not follow this strategy. For on the conception of proportionality that I elaborated earlier, proportionality does not involve incommensurable considerations.

The application of the doctrine of proportionality presupposes two prior findings. The first concerns whether a constitutional right has been infringed by interpreting the protections that a particular constitutional right affords in relation to its underlying purpose, securing the human dignity of those subject to law's authority. The second concerns whether the limitation pursues the kind of objective that can justify the infringement of a constitutional right, that is, an objective integral to the maintenance and refinement of a legal order committed to fulfilling the human dignity of all who are subject to its authority. If one of these preconditions remains unsatisfied, then proportionality lacks its condition of application: either no constitutional right has been infringed (which means that there is nothing to justify) or the infringement furthers an illicit objective (which means that no justification is possible). Alternately, if both of these conditions are satisfied, then commensurability obtains between the rights and limits to which the doctrine of proportionality applies. Constitutional rights and the objectives for which they may be justifiably limited are not discrete considerations, but specifications of a legal system's internal ideal of human dignity

[98] Alexy, *A Theory of Constitutional Rights*, 401–10; Matthias Klatt and Moritz Meister, *The Constitutional Structure of Proportionality* (Oxford: Oxford University Press, 2012), 58–66; Möller, "Proportionality: Challenging the Critics," 719–24; Paul-Erik N. Veel, "Incommensurability, Proportionality, and Rational Legal Decision-Making," *Law and Ethics of Human Rights* 4 (2010): 180; and especially Silva, "Comparing the Incommensurable: Constitutional Principles, Balancing, and Rational Decision," 301.

under law. The claim that proportionality involves the balancing of incommensurables overlooks the preconditions of the doctrine's application.[99]

This understanding is evident in the jurisprudence of Chief Justice Dickson. In introducing proportionality into Canadian constitutional jurisprudence, he proceeded from the text of Canada's limitation clause: 'The *Canadian Charter of Rights and Freedoms* guarantees the rights and freedoms set out in it subject only to such reasonable limits prescribed by law as can be demonstrably justified in a free and democratic society.'[100] Within this provision, the Chief Justice argued, the 'underlying values of a free and democratic society'[101] have a 'dual function.'[102] As he put the point in *R.* v. *Oakes*, the seminal Canadian case on the limitation of constitutional rights:

> The underlying values and principles of a free and democratic society are the genesis of the rights and freedoms guaranteed by the *Charter* and the ultimate standard against which a limit on a right or freedom must be shown, despite its effect, to be reasonable and demonstrably justified.[103]

For the Chief Justice, rights and justified limits are instances of a common set of constitutional values.[104] These values provide the touchstone for

[99] See, for example, Endicott, "Proportionality and Incommensurability." Endicott's focus is on administrative cases in the United Kingdom that involve a conflict between two discrete particulars, the right to family and private life, on one hand, and the public objective of deportation, on the other. Endicott offers neither an account of whether the rights in the *European Convention for the Protection of Human Rights and Fundamental Freedoms* instantiate a common norm regarding the relationship between collective force and individual freedom, nor an account of the kind of objectives for which rights may be justifiably limited. After bypassing these aspects of the analysis, Endicott asserts that proportionality involves balancing the unbalanceable. My argument moves in the opposite direction. Instead of looking to a particular conflict and then asking whether the right and the limit happen to instantiate a common norm, I begin by formulating the duty of the state to reconcile public authority with human dignity, and then explain how constitutional rights and admissible bases of limitation specify this duty. This theoretical approach finds its doctrinal reflection in the purposive interpretation of rights and the obligatory objective requirement. When this doctrinal methodology is followed, the commensurability of rights and limits is established prior to the application of the proportionality subtests. Proportionality, then, presupposes commensurability.

[100] *Canadian Charter of Rights and Freedoms*, s. 1, Part I of the Constitution Act, 1982, being Schedule B to the Canada Act 1982 (U.K.), 1982, c. 11, s. 1 [hereinafter *Charter*].

[101] *Slaight Communications Inc.* v. *Davidson*, [1989] 1 SCR 1038, 1056.

[102] *R.* v. *Keegstra* [1990] 3 SCR 697, 736. [103] *R.* v. *Oakes*, 136.

[104] Ibid. See also *Canada (Human Rights Commission)* v. *Taylor*, per Dickson C.J.: 'What is of utmost importance is a recognition that s. 1 both guarantees and limits Charter rights and freedoms by reference to principles fundamental in a free and democratic society.'

assessing both the extent to which a constitutional right is infringed and the significance of the countervailing objective. As I noted in the prior section, when the Chief Justice reached the proportionality *stricto sensu* stage in *R.* v. *Keegstra*, he held that the infringement was justified because hateful expression is 'only tenuously connected with the values underlying the guarantee of freedom of speech,' while the limitation made a contribution to bolstering equality, which is 'central to the concept of a free and democratic society.'[105] Thus, the limitation of freedom of expression was required by that right's underlying basis.

Alexy might deny that the unified theory of public law offers a competing conception of proportionality. On his view, proportionality is a structure that can be 'filled with moral arguments and considerations of weight and value that vary directly according to different perspectives.'[106] The unified theory is a substantive moral theory that directs the structure of proportionality to the fulfillment of human dignity. Accordingly, Alexy might conclude, the unified theory offers a way of *applying* the doctrine that he formulates, but it does not represent an alternative to it.

The claim that Alexy's structure can absorb the unified theory's conception of proportionality is mistaken for two reasons. The first concerns the structure of proportionality, while the second concerns that structure's moral significance.

First, from the standpoint of the conception of proportionality that I have elaborated, the structure of the doctrine that Alexy articulates is itself objectionable. Consider Alexy's account of the final stage of the analysis, proportionality *stricto sensu*:

> The principle of proportionality in the narrow sense as the third subprinciple of proportionality expresses the meaning of optimization relative to competing principles. It is identical with the Law of Balancing. This states: "The greater the degree of non-satisfaction of, or detriment to, one principle, the greater must be the importance of satisfying the other." This expresses the point that optimization relative to competing principles consists of nothing other than balancing.
>
> The Law of Balancing shows that balancing can be broken down into three stages. The first stage involves establishing the degree of non-satisfaction of, or detriment to, the first principle. This is followed by a second stage in which the importance of satisfying the competing principle is established. Finally, the third stage establishes whether the importance of satisfying the

[105] *R.* v. *Keegstra*, 787.

[106] Klatt and Meister, *The Constitutional Structure of Proportionality*, 56.

> competing principle justifies the detriment to, or non-satisfaction of, the first.[107]

For Alexy, proportionality *stricto sensu* calls for the optimization of the discrete principles that stand in a relation of opposition. The conception of proportionality that stems from the unified theory of public law culminates in a contrasting account. As I have argued, constitutional conflicts obtain not between competing particulars that must be optimized, but between conflicting determinations of an underlying norm. When such conflicts arise, the severity of the infringement to the constitutional right and the significance of the countervailing objective must be considered from the standpoint of the ideal that each instantiates. The duty of government is not to optimize each principle on its own terms, as in Alexy's Law of Balancing, but the underlying norm that each instantiates. Insofar as the Law of Balancing refers only to the competing principles and makes no reference to the underlying norm that each instantiates, it does not capture the understanding of proportionality *stricto sensu* that emerges from the unified theory.[108] Thus, the disagreement between these conceptions goes to the very structure of proportionality itself.[109]

[107] Alexy, *A Theory of Constitutional Rights*, 401.

[108] In an article published after a *Theory of Constitutional Rights*, Alexy suggests that the relative importance of two competing principles can be determined by looking to the 'common point of view' provided in the relevant constitution. Alexy, "On Balancing and Subsumption. A Structural Comparison," *Ratio Juris* 16 (2003): 442. If what is to be optimized is the common standpoint that each principle instantiates rather than each discrete principle on its own terms, then the Law of Balancing must be reformulated. However, in this article, the formulation of the Law of Balancing is identical to the one that appears in *A Theory of Constitutional Rights*. Ibid. 436–7 (introducing the Law of Balancing by quoting directly from *A Theory of Constitutional Rights*).

[109] The distinction between these understandings of proportionality's final subtest has significant ramifications for constitutional adjudication because laws infringing constitutional rights might stand or fall depending on how proportionality *stricto sensu* is conceptualized. Compare Chief Justice Dickson's judgment for the majority of the Supreme Court of Canada in *R.* v. *Keegstra* with the dissent of Justice McLachlin (as she then was). Whereas Chief Justice Dickson conceived of both the right and the limitation as instances of the legal order's commitment to realize a free and democratic society, Justice McLachlin conceived of both the right and the limitation as discrete values to be balanced directly against one another. Echoing Alexy's Law of Balancing, she explains that proportionality *stricto sensu* requires 'balancing the invasion of rights ... against the objective to which the limitation of those rights is directed.' Ibid. 846. When Justice McLachlin considers the severity of the infringement of freedom of expression in abstraction from the values of a free and democratic society, she deems the hateful character of the expression at issue to be of no significance in the proportionality analysis. Consequently, where Chief Justice Dickson finds the extent of the infringement

Second, in advancing a structural conception of proportionality, Alexy defends the view that proportionality is amoral and that the valuation of the competing principles requires an appeal to some extrinsic conception of morality. Instead of identifying a particular moral aim and then conscripting the doctrine of proportionality to advance it, my argument has expounded the moral significance of each of the conditions that precede and comprise the doctrine itself. Far from being an amoral structure, proportionality distills the doctrinal implications of a legal system's duty to conform to the demands of dignity in cases of constitutional conflict. If morality has something to say about the conditions that precede and form the doctrine of proportionality (in addition to what morality might say about the valuation of particular principles that stand in opposition), then proportionality itself has a moral structure. And if proportionality has a moral structure, that structure cannot be captured by an amoral (or structural) account.

Critics often dismiss the doctrine of proportionality as immoral and irrational. These objections merit the same response: even if they succeed against a structural conception of proportionality, they fail to offer a reason for rejecting the doctrine. For it remains possible to formulate a conception to which these objections do not apply. In developing the view that proportionality involves conflicts between instances of a common moral ideal, this chapter fleshes out that possibility.

7.4 Rights as trumps: an alternative?

Defenders and critics of proportionality often present Ronald Dworkin's rights as trumps model as a radical alternative to the doctrine.[110] This section considers the relationship between these approaches and argues

to be slight because the freedom to engage in hateful expression is antithetical to the values of a free and democratic society premised on the dignity of each of its members, Justice McLachlin holds that the infringement is severe because it imposes a content-based restriction on free expression. Having characterized the cost of the infringement as severe, McLachlin held that the infringement would not have survived the proportionality *stricto sensu* subtest.

110 See, for example, Alison L. Young, "Proportionality is Dead: Long Live Proportionality," 48; Barak, *Proportionality: Constitutional Rights and Their Limitations*, 365; Webber, *The Negotiable Constitution: On the Limitation of Rights*, 117; Neomi Rao, "On the Use and Abuse of Dignity in Constitutional Law," 238; Tsakyrakis, "Proportionality: An Assault on Human Rights," 489; Kai Möller, "Balancing and the Structure of Constitutional Rights," *International Journal of Constitutional Law* 5 (2007): 460; Mattias Kumm, "Constitutional Rights as Principles," 590–2; and Réaume, "Limitations on Constitutional Rights: The Logic of Proportionality."

that this view is mistaken. The rights as trumps model is not an alternative to proportionality, but an inchoate version of it. Thus, opponents of proportionality must look elsewhere for an ally. In what follows, I abstract from debates about how best to understand the evolution and unity of Dworkin's theory (or theories) of rights[111] and focus instead on his understanding of the conditions that justify the infringement of a right.

The rights as trumps model proceeds from the simple and appealing idea that fundamental rights have an elevated status with respect to collective goals asserted in the name of the public interest, utility, popular preference, nonprohibitive cost, or administrative convenience. As Dworkin puts the point, 'Individuals have rights when, for some reason, a collective goal is not a sufficient justification for denying them what they wish, as individuals, to have or to do, or not a sufficient justification for imposing some loss or injury on them.'[112] Instead of conceiving of rights as the freedom that remains after the government has enacted collective goals, Dworkin invites his readers to understand rights as limits on the pursuit of collective goals. To suppose otherwise, he insists, is to abandon the idea that the rights of individuals can constrain the conduct of their government.[113]

Once rights are understood in this way, the temptation to balance fundamental rights against collective goals must be resisted.[114] For if the nature of a right is that it overrides a collective goal, then rights and goals do not compete with one another on a common plane. Instead, any instance of a fundamental right prevails over any instance of a collective goal. Even in cases in which the marginal infringement of a right would

[111] For critical discussions of Dworkin's treatments of the nature and justification of rights, see, for example, Richard H. Pildes, "Dworkin's Two Conceptions of Rights," *Journal of Legal Studies* 29 (2000): 309–15 (distinguishing between rights as immunities that shield individuals from the preferences of the majority and rights as constraining the kind of reasons for which the majority may infringe individual interests); Paul Yowell, "Critical Examination of Dworkin's Theory of Rights," *American Journal of Jurisprudence* 52 (2007): 93–137 (distinguishing and emphasizing the incongruity between understanding rights as protecting shielded-interests and excluding external preferences); and Donald H. Regan, "Glosses on Dworkin: Rights, Principles, and Policies," *Michigan Law Review* 76 (1978): 1221 (identifying Dworkin's 'essays on external preferences as interesting digressions from the main current of' his theory of rights). For an interpretation that seeks to introduce greater consistency into Dworkin's theorizing on rights by aligning it solely with the constraint against appeals to external preferences, see Jeremy Waldron, "Pildes on Dworkin's Theory of Rights," *Journal of Legal Studies* 29 (2000): 301–7.

[112] *Taking Rights Seriously*, xi. [113] Ibid. 194.

[114] Ibid. 197–8. See also Ronald Dworkin, *A Bill of Rights for Britain* (London: Chatto & Windus, 1990), 10; Ronald Dworkin, *Is Democracy Possible Here? Principles for a New Political Debate* (Princeton: Princeton University Press, 2006), 27.

make a significant contribution to a collective goal, the enjoyment of the right may not be curtailed. Collective goals might violate rights, but there can be no conflict between them.

Critics of proportionality often appeal to the rights as trumps model in arguing that the doctrine fails to take rights seriously.[115] A right overrides other interests, including those that advance society's collective goals. In the eyes of its critics, proportionality balances rights against these very considerations. Thus, the doctrine reveals itself as – to borrow a phrase from Dworkin – 'a confusion that threatens to destroy the concept of individual rights.'[116]

Not all conceptions of proportionality are vulnerable to this objection. The thesis that rights trump collective goals of policy, preference, utility, nonprohibitive cost, or administrative convenience simply echoes the obligatory objective condition, articulated earlier. A constitutional right may not be justifiably limited for the sake of furthering 'objectives which are trivial or discordant with the principles of a free and democratic society.'[117] On this point, proponents of the rights as trumps model and proportionality may stand in agreement. The shared claim is not that rights typically outweigh such objectives, but that because such objectives are incapable of justifying the infringement of a right, a right cannot be balanced against them.

That rights trump certain kinds of considerations does not mean that rights cannot themselves be trumped. Thus, Dworkin claims that limits on freedom demand 'some special justification more powerful or compelling than the justification' that government must provide for 'other political decisions.'[118] In *Taking Rights Seriously*, he delineates the grounds on which rights may be justifiably constrained:

> I must not overstate the point. Someone who claims that citizens have a right against the Government need not go so far as to say that the State is *never* justified in overriding that right. He might say, for example, that although citizens have a right to free speech, the Government may override that right when necessary to protect the rights of others, or to prevent a catastrophe . . . What he cannot do is to say that Government is justified in overriding a right on the minimal grounds that would be sufficient if no

115 See, for example, Alison L. Young, "Proportionality is Dead: Long Live Proportionality," 48; Webber, *The Negotiable Constitution: On the Limitation of Rights*, 117; Neomi Rao, "On the Use and Abuse of Dignity in Constitutional Law," 238; and Tsakyrakis, "Proportionality: An Assault on Human Rights," 489.

116 *Taking Rights Seriously*, 199. 117 *R. v. Oakes*, 138–9.

118 *Sovereign Virtue: The Theory and Practice of Equality* (Cambridge: Harvard University Press, 2002), 127.

> such right existed. He cannot say that the Government is entitled to act on no more than a judgment that its act is likely to produce, overall, a benefit to the community. That admission would make his claim of a right pointless . . .[119]

For Dworkin, rights trump a range of subordinate considerations, but can nevertheless be constrained when a trump appears on the opposing side of the dispute. In these cases, a right might conflict with another right or with some goal of 'special urgency.'[120]

Dworkin's example of competing rights involves the law of defamation. In this domain, the fundamental right of free speech is limited in order to protect the 'right of others not to have their reputations ruined by a careless statement.'[121] Dworkin is adamant that defamation is not an isolated example: 'The individual rights that our society acknowledges often conflict in this way, and when they do it is the job of government to discriminate.'[122] Further, he holds that when considerations of this kind are in play, balancing is unobjectionable: '"Balancing" is appropriate when the Government must choose between competing claims of right.'[123]

Dworkin also accepts that there are objectives for which fundamental rights may be justifiably limited. He emphasizes that the 'ordinary routine goals of political administration' cannot justify a limitation – otherwise the claim that rights are trumps would be meaningless.[124] Dworkin characterizes an objective for which rights can be justifiably limited as a 'compelling reason' that 'is consistent with the suppositions on which the original right must be based.'[125] He explains that these suppositions concern 'the vague but powerful idea of human dignity' or 'the more familiar idea of political equality.'[126] Thus, Dworkin's claim is that the only kind of purpose capable of justifying the limitation of a particular fundamental right is one that coheres to the general normative basis on which all fundamental rights rest. His standard example of such a purpose is an emergency:

> A right may be regarded as a trump, moreover, even though it might not trump the general good in cases of emergency: when the competing interests are grave and urgent, as they might be when large numbers of

119 *Taking Rights Seriously*, 191–2. 120 Ibid., 92. 121 Ibid., 193. 122 Ibid.
123 Ibid., 199. 124 Ibid., 92.
125 Ibid., 200. On this point, see François du Bois, "Rights Trumped? Balancing in Constitutional Adjudication," *Acta Juridica* (2004): 160–1.
126 *Taking Rights Seriously*, 198. I contrast Dworkin's conception of human dignity with the one that I have elaborated in this book's conclusion.

> lives or the survival of a state is in question. Then, we might say, the trump gets trumped not by an ordinary justification but by a higher trump.[127]

On this point, the rights as trumps model is in lockstep with the doctrine of proportionality, as formulated in this chapter. Although there are a range of considerations that are incapable of justifying the limitation of rights, rights are not absolute. When the objective of the infringement stems from the underlying basis of the right, the justification of a limitation is possible.

A familiar question now resurfaces: What is the duty of government with respect to cases in which a trump is present on each side of the dispute? Distancing himself from the view that the presence of a conflict gives the government license to infringe any right to any extent,[128] Dworkin claims that the state acts contemptuously toward dignity and equality if it requires some to suffer a severe constraint on rights so that 'other men's risk of loss may be marginally reduced. If rights make sense, then the degrees of their importance cannot be so different that some count not at all when others are mentioned.'[129] In other words, Dworkin rejects the view that rights stand in a hierarchy in which some must always cede to others regardless of the extent of their relative infringements. Instead, he holds that when government is confronted by clashing rights, it must make the 'right choice' by protecting the 'more important of the two.'[130] But what is the standard for evaluating which is more important? Dworkin's answer seems to be that all fundamental rights and all admissible bases of limitation are instances of the state's general duty to protect dignity and equality.[131] Thus, the severity of a rights infringement and the importance of the countervailing objective must be considered from this common standpoint. A limitation is justified in those cases in which it serves the suppositions on which the right itself rests. Thus, it seems that the rights as trumps model elides with the normative architecture of the doctrine of proportionality.

[127] *Justice for Hedgehogs* (Cambridge: Harvard University Press, 2011), 473. See also *Sovereign Virtue: The Theory and Practice of Equality*, 127; and *Is Democracy Possible Here? Principles for a New Political Debate*, 50.

[128] *Taking Rights Seriously*, 203: 'Shall we say that some rights to protection are so important that the Government is justified in doing all it can to maintain them? Shall we therefore say that the Government may abridge the rights of others to act when their acts might simply increase the risk, by however slight or speculative a margin, that some person's right to life or property will be violated? ... [N]o society that purports to recognize a variety of rights, on the ground that a man's dignity or equality may be invaded in a variety of ways, can accept such a principle.'

[129] Ibid., 203–4. [130] Ibid., 194. [131] Ibid., 198.

To my knowledge, Dworkin nowhere explicitly discusses the doctrine of proportionality. When he encounters limitation clauses in human rights documents, he dismisses them as the product of 'political compromises' required to attract the assent of hesitant countries.[132] Nevertheless, Dworkin does consider cases in which he acknowledges that a conflict obtains between trumps, whether between rights or between a right and some appropriate objective.[133] And when he does, he reiterates the conditions that form the doctrine of proportionality. He echoes the rational connection requirement by insisting that if the relationship between the purpose that the law pursues and the rights-infringing means that it employs is one of mere 'speculation,' then rights are not taken seriously.[134] He echoes the minimal impairment requirement when he claims that the government 'may stop a man from exercising his right to speak when there is a clear and substantial risk that his speech will do great damage to the person or property of others, and *no other means of preventing this are at hand*, as in the case of the man shouting "Fire!" in a theater.'[135] And he echoes the proportionality *stricto sensu*

[132] *Is Democracy Possible Here? Principles for a New Political Debate*, 49

[133] I therefore reject the claim that Dworkin's rights as trumps model 'leaves no room for the possibility of conflicts that postulate the existence of two non-utilitarian arguments opposing each other.' See Zucca, *Constitutional Dilemmas: Conflicts of Fundamental Legal Rights in Europe and the USA*, xii. However, Dworkin does exhibit an eagerness to avoid the complexities of constitutional conflicts by acknowledging the presence of a right on one side of a dispute, while insisting that only considerations of popular preference lie on the other. Thus, his account of the right to pornography has been criticized for pitting freedom of speech against the community preferences that seek to silence it in order to avoid disgust or discomfort that such materials elicit. Dworkin thereby overlooks the possibility of a 'rights-based argument against pornography . . . As a rule, when he raises the possibility of any link between pornography and harm to women of a concrete and familiar sort, he fails to take it seriously.' Rae Langton, "Whose Right? Dworkin, Women and the Pornographers," *Philosophy & Public Affairs* 19 (1990): 326–7. Just as Dworkin avoids considering rights-based arguments for limiting the right to pornography, so too he avoids rights-based arguments for prohibiting hate speech. Restrictions on hate speech are generally motivated 'by concern for the rights of victims of hate speech not to be harmed unjustly by it, rather than, as Dworkin assumes, by moral disapproval of those who engage in, or willingly listen to, such speech.' Susan J. Brison, "The Autonomy Defense of Free Speech," *Ethics* 108 (1998): 325. Dworkin's discussion of hate speech recognizes the rights-claim of the speaker, but reduces rights-based arguments for restricting speech into nothing more than censorship for the sake of popular preference. Perhaps a similar charge could be raised against Dworkin's writings on affirmative action, but I cannot pursue this point here.

[134] Ronald Dworkin, *Life's Dominion: An Argument about Abortion, Euthanasia, and Individual Freedom* (New York: Alfred A. Knopf: 1993), 115. See also *Taking Rights Seriously*, 195; and *Is Democracy Possible Here? Principles for a New Political Debate*, 50.

[135] *Taking Rights Seriously*, 204 (my emphasis).

requirement when he adverts, in the terrorism context, to the wrongfulness of supposing 'that any act that improves our own security, no matter how marginally, is for that reason justified.'[136] Finally, he suggests that 'government should bear the onus of demonstrating that *any* interference with *any* part of the fundamental liberties is really necessary to secure some essential goal.'[137]

The doctrine of proportionality takes the various considerations to which Dworkin appeals in reasoning about the moral complexity of constitutional conflicts, and orders them into a sequence of conditions that government must satisfy to justify the limitation of a constitutional right. The result is that the doctrine of proportionality coheres with the rights as trumps model but offers doctrinal guidance that the model lacks. Accordingly, when critics of proportionality claim that the doctrine should be abandoned and replaced with Dworkin's model, they thereby affirm an inchoate version of the very position that they repudiate. As the legal practice of constitutional states around the world converges on proportionality, its critics have failed to unite around a shared alternative.

Conclusion

Proportionality is often understood as a doctrine that introduces exceptions to the constitutional order's commitment to uphold human dignity and fundamental rights. From this standpoint, proportionality stands in opposition to the modern constitutional project's aim of making human dignity and fundamental rights a justiciable constraint on state conduct. This chapter expounds and defends an opposing conception of proportionality. The distinguishing feature of this conception is that it generates each of the conditions that precede and comprise the doctrine from the overarching duty of a legal system to govern in conformity with dignity's demands. The doctrine of proportionality does not dilute this duty, but rather sets out the conditions for assessing government's conformity to it in cases in which the determinations of dignity conflict.

This book began with a skeptical challenge to modern constitutional practice. The challenge alleged that human dignity 'does not provide a universalistic, principled basis for judicial decision-making in the human

[136] *Is Democracy Possible Here? Principles for a New Political Debate*, 50.
[137] *A Bill of Rights for Britain*, 11.

rights context.'[138] This chapter concludes a sustained response to this challenge. By attending to the systematic implications of human dignity as equal freedom, a unified theory of the normative, constitutional, and doctrinal dimensions of public law emerges. As a matter of the normative dimension, public law is constituted and regulated by principles that establish the rights and duties of rulers and ruled. As a matter of the constitutional dimension, these principles demand the creation, maintenance, and refinement of a modern constitutional form of governance in which human dignity forms a justiciable constraint on the exercise of all public authority. As a matter of the doctrinal dimension, these principles demand the development of doctrines that connect the normative and constitutional dimensions to legal disputes surrounding, for example, constitutional amendments and the adjudication of constitutional rights. By attending to the implications of the concept of human dignity, the unified theory of public law justifies the doctrines that modern constitutional states employ in responding to these kinds of disputes. The concrete meaning of the concept of human dignity emerges not from applying the concept directly to a legal dispute, but by attending to the considerations apposite to the dimension that the dispute engages.

[138] "Human Dignity and Judicial Interpretation of Human Rights," *European Journal of International Law* 19 (2008): 655. See also McCrudden, ed., *Understanding Human Dignity* (Oxford: Oxford University Press, 2013), xi.

Conclusion

Public law in postwar theory and practice

In the decades since World War II, the theory and practice of public law have undergone a dramatic transformation. As a matter of legal theory, H.L.A. Hart's rejuvenation of legal positivism in the Anglo-American world motivated novel forms of nonpositivist thought, from Lon Fuller's conception of law's internal morality to Ronald Dworkin's interpretive model of adjudication. The result is that the classical problems of legal philosophy are now debated, in large part, from the standpoint of theoretical frameworks unknown to earlier generations. The practice of public law has undergone a similarly profound reorientation. Since the end of World War II, a diverse and growing number of states from around the world have converged on a versatile new model of constitutional ordering. The purpose of this modern constitutional paradigm is to establish the legal, institutional, and doctrinal conditions in which human dignity and fundamental rights form a justiciable constraint on all public power. The comparative constitutionalist Mauro Cappelletti characterized the 'unprecedented character of this ongoing development' as 'perhaps, the most phenomenal societal transformation trend that has ever occurred in human history.'[1]

When the postwar innovations in the theory and practice of public law are considered side by side, a puzzle emerges. While legal theory is often conceived of as an attempt to explain the fundamental ideas that structure and animate legal practice, the foremost legal theories of the postwar period are neither inspired by nor responsive to the emergence of modern constitutional practices. When Hart considers features of the American constitutional order that conform to this paradigm, he dismisses them as legal eccentricities that are confined to the singular case of

[1] Mauro Cappelletti, "Repudiating Montesquieu? The Expansion and Legitimacy of 'Constitutional Justice,'" *Catholic University Law Review* 35 (1986): 29–30.

the United States and that are, in any event, 'particularly hard to justify in a democracy.'[2] Fuller regards the institutional arrangements and substantive commitments of the modern constitutional state as needless because the ideal of legality that he defends can be fully satisfied in their absence. Dworkin's emphasis on individual rights and constitutional adjudication brings him into closer proximity with the modern constitutionalism paradigm, but he makes significant departures from the paradigm in the normative, institutional, and doctrinal dimensions of his project. The disjunction between the postwar theory and practice of public law raises the question: Why did public law's most innovative theorists regard the innovations in the postwar practice of public law as unacceptable, unnecessary, or as unworthy of theoretical exploration? More generally, is there some shared feature of these theories that left their originators unable to discern or appreciate the significance of the radical developments in governance that were emerging in their day?

I begin by discussing how Hart, Fuller, and Dworkin conceived of core components of modern constitutional practice, such as constitutional supremacy, the entrenchment of constitutional rights, and judicial review. I then argue that the reason why these theorists overlooked the groundbreaking significance of modern constitutional practices is systematic rather than incidental. Modern constitutionalism is a response to a fundamental problem inherent in the structure of public law. This problem concerns the interrelationship between the most basic aspects of a legal system: public authority and public justice. So long as their character and interrelation is not evident, the problem to which modern constitutionalism responds remains invisible. By sidestepping the fundamental theoretical problem in public law, the leading postwar legal theorists deprived themselves of the resources to appreciate the practices developing in the world around them.

Hart's essay, "American Jurisprudence through English Eyes: The Nightmare and the Noble Dream," appeared in 1977,[3] in the aftermath of the Warren Court's (ultimately unsuccessful) attempt to bring the United States into accord with the doctrinal commitments of the modern constitutional paradigm.[4] Hart explains that from the perspective of an

[2] Hart, "American Jurisprudence through English Eyes: The Nightmare and the Noble Dream," in *Essays in Jurisprudence and Philosophy* (Oxford: Oxford University Press, 1983), 125.

[3] *Essays in Jurisprudence and Philosophy* (Oxford: Oxford University Press, 1983).

[4] On the divergences that separate the modern constitutional paradigm from American understanding and doctrine, see Dieter Grimm, "German and American

English lawyer, the striking feature of the American legal system is the Supreme Court, which has 'a role and a status unlike that of any English court and indeed unlike any courts anywhere.'[5] The American Supreme Court enjoys the right to invalidate legislation, whether enacted by Congress or by state legislatures. Further, the grounds on which legislation may be invalidated extend from considerations of 'form or procedure' to the

> content of legislation, so that, to an English lawyer's astonishment, even a statute of Congress of impeccable clarity, passed by an overwhelming majority and conforming to all procedural requirements specified in the constitution, might still be held invalid because its interference with individual liberty or with property did not satisfy the requirement of a vague undefined standard of reasonableness or desirability, a doctrine which came to be called "substantive due process."[6]

Hart notes that the practice of exercising judicial review on substantive grounds has cast 'the American courts afloat on a sea of controversial moral judgments.'[7] Such a practice stands in need of justification both because it is 'something very different from what conventional legal thought in all countries conceives as the standard judicial function' and because the practice 'seems to the English lawyer' difficult to reconcile with democratic governance.[8]

In claiming that the United States alone enables courts to strike down legislation on the basis of its conformity to substantive norms, Hart indicates his unfamiliarity with the constitutional practices materializing in the world around him. As Cappelletti observed in his 1971 work, *Judicial Review in the Contemporary World*,

> Our own time has seen the burgeoning of "constitutional justice," which has in a sense combined the forms of legal justice and the substance of natural justice. Desirous of protecting the permanent will rather than the temporary whims of the people, many modern states have reasserted higher law principles through written constitutions. Thus there has been a synthesis of three separate concerns: the supremacy of certain higher law

Constitutionalism: A Comparison," *The Berlin Journal* 7 (2003): 8–14. Although the divergences that Grimm discerns in American constitutional jurisprudence are significant, they operate largely at the doctrinal dimension. Accordingly, what is needed to bring the United States into accordance with the modern constitutional paradigm is a shift in constitutional philosophy and judicial doctrine as opposed to a formal amendment of the constitution. I cannot elaborate on this important issue here.

5 Ibid., 124. 6 Ibid., 124–5. 7 Ibid., 125.

8 Ibid. I respond to the objection that modern constitutionalism is undemocratic in Chapter 5; Part IV.

> principles, the need to put even the higher law in written form, and the employment of the judiciary as a tool for enforcing the constitution against ordinary legislation. This union of concepts first occurred in the United States, but it has since come to be considered by many as essential to the rule of law (*Rechtsstaat*) anywhere.[9]

The constitutional innovations that Hart found so conspicuous in the United States had, since the end of World War II, become commonplace features of the postwar practice of public law. Within a handful of years after World War II, Austria, Germany, and Italy adopted written constitutions that bound all branches of government, placed substantive constraints on the amendment process, entrenched a bill of rights to regulate the relationship between the individual and state power, and established an independent judicial body to make constitutional norms justiciable.[10] By the time Hart observed the singularity of the Warren Court, modern constitutionalism had spread to Greece and Portugal and was influencing Eastern European reformers.[11] While Hart seems to be generally unaware of these broader developments, he does not seem, in principle, to oppose them. In discussing the judicial powers of American courts, Hart is content to ask how these developments are compatible with democratic governance and whether there is a 'general conception of the nature of law' that is compatible with them.[12]

Hart displays a similar ambivalence when he turns his attention to human rights. He acknowledges

> that a theory of right is urgently called for. During the last half century man's inhumanity to man has been such that the most basic and elementary freedoms and protections have been denied to innumerable men and women guilty, if of anything, only of claiming such freedoms and protections for themselves and others, and sometimes these have been denied to them on the specious pretence that this denial is demanded by the general welfare of a society. So the protection of a doctrine of basic human rights limiting what a state may do to its citizens seems to be precisely what the political problems of our age most urgently require, or at any rate they require this more urgently than a call to maximise general utility . . . The doctrine of human rights has at least temporarily replaced the doctrine of maximizing utilitarianism as the prime philosophical inspiration of political and social reform.[13]

9 (New York: Bobbs-Merrill, 1971), 42.
10 Cappelletti, "Repudiating Montesquieu? The Expansion and Legitimacy of 'Constitutional Justice,'" 5–6.
11 Ibid., 7–8.
12 *Essays in Jurisprudence and Philosophy*, 125.
13 Ibid., 196–7

Hart emphasizes the need for rights-based theories of government, but he also adds that the 'revived doctrines of basic rights, as currently presented, are in spite of much brilliance still unconvincing.'[14] Whether considering the substantive commitments or the constitutional structure of modern constitutional states, the leading legal theorist of his day found himself without a theory.

Fuller too viewed the emergence of modern constitutionalism with suspicion, but in his case the suspicion was rooted not in the disorienting features of a foreign practice, but in the commitments of his own legal theory. For Fuller, 'law is the enterprise of subjecting human conduct to the governance of rules.'[15] If human conduct is to be subject to the governance of rules, then those rules must be, at least to some extent, (1) general, (2) public, (3) prospective, (4) clear, (5) noncontradictory, (6) possible to obey, (7) constant in time, and (8) congruent with official action.[16] These requirements form a procedural ideal of legality, which Fuller calls the *internal morality of law*.

Fuller's procedural ideal of legality is indifferent to the substantive commitments of the modern constitutional state. In elaborating the procedural character of his legal ideal, Fuller explains that the internal morality of law 'is, over a wide range of issues, indifferent toward the substantive aims of law and is ready to serve a variety of such aims with equal efficacy.'[17] He notes that the internal morality of law has nothing to say about whether contraception should be prohibited[18] or even about the 'subjugation of women.'[19] The same cannot be said about modern constitutionalism, which directs all public authority toward a substantive aim, the realization of a legal system adequate to the dignity of each of its free and equal inhabitants.

Fuller could respond that his legal theory nevertheless shares the fundamental commitment of modern constitutionalism, that legal ordering must answer to the human dignity of those who are bound by the rules it promulgates:

> I have repeatedly observed that legal morality can be said to be neutral over a wide range of ethical issues. It cannot be neutral in its view of man himself. To embark on the enterprise of subjecting human conduct to the governance of rules involves of necessity a commitment to the view that man is, or can become, a responsible agent, capable of understanding and following rules, and answerable for his defaults. Every departure from the

[14] Ibid., 195.
[15] *The Morality of Law* (New Haven: Yale University Press, 1994), 96 and 106.
[16] Ibid., 39. [17] Ibid., 153. [18] Ibid. [19] Ibid., 96.

> principles of the law's inner morality is an affront to man's dignity as a responsible agent.[20]

Although Fuller embraces the term *human dignity*, he attributes his own distinctive meaning to it. For Fuller, dignity consists in the capacity of an agent to be subject to the governance of rules. The duty incumbent on government is to respect the capacity for agency by enacting rules that conform to the procedural principles that make up the internal morality of law.[21] From the standpoint of modern constitutional jurisprudence, Fuller's theory of the rule of law captures one aspect of dignity but overlooks another. As I have argued, human dignity involves not simply the capacity to be subject to *duties* imposed through the promulgation of authoritative legal rules. In the relationship between rulers and ruled, human dignity also involves the *right* of persons to be governed in accordance with norms of equal freedom. By making the satisfaction of this right the condition for the valid exercise of public authority, a modern constitutional state repudiates substantive aims that are fully compatible with Fuller's ideal of legality. Modes of legal ordering that deny the equality of persons on the basis of their gender or that impose arbitrary restrictions on freedom violate the right of persons to just governance. Accordingly, within a modern constitutional state, such arrangements cannot be valid.[22]

Given that Fuller's ideal of legality can be satisfied by laws and legal systems that pursue a range of substantive aims through a variety of lawgiving processes, democratic and otherwise, one would expect Fuller to hold that the internal morality of law sets out an ideal of legality that neither requires constitutional rights protection nor democratic modes of lawgiving, but is nevertheless compatible with them. Surprisingly, this is not the position that he adopts. In his reply to Hart, Fuller mentions that substantive norms may be enacted into ordinary statutes, but should be excluded from a written constitution in societies 'emerging from a period of violence.'[23] Fuller thus laments that the 'constitutions that have come into existence since World War II' typically 'incorporate a host of

[20] Ibid., 162. [21] Ibid., 40.

[22] For a discussion acknowledging the differing normative demands of modern constitutional states and Fuller's internal morality of law, see David Dyzenhaus, "The Juristic Force of Injustice," in *Calling Power to Account: Law, Reparations and the Chinese Head Tax*, ed. Dyzenhaus and Mayo Moran (Toronto: University of Toronto Press, 2005), 264 and 280–1.

[23] Fuller, "Positivism and Fidelity to Law – A Reply to Professor Hart," *Harvard Law Review* 71 (1958): 642.

economic and political measures.'[24] While the measures to which he refers are not entirely clear, the legal context suggests that what is at issue are constitutional provisions protecting socioeconomic rights and the democratic character of the constitutional order. Fuller seems to find such measures objectionable because he suspects that these substantive aims have been inserted into the constitution not because they are generally affirmed but because 'they would not be able to survive the vicissitudes of an ordinary exercise of parliamentary power.'[25] The danger that Fuller sees in the constitutional entrenchment of substantive aims that are not generally affirmed is that the internal morality of law requires congruence between legal rules and official action. But if the people who must effectuate the constitution are not committed to its substantive aims, discrepancies between rule and official action might emerge.

In *The Morality of Law*, Fuller extends his opposition to substantive constitutional norms beyond the special case of societies emerging from periods of violence. In discussing the American Constitution, he recognizes that it entrenches substantive norms but suggests that judges should avoid appealing to them in reviewing the constitutionality of legislation.[26] It is striking that having formulated a legal ideal that insists upon the importance of congruity between legal rule and official action, Fuller holds that judges should avoid invalidating legislation on the basis of its failure to conform to substantive norms entrenched within the constitution. His discussions of constitutionalism reveal a general indifference toward the substantive aims of law and a particular hostility to the inclusion of substantive aims in written constitutions.

Fuller's skepticism toward modern constitutional practice echoes Hart's, but does not stem from the same basis. Hart questions substantive judicial review because he cannot reconcile it with his own understanding of institutional roles within a democracy. Since Fuller's ideal of legality can be fully satisfied by a nondemocratic state, his opposition must have another source. Consider the relation between Fuller's procedural ideal of legality and the notion of a written constitution. Fuller describes the internal morality of law as 'essentially a branch of constitutional law, largely and properly developing outside the framework of our written constitutions.'[27] The internal morality of law is *constitutional* in nature because it concerns the 'authority to enact rules and to reach decisions that will be regarded as properly binding on those affected by them.'[28] The internal morality of law is the unwritten constitution of

[24] Ibid., 643. [25] Ibid. [26] *The Morality of Law*, 104–5. [27] Ibid., 128. [28] Ibid.

every legal order because the procedural principles that Fuller sets out accompany the subjection of human conduct to the governance of rules. But in conceiving of the internal morality of law as an *unwritten* constitution composed exclusively of procedural norms, Fuller seems to reject the propriety of a *written* constitution being committed to the pursuit of substantive norms. He holds that 'a written constitution defines basic lawmaking procedure' and suggests that a written constitution should be conceived of as 'establishing a basic procedural framework for future governmental action in the enactment and administration of laws.'[29] For Fuller, the features of a written constitution should not exceed the procedural parameters of the unwritten constitution common to legal systems as such. From this standpoint, modern constitutionalism is problematic: in making conformity to substantive norms the condition for the valid exercise of public power, modern constitutionalism distorts the morality that makes law possible.

Unlike Hart and Fuller, Dworkin was eager to affirm the model of constitutional governance that emerged in the United States in the 'halcyon days of the Warren Court.'[30] But as we saw in Chapter 5, Dworkin's justification of these arrangements is vulnerable to a devastating objection. Dworkin initially argued that judicial review is justified because of the morally beneficial outcomes that it produces: judicial review raises the level of public debate by formulating pressing issues as questions of political morality and then selects the morally best answer.[31] As Dworkin's critics were quick to point out, such a results-driven justification of judicial review cannot succeed. Judicial review cannot be elevated over competing arrangements by pointing to the benefits that Dworkin identifies because these benefits may be enjoyed when judicial review is absent and might fail to materialize when it is present. The criticism's strength was compounded by the fact that in the years since Dworkin began defending judicial review, the decisions of the US Supreme Court became increasingly objectionable in his own eyes.[32]

Rather than look to the design of well-ordered constitutional states for insights regarding institutional roles, Dworkin responded to his critics by diluting his own constitutional commitments. While maintaining his rejection of the view advanced by 'many lawyers and political scientists'

[29] Fuller, "Positivism and Fidelity to Law – A Reply to Professor Hart," *Harvard Law Review* 71 (1958): 642–3.

[30] Dworkin, *Freedom's Law* (Cambridge: Harvard University Press, 1996), 3.

[31] Ibid., 344 and 34.

[32] *Justice for Hedgehogs* (Cambridge: Harvard University Press, 2011), 399.

that 'judicial review is inevitably and automatically a defect in society,' Dworkin distanced himself from his earlier view that judicial review contributes to the legitimacy of a democratic state.[33] Within any given legal setting, the appropriateness of judicial review rests on pragmatic considerations 'that vary from place to place,' which include a country's track record in protecting individual and minority rights, as well as 'the strength of the rule of law, the independence of the judiciary, and the character of the constitution judges are asked to enforce.'[34]

With Dworkin's retreat to this more modest position, the space between him and his opponents shrinks in two important respects. First, Dworkin joins his opponents by conceiving of judicial review not as a constitutional essential of any well-ordered regime that is accountable to the inherent dignity and fundamental rights of each of its members, but as an arrangement that may be rightfully adopted or rejected.[35] Whether the United States will, in the final analysis, have chosen wisely by adopting judicial review depends, Dworkin explains, 'on the character of future Supreme Court nominations. We must keep our fingers crossed.'[36] Second, Dworkin accepts the standpoint of constitutional critics who frame the merits of the choice in terms of promoting the best outcome in a given factual context.[37] The remaining disagreement seems confined to the narrow question: What arrangements would produce the best outcome in relation to which facts? But once the question is framed in this way, it is more profitably explored by the empirical investigations of political scientists rather than the moral argumentation of legal and political philosophers. In a world in which judicial review had solidified as an integral feature of modern constitutional governance, Dworkin gave up on defending judicial review as a general feature of a well-ordered legal system.

Turning from the constitutional dimension of Dworkin's project to the doctrinal, he develops the view 'that political rights are trumps over otherwise adequate justifications for political action.'[38] Because the right as trumps model holds that rights are absolute against certain kinds of considerations, Dworkin is often taken to offer an alternative to the doctrine that modern constitutional states have developed to

[33] Ibid. [34] Ibid., 398.
[35] Waldron, "The Core of the Case Against Judicial Review," *Yale Law Journal* 115 (2006): 1360.
[36] *Justice for Hedgehogs*, 399.
[37] Waldron, "The Core of the Case Against Judicial Review," 1359 ff.
[38] *Justice for Hedgehogs*, 329.

adjudicate constitutional rights, proportionality. For this doctrine denies that rights are absolute by admitting that they may be justifiably limited. In Chapter 7, I explored Dworkin's rights as trumps model and argued that it shares the architecture of proportionality. On the one hand, he argues that rights may be justifiably constrained only in cases in which they conflict with the government duty with respect to another right[39] or an objective that is 'consistent with the suppositions on which the original right must be based.'[40] These suppositions, he explains, are rooted in ideas of human dignity and political equality.[41] In such cases, the right is mirrored by an opposing trump. On the other, in formulating an account of the duty of government in cases in which trumps conflict, Dworkin reaches for the very considerations that comprise the doctrine of proportionality. However, he neglects to consolidate these considerations into an ordered set of conditions that government must satisfy to justify the limitation of a constitutional right. Thus, his rights as trumps model resembles proportionality, but does not offer judges the guidance that the doctrine provides. Far from formulating an innovative approach to the adjudication of constitutional rights, Dworkin defended an embryonic version of a doctrine that had already crystallized in courts around the world.

As Dworkin developed his philosophic project, the notion of human dignity assumed an increasingly prominent role. He recognized that the 'idea of dignity has been stained by overuse and misuse' in the proliferation of political manifestos and the crossfire of political rhetoric.[42] Too often, the idea of human dignity 'is used almost thoughtlessly either to provide a pseudo-argument or just to provide an emotional charge.'[43] But he also maintained that the idea of human dignity is indispensable in making sense of the moral situation in which human beings find themselves.[44] In his words, human dignity is an idea from which 'any moral theory worth its salt needs to proceed.'[45]

Dworkin interpreted human dignity as an idea comprised of two dimensions or principles.[46] The first, the *principle of self-respect*, requires each person to recognize that it is 'objectively important' to live well.

[39] *Taking Rights Seriously*, 193. [40] Ibid., 200. [41] Ibid., 198.

[42] *Justice for Hedgehogs*, 204. [43] Ibid., 204.

[44] Dworkin, *Is Democracy Possible Here?* (Princeton: Princeton University Press, 2006), 9.

[45] Quoted in Stuart Jeffries, "Ronald Dworkin: 'We Have a Responsibility to Live Well'," *The Guardian*, 31 March 2011, www.theguardian.com/books/2011/mar/31/ronald-dworkin-morality-dignity-hedgehogs.

[46] *Is Democracy Possible Here?*, 9–10; and *Justice for Hedgehogs*, 235.

Each person must acknowledge that 'it is a matter of importance that his life be a successful performance rather than a wasted opportunity.'[47] The second, the *principle of authenticity*, demands that each person determine what a successful life involves and live in accordance with that vision.[48] Taken together, these principles hold that each person can live a valuable life and that each person must take responsibility for doing so. Human dignity calls for self-respect and authenticity.

Although Dworkin presents human dignity as an 'interpretive concept' that seeks to describe and justify a shared social practice,[49] his account cannot stand as an interpretation of the prevailing meaning of human dignity in modern constitutional jurisprudence. Dworkin conceives of human dignity as what one has by virtue of living as one should, that is, by adhering to the principles of self-respect and authenticity. Since it is not the case that every human adheres to these principles, not every human possesses dignity. Thus, Dworkin indicates that those who violate the principle of self-respect by denying the importance of living well 'lack dignity,'[50] as do those who fail to take responsibility for their lives.[51] Human dignity is *human*, then, only in the sense that it is a quality that humans can acquire or forfeit. Modern constitutional jurisprudence takes a different view: human dignity is inherent, each person possesses human dignity in equal measure, and it can neither be acquired nor forfeited through one's actions. Thus, the virtuous and the vicious are equal in their dignity. Even a small child, who neither has acknowledged the importance of living well nor formulated and pursued her own conception of a successful life, is equal in dignity to those who have led (what Dworkin would recognize as) a successful life.[52]

[47] *Justice for Hedgehogs*, 203. [48] Ibid., 204. [49] Ibid. [50] Ibid., 14.

[51] Ibid., 210 (my emphasis): 'The second principle of dignity demands both that I be responsible in the virtue sense and that I accept relational responsibility when appropriate. I do not treat an act as my own, as issuing from my personality and character, unless I regard myself as judgmentally responsible for it. People who blame their parents or other people or society at large for their own mistakes, or who cite some form of genetic determinism to absolve themselves of any responsibility for how they have acted, *lack dignity*, because dignity requires owning up to what one has done.'

[52] Just as the unified theory of public law rejects Dworkin's notion of human dignity, so too it rejects his ideal of equal concern and equal respect. See *Taking Rights Seriously* (Cambridge: Harvard University Press, 1978), 272–3. Dworkin's theory involves two kinds of goods: *equal concern* involves the human capacity for frustration and suffering; *equal respect* involves the capacity to determine and pursue one's own purposes. An implication of Dworkin's view is that the liberty that forms the subject of equal respect may be limited on the basis of the utilitarian considerations that form the subject of equal concern. By contrast, the unified theory rejects the view that freedom may be limited for

In short, since the end of World War II, the most prominent Anglo-American legal theorists created frameworks that either rejected postwar constitutionalism whole cloth or failed to recognize its significance for their own projects. This disjunction between the theory and practice of public law in the postwar era is not accidental. As I have argued, modern constitutionalism is a response to a problem inherent in the normative structure of public law. Because the theories of Hart, Fuller, and Dworkin do not perceive the problem, they fail to grasp how the innovations of modern constitutional practice systematically address it.

Any theory of public law must confront a fundamental problem. The practice of public law seems to involve the interrelationship of two ineliminable components, authority and justice, which appear to stand in a relationship of opposition. On the one hand, the practice seems to require persons to act in conformity with legal obligations enacted through the contingent exercise of public authority. On the other, the same practice seems to require persons to act in conformity with timeless ideals of public justice. The theoretical puzzle at the core of public law stems from the incompatibility of these convictions. Because enacted laws are often unjust and just laws are rarely enacted, persons often find themselves simultaneously pulled in one direction by the demands of public authority and pulled in another by the demands of public justice.

The unified theory of public law resolves this problem by drawing a pair of distinctions. The first delineates the juridical situation of the parties to the public law relationship. Public law is a juridical relationship between rulers and ruled in which each party bears distinctive rights and duties. The notion of public authority concerns the right of rulers to establish, interpret, and implement legal obligations that bind the ruled. The notion of public justice concerns the right of the ruled to governance that brings the existing legal order into conformity with the human dignity of all who are bound by it. Thus, it is not the case that persons are bound both by the particular laws that happen to have been enacted in their legal order and by general considerations of justice. Rather, persons are divided into rulers and ruled; the ruled have a duty to obey enacted law and the rulers have a duty to govern justly. The second distinction

the sake of any value extrinsic to it. A further difference concerns the relationship between the ideal of each theory and public authority. The unified theory establishes that the internal ideal of a legal system *as such* is equal freedom under law. By contrast, as I note below, Dworkin's interpretive model commits him to the view that the ideal of equal concern and respect is internal to some legal systems, but external to others.

involves the character of the principles that structure the public law relationship. The principle of authority that empowers rulers and binds the ruled is the *constitutive principle* of public law. A regime of public law consists in publicly authoritative institutions that establish, interpret, and implement legal obligations incumbent on the ruled. The principle of justice, which concerns the right of the ruled to just governance and the corresponding obligation of the rulers, is the *regulative principle* of public law. Whereas the principle of authority sets out the standard for determining whether something is a legal system, the principle of justice provides a standard for determining the adequacy of an existing legal system and directing its reform. Once the rights and duties of the parties to the public law relationship and the principles that constitute and regulate this relationship are untangled, the tension that lies at the heart of public law dissolves.

The distinguishing feature of the unified theory of public law is the view that the right of government to exercise public authority is always accompanied by a duty to create a regime of equal freedom. This duty emerges from the justification of public authority advanced in Chapter 2. Public authority requires justification because the division of persons into rulers and ruled clashes with our conviction that each person is his or her own ruler. Public authority can be justified because in the absence of institutions that make, interpret, and implement law, persons would be incapable of interacting with one another on terms of equal freedom. Such a justification of the right of government to exercise public authority implicates a particular conception of public justice. Since the justification of public authority is premised on the right of each person to equal freedom, internal to the justification of public authority is a conception of an ideal legal order and a duty to approximate it. A legal order is just to the extent that public authority is consistent with the right of every person bound by it to equal freedom. A legal order is governed justly to the extent that it directs the exercise of public authority toward the realization of equal freedom under law. So conceived, the principles of public law are mutually implicating. There is no right to exercise public authority that is not accompanied by a duty to govern justly. There is no possibility of just governance in the absence of publicly authoritative institutions.

In maintaining that the right of a ruler to exercise public authority is accompanied by a duty to create a regime of equal freedom, the unified theory of public law makes a critical departure from competing theories. While Hart describes a practice in which legal officials change the normative situation of others by exercising public authority over them, he avoids the problem of explaining how someone could have the moral authority to change the normative situation of another. Having provided a description of public authority rather than a justification of it, Hart treats the question of what moral purpose legal power should pursue as a wholly extrinsic one. Positivism, as a theory of law's nature, leaves its advocates free to affirm a range of competing visions about the demands of morality. Fuller conceives of the act of a ruler imposing obligations on the ruled as implicating a series of moral requirements that are internal to law and procedural in nature, but takes for granted that one person could have the right to impose obligations on others by ruling them. When pressed about the substantive purposes that law should pursue, Fuller holds that this issue belongs to the external morality of law.[53] For Fuller, as for Hart, a legal system as such does not contain its own implicit substantive moral aim.[54]

The same is true of Dworkin. Distancing his interpretive model from theories that articulate 'an abstract and timeless political morality' applicable to legal systems in all times and places,[55] he calls for the adoption of a standard of justification from among the purposes immanent to the contingent legal practice of a particular community.[56] Interpretation, as opposed to invention, must *fit* the general features of the practice that it seeks to illuminate. If that practice admits a plurality of divergent justifications that satisfy the requirement of fit, Dworkin asserts that the interpreter is to affirm the interpretation that casts the coercive practice of law in its best light by showing it 'as the best course of statesmanship possible.'[57] With respect to the American legal system, a variety of standards fit the practice, including communitarianism and utilitarianism,[58] but Dworkin argues that what he calls integrity 'provides the best constructive interpretation of the community's legal practice' by upholding the legality of legal propositions that 'figure in or follow from the

[53] *The Morality of Law*, 96.

[54] On this point, see Jennifer Nadler, "Hart, Fuller, and the Connection between Law and Justice," *Law and Philosophy* 27 (2008): 1–2.

[55] Ronald Dworkin, *Law's Empire* (Cambridge: Harvard University Press, 1986), 216.

[56] Ibid., 97.

[57] Dworkin, "Law's Ambitions for Itself," *Virginia Law Review* 71 (1985): 178. For Dworkin's view that law is a justification of coercion based on past practice, see *Law's Empire*, 93, 97, and 103. On the tension between Dworkin's interpretive model and his theory of law's authority, see T.R.S. Allan, "Law, Justice, and Integrity: The Paradox of Wicked Laws," *Oxford Journal of Legal Studies* 29 (2009): 705–28.

[58] Ibid., 216.

principles of justice, fairness, and procedural due process.'[59] Other standards, such as Marxism and fascism, are excluded because they fail to fit the contours of American legal practice.[60] Since the appropriate standard of justification emerges from the interpreter's engagement with the contingent features of an existing legal practice, Dworkin does not exclude the possibility that these and other illiberal ideologies may justify legal systems with divergent practices. As he explains, the justificatory norms immanent to particular legal systems 'are much more contingent than those of justice, and they are often matters of regret.'[61] Dworkin emphasized that, on his view, what law is in a particular legal system depends in part on what law ought to be.[62] A less welcome feature of his interpretive model is that what law ought to be in a particular legal system depends in part on what law is.[63]

The unified theory of public law avoids the variability of Dworkin's legal ideal. Instead of framing a legal morality that happens to fit the 'brute facts of legal history' that confront an interpreter situated in a particular place and time,[64] the unified theory holds that the morality immanent to a legal system follows from a feature common to legal systems as such, the right of government to exercise public authority over free and equal persons. The justification of public authority – the constitutive feature of a legal system – indicates the ideal of governance to which its exercise must be directed. The same strategy also provides an alternative to the substantive moral indeterminacy of the legal theories of Hart and Fuller. Every exercise of public authority is accompanied by a duty to realize a regime of equal freedom. This duty is the subject of Chapter 4.

59 *Law's Empire*, 225. 60 Ibid., 408.

61 Ibid., 406 (contrasting the abstraction of *pure* integrity (in which a judge would 'consider what the law would be if judges were free simply to pursue coherence in the principles of justice that flow through and unite different departments of law') with *inclusive* integrity (which takes place in the contingent setting of an existing legal system and requires a judge to 'give effect to statutes that pull against substantive coherence and to precedents and local priorities that stand in the way of consistency over different departments of law')).

62 *Taking Rights Seriously*, vii; *A Matter of Principle*, 4; *Law's Empire*, 52; "Law's Ambitions for Itself," 175–6; and *Freedom's Law: The Moral Reading of the American Constitution* (Cambridge: Harvard University Press, 1996), 37–8.

63 As Hart observed, Dworkin's approach to justification may amount to nothing more than the 'least odious of morally unacceptable principles.' See Hart, *Essays on Bentham: Studies in Jurisprudence and Political Theory* (Oxford: Oxford University Press, 1982), 151; and Philip Soper, "Dworkin's Domain," *Harvard Law Review* 100 (1987): 1167.

64 *Law's Empire*, 255 and 90–1.

Once public law is conceived of in terms of mutually implicating principles of authority and justice, the justification of the legal and institutional structure of a modern constitutional state comes into view. As I explained in Chapter 5, the problem of accountability is that even though each person subject to public authority has a right to just governance, the legal structure of all precursors to modern constitutionalism leaves one or more persons without legal recourse in the event that this right is violated. The problem persists so long as public authority rests in the hands of a single person (as in a monarchy), a few persons (as in an aristocracy), or many persons (as in a majoritarian democracy). A monarchy is unaccountable to every person bound by its lawgiving, an aristocracy is unaccountable to the many, and a majoritarian democracy is unaccountable to the few. The problem of accountability is not that these forms of government necessarily exercise public authority in an unjust manner, but that one or more persons within them lack the legal capacity to constrain the exercise of public authority to the terms of its justification. Because every legal order has a duty to bring itself into the closest possible conformity with public justice, every legal system must ultimately address the problem of accountability.

The modern constitutional state is a systematic legal framework for rendering the exercise of public authority accountable neither to the many nor to the few, but to the right of every member of the legal order to just governance. Such a state addresses the problem of accountability by transforming the right of the ruled to just governance from a mere moral imperative into a legal constraint on the exercise of all public power. To this end, the modern constitutional state involves (1) a constitution that exhaustively specifies the conditions for the valid exercise of public authority by any branch of government, (2) a body of constitutional norms establishing that conformity to the right of each individual to just governance is the condition for the valid exercise of all public authority, and (3) a judicial institution that is both politically independent and constitutionally required to uphold constitutional norms by enabling any individual in the legal order who believes that his or her right to just governance has been infringed to bring a constitutional complaint challenging the validity of an authoritative act. Any legal system might succeed in enacting just law, but only a modern constitutional state renders the exercise of public authority accountable to the right of every person within the legal order to just governance. Judicial review is integral to modern constitutionalism not because it produces desirable outcomes that could nevertheless be realized in its absence, as

Dworkin would have it, but because it contributes to creating the conditions in which any individual within the legal order can challenge the validity of an authoritative act on the basis of its failure to conform to the duty of just governance. The revolution in postwar constitutionalism consists in the legal innovations that render the exercise of public authority accountable neither to the many nor to the few, but, for the first time in the long history of public law, to the right of every inhabitant of the legal order to just governance. In a modern constitutional state, everyone who exercises public authority must be answerable to anyone who is subject to it.

Competing theories fail to appreciate the innovations of modern constitutionalism because they lack the theoretical resources to discern the problem to which this practice responds. Because competing theories fail to recognize that the right of government to exercise public authority must always be directed toward fulfilling the right of persons to just governance, they fail to observe the problem of accountability. And if the problem of accountability remains unearthed, so too does the systematic way in which modern constitutional states respond. Hart fails to discern the problem of accountability because he seeks to explicate law's authority in abstraction from moral concepts. If morality is extrinsic to legality, then the question of how the exercise of public authority can be constrained to the moral boundaries of its own justification cannot arise. Fuller, by contrast, holds that law contains its own internal standard of adequacy. But by characterizing this standard as wholly procedural, Fuller maintains that it is possible for legal systems that are neither democratic nor rights-protecting to fully satisfy this ideal. Finally, Dworkin's interpretive model commits him to the view that the features of an existing legal practice set the parameters for its justification. This means that the justificatory standard immanent to a legal system may be liberal or illiberal. But even in a legal system that happens to be infused with liberal political morality, constitutionalism remains an extraneous feature of Dworkin's theory. Having attempted to justify a modest set of constitutional practices by pointing to beneficial outcomes that are realizable apart from them, Dworkin is ultimately pressed to concede that those practices are not integral to a well-ordered legal system.

This book responds to a skeptical challenge concerning the relationship between human dignity and modern constitutional governance. The challenge alleges that human dignity is either an empty idea or an illiberal one. In either case, it fails to justify the distinctive practices of constitutional states that invoke it. This book offers a sustained response to this challenge. By attending to the systematic implications of the concept of human dignity, conceived of in terms of the right of each person to equal freedom, a unified theory of the normative, institutional, and doctrinal dimensions of public law emerges. As a normative matter, public law is constituted and regulated by principles that establish the rights and duties of rulers and ruled. As an institutional matter, these principles demand the creation, maintenance, and refinement of a modern constitutional form of governance in which human dignity forms a justiciable constraint on the exercise of all public authority. As a doctrinal matter, a modern constitutional state requires the development of doctrines that connect these normative and constitutional commitments to instances arising in legal practice. By attending to the dimensions of human dignity, the practice of modern constitutionalism becomes intelligible.

In the postwar world, the theory and practice of public law seem to be moving in opposite directions. As a matter of practice, since the end of World War II, a growing chorus of lawyers, judges, and statesmen from around the world have observed the emergence of a new paradigm of constitutional governance. In countries as diverse as Germany, South Africa, and Canada, the distinguishing mark of this versatile new paradigm is the creation of constitutional norms, institutional arrangements, and legal doctrines that transform the right of persons to just governance from an empty ideal into an effective constraint on the exercise of public power. In the practice of legal systems around the world, modern constitutionalism has established itself as the leading response to the various pathologies of public law, from the barbarism of failed states to the injustices of majoritarian ones. But as a matter of constitutional theory, modern constitutionalism is increasingly subject to criticism from theorists committed to earlier models of government, which fail to render the exercise of public power accountable to the right of each and every member of the legal order to just governance. The result is a chasm that separates the practice of modern constitutionalism from a theory that could explain and guide it. Consequently, legal practitioners seeking to cultivate modern constitutional governance in a variety of settings have had to find their way without theoretical illumination.

The overarching purpose of this book has been to take the first steps in bringing the theory and practice of public law back together. By resolving the conflict between notions of authority and justice that lies at the heart of public law, the unified theory exposes a problem latent in the structure of public law to which modern constitutionalism systematically responds. Earlier systems of public law succeeded in making public authority accountable to the few or to the many. The groundbreaking significance of the modern constitutional state consists in creating the legal conditions in which the exercise of public authority is accountable to the dignity of each free and equal person subject to law's dominion. In articulating the duty of existing states to bring themselves into increasing conformity with the modern constitutional paradigm, the unified theory connects the general normative structure of public law to the most innovative practices of the postwar world. Such a connection can be forged because what a legal system is indicates what a legal system must become.

BIBLIOGRAPHY

Abel, Corey, and Timothy Fuller. *The Intellectual Legacy of Michael Oakeshott*. Charlottesville: Imprint Academic, 2005.

Ackerman, Bruce. "Higher Lawmaking." In *Responding to Imperfection: The Theory and Practice of Constitutional Amendment*, edited by Sanford Levinson. 63–88. Princeton: Princeton University Press, 1995.

"Rooted Cosmopolitanism." *Ethics* 104, no. 3 (1994): 516–35.

We the People. Cambridge, Mass.: Belknap Press of Harvard University Press, 1991.

Ackermann, Lourens W.H. "The Legal Nature of the South African Constitutional Revolution." *New Zealand Law Review*, no. 4 (2004): 633–79.

"The Soul of Dignity: A Reply to Stu Woolman." In *Constitutional Conversations*, edited by Stu Woolman and Michael Bishop. 217–30. Pretoria: Pretoria University Press, 2008.

Albert, Richard. "Nonconstitutional Amendments." *Canadian Journal of Law and Jurisprudence* 22, no. 1 (2009): 5–47.

Aleinikoff, T. Alexander. "Constitutional Law in the Age of Balancing." *Yale Law Journal* 96, no. 5 (1987): 943–1005.

Alexy, Robert. *The Argument from Injustice: A Reply to Legal Positivism*. Oxford: Clarendon Press, 2002.

"Discourse Theory and Human Rights." *Ratio Juris* 9, no. 3 (1996): 209–35.

"Effects of Defects – Action or Argument? Thoughts about Deryck Beyleveld and Roger Brownsword's Law as a Moral Judgment." *Ratio Juris* 19, no. 2 (2006): 169–79.

"On Balancing and Subsumption. A Structural Comparison." *Ratio Juris* 16, no. 4 (2003): 433–49.

"On Necessary Relations between Law and Morality." *Ratio Juris* 2, no. 2 (1989): 167–83.

"On the Concept and the Nature of Law." *Ratio Juris* 21, no. 3 (2008): 281–99.

A Theory of Constitutional Rights. Oxford: Oxford University Press, 2002.

"Thirteen Replies." In *Law, Rights and Discourse: The Legal Philosophy of Robert Alexy*, edited by George Pavlakos. 333–66. Oxford: Hart Publishing, 2007.

Allan, T.R.S. "Law, Justice and Integrity: The Paradox of Wicked Laws." *Oxford Journal of Legal Studies* 29, no. 4 (2009): 705–28.

Almond, Gabriel A., Marvin Chodorow, and Roy Harvey Pearce. "Progress and Its Discontents." *Bulletin of the American Academy of Arts and Sciences* 35, no. 3 (1981): 4–23.

Amar, Akhil Reed. "Popular Sovereignty and Constitutional Amendment." In *Responding to Imperfection: The Theory and Practice of Constitutional Amendment*, edited by Sanford Levinson. 89–116. Princeton: Princeton University Press, 1995.

Anderson, Elizabeth. *The Imperative of Integration*. Princeton: Princeton University Press, 2010.

"Toward a Non-Ideal, Relational Methodology for Political Philosophy: Comments on Schwartzman's 'Challenging Liberalism'." *Hypatia* 24, no. 4 (2009): 130–45.

Arad, Yitzhak, Israel Gutman, and Abraham Margaliot. *Documents on the Holocaust: Selected Sources on the Destruction of the Jews of Germany and Austria, Poland, and the Soviet Union*. 8th ed. Lincoln: University of Nebraska Press, 1999.

Aristotle. "Politics." Translated by Hippocrates G. Apostle and Lloyd P. Gerson. In *Selected Works*. 557–615. Iowa: The Peripatetic Press, 1991.

Aron, Raymond. *Main Currents of Sociological Thought*. New Brunswick, N.J.: Transaction Publishers, 2009.

Austin, John. *Lectures on Jurisprudence, or, the Philosophy of Positive Law*. New York: H. Holt, 1875.

The Province of Jurisprudence Determined. London: J. Murray, 1832.

Bagaric, Mirko, and James Allan. "The Vacuous Concept of Dignity." *Journal of Human Rights* 5 (2006): 257–70.

Barak, Aharon. "Human Dignity: The Constitutional Value and the Constitutional Right." In *Understanding Human Dignity*, edited by Christopher McCrudden. 361–80. Oxford: Oxford University Press, 2013.

"Proportional Effect: The Israeli Experience." *The University of Toronto Law Journal* 57, no. 2 (2007): 369–82.

Proportionality: Constitutional Rights and Their Limitations. Cambridge: Cambridge University Press, 2012.

"Unconstitutional Constitutional Amendments." *Israel Law Review* 44 (2011): 321–41.

Beatty, David M. *The Ultimate Rule of Law*. Oxford: Oxford University Press, 2004.

Benda, Ernst. "Foreword by the Federal President." In *Basic Law for the Federal Republic of Germany*. 5–6. Berlin: Bundestag, 2001.

Bentham, Jeremy. *A Fragment on Government*. Cambridge: Cambridge University Press, 2001.

An Introduction to the Principles of Morals and Legislation. Oxford: Clarendon Press, 1879.

Berkowitz, Roger. "Dignity Jurisprudence: Building a New Law on Earth." In *The Dignity Jurisprudence of the Constitutional Court of South Africa*, edited by Drucilla Cornell, Stu Woolman, Sam Fuller, Jason Brickhill, Michael Bishop, and Diana Dunbar. 65–72. New York: Fordham University Press, 2013.

Berman, Harold Joseph. *Law and Revolution: The Formation of the Western Legal Tradition*. Cambridge, Mass.: Harvard University Press, 1983.

Bertea, Stefano. "How Non-Positivism Can Accommodate Legal Certainty." In *Law, Rights, and Discourse: The Legal Philosophy of Robert Alexy*, edited by George Pavlakos. 69–82. Oxford: Hart Publishing, 2007.

Bickel, Alexander M. *The Least Dangerous Branch: The Supreme Court at the Bar of Politics*. Indianapolis: Bobbs-Merrill, 1962.

Bilchitz, David. "Does Balancing Adequately Capture the Nature of Rights?" *South African Public Law* 25 (2010): 423–44.

Bluntschli, Johann Caspar. *Politik Als Wissenschaft*. Stuttgart: Verlag der J.G. Cotta'schen Buchhandlung, 1876.

Bodenheimer, Edgar. "Significant Developments in German Legal Philosophy since 1945." *The American Journal of Comparative Law* 3, no. 3 (1954): 379–96.

Bois, François du. "Rights Trumped? Balancing in Constitutional Adjudication." *Acta Juridica* (2004): 155–81.

Bork, Robert H. *Slouching Towards Gomorrah: Modern Liberalism and American Decline*. New York: ReganBooks, 1996.

Bradley, K.R. *Slavery and Society at Rome*. Cambridge: Cambridge University Press, 1994.

Brecht, Arnold. *Federalism and Regionalism in Germany – the Division of Prussia*. New York: Oxford University Press, 1945.

Brison, Susan J. "The Autonomy Defense of Free Speech." *Ethics* 108, no. 2 (1998): 312–39.

Browning, Christopher R. *Ordinary Men: Reserve Police Battalion 101 and the Final Solution in Poland*. New York, N.Y.: Aaron Asher Books, 1992.

Brudner, Alan. "What Theory of Rights Best Explain the Oakes Test?" In *The Limitation of Charter Rights: Critical Essays on R. V. Oakes*, edited by Grégoire C.N. Webber and Luc Tremblay. 59–74. Montreal: Les Editions Themis, 2009.

Byk, Christian. "Is Human Dignity a Useless Concept?: Legal Perspectives." In *The Cambridge Handbook of Human Dignity: Interdisciplinary Perspectives*, edited by Marcus Düwell. 362–7. Cambridge: Cambridge University Press, 2014.

Caenegem, R.C. van. *An Historical Introduction to Western Constitutional Law*. Cambridge: Cambridge University Press, 1995.

Calhoun, John C. "A Discourse on the Constitution and Government of the United States." In *John C. Calhoun: Selected Writings and Speeches*, edited by H. Lee Cheek Jr. 61–222. Washington: Regnery Publishing, 2003.

"Slavery a Positive Good." http://teachingamericanhistory.org/library/document/slavery-a-positive-good/.

Campbell, Juan Colombo. "Constitutional Court Judges' Roundtable." *International Journal of Constitutional Law* 3, no. 4 (2005): 544–50.

Cancik, Hubert. "'Dignity of Man' and 'Persona' in Stoic Anthropology: Some Remarks on Cicero, De Officiis I 105–107." In *The Concept of Human Dignity in Human Rights Discourse*, edited by Eckart Klein and David Kretzmer. 19–39. Dordrecht: Kluwer Law International, 2002.

Caplan, Arthur L. *When Medicine Went Mad: Bioethics and the Holocaust*. Totowa, N.J.: Humana Press, 1992.

Cappelletti, Mauro. "The Expanding Role of Judicial Review in Modern Societies." In *The Role of Courts in Society*, edited by Simon Shetreet. 79–96. Dordrecht: Martinus Nijhoff Publishers, 1988.

"Judicial Review in Comparative Perspective." *California Law Review* 58, no. 5 (1970): 1017–53.

Judicial Review in the Contemporary World. New York: Bobbs-Merrill, 1971.

"Repudiating Montesquieu? The Expansion and Legitimacy of 'Constitutional Justice'." *Catholic University Law Review* 35 (1986): 1–32.

Carozza, Paolo G. "Human Dignity in Constitutional Adjudication." In *Comparative Constitutional Law*, edited by Tom Ginsberg and Rosalind Dixon. 459–72. Cheltenham: Edward Elger, 2011.

"Human Rights, Human Dignity, and Human Experience." In *Understanding Human Dignity*, edited by Christopher McCrudden. 615–30. Oxford: Oxford University Press, 2013.

Chaskalson, Arthur. "From Wickedness to Equality: The Moral Transformation of South Africa Law." *International Journal of Constitutional Law* 1 (2003): 590–609.

"Human Dignity as a Constitutional Value." In *The Concept of Human Dignity in Human Rights Discourse*, edited by David Kretzmer and Eckart Klein. 133–44. The Hague: Kluwer Law International, 2002.

"Human Dignity as a Foundational Value of Our Constitutional Order." *South African Journal on Human Rights* 16 (2000): 193–205.

Cohen-Eliya, Moshe, and Iddo Porat. "Proportionality and the Culture of Justification." *The American Journal of Comparative Law* 59, no. 2 (2011): 463–90.

Coleman, Jules L., and Brian Leiter. "Legal Positivism." In *A Companion to Philosophy of Law and Legal Theory*, edited by Dennis Patterson. 228–48. Oxford: Basil Blackwell, 1999.

Coleman, Jules L., and Scott Shapiro. *The Oxford Handbook of Jurisprudence and Philosophy of Law*. Oxford: Oxford University Press, 2004.

Cooley, Thomas M. "The Power to Amend the Federal Constitution." *Michigan Law Journal* 2 (1893): 109–20.

Cornell, Drucilla, and Sam Fuller. "Introduction." In *Dignity Jurisprudence of the Constitutional Court of South Africa*, edited by Drucilla Cornell, Stu Woolman, Sam Fuller, Jason Brickhill, Michael Bishop, and Diana Dunbar. 3–20. New York: Fordham University Press, 2013.

Cotler, Irwin. "Jewish NGOS and Religious Human Rights: A Case Study." In *Religious Human Rights in Global Perspective*, edited by John Witte Jr. and Johan D. van der Vyver. 235–94. The Hague: Kluwer Law International, 1996.

Cover, Robert. *Justice Accused: Antislavery and the Judicial Process*. New Haven: Yale University Press, 1975.

Currie, David P. *The Constitution of the Federal Republic of Germany*. Chicago: University of Chicago Press, 1994.

Dahl, Robert Alan. *Polyarchy: Participation and Opposition*. New Haven: Yale University Press, 1971.

Dan-Cohen, Meir. "Introduction: Dignity and Its (Dis)Contents." In *Dignity, Rank, and Rights*, edited by Meir Dan-Cohen. 3–10. Oxford: Oxford University Press, 2012.

Davis, David Brion. *The Problem of Slavery in Western Culture*. Ithaca, N.Y.: Cornell University Press, 1966.

Davis, Dennis. "Equality: The Majesty of Legoland Jurisprudence." *South African Law Journal* 116 (1999): 398–414.

Deák, István. "Holocaust Views: The Goldhagen Controversy in Retrospect." *Central European History* 30, no. 2 (1997): 295–307.

Del Duca, Louis, and Patrick Del Duca. "An Italian Federalism? The State, Its Institutions and National Culture as Rule of Law Guarantor." *American Journal of Comparative Law* 54 (2006): 1–48.

De Ste. Croix, G. E. M. *The Class Struggle in the Ancient Greek World: From the Archaic Age to the Arab Conquests*. Ithaca, N.Y.: Cornell University Press, 1981.

de Toqueville, Alexis. *Democracy in America*. New York: Alfred A. Knopf, 1994.

Dietze, Gottfried. "Unconstitutional Constitutional Norms? Constitutional Development in Postwar Germany." *Virginia Law Review* 42 (1956): 1–22.

Dixon, Rosalind. "Constitutional Amendment Rules: A Comparative Perspective." In *Comparative Constitutional Law*, edited by Tom Ginsberg and Rosalind Dixon. 86–111. Cheltenham: Edward Elgar, 2011.

Douglass, Frederick. "The Address of Southern Delegates in Congress to Their Constituents or, the Address of John C. Calhoun and Forty Other Thieves." *The North Star*, February 9, 1849.

"Change of Opinion Announced." *The North Star*, May 23, 1851.
Life and Times of Frederick Douglass. New York: Cosimo, 2008.
Dreben, Burton. "On Rawls and Political Liberalism." In *The Cambridge Companion to Rawls*, edited by Samuel Freeman. 316–46. Cambridge: Cambridge University Press, 2003.
Dreier, Horst. "Human Dignity in German Law." In *The Cambridge Handbook of Human Dignity: Interdisciplinary Perspectives*, edited by Marcus Düwell. 375–85. Cambridge: Cambridge University Press, 2014.
Dupré, Catherine. "Human Dignity in Europe: A Foundational Constitutional Principle." *European Public Law* 19, no. 2 (2013): 319–40.
Dürig, Günter. "An Introduction to the Basic Law of the Federal Republic of Germany." In *The Constitution of the Federal Republic of Germany*, edited by Ulrich Karpen. 11–24. Baden-Baden: Nomos Verlagsgesellschaft, 1988.
Dworkin, Ronald. *A Bill of Rights for Britain*. London: Chatto & Windus, 1990.
Freedom's Law: The Moral Reading of the American Constitution. Cambridge, Mass.: Harvard University Press, 1996.
Is Democracy Possible Here?: Principles for a New Political Debate. Princeton, N.J.: Princeton University Press, 2006.
Justice for Hedgehogs. Cambridge, Mass.: Belknap Press of Harvard University Press, 2011.
Justice in Robes. Cambridge, Mass.: Belknap Press of Harvard University, 2006.
"Law's Ambitions for Itself." *Virginia Law Review* 71, no. 2 (1985): 173–87.
Law's Empire. Cambridge, Mass.: Belknap Press, 1986.
Life's Dominion: An Argument About Abortion, Euthanasia, and Individual Freedom. New York: Alfred A. Knopf, 1993.
A Matter of Principle. Cambridge, Mass.: Harvard University Press, 1985.
Sovereign Virtue: The Theory and Practice of Equality. Cambridge, Mass.: Harvard University Press, 2000.
Taking Rights Seriously. Cambridge: Harvard University Press, 1977.
"Thirty Years On." *Harvard Law Review* 115 (2002): 1655–87.
Dyzenhaus, David. "Constitutionalism in an Old Key: Legality and Constituent Power." *Global Constitutionalism* 1 (2012): 229–60.
Hard Cases in Wicked Legal Systems: Pathologies of Legality. 2nd ed. Oxford; New York: Oxford University Press, 2010.
"How Hobbes Met the 'Hobbes Challenge'." *The Modern Law Review* 72, no. 3 (2009): 488–506.
Recrafting the Rule of Law: The Limits of Legal Order. Oxford: Hart, 1999.
Dyzenhaus, David, and Mayo Moran. *Calling Power to Account: Law, Reparations and the Chinese Canadian Head Tax Case*. Toronto: University of Toronto Press, 2005.
Dyzenhaus, David, and Thomas Poole. *Hobbes and the Law*. Cambridge: Cambridge University Press, 2012.

Ebbinghaus, Julius. "The Law of Humanity and the Limits of State Power." *The Philosophical Quarterly* 3, no. 10 (1953): 14–22.

Eberle, Edward J. "The German Idea of Freedom." *Oregon Review of International Law* 10 (2008): 1–76.

"Human Dignity, Privacy and Personality in German and American Constitutional Law." *Utah Law Review* (1997): 964–1056.

Eckert, Joern. "Legal Roots of Human Dignity in German Law." In *The Concept of Human Dignity in Human Rights Discourse*, edited by Eckart Klein and David Kretzmer. 41–53. Dordrecht: Kluwer Law International, 2002.

Eddy, Katherine. "Against Ideal Rights." *Social Theory and Practice* 34 (2008): 463–81.

Eisgruber, Christopher L. *Constitutional Self-Government*. Cambridge: Harvard University Press, 2001.

Elliot, Jonathan, ed. *Debates on the Adoption of the Federal Constitution*. New York: Burt Franklin, 1888.

Enders, Christoph. "A Right to Have Rights – the German Constitutional Concept of Human Dignity in German Basic Law." *Revista de Estudos Constitucionais, Hermenêutica e Teoria do Direito* 2, no. 1 (2010): 1–8.

Endicott, Timothy. "Proportionality and Incommensurability." In *Proportionality and the Rule of Law: Rights, Justification, and Reasoning*, edited by Bradley W. Miller Grant Huscroft, Grégoire Webber. 311–42. Cambridge: Cambridge University Press, 2014.

Evans, Richard J. *The Third Reich in History and Memory*. Oxford: Oxford University Press, 2015.

Ewing, K.D. "The Human Rights Act and Parliamentary Democracy." *Modern Law Review* 62, no. 1 (1999): 79–99.

Farrand, Max, and David Maydole Matteson, ed. *The Records of the Federal Convention of 1787*. 4 vols. New Haven: Yale University Press, 1966.

Farrelly, Colin. "Justice in Ideal Theory: A Refutation." *Political Studies* 55 (2007): 844–64.

Favoreu, Louis. "Justicia Y Jueces Constitucionales." *Revista de Derecho Publico* 61 (1999): 10–16.

Feinberg, Joel. "Duty and Obligation in the Non-Ideal World by John Rawls." *The Journal of Philosophy* 70, no. 9 (1973): 263–75.

Ferreres, Víctor Comella. *Constitutional Courts and Democratic Values: A European Perspective*. New Haven: Yale University Press, 2009.

Finley, M.I. *Slavery in Classical Antiquity: Views and Controversies*. Cambridge: W. Heffer, 1964.

Fletcher, G.P. "Human Dignity as a Constitutional Value." *University of Western Ontario Law Review* 22 (1984): 171–82.

Ford, P.L., ed. *The Writings of Thomas Jefferson*. Vol. 10, 1899.

Fox, Gregory H., and George Nolte. "Intolerant Democracies." *Harvard International Law Journal* 36 (1995): 1–70.

Fraenkel, Ernst. *The Dual State: A Contribution to the Theory of Dictatorship*. Translated by E.A. Shils, Edith Lowenstein, and Klaus Knorr. New York: Oxford University Press, 1941.
Freehling, William W. *The Road to Disunion*. 2 vols. Oxford: Oxford University Press, 1990.
Freeman, Samuel. *The Cambridge Companion to Rawls*. Cambridge: Cambridge University Press, 2003.
"Constitutional Democracy and the Legitimacy of Judicial Review." *Law and Philosophy* 9, no. 4 (1990): 327–70.
Friedländer, Saul. "From Anti-Semitism to Extermination: An Historiographical Study of Nazi Policies toward the Jews and an Essay in Interpretation." *Yad Vashem Studies* 16 (1984): 1–50.
Nazi Germany and the Jews. New York: HarperCollins, 1997.
Friedrich, Carl J. "The Issue of Judicial Review in Germany." *Political Science Quarterly* 43, no. 2 (1928): 188–200.
"The Political Theory of the New Democratic Republic." *Review of Politics* 12, no. 2 (1950): 215–24.
"Rebuilding the German Constitution, II." *American Political Science Review* 43 (1949): 704–20.
Fukuyama, Francis. *The Origins of Political Order: From Prehuman Times to the French Revolution*. New York: Farrar, Straus and Giroux, 2011.
Fuller, Lisa L. "Burdened Societies and Transitional Justice." *Ethical Theory and Moral Practice* 15, no. 3 (2012): 369–86.
Fuller, Lon L. *The Morality of Law*. New Haven: Yale University Press, 1964.
"Positivism and Fidelity to Law: A Reply to Professor Hart." *Harvard Law Review* 71, no. 4 (1958): 630–72.
"Reason and Fiat in Case Law." *Harvard Law Review* 59, no. 3 (1946): 376–95.
Gardbaum, Stephen. "The Case for the New Commonwealth Model of Constitutionalism." *German Law Journal* 14, no. 12 (2013): 2229–48.
"The New Commonwealth Model of Constitutionalism." *American Journal of Comparative Law* 49 (2001): 707–60.
"Reassessing the New Commonwealth Model of Constitutionalism." *International Journal of Constitutional Law* 8, no. 2 (2010): 167–206.
Gardner, John. "Legal Positivism: 5½ Myths." *The American Journal of Jurisprudence* 46 (2001): 199–227.
Garlicki, Lech, and Zofia A. Garlicka. "External Review of Constitutional Amendments? International Law as a Norm of Reference." *Israel Law Journal* 44 (2011): 343–68.
Garner, James Wilford. *Introduction to Political Science*. New York: American Book Company, 1910.
Garnsey, Peter. *Ideas of Slavery from Aristotle to Augustine*. Cambridge: Cambridge University Press, 1996.

Gierke, Otto von. "German Constitutional Law in Its Relation to the American Constitution." *Harvard Law Review* 23, no. 4 (1910): 273–90.

Gilabert, Pablo. "Global Justice and Poverty Relief in Nonideal Circumstances." *Social Theory and Practice* 34 (2008): 411–38.

Goldhagen, Daniel Jonah. *Hitler's Willing Executioners: Ordinary Germans and the Holocaust*. New York: Alfred A. Knopf, 1996.

Goodin, Robert E. "Political Ideals and Political Practice." *British Journal of Political Science* 25, no. 1 (1995): 37–56.

Goos, Christoph. "Würde Des Menschen: Restoring Human Dignity in Post-Nazi Germany." In *Understanding Human Dignity*, edited by Christopher McCrudden. 79–93. Oxford: Oxford University Press, 2013.

Graumann, Sigrid. "Human Dignity and People with Disabilities." In *The Cambridge Handbook of Human Dignity: Interdisciplinary Perspectives*, edited by Marcus Düwell. 484–91. Cambridge: Cambridge University Press, 2014.

Green, Leslie. *The Authority of the State*. Oxford: Clarendon Press, 1990.

"Law and Obligations." In *The Oxford Handbook of Jurisprudence and Philosophy of Law*, edited by Jules L. Coleman, Scott Shapiro, and Kenneth Einar Himma. 514–47. Oxford: Clarendon Press, 2004.

Griffin, Stephen M. "Constitutionalism in the United States: From Theory to Politics." In *Responding to Imperfection: The Theory and Practice of Constitutional Amendment*, edited by Sanford Levinson. 37–62. Princeton: Princeton University Press.

Grimm, Dieter. "The Achievement of Constitution and Its Prospects in a Changed World." In *The Twilight of Constitutionalism?*, edited by Petra Dobner and Martin Loughlin. 3–22. Oxford: Oxford University Press, 2010.

"The Basic Law at 60 – Identity and Change." *German Law Journal* 11 (2010): 33–46.

"Constitutional Adjudication and Democracy." *Israel Law Review* 33, no. 2 (2000): 193–215.

"Dignity in a Legal Context: Dignity as an Absolute Right." In *Understanding Human Dignity*, edited by Christopher McCrudden. 381–92. Oxford: Oxford University Press, 2013.

"Freedom of Speech in a Globalized World." In *Extreme Speech and Democracy*, edited by Ivan Hare and James Weinstein. 11–22. Oxford: Oxford University Press, 2009.

"German and American Constitutionalism: A Comparison." *The Berlin Journal* 7 (2003): 8–12.

"Human Rights and Judicial Review in Germany." In *Human Rights and Judicial Review*, edited by David M. Beatty. 269–95. Dordrecht: Martinus Nijhoff Publishers, 1994.

"Proportionality in Canadian and German Constitutional Jurisprudence." *The University of Toronto Law Journal* 57, no. 2 (2007): 383–97.

"Values in German Constitutional Law." Unpublished, *on file with author.*
Habermas, Jürgen. *Between Facts and Norms: Contributions to a Discourse Theory of Law and Democracy.* Cambridge, Mass.: MIT Press, 1996.
Haldemann, Frank. "Gustav Radbruch vs. Hans Kelsen: A Debate on Nazi Law." *Ratio Juris* 18 (2005): 162–78.
Hale, Brenda. "Preface." In *Understanding Human Dignity*, edited by Christopher McCrudden. xv–xvii. Oxford: Oxford University Press, 2013.
Halmai, Gábor. "Unconstitutional Constitutional Amendments: Constitutional Courts as Guardians of the Constitution?" *Constellations* 19 (2012): 182–203.
Hamilton, Alexander, James Madison, Henry B. Dawson, John Jay, and John C. Hamilton. *The Federalist a Commentary on the Constitution of the United States: A Collection of Essays.* Philadelphia: J.B. Lippincott, 1864.
Harel, Alon. *Why Law Matters.* Oxford: Oxford University Press, 2014.
Harel, Alon, and Tsvi Kahana. "The Easy Core Case for Judicial Review." *Journal of Legal Analysis* 2, no. 1 (2010): 227–56.
Hart, H.L.A. *The Concept of Law.* Oxford: Clarendon Press, 1963.
Essays in Jurisprudence and Philosophy. Oxford: Oxford University Press, 1983.
Essays on Bentham: Studies in Jurisprudence and Political Theory. Oxford: Oxford University Press, 1982.
"Legal and Moral Obligation." In *Essays in Moral Philosophy*, edited by Abraham Irving Melden. 82–107. Seattle: University of Washington Press, 1958.
"Positivism and the Separation of Law and Morals." *Harvard Law Review* 71, no. 4 (1958): 593–629.
Havel, Václav. *The Art of the Impossible: Politics as Morality in Practice: Speeches and Writings, 1990–1996.* Toronto: Alfred A. Knopf, 1997.
Hayek, Friedrich A. *The Constitution of Liberty.* Chicago: University of Chicago Press, 1960.
Hendrix, Burke A. "Where Should We Expect Social Change in Non-Ideal Theory?" *Political Theory* 41, no. 1 (2013): 116–43.
Hershovitz, Scott. *Exploring Law's Empire: The Jurisprudence of Ronald Dworkin.* Oxford; New York: Oxford University Press, 2006.
Heyman, Steven J. "The Dark Side of the Force: The Legacy of Justice Holmes for First Amendment Jurisprudence." *William & Mary Bill of Rights Journal* 19 (2011): 661–723.
Hickman, Tom. "Proportionality: Comparative Law Lessons." *Judicial Review* 12, no. 1 (2007): 31–55.
Himma, Kenneth Einar. "Positivism and the Problem of Explaining Legal Obligation." *American Philosophical Association Newsletter* 5 (2006): 13–18.

Hinks, Peter P., John R. McKivigan, and R. Owen Williams. *Encyclopedia of Antislavery and Abolition*. Greenwood Milestones in African American History. Westport, Conn.: Greenwood Press, 2007.

Hobbes, Thomas. *De Cive; or, the Citizen*, edited by Sterling P. Lamprecht. New York: Appleton-Century-Crofts, 1949.

Leviathan: With Selected Variants from the Latin Edition of 1668. Indianapolis, Ind.: Hackett, 1994.

Hogg, Peter W. *Constitutional Law of Canada*. 5th ed. 2 vols. Scarborough, Ont.: Thomson Carswell, 2007.

Holmes, Stephen, and Cass R. Sunstein. "The Politics of Constitutional Revision in Eastern Europe." In *Responding to Imperfection: The Theory and Practice of Constitutional Amendment*, edited by Sanford Levinson. 275–306. Princeton: Princeton University Press, 1995.

Hughes, Anne. *Human Dignity and Fundamental Rights in South Africa and Ireland*. Pretoria: Pretoria University Press, 2014.

Hume, David. "Of the Original Contract." In *Essays, Moral, Political, Literary*, edited by E.F. Miller. 465–87. Indianapolis: Liberty Classics, 1985.

Huscroft, Grant. "Proportionality and Pretense." *Constitutional Commentary* 29, no. 2 (2014): 229–56.

Huscroft, Grant, Bradley W. Miller, and Grégoire Webber, eds. *Proportionality and the Rule of Law: Rights, Justification, Reasoning*. Cambridge: Cambridge University Press, 2014.

Israel, Jonathan. *A Revolution of the Mind: Radical Enlightenment and the Intellectual Origins of Modern Democracy*. Princeton, N.J.: Princeton University Press, 2010.

Jacobsohn, Gary J. "Abraham Lincoln 'on This Question of Judicial Authority': The Theory of Constitutional Aspiration." *Western Political Science Association* 36 (1983): 52–70.

"An Unconstitutional Constitution? A Comparative Perspective." *International Journal of Constitutional Law* 4 (2006): 460–87.

Jeffries, Stuart. "Ronald Dworkin: 'We Have a Responsibility to Live Well'." *The Guardian*, March 31, 2011.

Joly, Fábio Duarte. "Spartacus Revolt." In *Encyclopedia of Antislavery and Abolition*, edited by Peter Hinks, John McKivigan, and R. Owen Williams. 648–51. Westport: Greenwood Press, 2007.

Kant, Immanuel. *Anthropology from a Pragmatic Point of View*. Cambridge: Cambridge University Press, 2006.

Practical Philosophy. The Cambridge Edition of the Works of Immanuel Kant. Cambridge: Cambridge University Press, 1996.

Kateb, George. *Human Dignity*. Cambridge: Harvard University Press, 2011.

Kavanagh, Aileen. "Constitutional Review, the Courts, and Democratic Scepticism." *Current Legal Problems* 62, no. 1 (2009): 102–35.

Kelbley, Charles L. "Are There Limits to Constitutional Change? Rawls on Comprehensive Doctrines, Unconstitutional Amendments, and the Basis of Equality." *Fordham Law Review* 72 (2004): 1487–536.

Kelsen, Hans. *An Introduction to the Problems of Legal Theory*. Oxford: Oxford University Press, 1992.

"The Natural-Law Doctrine before the Tribunal of Science." *Western Political Science Quarterly* 2 (1949): 481–513.

Kershaw, Ian. *Popular Opinion and Political Dissent in the Third Reich, Bavaria 1933–1945*. Oxford: Oxford University Press, 1983.

Khosla, Madhav. "Proportionality: An Assault on Human Rights?: A Reply." *International Journal of Constitutional Law* 8 (2010): 298–306.

Klatt, Matthias. "An Egalitarian Defense of Proportionality-Based Balancing: A Reply to Luc B. Tremblay." *International Journal of Constitutional Law* 12, no. 4 (2014): 891–99.

Klatt, Matthias, and Moritz Meister. *The Constitutional Structure of Proportionality*. Oxford: Oxford University Press, 2012.

Klein, Claude. "Introduction." *Israel Law Review* 44 (2011): 318–20.

Klein, Eckart. "Human Dignity in German Law." In *The Concept of Human Dignity in Human Rights Discourse*, edited by David Kretzmer and Eckart Klein. 145–59. The Hague: Kluwer Law International, 2002.

Kleingeld, Pauline. "Kant, History, and the Idea of Moral Development." *History of Philosophy Quarterly* 16, no. 1 (1999): 59–80.

Klemperer, Victor. *I Will Bear Witness: A Diary of the Nazi Years*. New York: Random House, 1998.

Kommers, Donald P. "The Basic Law: A Fifty Year Assessment." In *Fifty Years of German Basic Law: The New Departure for Germany*, edited by AICGS Conference Report. Baltimore: Johns Hopkins University Press, 1999.

"German Constitutionalism: A Prolegomenon." *Emory Law Journal* 40 (1991): 837–73.

Kommers, Donald P., and Russell A. Miller. *The Constitutional Jurisprudence of the Federal Republic of Germany*. 3rd ed. Durham, N.C.: Duke University Press, 2012.

Koonz, Claudia. *The Nazi Conscience*. Cambridge, Mass.: Belknap Press of Harvard University Press, 2003.

Korsgaard, Christine M. "The Right to Lie: Kant on Dealing with Evil." *Philosophy & Public Affairs* 15, no. 4 (1986): 325–49.

Kretzmer, David, and Eckart Klein. *The Concept of Human Dignity in Human Rights Discourse*. The Hague: Kluwer Law International, 2002.

Krishnaswamy, Sudhir. *Democracy and Constitutionalism in India: A Study of the Basic Structure Doctrine*. New Delhi: Oxford University Press, 2009.

Kumm, Mattias. *The Best of Times and the Worst of Times: Between Constitutional Triumphalism and Nostalgia*, edited by Petra Dobner and Martin Loughlin. 201–19. Oxford: Oxford University Press, 2010.

"Constitutional Rights as Principles: On the Structure and Domain of Constitutional Justice. Review of a Theory of Constitutional Rights, by Robert Alexy." *International Journal of Constitutional Law* 2 (2004): 574–96.

"The Idea of Socratic Contestation and the Right to Justification: The Point of Rights-Based Proportionality Review." *Law & Ethics of Human Rights* 4 (2010): 141–75.

"Political Liberalism and the Structure of Rights: On the Place and Limits of the Proportionality Requirement." In *Law, Rights, and Discourse*, edited by George Pavlakos. 131–66. Oxford: Hart Publishing, 2007.

Langton, Rae. "Whose Right? Ronald Dworkin, Women, and Pornographers." *Philosophy & Public Affairs* 19, no. 4 (1990): 311–59.

Laws, Sir John. "The Good Constitution." *Cambridge Law Journal* 71, no. 3 (2012): 567–82.

Leiter, Brian. "The Radicalism of Legal Positivism." Available at SSRN: http://ssrn.com/abstract=1568333.

"Why Legal Positivism?" Available at SSRN: http://ssrn.com/abstract=1521761.

Lenoir, J.J. "Judicial Review in Germany under the Weimar Constitution." *Tulane Law Review* 14, no. 3 (1940): 361–83.

Levinson, Sanford, ed. *Responding to Imperfection: The Theory and Practice of Constitutional Amendment*. Princeton: Princeton University Press, 1995.

Levy, Jacob T. "Not So Novus an Ordo: Constitutions without Social Contracts." *Political Theory* 37, no. 2 (2009): 191–217.

Limbach, Jutta. "The Concept of the Supremacy of the Constitution." *The Modern Law Review* 64, no. 1 (2001): 1–10.

Lincoln, Abraham. *Abraham Lincoln: His Speeches and Writings*. New York: Da Capo, 1946.

Collected Works, edited by Roy P. Basler. 11 vols. New Brunswick, N.J., 1953.

Loughlin, Martin. "The Concept of Constituent Power." *European Journal of Political Theory* 13 (2014): 218–37.

The Idea of Public Law. Oxford: Oxford University Press, 2003.

Loughlin, Martin, and Neil Walker. *The Paradox of Constitutionalism: Constituent Power and Constitutional Form*. Oxford: Oxford University Press, 2007.

Loughlin, Martin, and Petra Dobner. *The Twilight of Constitutionalism?* Oxford: Oxford University Press, 2010.

Lunau, Henry. "The Threat of Nazi Law to All Fundamental Legal Principles." *Proceedings of the American Foreign Law Association* 23 (1942): 1–11.

Lutz, Donald. "Toward a Theory of Constitutional Amendment." In *Responding to Imperfection: The Theory and Practice of Constitutional Amendment*, edited by Sanford Levinson. 237–76. Princeton: Princeton University Press, 1995.

Mahlmann, Matthias. "The Basic Law at 60 – Human Dignity and the Culture of Republicanism." *German Law Journal* 11 (2010): 9–32.

"The Good Sense of Dignity: Six Antidotes to Dignity Fatigue in Ethics and Law." In *Understanding Human Dignity*, edited by Christopher McCrudden. Oxford: Oxford University Press, 2013.

"Human Dignity and Autonomy in Modern Constitutional Orders." In *The Oxford Handbook of Comparative Constitutional Law*, edited by Michel Rosenfeld and András Sajó. 370–95. Oxford: Oxford University Press, 2012.

Mandela, Nelson. *Long Walk to Freedom: The Autobiography of Nelson Mandela*. London: Abacus, 2009.

Marbury, William L. "The Limitations Upon the Amending Power." *Harvard Law Review* 33 (1919): 223–35.

Martin, Douglas. "Sidney Morgenbesser, 82, Kibitzing Philosopher, Dies." *The New York Times*, 2004.

Martin Jr., Waldo E. *The Mind of Frederick Douglass*. Chapel Hill: University of North Carolina Press, 1984.

Mason, Andrew. "Just Constraints." *British Journal of Political Science* 34, no. 2 (2004): 251–68.

McCrudden, Christopher. "Human Dignity and Judicial Interpretation of Human Rights." *European Journal of International Law* 19 (2008): 655–724.

Mendes-Flohr, Paul R., and Jehuda Reinharz. *The Jew in the Modern World: A Documentary History*. 2nd ed. Oxford: Oxford University Press, 1995.

Mertens, Thomas. "Darker Legacies of Law in Europe: The Shadow of National Socialism and Fascism over Europe and Its Legal Traditions." *Ratio Juris* 18 (2005): 285–91.

"Nazism, Legal Positivism and Radbruch's Thesis on Statutory Injustice." *Law and Critique* 14 (2003): 277–95.

Meyerson, Denise. "Does the Constitutional Court of South Africa Take Rights Seriously? The Case of S v Jordan." *Acta Juridica* (2004): 138–54.

Mill, John Stuart. *The Subjection of Women*. New York: Dover, 1997.

Miller, Bradley W. "Proportionality's Blind Spot: 'Neutrality' and Political Philosophy." In *Proportionality and the Rule of Law: Rights, Justification, Reasoning*, edited by Grant Huscroft, Bradley W. Miller and Grégoire Webber. 370–96. Cambridge: Cambridge University Press, 2014.

Mills, Charles W. "'Ideal Theory' as Ideology." *Hypatia* 20, no. 3 (2005): 165–84.

Möller, Kai. "Balancing and the Structure of Constitutional Rights." *International Journal of Constitutional Law* 5 (2007): 453–68.

Morsink, Johannes. "World War Two and the Universal Declaration." *Human Rights Quarterly* 15 (1993): 357–405.

Moses, A.D. "Structure and Agency in the Holocaust: Daniel J. Goldhagen and His Critics." *History and Theory* 37 (1998): 194–99.

Moyn, Samuel. "The Secret History of Constitutional Dignity." In *Understanding Human Dignity*, edited by Christopher McCrudden. 95–112. Oxford: Oxford University Press, 2013.

Müller, Ingo. *Hitler's Justice: The Courts of the Third Reich*. Translated by Deborah Lucas Schneider. London: Tauris, 1991.

Mureinik, Etienne. "A Bridge to Where? Introducing the Interim Bill of Rights." *South African Journal on Human Rights* 10 (1994): 31–48.

Murphy, Liam B. *Moral Demands in Nonideal Theory*. Oxford: Oxford University Press, 2000.

Murphy, Walter F. "Consent and Constitutional Change." In *Comparative Constitutional Law*, edited by Vicki C. Jackson and Mark Tushnet. New York: Foundation Press, 1999.

"Slaughter-House, Civil Rights, and Limits on Constitutional Change." *American Journal of Jurisprudence* 32 (1987): 1–22.

Neiman, Susan. *Moral Clarity: A Guide for Grown-up Idealists*. Orlando, Fla.: Harcourt, Inc., 2008.

Nohlen, Nicolas. "Germany: The Electronic Eavesdropping Case." *International Journal of Constitutional Law* 3 (2005): 680–86.

Noorani, A.G. "Behind the 'Basic Structure Doctrine': On India's Debt to a German Jurist." *Frontline* 18 (2001), www.hinduonnet.com/fline/ fl1809/18090950 .htm (last visited July 10, 2015).

Oakeshott, Michael. *On History and Other Essays*. Oxford: Basil Blackwell, 1983.

Oliver, Dawn, and Carlo Fusaro. "Towards a Theory of Constitutional Change." In *How Constitutions Change: A Comparative Study*, edited by Carlo Fusaro and Dawn Oliver. 405–34. Oxford: Hart Publishing, 2013.

Paine, Thomas. "African Slavery in America." *Pennsylvania Journal and the Weekly Advertiser*, March 8, 1775.

The Rights of Man in Rights of Man, Common Sense, and Other Political Writings. Oxford: Oxford University Press, 1998.

Panaccio, Charles-Maxime. "In Defence of Two-Step Balancing and Proportionality in Rights Adjudication." *Canadian Journal of Law and Jurisprudence* 24 (2011): 109–28.

Pappe, H.O. "On the Validity of Judicial Decisions in the Nazi Era." *The Modern Law Review* 23, no. 3 (1960): 260–74.

Patterson, Dennis M. *A Companion to Philosophy of Law and Legal Theory*. Cambridge, Mass.: Blackwell Publishers, 1999.

Paulson, Stanley L. "On the Background and Significance of Gustav Radbruch's Post-War Papers." *Oxford Journal of Legal Studies* 26, no. 1 (2006): 17–40.

"Radbruch on Unjust Laws: Competing Earlier and Later Views?" *Oxford Journal of Legal Studies* 15 (1995): 489–500.

"Review of Law as a Moral Judgment, by Deryck Beyleveld and Roger Brownscord." *Ratio Juris* 7 (1994): 111–16.

Pavlakos, George, ed. *Law, Rights and Discourse: The Legal Philosophy of Robert Alexy*. Oxford: Hart Publishing, 2007.

Perry, Stephen. "Associative Obligations and the Obligation to Obey the Law." In *Exploring Law's Empire: The Jurisprudence of Ronald Dworkin*, edited by Scott Hershovitz. 183–206. Oxford: Oxford University Press, 2006.

"Political Authority and Political Obligation." In *Oxford Studies in Philosophy of Law*, edited by Leslie Green and Brian Leiter. 1–74. Oxford: Oxford University Press, 2013.

Pettit, Phillip. *Republicanism: A Theory of Freedom and Government*. Oxford: Oxford University Press, 2010.

Phillips, Michael. "Reflections on the Transition from Ideal to Non-Ideal Theory." *Noûs* 19, no. 4 (1985): 551–70.

Pildes, Richard H. "Dworkin's Two Conceptions of Rights." *The Journal of Legal Studies* 29, no. 1 (2000): 309–15.

Pinker, Stephen. "The Stupidity of Dignity." *The New Republic*, 28 May 2008.

Plato. *Complete Works*. Indianapolis, Ind.: Hackett, 1997.

Pogge, Thomas. "Is Kant's Rechtslehre a 'Comprehensive Liberalism'?" In *Kant's Metaphysics of Morals*, edited by Mark Timmons. 133–58. Oxford: Oxford University Press, 2002.

Preuss, Ulrich K. "The Implications of 'Eternity Clauses': The German Experience." *Israel Law Review* 44 (2001): 429–48.

Quirk, Patrick. "An Australian Looks at German 'Proportionality'." *University of Notre Dame Australia Law Review* 1 (1999): 39–55.

Radbruch, Gustav. "Five Minutes of Legal Philosophy (1945)." *Oxford Journal of Legal Studies* 26, no. 1 (2006): 13–15.

Kulturlehre Des Sozialismus Ideologische Betrachtungen. 4. Aufl ed. Frankfurt am Main: Athenäum, 1970.

"Legal Philosophy." In *The Legal Philosophies of Lask, Radbruch, and Dabin*, edited by Kurt Wilk. Cambridge: Harvard University Press, 1950.

"Statutory Lawlessness and Supra-Statutory Law (1946)." *Oxford Journal of Legal Studies* 26, no. 1 (2006): 1–11.

Radin, Margaret Jane. "Lacking a Transformative Social Theory: A Response." *Stanford Law Review* 45, no. 2 (1993): 409–24.

Rao, Neomi. "On the Use and Abuse of Dignity in Constitutional Law." *Columbia Journal of European Law* 14, no. 2 (2008): 201–55.

Rawls, John. *Justice as Fairness: A Restatement*. Cambridge, Mass: Harvard University Press, 2001.

The Law of Peoples. Cambridge, Mass.: Harvard University Press, 1999.

Political Liberalism. New York: Columbia University Press, 1996.

"Political Liberalism: Reply to Habermas." *The Journal of Philosophy* 92, no. 3 (1995): 132–80.

A Theory of Justice. Cambridge, Mass.: Belknap Press of Harvard University Press, 1971.

Raz, Joseph. "Authority and Justification." *Philosophy & Public Affairs* 14, no. 1 (1985): 3–29.

The Authority of Law: Essays on Law and Morality. 2nd ed. Oxford: Oxford University Press, 2009.

Authority. Readings in Social and Political Theory. New York: New York University Press, 1990.

"Kelsen's Theory of the Basic Norm." *American Journal of Jurisprudence* 19 (1974): 94–111.

The Morality of Freedom. Oxford: Oxford University Press, 1986.

Réaume, Denise G. "Limitations on Constitutional Rights: The Logic of Proportionality (August 2009)." *Oxford Legal Studies Research Paper No. 26/2009*. http://ssrn.com/abstract=1463853; http://dx.doi.org/10.2139/ssrn.1463853.

Reeves, Anthony R. "Judicial Practical Reason: Judges in Morally Imperfect Legal Orders." *Law and Philosophy* 30, no. 3 (2011): 319–52.

Regan, Donald H. "Glosses on Dworkin: Rights, Principles, and Policies." *Michigan Law Review* 76, no. 8 (1978): 1213–64.

Ripstein, Arthur. "Authority and Coercion." *Philosophy & Public Affairs* 32, no. 1 (2004): 2–35.

Force and Freedom: Kant's Legal and Political Philosophy. Cambridge, Mass.: Harvard University Press, 2009.

Robeyns, Ingrid. "Ideal Theory in Theory and Practice." *Social Theory and Practice* 34 (2008): 341–62.

Rosen, Michael. *Dignity: Its History and Meaning*. Cambridge, Mass.: Harvard University Press, 2012.

"Dignity: The Case Against." In *Understanding Human Dignity*, edited by Christopher McCrudden. 143–54. Oxford: Oxford University Press, 2013.

Roth, Götz Aly, and Karl Heinz. "The Legalization of Mercy Killings in Medical and Nursing Institutions in Nazi Germany from 1939 until 1941." *International Journal of Law and Psychiatry* 7 (1985): 145–63.

Rousseau, Jean-Jacques, and Donald A. Cress. *Basic Political Writings*. Indianapolis, Ind.: Hackett, 1987.

Roznai, Yaniv. "Legisprudence Limitations on Constitutional Amendments? Reflections on the Czech Constitutional Court's Declaration of Unconstitutional Constitutional Act." *Vienna Journal on International Constitutional Law* 7 (2014): 29–57.

"Unconstitutional Constitutional Amendments – the Migration and Success of a Constitutional Idea." *American Journal of Comparative Law* 61 (2013): 657–719.

Rubenfeld, Jed. *Freedom and Time: A Theory of Constitutional Self-Government.* New Haven: Yale University Press, 2001.

Rundle, Kristen. "The Impossibility of an Exterminatory Legality: Law and the Holocaust." *University of Toronto Law Journal* 59, no. 1 (2009): 65–125.

Russell, Bertrand. *Unpopular Essays.* New York: Routledge, 2009.

Sachs, Albie. "South Africa's Unconstitutional Constitution: The Transition from Power to Lawful Power." *St. Louis University Law Journal* 41 (1997): 1249–57.

The Strange Alchemy of Life and Law. Oxford: Oxford University Press, 2009.

Sadurski, Wojciech. "Judicial Review and the Protection of Constitutional Rights." *Oxford Journal of Legal Studies* 22, no. 2 (2002): 275–99.

Sartori, Giovanni. *Democratic Theory.* New York: Praeger, 1965.

Schapiro, Tamar. "Compliance, Complicity, and the Nature of Nonideal Conditions." *The Journal of Philosophy* 100, no. 7 (2003): 329–55.

Schleunes, Karl A. *Legislating the Holocaust: The Bernard Loesener Memoirs and Supporting Documents.* Boulder, Colo.: Westview Press, 2001.

Schlink, Bernard. "Proportionality in Constitutional Law: Why Everywhere but Here?" *Duke Journal of Comparative and International Law* 22, no. 2 (2012): 291–302.

Schmidtz, David. "Nonideal Theory: What It Is and What It Needs to Be." *Ethics* 121, no. 4 (2011): 772–96.

Schmitt, Carl. *Constitutional Theory.* Translated by Jeffrey Seitzer. Durham: Duke University Press, 2008.

Schopenhauer, Arthur. *The Basis of Morality.* Translated by Arthur Brodrick Bullock. New York: MacMillan, 1915.

Sen, Amartya. "What Do We Want from a Theory of Justice?" *The Journal of Philosophy* 103, no. 5 (2006): 215–38.

Sensen, Oliver. "Human Dignity in Historical Perspective: The Contemporary and Traditional Paradigms." *European Journal of Political Theory* 10, no. 1 (2011): 71–91.

Shapiro, Scott. *Legality.* Cambridge, Mass.: Harvard University Press, 2011.

"What Is the Internal Point of View?" *Fordham Law Review* 75 (2006): 1157–70.

Sher, George. *Approximate Justice: Studies in Non-Ideal Theory.* Lanham: Rowman & Littlefield Publishers, 1997.

Shetreet, Shimon. *The Role of Courts in Society.* Dordrecht: M. Nijhoff Publishers, 1988.

Sieyès, Emmanuel Joseph. *Political Writings: Including the Debate between Sieyès and Tom Paine in 1791.* Translated by Michael Sonenscher. Indianapolis, Ind.: Hackett, 2003.

Silva, Virgílio Afonso da. "Comparing the Incommensurable: Constitutional Principles, Balancing, and Rational Decision." *Oxford Journal of Legal Studies* 31, no. 2 (2011): 273–301.

Simmons, A. John. "Ideal and Nonideal Theory." *Philosophy & Public Affairs* 38, no. 1 (2010): 5–36.

"Justification and Legitimacy." *Ethics* 109, no. 4 (1999): 739–71.

"The Principle of Fair Play." *Philosophy & Public Affairs* 8, no. 4 (1979): 307–37.

Slynn of Hadley, Gordon, Mads Tønnesson Andenæs, and Duncan Fairgrieve. *Judicial Review in International Perspective*. The Hague: Kluwer Law International, 2000.

Smith, Eivind. "Old and Protected? On the 'Supra-Constitutional' Clause in the Constitution of Norway." *Israel Law Journal* 44 (2011): 369–88.

Soper, Philip. "Dworkin's Domain." *Harvard Law Review* 100, no. 5 (1987): 1166–86.

Sorabjee, Soli. "The Ideal Remedy: A Valediction." In *The Supreme Court Versus the Constitution*, edited by Pran Chopra. New Delhi: Sage Publications, 2006.

Sreenivasan, Gopal. "Non-Ideal Theory: A Taxonomy with Illustration." In *Global Justice and Bioethics*, edited by Joseph Millum and Ezekiel J. Emmanuel. 135–52. Oxford: Oxford University Press, 2012.

Stemplowska, Zofia "What's Ideal About Ideal Theory?" *Social Theory and Practice* 34 (2008): 319–40.

Stolleis, Michael. *The Law under the Swastika: Studies on Legal History in Nazi Germany*. Chicago: University of Chicago Press, 1998.

Stone, Martin. "Legal Positivism as an Idea About Morality." *The University of Toronto Law Journal* 61, no. 2 (2011): 313–41.

Stone Sweet, Alec, and Jud Mathews. "Proportionality Balancing and Global Constitutionalism." *Columbia Journal of Transnational Law* 47 (2008): 73–165.

Swift, Adam. "The Value of Philosophy in Nonideal Circumstances." *Social Theory and Practice* 34 (2008): 363–87.

Szente, Zoltan. "The Historic Origins of the National Assembly in Hungary." *Historia Constitutional* 8 (2007): 228–44.

Taylor, C.C.W. "A Note on Ancient Attitudes Towards Slavery." *Analysis* 43 (1983): 40–43.

Tremblay, Luc B. "An Egalitarian Defense of Proportionality-Based Balancing," International Journal of Constitutional Law." *International Journal of Constitutional Law* 12, no. 4 (2014): 864–90.

Tribe, Laurence. *The Invisible Constitution*. Oxford: Oxford University Press, 2008.

Trudeau, Pierre Elliot. *The Essential Trudeau*. Toronto: McClelland and Stewart, 1998.

Tsakyrakis, Stavros. "Proportionality: An Assault on Human Rights." *International Journal of Constitutional Law* 7 (2009): 468–93.

Ullrich, Dierk. "Concurring Visions: Human Dignity in the Canadian Charter of Rights and Freedoms and the Basic Law of the Federal Republic of Germany." *Global Jurist Frontiers* 3, no. 1 (2003): 1535–653.

Unger, Aryeh L. "The Public Opinion Reports of the Nazi Party." *The Public Opinion Quarterly* 29, no. 4 (1965): 565–82.

Urbina, Francisco J. "A Critique of Proportionality." *American Journal of Jurisprudence* 57, no. 1 (2012): 49–80.

Valentini, Laura. "On the Apparent Paradox of Ideal Theory." *The Journal of Political Philosophy* 17 (2009): 332–55.

Vallentyne, Peter, and Bas van der Vossen. "Libertarianism." *Stanford Encyclopedia of Philosophy*, edited by Edward N. Zalta (Fall 2014 edition), http://plato.stanford.edu/archives/fall2014/entries/libertarianism/.

Veel, Paul-Erik N. "Incommensurability, Proportionality, and Rational Legal Decision-Making." *Law and Ethics of Human Rights* 4, no. 2 (2010): 178–228.

Venter, Francois. *Constitutional Comparison: Japan, Germany, Canada and South Africa as Constitutional States.* Cape Town: Kluwer Law International, 2000.

von Krauss, Rupprecht. *Der Grundsatz Der Verhältnismässigkeit in Seiner Bedeutung Für Die Notwendigkeit Des Mittels in Verwaltungsrecht.* Hamburg, 1955.

Waldron, Jeremy. "The Core of the Case against Judicial Review." *Yale Law Journal* 115, no. 6 (2006): 1346–406.

The Dignity of Legislation. Cambridge: Cambridge University Press, 1999.

Dignity, Rank, and Rights. New York: Oxford University Press, 2012.

"Five to Four: Why Do Bare Majorities Rule on Courts?" *Yale Law Journal* 123, no. 6 (2014): 1692–1730.

"Freeman's Defense of Judicial Review." *Law and Philosophy* 13, no. 1 (1994): 27–41.

"Judicial Review and the Conditions of Democracy." *Journal of Political Philosophy* 6, no. 4 (1998): 335–55.

Law and Disagreement. Oxford: Oxford University Press, 1999.

"Pildes on Dworkin's Theory of Rights." *Journal of Legal Studies* 29, no. 1 (2000): 301–7.

"Positivism and Legality: Hart's Equivocal Response to Fuller." *New York University Law Review* 83 (2008): 1135–69.

"A Rights-Based Critique of Constitutional Rights." *Oxford Journal of Legal Studies* 13, no. 1 (1993): 18–51.

Theories of Rights. Oxford: Oxford University Press, 1984.

Walen, Alec. "Judicial Review in Review." *International Journal of Constitutional Law*, no. 7 (2009): 329–54.

Wall, Ilan rua. "Notes on an 'Open' Constituent Power." *Law, Culture and the Humanities* (2013): 1–15.

Walzer, Michael. "Philosophy and Democracy." *Political Theory* 9, no. 3 (1981): 379–99.

Washington, George. "Letter to Bushrod Washington, November 10, 1787." In *The Writings of George Washington*, edited by John C. Fitzpatrick. 309–12. Washington: Government Printing Office, 1944.

Webber, Grégoire C.N. *The Negotiable Constitution: On the Limitation of Rights*. Cambridge: Cambridge University Press, 2012.

"Proportionality, Balancing, and the Cult of Constitutional Rights Scholarship." *Canadian Journal of Law and Jurisprudence* 23 (2010): 179–202.

Weinrib, Ernest Joseph. *Corrective Justice*. Oxford: Oxford University Press, 2012.

The Idea of Private Law. Cambridge, Mass.: Harvard University Press, 1995.

Weinrib, Jacob. "Permissive Laws and the Dynamism of Kantian Justice." *Law and Philosophy* 33 (2014): 105–36.

Weinrib, Lorraine E. "Canada's Constitutional Revolution: From Legislative to Constitutional State." *Israel Law Review* 33 (1999): 13–50.

"'Do Justice to Us!' Jews and the Constitution of Canada." In *Not Written in Stone: Jews, Constitutions, and Constitutionalism in Canada*, edited by Daniel J. Elazar, Michael Brown, and Ira Robinson. 33–68. Ottawa: University of Ottawa Press, 2003.

"Human Dignity as a Rights-Protecting Principle." *National Journal of Constitutional Law* 17 (2004): 325–45.

Wermiel, Stephen J. "Law and Human Dignity: The Judicial Soul of Justice Brennan." *William & Mary Bill of Rights Journal* 7, no. 5 (1998): 223–39.

Westermann, William Linn. "Between Slavery and Freedom." *American Historical Review* 50 (1945): 213–27.

Williams, Bernard. *Shame and Necessity*. Berkeley, Calif.: University of California Press, 2008.

Willis, Hugh Evander. *Constitutional Law of the United States*. Bloomington, Ind.: Principia Press, 1936.

Wolff, Jonathan. *An Introduction to Political Philosophy*. Oxford: Oxford University Press, 1996.

Wood, Allen. "Human Dignity, Right and the Realm of Ends." *Acta Juridica* (2008): 47–65.

Woolman, Stu. "The Architecture of Dignity." In *The Dignity Jurisprudence of the Constitutional Court of South Africa*, edited by Stu Woolman, Drucilla Cornell, Sam Fuller, Jason Brickhill, Michael Bishop, and Diana Dunbar. 73–123. New York: Fordham University Press, 2013.

Young, Alison L. "Proportionality Is Dead: Long Live Proportionality." In *Proportionality and the Rule of Law: Rights, Justification, and Reasoning*, edited by Grant Huscroft, Bradley W. Miller, and Grégoire Webber. 43–66. Cambridge: Cambridge University Press, 2014.

Yowell, Paul. "Critical Examination of Dworkin's Theory of Rights." *American Journal of Jurisprudence* 52, no. 1 (2007): 93–137.
Zipursky, Benjamin C. "Legal Obligations and the Internal Aspect of Rules." *Fordham Law Review* 75, no. 3 (2006): 1229–53.
Zucca, Lorenzo. *Constitutional Dilemmas: Conflicts of Fundamental Legal Rights in Europe and the USA*. Oxford: Oxford University Press, 2007.

INDEX

Lightning Source UK Ltd.
Milton Keynes UK
UKOW06n0602040916

282132UK00005B/84/P

9 781107 084285